Study Guide
to Accompany

Business Law Today
Second Edition

Roger LeRoy Miller
Center for Policy Studies
Clemson University
and School of Law
University of Miami

Gaylord A. Jentz
Herbert D. Kelleher
Professor in Business Law
MSIS Department
University of Texas at Austin

Prepared by

Nancy L. Hart
Midland College, Texas

West Publishing Company
St. Paul New York Los Angeles San Francisco

COPYRIGHT © 1991 by   WEST PUBLISHING CO.
50 W. Kellogg Boulevard
P.O. Box 64526
St. Paul, MN 55164-1003

98 97 96 95 94 93 92 91   8 7 6 5 4 3 2 1

ISBN 0-314-81758-1

<u>DEDICATION</u>

This edition is dedicated
(alphabetically)
to
Gloria, Lacey, Peggy and Wayne.

CONTENTS

Our Legal Heritage

General Principles

Law is a set of rules which can be enforced by the government. These rules establish proper conduct between individuals in a society and between individuals and their society. The rules come from cases, statutes, constitutions and administrative agencies. The government enforces the rules through court decisions.

Business law is the set of rules which governs commercial transactions. The Commerce Clause of the United States Constitution governs some aspects of business law but state law is the primary source. Because state laws may differ, the Uniform Commercial Code attempts to create a set of business rules which apply in every state.

Chapter Summary

I.   Sources of Law

    A.   Early Courts of Law--Initially, legal disputes were settled by local custom. In 1066, England established the king's court (Curia Regis) which established uniform or common customs for the whole country. Judges of the king's court used earlier decisions, published in Year Books, as guides for solving disputes. The king's court is the origin of modern common law.

    B.   General--Our law originates from four sources.

        (1)   Common Law--May also be called case law or judge-made law. Law is created when a judge makes a decision in a lawsuit. In a common law system, the judge looks for earlier cases or precedent (from the word "precede") which have similar facts and follows the rule of the earlier cases. This process is stare

1

<u>decisis</u>. Stare decisis promotes fair decisions because people in similar circumstances will receive similar decisions. It is also faster and easier for the judge if he or she has guidelines to follow. The law is also more stable and predictable because of this adherence to past rules.

(2)   <u>Constitutional Law</u>--The U.S. Constitution is the highest law in the country. Any other law which conflicts with its principles will be declared unconstitutional. State constitutions are the highest law within each state but are inferior to the U.S. Constitution.

(3)   <u>Statutory Law (Legislation)</u>--Created by the U.S. Congress and state legislatures.

(4)   <u>Administrative Law</u>--Administrative agencies are created when an executive or legislative branch of government turns over some of its regulatory power. Administrative law governs a dispute between an individual and an agency. The first person who will try to resolve this type of dispute is an agency employee called an administrative law judge. Administrative process refers to the control of law by administrative agencies; judicial process refers to the control of law by the courts.

C.   <u>American Commercial Law</u>--The four sources listed above are also sources of business or commercial law. However, because business tends to cross state lines, uniform or model laws are created by experts in the field. The model laws are proposed as legislation in each state and a state can adopt all, some, or none of the model law. The Uniform Commercial Code is an example of a uniform law.

II.   <u>Finding the Law</u>

A.   <u>State Court Decisions</u>--Trial court decisions usually are not published but decisions by appellate courts are.

(1)   <u>State Reports</u>--Books published by each state.

(2)   <u>National Reporter System</u>--Published by West Publishing Co. States are grouped into geographical areas and decisions are published in regional reporters. The seven regional reporters are the Atlantic, South Eastern, South Western, North Western, North Eastern, Southern and Pacific.

<u>Citation Form</u>--A legal citation states where a particular case may be found. The citation consists of three parts: the volume number, reporter name, and page number. (Older cases do not follow this citation pattern.) Some states do not publish the decisions of their courts, but

use the National Reporter System. If a state does publish court decisions, both citations are used and they are called parallel citations.

B.   Federal Court Decisions

(1)   Decisions of Lower Courts--Published by West Publishing Co. Trial court decisions are found in the Federal Supplement. Intermediate appellate court decisions are found in the Federal Reporter. Cases involving bankruptcy law are found in the Bankruptcy Reporter.

(2)   Decisions of the United States Supreme Court--U.S. Reports is published by the federal government. It is the official publication. Unofficial publications, which are printed by private companies, include Lawyers' Edition (Lawyers' Cooperative Publishing Company) and Supreme Court Reporter (West Publishing Company). The Supreme Court Reporter and other reporters printed by West Publishing Co. use headnotes (or summaries of the law involved in a case). The points of law contained in the headnotes are classified by subject and by number and every case on a similar point will have the same headnote subject and number. This classification system allows lawyers to find all cases (precedent) which deal with the same points of law.

C.   State and Federal Codes and Regulations--Statutes passed by state and federal legislators are also published. Originally, they are published in chronological order (e.g. United States Statutes at Large). Later, these statues are arranged by subject matter and are published in codes, revisions, or compilations). The citation form of a code includes a title number or title name and a section number. The official publication of federal statutes is the United States Code (U.S.C.). Private publishing companies may print unofficial codes.

Federal administrative rules and regulations are published in the Code of Federal Regulations (C.F.R.) and follow a similar citation pattern, using title and section numbers.

III.   Analyzing Case Law

A.   Case Titles--Also called the style of the case. Usually consists of two names, one "versus" another. If the decision being reported is by a trial court the plaintiff's name is always first. If the decision is by a higher court, the name of the party appealing may come first.

B.   Terminology

(1)   Decisions and Opinions--A written court decision contains the

rules of law that apply in the case, the judgment of the court, and the court's opinion (the reasons for the court's decision). The court may have more than one judge. When all the judges agree, the opinion is unanimous. When all the judges do not agree, a majority and sometimes a minority, or dissenting, opinion is written. A judge who agrees with the majority opinion, but wants to add his or her own thoughts, will write a concurring opinion.

(2)   <u>Judges and Justices</u>--These two terms are often used interchangeably. Some states save the title of "justice" for judges who sit on appellate or supreme courts.

(3)   <u>Appellant and Appellee</u>--The appellant, or petitioner, is the loser in trial court and is the party who appeals that decision. The appellee, or respondent, is the winner in trial court.

(4)   <u>New Computerized Legal Research</u>--WESTLAW and LEXIS are examples of computerized law libraries that are available to attorneys via a computer terminal. The user types in a search request or query; the computer searches its library (data base) and displays the cases, statutes, and other material which contain information about the request. The user can store the information on a diskette or print out a hard (paper) copy.

IV.   <u>The Constitution As It Affects Business</u>

A.   <u>The Commerce Clause</u>--The federal government has the power to regulate business dealings if such actions "affect" interstate commerce (affectation doctrine). The business dealings do not have to cross state borders. Each state has police powers which give it the right to regulate the health, safety and public welfare. However, if a state law based on police power interferes with interstate commerce, the necessity of the law will be weighed against the burden placed on commerce.

B.   <u>Interstate Commerce Act</u>--Created in 1887 to curb abuses in the railroad industry. Established the Interstate Commerce Commission--the first federal regulatory agency. Initially, this agency had little power, but in the first half of the twentieth century, its power grew. Since 1980, Congress has enacted legislation which reduces the power of the ICC.

C.   <u>The Bill of Rights</u>--The first ten amendments to the Constitution; designed to protect individuals from interference by the government. Originally included only actions by the federal government, but the Fourteenth Amendment, through selective incorporation, has been applied to actions by state governments.

(1)   <u>Freedom of Speech</u>--Not all speech is protected. Obscenity and words likely to incite fights or riots are not protected at all. Advertising and other forms of commercial speech are less protected than non-commercial speech. A defamatory statement is protected if an honest error led to the offending speech.

(2)   <u>Freedom of Religion</u>--Involves both an individual's right to practice religion and a ban on a government-created religion. (The latter is the establishment clause.) A regulation which affects religion is valid as long as it does not promote a particular religion or place a significant burden on religion. Examples of valid laws include Sunday closing laws and provisions for municipally-funded Nativity scenes. An employer must make reasonable accommodations for an employee's religion.

Study Questions

Fill-in-the-Blank Questions

A law passed by the U.S. Congress is an example of ___Statutory_____
_____ law.   (common/statutory)

A regulation adopted by the Internal Revenue Service is an example of
___administrative_____ law.
          (common/administrative)

The commerce clause is an example of ___Constitutional_____
law.   (constitutional/statutory)

True-False Questions

1.   "Codes" are publications of cases decided by federal courts. ___F____

2.   "Stare decisis" is the process of using earlier cases as guidelines in resolving current disputes. ___T____

3.   The Uniform Commercial Code was passed by the United States Congress. ___F____

4.   Administrative agencies are created by the executive or legislative branches of government. ___T____

5.   An employer must make whatever changes are necessary to accommodate a worker's religion. ___F____

6.   Commercial speech is absolutely protected by the United States Constitution. _____

7.   A law passed by the Oregon legislature which conflicts with the provisions of the United States Constitution will be held unconstitutional. ___T___

8.   A state's police powers are its powers to regulate the health and safety of its citizens. ___T___

9.   Case law is a synonym for statutory law. _____

10.   The "affectation doctrine" is used in freedom of religion cases. ___F___

11.   Decisions made by federal trial courts usually are published. ___T___

12.   The Interstate Commerce Act was passed in order to regulate the railroad industry. ___T___

13.   A parallel citation means that a case is published in more than one book. _____

14.   A unanimous opinion is issued when all the judges agree on the decision made by the court as a whole. ___T___

15.   The name of the plaintiff always comes first in the case name of a decision published by an appellate court. ___F___

16.   LEXIS is the title of a set of books which publishes the decisions of the United States Supreme Court. _____

17.   Administrative process refers to cases decided by lower court judges. ___F___

Multiple-Choice Questions

1.   The right to regulate commerce between the several states is found in:

            a.   a law passed by Congress.
            b.   the Uniform Commercial Code.
            c.   the United States Constitution.
            d.   common law.

2.   Jones v. Smith is a contract case decided in 1965. Johns v. Teller is a similar case being decided today. The Jones case is _____ for the Teller case.

            a.   precedent
            b.   stare decisis
            c.   preface
            d.   premise

3.   American common law is based on law in:

    a.   France.
    b.   Germany.
    c.   England.
    d.   Canada.

4.   The commerce clause regulates:

    a.   intrastate commerce only.
    b.   interstate commerce only.
    c.   foreign commerce only.
    d.   all of the above if interstate commerce is burdened.

5.   The supreme or highest law of the land is:

    a.   legislation passed by Congress.
    b.   the United States Constitution.
    c.   common law.
    d.   administrative law.

6.   Federal administrative regulations are published in the:

    a.   National Reporter System.
    b.   Federal Supplement.
    c.   Code of Federal Regulations.
    d.   United States Statutes at Large.

7.   Watkins sued Griffin for breach of contract. Watkins lost in trial court and has appealed the case to a state court of appeal. Watkins is the:

    a.   plaintiff and appellant.
    b.   plaintiff and appellee.
    c.   defendant and appellee.
    d.   defendant and petitioner.

8.   "358 N.W.788" means that a case can be found at:

    a.   volume 788, page 358 of the North Western Reporter.
    b.   volume 358, page 788 of the North Western Reporter.
    c.   section 358, page 788 of the North Western Reporter.
    d.   section 788, volume 358 of the North Western Reporter.

9.   <u>Watkins v. Griffin</u> was decided by a court of appeals consisting of nine judges. Judges A, B, C, D, and E decided for Watkins, although E wrote his own opinion. Judges F, G, H & I decided for Griffin. Judge E's separate opinion is called a _____ decision.

    a.   concurring

        b.   dissenting
        c.   majority
        d.   minority

10.   If Judge F wrote an opinion, it would be a _____ opinion.

        a.   concurring
        b.   dissenting
        c.   majority
        d.   minority

Answers to Study Questions

Fill-in-the-Blank Questions

A law passed by the U.S. Congress is an example of statutory law or legislation; common law is case law. A regulation adopted by the Internal Revenue Service is an example of administrative law. The commerce clause is part of the United States Constitution.

True-False Questions

1.   F. "Codes" are publications of statutes arranged by subject matter.

2.   T.

3.   F. The UCC is a uniform law which is passed or rejected by the legislature of each state.

4.   T.

5.   F. An employer need only make reasonable accommodations.

6.   F. It is protected but to a lesser extent than other forms of speech.

7.   T.

8.   T.

9.   F. Case law is a synonym for common law.

10.   F. It is used in cases involving the commerce clause.

11.   T.

12.   T.

13.   T.

14.   T.

15.   F. If a trial court decision is being published, the plaintiff's name is always first. If an appellate court decision is being published, the name of the appellant _may_ come first.

16.   F. LEXIS is a computerized legal research system.

17.   F. Administrative process refers to administration of law by administrative agencies.

Multiple-Choice Questions

1.   c
2.   a
3.   c
4.   d
5.   b
6.   c
7.   a
8.   b
9.   a
10.   b

Courts and Procedures

General Principles

The American judicial system is composed of 2 sets of courts: state and federal. The federal courts hear only certain types of cases; most disputes are settled in state courts. Each system has three levels: a trial court, a middle-level or appeals court and a supreme court.

The formal process of litigation is similar in each state. Modern procedure attempts to settle disputes quickly and fairly. Note that a case can end before the parties have reached the courtroom. Arbitration and other forms of non-judicial dispute resolution are becoming more prevalent.

Chapter Summary

I.   <u>Jurisdiction</u>--Jurisdiction is technically the power of a court to hear a case. It can refer to a court's geographical boundaries or to the subject matter of cases. As a practical matter, it tells a lawyer in which court to file a case.

     A.   <u>Jurisdiction over Persons and Property</u>--The power of a state court is normally limited to its geographic boundaries. A defendant has a right to be sued in his or her home state. Long-arm statutes are exceptions to this rule. Typical long-arm statutes involve a corporation who may be sued in the state in which it is incorporated, where it has its main plant and any state where it does business.

     B.   <u>Jurisdiction over Subject Matter</u>--A court's power to hear a case may be limited by the type of case or the money amount involved. A court with restricted powers has <u>limited</u> jurisdiction; a court which hears most types of cases has <u>general</u> jurisdiction.

C.   Original v. Appellate Jurisdiction--Trial courts which hear the case for the first time have original jurisdiction. Courts of appeal and supreme courts, which hear the case only after it has been tried, have appellate jurisdiction.

D.   Venue--Venue determines the geographic location of a suit within a judicial district. Generally, venue is proper where the parties live or where the case arose.

Jurisdiction over the person tells the lawyer in which state a suit may be brought. Jurisdiction over the subject matter determines which kind of court will hear the case. All three requirements must be satisfied.

Example: A resident of Houston, Texas receives a traffic ticket. Jurisdiction over the subject matter is in the municipal court and the venue is Houston.

II.   The State Court System

A.   Trial Courts--May have limited jurisdiction (probate courts) or general jurisdiction (county or district courts). Small claims courts have limited jurisdiction based on the amount of the claim. (Usually less than $2500). Lawyers are not required. They are courts of original jurisdiction because they hear cases when they are first brought.

B.   Courts of Appeal--Most states have three levels of courts: trial, intermediate courts of appeal, and a supreme court. These upper-level courts do not try cases. The judges examine the record of case in the trial court to determine if a mistake was made. The supreme court of a state rules finally on cases involving state law. Its opinion cannot be challenged, even by the United States Supreme Court (unless the case involves federal law).

III.   The Federal Court System

A.   Trial Courts--U.S. district courts have original jurisdiction in cases involving federal law. There are other trial courts with special subject-matter jurisdiction (e.g., U.S. tax court).

B.   U.S. Courts of Appeals--Twelve judicial circuits. Hear appeals from district courts and from federal administrative agencies.

C.   The U.S. Supreme Court--Created by the Constitution. Nine justices are nominated by the president and confirmed by the Senate.

IV.   Jurisdiction of the Federal Courts and Judicial Review

A.   Constitutional Boundaries--Creates U.S. Supreme Court but gives the

Congress the right to create lower federal courts. Original jurisdiction of the high court is established by the Constitution; Congress regulates appellate jurisdiction. Courts can also limit the types of cases they will hear.

B.   Diversity Jurisdiction--Plaintiff and defendant are from different states and the amount in dispute is more than $50,000.

C.   Federal Question--Case involving a federal statute, the U.S. Constitution, or a treaty. A case can involve both state and federal law. In such a case, a federal court and a state court would have concurrent jurisdiction. If only one court can hear a case, that court has exclusive jurisdiction. Federal courts have exclusive jurisdiction of certain kinds of cases (e.g. bankruptcy, patents).

D.   Judicial Review--The power of the courts to determine if laws passed by Congress conflict with the provisions of the United States Constitution. If so, the law will be held to be unconstitutional.

V.   How Cases Reach the Supreme Court--In the federal court system, the party who loses at trial has the right to take the case to a middle-level court of appeals for review. After a decision by that court, the losing party may ask the Supreme Court to hear the case by filing an application for a writ of certiorari. The Court does not have to hear the case and most cases are not heard. Usually only cases involving important Constitutional issues are heard, and even then, four of the nine justices must vote to hear the case.

VI.   Following a Case through the State Courts--Our system of courts is adversarial, meaning that both sides of the case are presented by opposing parties. The judge is neutral and usually passive, although he or she may ask questions. Court procedure may be outlined as follows:

A.   The Pleadings--The initial documents filed by a plaintiff and a defendant.

(1)   Complaint (Petition)--Filed by the plaintiff. Must state the facts, the rule of law violated by the defendant and the remedy sought.

(2)   Summons--Notice of the suit and a copy of the petition is given to the defendant. Usually served in person.

(3)   Answer, Counterclaim or Motion to Dismiss--Possible responses by the defendant after receipt of summons and complaint.

(a)   Default Judgment--If the defendant does not answer, the plaintiff wins automatically.

(b)   <u>Motion to Dismiss (or Demurrer)</u>--Asks the judge to dismiss the case because plaintiff's petition does not show a legal wrong. If it is granted, the case ends and the loser may appeal.

(c)   <u>Answer</u>--May deny what the plaintiff claims or admit that the facts of the petition are true but there is another reason the defendant should not be liable (affirmative defense). Examples of affirmative defenses are statute of limitations, contributory negligence, and fraud.

(d)   <u>Counterclaim</u>--The defendant not only denies liability but claims that the plaintiff is liable.

B.   <u>Judgment on the Pleadings and Summary Judgment</u>--A motion for judgment on the pleadings asks the judge to look at the initial documents filed by both parties and to decide the case. A motion for summary judgment is similar; however, the judge may look at other evidence such as sworn statements or affidavits. A motion for summary judgment will be granted only if the facts are not in dispute.

C.   <u>Discovery</u>--The attorneys trade information about the case. It is designed to make trials shorter and equitable. There are five broad methods of discovery.

(1)   <u>Depositions</u>--Witness answers questions posed by both attorneys at an informal meeting. A court reporter swears in the witness and takes down the testimony. This testimony can be used at trial if the witness is unavailable or if the witness tells a different version of the story at trial.

(2)   <u>Interrogatories</u>--Written questions answered under oath by parties and their attorneys. Interrogatories may be sent to parties only; they may not be used to question witnesses. Interrogatories are less expensive than depositions.

(3)   <u>Other Information</u>

(a)   <u>Request for Admissions</u>--One party sends the other a written set of statements pertaining to the litigation. The recipient may admit or deny the statements. Anything admitted will not have to be proven at trial. Therefore, this form of discovery is usually used to dispose of unimportant or uncontested issues.

(b)   <u>Request for Production of Documents or Objects and Request for Entry upon Land</u>--Parties can examine relevant documents or objects not in their possession.

If a particular location is important to the litigation, a party may also request entry on the property.

    (c)   <u>Physical and Mental Examination</u>--Available <u>only</u> if one party is claiming health-related injury, cause of action, or defense.

(4)   <u>Compliance with Discovery Requests</u>--If a party does not cooperate with discovery requests, the court may order him or her to do so. If the party still refuses, the court may order a fine, imprisonment, payment of costs, or a default judgment.

D.   <u>Pretrial Hearing</u>--If a case has not been settled, the judge and the attorneys meet to plan the trial and resolve disputes over evidence and other matters.

E.   <u>Trial by Jury</u>--In almost all cases, the parties are entitled to a jury trial. The case can be decided by a judge if neither party requests a jury.

F.   <u>Voir Dire (Jury Selection)</u>--The lawyers select the jury from a panel by asking questions. The questions are designed to show if a juror is biased in favor of one side or the other. Potential jurors may be eliminated by strikes. Strikes for cause are based on a showing that a juror should not serve; peremptory strikes (limited in number) eliminate jurors without a reason being given.

A petit jury is a trial court jury. A grand jury is used in criminal proceedings and hears only the state's side of a case. A grand jury determines if there is probable cause to bring a criminal defendant to trial.

G.   <u>At the Trial</u>

(1)   <u>Plaintiff's Case</u>--Because the plaintiff initiated the lawsuit, he or she has the burden of proof and must proceed first. The procedure is the same for all witnesses; the plaintiff's attorney asks questions on direct examination and the defendant's attorney cross-examines the witnesses. The plaintiff's attorney may then ask questions of the same witness on redirect examination and the defendant's attorney may ask questions on re-cross examination. At this time, the plaintiff also introduces exhibits or relevant items.

(2)   <u>Motion for Directed Verdict</u>--At the end of the plaintiff's evidence, the defendant may claim that the plaintiff has failed to make out a case. If the judge agrees and grants the motion, the case ends.

(3)   Defendant's Evidence--If a directed verdict is not granted, the defendant must present his or her evidence. At this stage, the defendant conducts direct examination of his or her witnesses and the plaintiff conducts cross-examination.

(4)   Rebuttal and Rejoinder--The plaintiff is given a chance to refute the defendant's evidence on rebuttal. The defendant is then entitled to do the same on rejoinder.

(5)   Closing Arguments--Each side is given opportunity to summarize the evidence and persuade the jury

(6)   Instructions (Court's Charge)--The judge tells the jury the rules of law to be used in deciding the case, and the definitions of legal terms.

(7)   Jury's Verdict

(8)   a.   Motion for New Trial or J.N.O.V.--After the jury has decided the case, the loser may ask the judge to grant a new trial.

         b.   Motion for Judgment N.O.V.--A motion may also be made to reverse the jury's verdict. If the motion for j.n.o.v. is granted, the loser becomes the winner.

VII.   The Appeal--The loser has the right to ask a middle-level appeals court to hear the case. The loser's attorney submits the record on appeal which consists of the documents in the case, the testimony of the witnesses, and the attorneys' written arguments or briefs. The attorneys may also choose to appear before the appellate court for oral argument.

The appellate court can reach three possible decisions:

(1)   Affirm--The trial court decision stands because the appellate court agrees with the verdict reached at trial.

(2)   Reverse--The trial court decision is overturned or reversed if a mistake was made at trial. The loser at trial court becomes the winner.

(3)   Remand--The appellate court sends the case back for a new trial.

         After an intermediate appellate court makes a decision, a party can attempt to appeal to a state's supreme court. However, these appeals are usually limited by a process similar to a petition for a writ of certiorari in the federal system.

VIII.   <u>Alternative Dispute Resolution (ADR)</u>--Less formal, non-judicial resolution of legal disputes. A disinterested third party listens to both parties. ADR is becoming more popular because it is less expensive and less time-consuming than a trial. Court systems and private industries are experimenting with ADR programs.

A.   <u>Mediation</u>--The parties reach the decision by working with a third party.

B.   <u>Arbitration</u>--A more formal hearing in which the third party or arbitrator makes the decision or award. A contract may specify that a dispute will be settled by arbitration; this contractual obligation will be enforced by the state and federal governments. Arbitration services provide panels of experts who will arbitrate disputes.

C.   <u>Summary Jury Trial</u>--Used in federal court. Parties present arguments without witnesses. A jury issues a non-binding decision and after the decision, the court orders more negotiations. If a settlement is not reached, either side can ask for a standard jury trial.

Study Questions

Fill-in-the-Blank Questions

Mary claims that John owes her money and John refuses to pay. Mary decides to sue. The document that Mary's lawyer will file to start the suit is a _____.
(complaint/demurrer)

John's lawyer claims that Mary has no case and asks the judge to bar Mary's claim and end the suit. The document that John's lawyer will file is a(n) _____.
(answer/motion to dismiss/counterclaim)

If the case goes to trial and Mary wins, John's lawyer may file a document asking the court to reverse the jury's verdict. This document is a motion for a _____.
(directed verdict/judgment n.o.v.)

True-False Questions

1.   Congress can place some limits on the jurisdiction of the United States Supreme Court. _____

2.   When a plaintiff's attorney questions a witness for the defendant, he or she is conducting rebuttal. _____

3.   A synonym for the instructions given to the jury is the court's charge. _____

4.   The federal courts have limited jurisdiction. _____

5.   A long-arm statute is used by lawyers in selecting a jury. _____

6.   When two or more courts could hear the same case, the courts have appellate jurisdiction. _____

7.   If a party makes a motion for summary judgment and the judge grants the motion, the case will be decided by a jury. _____

8.   Most states have a two-tiered court system. _____

9.   An application for a writ of certiorari is filed in trial court. _____

10.   In an arbitration proceeding, a third party decides who will win the case. _____

11.   A lawyer who demonstrates that a potential juror is biased will be entitled to use a peremptory strike in order to remove that person from the jury. _____

12.   Arbitration clauses in a contract are usually not enforceable. _____

13.   A grand jury is used in arbitration proceedings. _____

Multiple-Choice Questions

1.   Which of the following are in correct chronological order?

a.   Voir dire, motion for summary judgment, summons, motion for j.n.o.v.
b.   Voir dire, summons, motion for summary judgment, motion for j.n.o.v.
c.   Summons, motion for summary judgment, voir dire, motion for j.n.o.v.
d.   Summons, motion for j.n.o.v., voir dire, motion for summary judgment

2.   When a case can only be brought in one court, that court has _____ of the case.

a.   original jurisdiction
b.   concurrent jurisdiction
c.   limited jurisdiction
d.   exclusive jurisdiction

3.   If the defendant's lawyer asks the judge to decide the case immediately after the plaintiff has presented evidence at trial, he or she will ask for a:

   a.   counterclaim.
   b.   directed verdict.
   c.   new trial.
   d.   voir dire.

4.   The decision made by an arbitrator is called a(n):

   a.   verdict.
   b.   award.
   c.   motion.
   d.   none of the above.

5.   Mary bought a microwave oven from AAA Appliance, a company which is incorporated in Delaware, has its main office in Atlanta, Georgia, and does business in Milwaukee, Wisconsin, where Mary purchased her oven. If the oven malfunctions and Mary decides to sue, in which states can she sue AAA?

   a.   Delaware only
   b.   Delaware or Georgia only
   c.   Wisconsin only
   d.   Delaware, Georgia or Wisconsin

6.   Written questions answered by a party and his or her lawyer as a part of discovery are called:

   a.   interrogatories.
   b.   interrogations.
   c.   depositions.
   d.   dispositions.

7.   Which of the following documents would not be filed by a defendant to a lawsuit?

   a.   counterclaim
   b.   motion to dismiss
   c.   answer
   d.   complaint

8.   Bob owns a video rental store in Santa Fe, New Mexico. He recently agreed to purchase $5,000 of video equipment from a supplier in New York City. If the supplier breaches the contract, Bob:

   a.   can sue in federal court because of diversity of citizenship.
   b.   can sue in federal court because a federal question is involved.

      c.   can sue in federal court because federal courts have general jurisdiction.

      d.   cannot sue in federal court.

9.   Which of the following are in correct chronological order?

      a.   summons, motion for directed verdict, pre-trial hearing, counterclaim

      b.   summons, pre-trial hearing, counterclaim, motion for directed verdict

      c.   summons, counterclaim, motion for directed verdict, pre-trial hearing

      d.   summons, counterclaim, pre-trial hearing, motion for directed verdict

10.   Which of the following statements best describes Congress's role in determining jurisdiction of the federal courts?

      a.   Congress determines the complete jurisdiction of all federal courts, including the complete jurisdiction of the United States Supreme Court.

      b.   Congress determines the jurisdiction of the lower federal courts and the appellate jurisdiction of the United States Supreme Court.

      c.   Congress determines the jurisdiction of the lower federal courts and the original jurisdiction of the United States Supreme Court.

      d.   Congress has no power to determine the jurisdiction of the federal courts.

11.   Peter sued Cynthia in trial court and Peter won the case. Cynthia has decided to appeal. If the court of appeals agrees with the decision of the trial court, the case will be:

      a.   affirmed.

      b.   remanded.

      c.   reversed.

      d.   none of the above.

12.   If the court of appeals disagrees with the decision of the trial court and decides that Cynthia should win, the case will be:

      a.   affirmed.

      b.   remanded.

      c.   reversed.

      d.   none of the above.

13.   If the defendant in a lawsuit fails to respond to a summons, the plaintiff will receive:

      a.   an award from an arbitrator.

      b.   a new trial.

      c.   a default judgment.

      d.   a directed verdict.

14.   The prisoners in a county jail want to file suit against the county because they are not allowed to drink coffee in jail. The prisoners claim that the ban on coffee is in violation of the Eighth Amendment of the United States Constitution. The prisoners:

a.   can sue in federal court because of diversity of citizenship.
b.   cannot sue in federal court because there is no diversity of citizenship.
c.   can sue in federal court because a federal question is at issue.
d.   cannot sue in federal court because a federal question is at issue.

15.   The power of a court to hold a statute or law unconstitutional is:

a.   judicial review.
b.   judicial arbitration.
c.   exclusive jurisdiction.
d.   writ of certiorari.

16.   The geographic region within a judicial district where a case can be brought is:

a.   jurisdiction over the person.
b.   jurisdiction over the subject matter.
c.   venue.
d.   federal question.

17.   If a party loses a case at trial and on the first appeal and wants a supreme court to hear the case, he or she:

a.   can file an appeal and the court must hear the case.
b.   can file an application for a writ of certiorari which the court may or may not grant.
c.   cannot file another appeal.
d.   can file an application for a writ of certiorari and the court must hear the case.

18.   A trial court which can hear most types of cases has:

a.   appellate jurisdiction.
b.   exclusive jurisdiction.
c.   limited jurisdiction.
d.   general jurisdiction.

19.   When the plaintiff's attorney questions a witness for the defense for the first time, he or she is conducting:

a.   cross-examination.
b.   direct examination.
c.   recross examination.
d.   redirect examination.

20.   There are several points during a case when it can end at the trial stage. Which of the following, if granted by the judge, will <u>not</u> end the trial?

    a.   motion for directed verdict
    b.   counterclaim
    c.   motion for summary judgment
    d.   motion to dismiss

21.   Judicial review:

    a.   is the power of Congress to limit the kinds of cases that federal courts may hear.
    b.   is the power of the federal courts to hear cases involving state law.

    c.   is the power of the federal courts to determine if a law passed by Congress is unconstitutional.
    d.   is the power of the Senate to confirm a president's choice for justice of the United States Supreme Court.

22.   Which of the following is in correct chronological order?

    a.   instructions to the jury, motion for a new trial, appeal to the court of appeals, application for a writ of certiorari
    b.   motion for new trial, appeal to the court of appeals, instructions to the jury, application for a writ of certiorari
    c.   application for a writ of certiorari, motion for new trial, instructions to the jury, appeal to the court of appeals
    d.   instructions to the jury, motion for a new trial, application for a writ of certiorari, appeal to the court of appeals

23.   Which of the following are pleadings in a civil trial?

    a.   complaint and motion for summary judgment
    b.   complaint and answer
    c.   complaint and motion for j.n.o.v.
    d.   motion to dismiss and motion for summary judgment

24.   Madeline sues Patsy for negligence. Patsy's lawyer files a motion for judgment on the pleadings. If the judge grants the motion, who will win the case?

    a.   Patsy
    b.   Madeline
    c.   No one, the jury must still hear the case
    d.   No one, the judge must still hear the case

25.   Which of the following facts about arbitration is <u>false</u>?

    a.   The parties can use arbitration in insurance law cases.

b.   Arbitration is a form of alternative dispute resolution.
c.   Arbitration must follow the court rules of evidence and procedure.
d.   The arbitrator, not the parties, decides the case.

26.   Paula and Susan are involved in an automobile accident. Jerry is a witness. Paula sues Susan in negligence. Which of the following statements regarding possible discovery in the case is <u>false</u>?

a.   Paula may send interrogatories to Susan, but she may not send them to Jerry.
b.   Susan will be able to obtain copies of the repair bills for Paula's car.
c.   Paula may not send a request for admissions to Jerry because he is not a party to the suit.
d.   Susan may not request Jerry's deposition because he is not a party to the suit.

27.   A form of arbitration in which a party argues a case but does not call witnesses is:

a.   mediation.
b.   summary jury trial.
c.   directed verdict.
d.   no-bill.

28.   A grand jury:

a.   decides civil cases only.
b.   determines if there is enough evidence to bring a criminal case to trial.
c.   decides criminal cases in a summary jury trial.
d.   decides criminal and civil cases.

29.   Which of the following is <u>not</u> a form of discovery?

a.   request for admissions
b.   interrogatory
c.   peremptory strikes
d.   deposition

30.   The "rule of four" states that:

a.   four out of twelve jurors are needed to decide a case.
b.   four court of appeals judges must agree in order to reverse a trial court decision.
c.   four justices of the United States Supreme Court must agree to grant a writ of certiorari.
d.   only four jurors may be struck for cause in any one case.

Answers to Study Questions

Fill-in-the-Blank Questions

Mary's lawyer will file a complaint. A demurrer or motion to dismiss would be filed by the defendant if he or she thought that there was not basis for the suit.

John's lawyers will file a motion to dismiss. An answer denies the facts in the plaintiff's petition but does not ask the judge to dismiss the case. A counterclaim is filed by a defendant if he or she not only denies responsibility but sues the plaintiff.

John's lawyers will file a motion for a judgment n.o.v. A judgment n.o.v. asks the court to disregard the jury's verdict and to reverse the jury's decision. A motion for directed verdict is filed at the conclusion of the plaintiff's evidence, in the middle of the lawsuit.

True-False Questions

1.   T.

2.   F. This is a description of cross-examination. Rebuttal is the plaintiff's chance to present more evidence after the defendant has presented his or her case.

3.   T.

4.   T.

5.   F. A long-arm statute allows a non-resident defendant to be sued in the plaintiff's home state.

6.   F. They have concurrent jurisdiction. Appellate jurisdiction is the power of a court to hear a case on appeal.

7.   F. Summary judgment is used when the facts of the case are not in dispute. If the facts are not in dispute, there is no need for a jury.

8.   F. Most states have a three-tiered system: trial court, court of appeals, and supreme court.

9.   F. It is filed in a supreme court.

10.   T.

11.   F. If a lawyer can prove bias, he or she will use a strike for cause. A peremptory strike can be used without demonstrating bias.

12.   F.   An arbitration clause is usually enforceable by the state or federal government.

13.   F.   A grand jury determines if there is enough evidence to try a person accused of a crime.

Multiple-Choice Questions

1.	c	16.	c
2.	d	17.	b
3.	b	18.	d
4.	b	19.	a
5.	d	20.	b
6.	a	21.	c
7.	d	22.	a
8.	d	23.	b
9.	d	24.	a
10.	b	25.	c
11.	a	26.	d
12.	c	27.	b
13.	c	28.	b
14.	c	29.	c
15.	a	30.	c

3

Torts

General Principles

A tort is a wrong involving an injury committed by one private party against another. A person may be liable under both civil and criminal law if his or her actions constitute a tort and a crime. An injury may include physical injury, emotional distress, injury to property, and injury to a person's reputation.

There are three kinds of torts: intentional injury, negligence, and strict liability. The difference depends on the state of mind of the person committing the tort. An intentional tort requires a conscious, deliberate action, although not necessarily the intent to do the harm which results. Negligence is based on carelessness; strict liability is no-fault liability.

A plaintiff will not be successful in a tort suit unless he or she can provide the <u>elements</u> of the tort. Each tort has separate elements and each element must be met. If one or more elements is missing, that tort has not occurred.

Chapter Summary

I.   <u>Intentional Torts against Persons</u>--The defendant or tortfeasor must intend an act and the act must cause an injury to the body, welfare or reputation of another. It does not matter that the tortfeasor desired a different result; the law presumes that a person intends the normal consequences of his or her actions.

    A.   <u>Assault</u>--The elements are:

        (1)   An intentional act

        (2)   The act causes fear or apprehension

        (3)   The fear of immediate bodily contact

        (4)   The contact would be harmful or offensive to a reasonable person

B.   <u>Battery</u>--The elements are:

        (1)   An intentional act

        (2)   The act is unexcused

        (3)   Bodily contact (includes items closely connected with a person)

        (4)   The contact would be harmful or offensive to a reasonable person

C.   <u>Defenses to Assault and Battery</u> include:

        (1)   Consent by the plaintiff to the touching (e.g. participation in football games or other contact sports)

        (2)   Self-defense or defense of another if reasonable force is used to repel an attack; the defense is valid even if there is no real danger if a <u>reasonable</u> person would have thought that the danger existed.

        (3)   Defense of property if reasonable force is used, but never force which would cause serious bodily injury or death.

D.   <u>False Imprisonment</u>--The elements are:

        (1)   Intentional

        (2)   Unjustified

        (3)   <u>Confinement or restraint of another</u>--May be accomplished by actual physical restraint or threats, if the threats are of physical force.

In most states, a merchant protection statute allows store owners to detain suspected shoplifters if there is probable cause to stop the customer and if the detention is reasonable.

E.   <u>Infliction of Mental Distress</u>--The elements are:

        (1)   An intentional act

        (2)   The act is outrageous or extreme

(3)   The act causes serious emotional distress

(4)   Physical symptoms of distress (some states)

F.   <u>Defamation</u>--Protects injury to reputation. Disparagement of goods and slander of title protect injury to the reputation of a person's property. Oral defamation is slander; written defamation is libel. The elements are:

(1)   A statement (stated by one person <u>or</u> repeated by another)

(2)   Statement would cause a person to hate or ridicule the plaintiff

(3)   The statement is made to a third party (publication). Does not matter that the statement was not intended to be overheard; an eavesdropper can satisfy this requirement.

(4)   Damages based on (b). Some statements automatically satisfy this element (defamation per se).

<u>Defenses</u>:

(1)   Truth

(2)   Absolute privilege--Statement made on the floor of Congress by members of Congress or statements made by judges or attorneys during trial

(3)   Public figure--If the plaintiff is a public figure, malice or reckless disregard of the truth, must be shown.

G.   <u>Invasion of Privacy</u> (4 types)

(1)   Unpermitted use of a person's picture or likeness

(2)   Intrusion on a person's affairs

(3)   Public disclosure of private and objectionable facts (not necessarily false)

(4)   Disclosure of information which misleads the public about a person

H.   <u>Misrepresentation</u>--The elements are:

(1)   Misrepresentation of material facts--Puffing and opinions will not suffice, the fact misrepresented must have been important.

(2)   Misrepresentation is made in order to induce reliance

(3)   Justifiable reliance by the plaintiff (Would a reasonable person have relied?)

(4)   Damages

(5)   The damages were caused by or related to the misrepresentation. If damages were suffered because of some other reason, there may be a case for negligence or strict liability but not for misrepresentation.

II.   Intentional Torts against Property--Property is either real estate (land or items permanently attached to it such as a carport or fence) or personal (everything else).

A.   Trespass to Land--The elements are:

(1)   Unpermitted (owner or rightful possessor does not consent)
(2)   Intrusion above, on, or under land
(3)   The land belongs to another
(4)   Injury is not required but the amount of damages depends on the extent of the injury.

Defenses are few, but the defendant's conduct may be excused if he or she entered the property in an emergency or if he or she can prove that the plaintiff does not own the land.

B.   Trespass to Personal Property--The elements are:

(1)   Unjustified and intentional

(2)   Interference

(3)   With the personal property of another

The defenses are the same as for trespass to land. Note that the property does not have to be moved and distinguish:

C.   Conversion--The civil wrong corresponds to the criminal wrong of theft. The elements are:

(1)   Unjustified and intentional

(2)   Taking--removal

(3)   The property belongs to another

III.   Negligence--The actions of the defendant do not have to be deliberate; carelessness is the standard. Most auto accidents are caused by negligence. The elements are:

    A.   Duty owed by the Plaintiff to the Defendant--May be extremely broad such as the duty one driver owes another to drive safely. Certain persons, such as parents and children, owe a duty of care to each other as a consequence of their relationship.

    B.   Breach of Duty--Ask yourself if the defendant acted carelessly. The standard is a reasonable man in the defendant's position. E.g. a lawyer must act as a reasonable lawyer would act.

    C.   Injury--The plaintiff must have suffered some (although not necessarily physical) injury.

    D.   Causation

        (1)   Cause in Fact--The defendant's action must have been the physical cause of the injury. The "but for" test is used to see if this element has been met. Ask yourself: "If the defendant had not acted, would the injury have occurred?" (But for the defendant's conduct, the injury would not have occurred.)

        (2)   Proximate or Legal Cause--Based on the idea that a defendant should only be responsible for injuries that can be foreseen to result from his or her careless conduct. Distinguish intentional torts where the defendant is liable whether the injuries are foreseeable or not. Determine the breach committed by the defendant and ask yourself what type of injuries are foreseeable from this type of conduct. If the injury suffered is foreseeable, there is proximate cause; if not, there is no proximate cause.

            A superseding or intervening force may break the chain of causation. No liability if this force could not have been foreseen. However, defensive maneuvers and rescue of a person in danger can be foreseen and will not break the chain.

            Res Ipsa Loquitur--Helps a plaintiff prove negligence when the injury obviously occurred as a result of carelessness. The plaintiff must also show that the cause of the negligence was under the defendant's sole control. If this rule is applied, then the defendant has the burden of proving that he or she was not negligent.

    E.   Defenses to Negligence

        (1)   Assumption of Risk--The plaintiff knows that his or her

conduct involves risk but voluntarily decides to act. The "voluntariness" element does not apply if the plaintiff acts in an emergency or if the risk is greater or different than a reasonable person would expect.

(2)   <u>Contributory Negligence</u>--If the plaintiff is also negligent, contributory negligence bars any suit by the plaintiff regardless of which party was more at fault.

(3)   <u>Comparative Negligence</u>--Most states have adopted a comparative negligence standard. The negligence of the plaintiff and the defendant are compared. In the <u>pure</u> form of comparative negligence, the plaintiff may sue regardless of the amount of fault. In other states, if the plaintiff is more than 50 percent at fault, the suit is barred.

(4)   <u>Last Clear Chance</u>--Used when both parties are negligent. The person who had the last opportunity to avoid the injury will be responsible for damage to the other party. This was used frequently in cases involving contributory negligence; otherwise, a slightly negligent plaintiff would not be able to sue at all. This rule has been adopted in most states where comparative negligence is used.

IV.   <u>Strict Liability</u>--No-fault liability. It is not necessary to find that the defendant breached a duty. It is used with high-risk activities such as blasting and keeping wild animals and is a cost of that type of business. Assumption of risk is a defense; comparative and contributory negligence are not.

Study Questions

Fill-in-the-Blank Questions

Thomas Tortfeasor is shopping in the grocery store. He becomes impatient with two ladies blocking the aisle. He forcibly bumps one lady with his cart. She falls down and breaks her hip. He swings his fist at the other lady but misses.

When Thomas bumped the woman with his cart, he committed

_____.
(assault/battery/neither)

When Thomas attempted to hit the second woman, he committed

_____.
(assault/battery/both)

Thomas _____ responsible for the woman's broken hip.
                (is/is not)

True-False Questions

1.   Trespass to land is an intentional tort. _____

2.   A teacher asks a student into her office, closes the door, and calls him a "cheat". Assuming that the statement is false and that only the student heard the remark, the teacher has committed slander. _____

3.   Assumption of risk is a defense to negligence. _____

4.   Strict liability is a synonym for no-fault liability. _____

5.   Necessity is a defense to trespass to land. _____

6.   The difference between trespass to personal property and conversion is that in conversion, the property must be moved. _____

7.   Public disclosure of true but embarrasing facts is a form of invasion of privacy. _____

8.   A "posted" sign is necessary to prove that a burglar is a trespasser. _____

9.   Proximate cause is an element of every intentional tort. _____

10.   In order for a plaintiff to recover for the tort of false imprisonment case, he or she must show that the defendant used physical restraint. _____

Multiple-Choice Questions

1.   Mrs. Harris buys a new toaster. The first time she uses it, she notices that sparks are flying from the toaster. She continues to use the toaster and is severely burned. If Mrs. Harris sues the toaster manufacturer in negligence, it can use which of the following defenses to defeat her claim?

    a.   Contributory negligence only
    b.   Assumption of risk only
    c.   Both contributory negligence and assumption of risk
    d.   Neither contributory negligence nor assumption of risk

2.   Which of the following is not a defense to assault?

    a.   Consent
    b.   Necessity
    c.   Self-defense
    d.   Defense of property

3.   Nancy is walking her dog without a leash. The dog sees a cat, chases it, and tramples a neighbor's rose bush. The neighbor witnesses the chase and suffers a heart attack. Nancy is responsible for:

   a.   the damage to the rose bush.
   b.   the neighbor's medical bills.
   c.   the damage to the rose bush and the neighbor's medical bills.
   d.   neither the damage to the rose bush nor the neighbor's medical expenses.

4.   Susan is shopping for a new car. A car salesman tells her that the car she has selected is the best car in the price range. After Susan buys the car, she discovers that another car in the price range gets better gas mileage and has more safety features. If Susan sues the salesman for misrepresentation:

   a.   she will succeed because the second car was better.
   b.   she will succeed because she was induced to buy the first car.
   c.   she will not succeed because she was not induced to buy the car.
   d.   she will not succeed because the salesman did not misrepresent a fact.

5.   Molly's ex-husband tells his drinking buddies that she had a baby out of wedlock. Assuming that the statement is true, Molly can sue her ex-husband for:

   a.   defamation.
   b.   false light.
   c.   public disclosure of private facts.
   d.   defamation and public disclosure of private facts.

6.   Judith owns a grocery store. One of her employees tells her that he saw Mr. Jones put a steak under his shirt. As Mr. Jones is leaving the store, Judith stops him, takes him to the store office, locks the door and calls the police. The police arrive 10 minutes later and discover that Mr. Jones is not guilty. If Mr. Jones sues Judith for false imprisonment, he will:

   a.   succeed because he was confined intentionally.
   b.   succeed because Judith lacked probable cause to detain him.
   c.   not succeed because the confinement was reasonable.
   d.   not succeed because Judith did not intend to confine him for a long period of time.

7.   Tony's Pizza sends out a false press release which states that several people who ate at a competitor's restaurant have contracted food poisoning. The competitor can sue Tony's for:

   a.   assault.
   b.   disparagement of goods.
   c.   negligence.
   d.   public disclosure of private facts.

8.   Two students find their teacher's business law book. They pour ink on the torts chapter. The students have committed:

         a.   trespass to personal property.
         b.   conversion.
         c.   trespass to personal property and conversion.
         d.   neither trespass to personal property nor conversion.

9.   Paul owns a construction company. He carelessly sets out dynamite. When a blast occurs, the windows in a nearby house shatter. The owner of the house can sue Paul for:

         a.   negligence only.
         b.   strict liability only.
         c.   negligence and strict liability.
         d.   neither negligence nor strict liability.

10.   Mr. Smith sees a man collapse on the sidewalk. Mr. Smith rushes past without stopping. The man suffers serious injuries because he remained on the sidewalk until someone took him to the hospital two hours later. If the man sues Mr. Smith, he will not succeed because one of the following elements is missing. Which one?

         a.   Duty of care from Mr. Smith to the injured man
         b.   Cause in fact
         c.   Contributory negligence
         d.   Injury

11.   Bill sees Sandra's new bicycle in the driveway. He takes the bicycle and rides to the store. Sandra can sue Bill for:

         a.   theft only.
         b.   conversion only.
         c.   theft and conversion.
         d.   trespass to personal property and conversion.

12.   Linda carelessly parks her car on a hill and forgets to set the parking brake. While Linda is gone, a flood occurs and her car is swept through a store window. Linda's best argument against a negligence suit by the store owner is:

         a.   contributory negligence.
         b.   assumption of risk.
         c.   last clear chance.
         d.   superseding cause.

13.   Robert is shopping with his 3 year-old son. Robert allows the boy to wander through the store. A stockboy sees the child approaching a meat grinder but does nothing. The child is seriously injured when he sticks his hand in the

meat grinder. If Robert sues the store for negligence, the store's best defense is:

a.   contributory negligence on Robert's part.
b.   assumption of risk.
c.   last clear chance.
d.   intervening cause.

14.   Alice is involved in an auto accident and sues the other driver, Carl. The jury finds that the accident was 30 percent Alice's fault. If Alice lives in a state that recognized contributory negligence, Alice will recover:

a.   100 percent of her damages.
b.   70 percent of her damages.
c.   30 percent of her damages.
d.   nothing.

15.   If Alice lives in a state that recognized comparative negligence, Alice will recover:

a.   100 percent of her damages.
b.   70 percent of her damages.
c.   30 percent of her damages.
d.   nothing

16.   The mayor of Cantonville, who is running for re-election, is suing the local paper for a story leaked to the paper by members of the opposing political party. Assuming that the story is false, the mayor will win the suit if he can show that:

a.   the reporter who wrote the story was negligent in checking her sources.
b.   the reporter who wrote the story knew that the story was false when she wrote it.
c.   the paper printed the story and the intentions of the reporter do not matter.
d.   the story was false and the intentions of the reporter do not matter.

17.   Which of the following is a defense to strict liability?

a.   Comparative negligence
b.   Assumption of risk
c.   Necessity
d.   None of the above; there are no defenses to strict liability

18.   Louise purchases a new food processor from Gourmet Emporium. The salesman tells her the food processor will grind anything, including nuts in the shell. Louise tries the food processor, discovers that it will not grind unshelled nuts and the shells ruin the food processor. If Louise sues Gourmet

Emporium for misrepresentation, the store's best defense will be:

a. the salesman did not misrepresent a fact but merely expressed an opinion.

b. Louise has not suffered any damages.

c. the salesman did not intend for Louise to rely on his statement.

d. Louise's reliance was unjustifiable, because a reasonable person would not believe that a food processor could grind nuts in the shell.

19. Texas Tamales, Inc. is a manufacturer of Mexican food. Barbara purchased a can of the company's Coahuila Chili. When she opened the can, she discovered a dead fly in the chili. When Barbara sued for negligence, a Texas Tamale supervisor proved that the company took reasonable measures to ensure that foreign objects were removed from the chili. Barbara lost the case. Which element was missing?

a. Texas Tamales did not owe a duty to Barbara.

b. It is unforeseeable that a fly would be found in a can of chili.

c. Texas Tamales did not breach its duty to Barbara.

d. None, Barbara should not have lost the case.

20. There have been several robberies in Sidney's neighborhood. When Sidney goes on vacation, he leaves a loaded rifle attached to a trip wire. A burglar opens the door and is seriously injured. The burglar sues Sidney for battery.

a. The burglar will win because the use of a deadly weapon is not permitted to protect property.

b. The burglar will lose because a battery did not occur.

c. The burglar will lose because Sidney acted in self-defense.

d. The burglar will lose because Sidney did not intend to injure the burglar but only to frighten him.

21. Amy owns a small airplane and as a practical joke she flies over Rose's house at a low altitude. After two weeks, Rose threatens to sue Amy for trespass to land if she does not stop. If Rose decides to sue, she will:

a. lose because she has not suffered any monetary loss.

b. lose because Amy flies over Rose's house and does not touch it.

c. lose because Amy only intended to play a joke.

d. win because all the elements are satisfied.

22. Which of the following is not an element of negligence?

a. Duty from the defendant to the plaintiff

b. Proximate cause

c. Superseding cause

d. Injury caused by the defendant's actions

23.   In which of the following cases would "res ipsa loquitur" be appropriate?

    a.   A tenant sues a landlord when the building collapses.
    b.   One driver sues another for damages resulting from a car accident.
    c.   A student sues his principal for battery after the principal paddles him.
    d.   A candidate for city council sues an editor of a newspaper for defamation.

24.   Gloria sees Greg playing basketball in the middle of the street. Gloria swerves to avoid him and runs into a tree owned by Mrs. Smith. The tree and the car are both damaged. Which of the following statements is true?

    a.   Mrs. Smith cannot sue Greg for the damage to her tree.
    b.   Gloria cannot sue Greg because she caused the damage to her car.
    c.   Gloria and Mrs. Smith can both sue Greg.
    d.   Mrs. Smith cannot sue anyone, because the destruction of her tree was an accident.

25.   Lacey, a United States senator, is debating on the floor of Congress. She becomes angry and states that her opponent lets pigs eat at his dinner table.

    a.   Lacey is liable for defamation unless her statement is true.
    b.   Lacey is liable for defamation even if her statement is true.
    c.   Lacey is not liable; her statement is protected by a qualified privilege.
    d.   Lacey is not liable; her statement is protected by an absolute privilege.

Answers to Study Questions

Fill-in-the-Blank Questions

When Thomas bumped the woman with his cart, he committed battery. Battery is an unexcused, intentional harmful or offensive touching. If the woman saw Thomas threatening to bump her with the cart, he may also have committed assault.

When Thomas attempted to hit the second woman, he committed assault. Assault differs from battery in that no touching is required, but the victim must be aware of the defendant's act.

Thomas is responsible for the broken hip. This is true even though he did not intend serious injury. It is also irrelevant that the broken hip may or may not have been foreseeable. Proximate cause is an element of negligence but not of intentional torts.

True-False Questions

1.   T.

2.   F. The publication requirement has not been met.

3.   T.

4.   T.

5.   T.

6.   T.

7.   T.

8.   F. A burglar is presumed to be on property without the consent of the owner.

9.   F. It is an element of negligence.

10.   F. Threat of physical restraint may be enough.

Multiple-Choice Questions

1.	c		14.	d
2.	b		15.	b
3.	a		16.	b
4.	d		17.	b
5.	c		18.	d
6.	c		19.	c
7.	b		20.	a
8.	a		21.	d
9.	c		22.	c
10.	a		23.	a
11.	d		24.	c
12.	d		25.	d
13.	a			

Business Torts and Computer Law

4

General Principles

All torts are forms of personal injury. Remember that personal injury can include injury to reputation and injury to property. The first part of this chapter deals with injury to a business, including injury to intellectual property rights (e.g. copyright). The same "element analysis" used in the last chapter applies here also.

The invention and widespread use of computers in business has caused some intellectual property rights laws to become outdated. Patenting computer software programs provides some protection, but some procedures cannot be patented. Courts are deciding how much of a software program can be copyrighted and how much of another's software program can be used to develop new programs.

Chapter Summary

I.   Business Torts

      A.   Wrongful Interference with a Contractual Relationship--The elements are:

            (1)   A valid contract between A & B.
            (2)   C knows that the contract exists.
            (3)   C intentionally causes A or B to break the contract. The plaintiff must show that the contract would not have been broken without the interference of C.

                 Note that the outsider is sued for this tort. The party to the contract that acted wrongfully may be sued for breach of contract. Defense to wrongful interference with a contractual or business relationship is justification--genuine competitive behavior.

B.   Wrongful Interference with a Business Relationship--Same elements as above but a business relationship instead of a contract exists between A & B. Usually occurs when the defendant harasses the plaintiff's customers.

C.   Wrongfully Entering into Business--The defendant enters into business with the sole intention of ruining the plaintiff's business.

D.   Infringement of Copyright, Trademark and Patents --Occurs with unauthorized and unjustified use of the owner's rights.

   (1)   Trademark--A mark or motto that identifies the goods. Protects the consumer from similar products by others. If a word is used, it must be fanciful and not generic. A service mark is used to distinguish services rather than products. A trade name relates to a business name.

   (2)   Patent--Protects a device, design or process.

   (3)   Copyright--Applies only to literary or artistic creations; an idea cannot be protected. The method of expression is protected. The "fair use" defense allows a person to reproduce copyrighted materials without infringement if used for purposes of commentary, news reporting or teaching.

   (4)   The most common unauthorized use is "passing off", where the defendant represents his product as that of another, usually because the other product is more famous or better quality. The plaintiff, or true owner, will win the case if he can show that an ordinary customer would confuse the two products.

E.   RICO--Racketeer Influenced and Corrupt Organizations Act--Passed by Congress to prevent organized crime from contaminating legal businesses. However, the act is so broad that it has been used in many business fraud cases. The defendant can be prosecuted for committing a crime or be sued in a civil case. If a plaintiff is successful, he or she can win treble (triple) damages and attorneys' fees.

II.   Computers and the Law--In this area, the laws have not kept up with scientific discovery. New technology creates new legal problems.

A.   Protection of Property Rights in Software--The courts have decided that software development is a creative process entitled to copyright and patent protection. However, the scope of application is in doubt.

   (1)   Patents--Protection for some software is available but the time

required to obtain a patent is a drawback to this method of protection.

(2)   Copyrights--Amendments to the federal copyright laws have extended protection to computer programs but there are still some difficulties.

Computer programs are defined as a set of statements or instructions to be used with a computer to produce a specific result. Some programs are mathematical equations or shortcuts of longer programs-- items that usually cannot be copyrighted.

B.   Software Piracy--This is the unauthorized copying or theft of software programs. It is illegal (a form of larceny) but for reasons stated above, it is difficult to prosecute. Security systems are expensive to create and can be breached by sophisticated users. Some companies have used service support to authorized users to discourage piracy. Other companies have sued unauthorized users in a civil action for copyright or patent infringement.

C.   Semiconductor Chip Protection Act--Protects mask works, which are images of patterns of semiconductor chips. Creator must register the work with the U.S. Copyright Office within two years in order to gain ten years' protection.

D.   Defamation by Computer--Can occur by publication of erroneous information.

Study Questions

Fill-in-the-Blank Questions

Gloria, a software designer, obtains a "free copy" of some word processing software from Jack. She uses the software to do her English homework. While she is using the software, Gloria develops a process that allows the word processing software to be used with a database software.

When Gloria uses a "free copy of the word processing software, she is committing

_____.
        (software piracy/defamation by computer)

Gloria's use of this same software _____ protected by the fair use doctrine.
                                    (is/is not)

If Gloria had purchased the software and then developed the adaptation, under most recent court decisions, Gloria's addition _____ by copyrighted.   (could/could not)

True-False Questions

1.   Federal copyright laws have been expanded to include computer programs. _____

2.   The unauthorized use or copying of computer programs is known as software piracy. _____

3.   Paul and Susan have a contract. Paul knows of the contract and induces Susan to break it. Susan can be sued for wrongful interference with a contractual relationship. _____

4.   "The Whopper" is a trade name. _____

5.   The "fair use doctrine" is a defense to defamation. _____

6.   Patent rights are becoming increasingly important in licenses to use computer software. _____

7.   The intellectual property rights of computer software are determined by legislation alone; courts do not need to interpret the statutes. _____

8.   Disparagement of goods can be a form of computer defamation. _____

9.   Wrongfully entering into business is a crime, but is not a tort. _____

10.   Under RICO, only the government, not private citizens, may sue. _____

11.   "Passing off" is one form of invasion of privacy. _____

Multiple-Choice Questions

1.   Tony's Pizza sends out a false press release which states that several people who ate at a competitor's restaurant have contracted food poisoning. The competitor can sue Tony's for:

   a.   slander of title.
   b.   disparagement of goods.
   c.   negligence.
   d.   public disclosure of private facts.

2.   Which of the following protections against software piracy has diminished in recent years?

   a.   Encoding security systems in the software program.
   b.   Increased user support to authorized buyers.
   c.   Civil suits for copyright infringement.

3.   Which of the following would <u>not</u> be an issue in copyright cases involving computer programs?

a.   Some programs are mathematical questions and cannot be copyrighted.
b.   The federal copyright law does not apply to software.
c.   Some programs are faster versions of jobs that can be done without computers.
d.   None, because all of the above are issues in copyright cases involving computer programs.

4.   Betty is a book reviewer for a magazine. In the last issue, she criticized a new novel by Larry Lucas and emphasized her point by quoting from the second chapter. If Larry sues Betty for copyright infringement, her best defense will be:

a.   absolute privilege.
b.   the fair use doctrine.
c.   truth, because she really believed that the book was poorly written.
d.   conditional privilege, because Larry is a public figure.

5.   Skaggs Alpha Beta is a well-established supermarket chain in the southwestern United States. A competitor opens a new chain of stores called "Skaggs Alpha Zeta". Skaggs Alpha Beta should sue the newcomer for:

a.   infringement of a trade name.
b.   infringement of a trademark.
c.   infringement of a service mark.
d.   infringement of a copyright.

Sam, a salesman for Best Computer Company, is upset over the new sales route to which he has been assigned. Oscar, the owner of a rival computer company, sees Sam in a restaurant and tells Sam, "If you ever decide to leave Best, come see me." Sam quits working for Best two days later and goes to work for Oscar. If Best sues Oscar for wrongful interference with a contractual relationship, Best will:

a.   win if Sam had a contract with Best because Oscar knew that Sam worked for Best.
b.   win even if Sam had no contract because Oscar knew that Sam worked for Best.
c.   lose even if Sam had a contract with Best because Oscar did not induce Sam to quit.
d.   lose even if Sam had a contract because Oscar was negligent in speaking with Sam.

7.   Which of the following statements about RICO is <u>false</u>?

a.   RICO was passed in order to prevent business fraud.
b.   A lawsuit filed under RICO may be criminal or civil.

     c.   RICO is a federal law.

     d.   A plaintiff in a RICO suit may recover three times his or her actual damages.

8.   RICO stands for:

     a.   Robbery and Intentional Corruption by Organized Crime.

     b.   Racketeering and Intentional Corruption by Organized Crime.

     c.   Racketeering Influenced and Corrupt Organization.

     d.   Racketeering Influenced by Corruption and Organized Crime.

9.   Images of patterns created by semiconductor chips are called:

     a.   mask works.

     b.   software.

     c.   computer security systems.

     d.   computer coding.

10.   Wrongfully interfering with a business relationship is also known as:

     a.   negligent behavior.

     b.   predatory behavior.

     c.   piracy.

     d.   infringement.

11.   Alan opens a hamburger stand next door to Bill's Burgers. Alan advertises an opening day special which offers 10 burgers for $1. If Bill sues Alan for wrongful interference with a business relationship, Alan's best defense would be:

     a.   self-defense.

     b.   fair use.

     c.   privilege.

     d.   justification.

12.   If Bill could prove that Alan started his business solely in order to harm Bill, Alan would:

     a.   be liable for wrongfully entering into business.

     b.   be liable for wrongfully interfering with a contractual relationship.

     c.   be liable for business infringement.

     d.   not be liable; Alan has committed no tort.

13.   Copyrights and trademarks are examples of:

     a.   intellectual personal rights.

     b.   intellectual property rights.

     c.   infringement rights.

     d.   fair use rights.

14.   Drawbacks to using patents to protect computer software rights include:

    a.   the length of time it takes to procure a patent.
    b.   the fact that some processes may not be patented.
    c.   both a & b.
    d.   neither a nor b.

15.   Robert begins production and sales of a new "Miss Hoggy" doll, which looks very similar to the Muppets "Miss Piggy". The creator of the muppets should sue Robert for:

    a.   copyright infringement.
    b.   trademark infringement.
    c.   intellectual property piracy.
    d.   wrongful interference with a contractual relationship.

16.   Robert's actions in Question 15 constitute:

    a.   trading off.
    b.   passing off.
    c.   piracy.
    d.   none of the above.

17.   "Approved by the American Medical Association" is an example of a:

    a.   service mark.
    b.   trademark.
    c.   certification mark.
    d.   patent mark.

18.   An example of a trade name which has fallen into generic use and is no longer protected by intellectual property laws is:

    a.   Coca-Cola.
    b.   Corn Flakes.
    c.   Safeway.

19.   Which of the following statements is true?

    a.   Ideas may be copyrighted but expressions of ideas may not be copyrighted.
    b.   Expressions of ideas may be copyrighted but ideas may not be copyrighted.
    c.   Both ideas and expressions of ideas may be copyrighted.
    d.   Ideas and expressions of ideas may be patented but may not be copyrighted.

20.   Lacey writes a best seller, "Why Is An Alien In My Swamp?" She follows the proper procedure for copyrighting the book. Lacey's rights are protected for:

a.   ten years.
b.   fifty years.
c.   the length of her life plus fifty years.
d.   the length of her life plus seventy-five years.

21.   Which of the following facts about RICO is <u>false</u>?

a.   RICO regulates "racketeering" crimes.
b.   RICO has been praised for its widespread application.
c.   RICO may involve a civil suit and a criminal suit.
d.   RICO is a federal law.

22.   Software piracy is difficult to prosecute as a crime for all of the following reasons, <u>except</u>:

a.   software is intangible property and most criminal laws involve tangible property.
b.   software piracy is difficult to detect.
c.   software programs are not protected under federal law.
d.   software cannot be patented.

23.   If patent infringement is proven, the plaintiff may request which of the following remedies:

a.   Damages
b.   Injunction
c.   Destruction of all illegal copies
d.   All of the above are available remedies.

24.   Pauline works as a designer for Paris-Like Fashions, Inc. She has a two-year employment contract with the firm. Renaldo, who owns a competing firm, knows about Pauline's two-year commitment but promises her more wages and better benefits if she will break the contract. Pauline does so. Paris-Like Fashions should sue Renaldo for:

a.   breach of contract.
b.   contract infringement.
c.   intellectual property infringement.
d.   wrongful interference with a contractual relationship.

25.   Paris-Like Fashions should sue Pauline for:

a.   breach of contract.
b.   wrongful interference with a contract.
c.   both of the above.
d.   nothing, Pauline is not liable but Renaldo is.

Answers to Study Questions

Fill-in-the-Blank Questions

Gloria is committing software piracy when she uses an unauthorized copy of Jack's software. Defamation by computer occurs when erroneous computer data is published. Gloria's use of the software is <u>not</u> protected by the fair use doctrine; the fair use doctrine relates to the use of copyrighted material for educational use or for critical review. Gloria's addition, under recent court decisions, could be copyrighted.

True-False Questions

1.   T.

2.   T.

3.   F. Susan can be sued for breach of contract. Paul can be sued for wrongful interference with a contractual relationship.

4.   F. It is a trademark; a trade name refers to the name of a company.

5.   F. It is a defamation to copyright infringement.

6.   T.

7.   F. Courts are interpreting the old and new statutes.

8.   T.

9.   F. It is a tort.

10.   F. Private citizens may also sue.

11.   F. It is a form of intellectual property infringement.

Multiple-Choice Questions

1.	b		14.	c
2.	a		15.	b
3.	d		16.	b
4.	b		17.	c
5.	a		18.	b
6.	c		19.	b
7.	a		20.	c
8.	c		21.	b
9.	a		22.	d
10.	b		23.	d
11.	d		24.	d
12.	a		25.	a
13.	b			

Criminal Law

General Principles

Some actions may be the basis for a tort in a civil action and for a crime in a criminal prosecution. Crimes, however, are committed against society and it is the government which sues to enforce the criminal laws.

The defendant in a criminal case is afforded several safeguards against wrongful prosecution. Some forms of protection are procedural (probable cause is required for an arrest); some are substantive (defenses and guilt beyond a reasonable doubt).

Chapter Summary

I. ## What Is a Crime? (Crimes v. Torts)

Crimes	Torts
1. Committed against society as a whole.	1. Committed against an individual.
2. The plaintiff is the government.	2. The plaintiff is a private individual.
3. Punishment is a fine, imprisonment or both.	3. The plaintiff may recover money damages, but there is no punishment unless punitive damages are assessed. Even then punitive damages are paid to the injured party and not to the government.

4. Primarily statutory law.	4. Primarily common law.

II.   <u>Classification of Crimes</u>--The classification of crimes is established by the legislature or Congress and is defined by statute.

    A.   <u>Felonies</u>--The most serious crimes. Usually punishable by imprisonment in a penitentiary.

    B.   <u>Misdemeanors</u>--Less serious crimes. Usually punishable by confinement in the county or city jail for a short period of time (less than one year).

    C.   <u>Petty Offenses</u>--Usually not considered a crime although the offenses are defined in the criminal statutes. Includes parking and traffic violations.

III.   <u>What Is Criminal Liability?</u>--Requires an act which is prohibited by statute and the required mental state. The required mental state is defined as part of the crime.

IV.   <u>Defenses to Criminal Liability</u>--Most negate the required state of mind.

    A.   <u>Infancy</u>--Children under seven are exempt from criminal prosecution because it is assumed that they lack the required mental intent. Between seven and fourteen, children are presumed to lack mental intent, but the prosecution may prove otherwise. At age fourteen, children may be prosecuted but may prove that they lacked the mental intent.

    B.   <u>Intoxication</u>--Involuntary intoxication, including unknowingly taking liquor or drugs, acts as a complete defense, if the defendant was so intoxicated that he or she did not know that a crime had been committed. Voluntary intoxication is not a complete defense, but the defendant may be able to lessen the degree of the crime by showing that he or she did not act intentionally.

    C.   <u>Insanity</u>

        (1)   <u>M'Naghten Test</u>--Most strict. Defendant must prove that he or she lacked the understanding to know what occurred or that he or she did not know that it was wrong.

        (2)   <u>Irresistible Impulse</u>--Because of disease, the defendant was unable to conform his or her conduct to the norm.

        (3)   <u>Model Penal Code</u>--Most liberal. Combines the M'Naghten and irresistible impulse tests. Behavior can be excused if the result of mental disease <u>or</u> defect. Defendant need not lack total understanding of the circumstances but only the substantial capacity to understand.

D.   <u>Mistake</u>--Mistake of fact is a defense if the defendant lacked the required mental state. Mistake of law is excused only if the law has not been widely published or if the individual relies on the advice of a government official.

E.   <u>Consent</u>--Available as a defense only if one element of the crime is "against the will of the victim".

F.   <u>Duress</u>--The defendant is forced to commit a crime against his or her will because of threats by another. The harm threatened must be more serious than the crime that the defendant is forced to commit.

G.   <u>Self-Defense/Defense of Others/Defense of Property</u>--As with torts, force is justifiable if used to repel an attack by another. Deadly force is only justifiable if the defendant is threatened with immediate death or serious bodily injury.

H.   <u>Entrapment</u>--A government official, such as a policeman, suggests to the defendant that a crime be committed <u>and</u> persuades the defendant to commit the crime. The test is whether the defendant would have committed the crime anyway (predisposition). If so, the entrapment defense fails.

I.   <u>Statute of Limitations</u>--After a set period of time, a defendant cannot be prosecuted for a crime. As a general rule, more serious crimes have longer statutes of limitations.

J.   <u>Immunity</u>--Part of the plea bargaining process. One defendant is protected from prosecution or given a reduced sentence in return for testimony against other wrongdoers.

V.   <u>Procedure in Criminal Law</u> Note the safeguards involving independent decision makers.

A.   <u>Constitutional Safeguards</u>--Designed to protect the individual from wrongful action by the government. Applies to state and federal courts. All are found in amendments to the United States Constitution.

The Fourth Amendment provides protection from unreasonable search and seizure and states that any arrest or search must be based on probable cause. The Fifth Amendment prevents a person from being tried twice for the same crime and ensures that the defendant is given a chance to contest the charges (due process). The Sixth Amendment guarantees that a criminal defendant has the right to a speedy and public trial, the right to question witnesses, and the right to be represented by an attorney. The Eighth Amendment deals with bail and cruel and unusual punishment.

B.   (1)   <u>Arrest</u>--A warrant will be issued only if an independent judge or magistrate is convinced that there is probable cause or a considerable possibility that the defendant has committed a crime. A police officer can act without a warrant if there is not time to get one and his or her belief meets the probable cause test.

(2)   <u>Indictment/Information</u>--The defendant is formally charged with a crime. A grand jury made up of impartial citizens issues an indictment for felony crimes. A magistrate issues an indictment for misdemeanor crimes.

(3)   <u>Trial</u>--The prosecution must prove that the defendant is guilty beyond a reasonable doubt. Compare the burden of proof in civil cases where the plaintiff must prove his or her case by a preponderance of the evidence (more likely than not). The defendant in a criminal action has the burden of proving a defense if the government meets its burden.

VI.   <u>Crimes Affecting Business</u>

A.   <u>Forgery</u>--The defendant must fraudulently make or alter a writing that changes the legal rights and liabilities of another. Forgery includes altering a legal document. Forgery also includes passing forged writing to another if the defendant knows it has been forged.

B.   <u>Robbery</u>--Robbery is larceny accomplished through the use of force or intimidation.

C.   <u>Burglary</u>--The defendant must enter property owned by another with the intent to commit a crime. Note that the crime does not have to be completed. Most states have eliminated the requirement of breaking and entering.

D.   <u>Larceny</u>--The wrongful or fraudulent taking of the property of another.

E.   <u>False Pretenses</u>--The defendant receives goods based on a false or fraudulent representation.

F.   <u>Receiving Stolen Goods</u>--The defendant must know or have reason to know that the goods have been stolen.

G.   <u>Embezzlement</u>--The defendant must be an agent of the victim or otherwise be entrusted with the stolen property. Embezzlement was created to fill in gaps left by theft statutes. Assume that a teller jimmies the books or receives money from a customer but does not turn the money over to the bank. Who owns the money at that point in time? Embezzlement is not often prosecuted.

H.   Arson--Intentional burning of building or property.

I.   Mail Fraud--Use of the mail to commit a deceptive practice, e.g. mailing out fake contests, prize announcements.

VII.   White Collar Crime

A.   Computer Crime

(1)   Definition--Some old theft statutes have been expanded to include theft of intangible property and theft of services. The American Bar Association definition is much broader and covers all forms of computer abuse and use of computers to commit crime.

(2)   Prosecution Problems--Difficult to detect because impact is not realized immediately.   Also, computer can be used anonymously. Furthermore, criminals of this type are more sophisticated computer users than are law enforcement officials.

(3)   Types

(a)   Financial Crimes--Using the computer network to transfer or remove funds.

(b)   Property Theft--Theft of computer hardware and using the computer to alter inventory records.

(c)   Vandalism and Destructive Programming--Can involve physical destruction of hardware or erasure/alteration of records.

(d)   Theft of Data/Services--Unauthorized use of computer time, information or hardware. Because this crime does not involve tangible items, it is difficult to prosecute under normal larceny statutes.

B.   Bribery

(1)   Public Officials--The recipient of the bribe must be a public officeholder and the defendant must intend to gain some private advantage.

(2)   Foreign Officials--Same standard as above. Covered by federal law.

(3)   Commercial--Wrongful business practices accomplished by payoffs to the defendant.

Note that in all cases, the offer of the bribe is sufficient; the intended recipient does not have to accept the bribe.

C.   Bankruptcy Fraud

(1)   False Claims of Creditors--A creditor who realizes that he or she may only receive a portion of the money owed by the debtor increases his or her claim in order to gain more money when the debtor's assets are distributed.

(2)   Fraudulent Transfer of Property--Shortly before bankruptcy, the debtor conveys property to a relative or friend. When the debtor declares bankruptcy, the property would not be considered part of the debtor's estate which is used to pay creditors. Therefore, the creditors are deprived of an asset to the estate.

(3)   Scam Bankruptcy--Planned by debtor in advance. The debtor establishes a business with a high turnover rate and good credit rating with suppliers. At some point when the creditors have advanced inventory or supplies, the defendant sells the inventory, closes the business, and leaves town with the only assets that could be used to satisfy the creditors.

D.   Corporate Crime--Impossible for a corporation to have criminal intent or to be imprisoned. Usually officers of the corporation are tried for the crime. The corporation itself may be tried and convicted if the punishment is a fine.

E.   RICO--The criminal action requires racketeering activity or the conspiracy to commit a crime via racketeering. Can be used in mail or securities fraud cases.

Study Questions

Fill-in-the-Blank Questions

The following events took place over the course of a year at Walt's Drug Store. Mr. Jones wrote a check to Walt's on an account he knew he had closed the month before. Mr. Jones' nine year-old son took a comic book from the rack without paying for it. Daniel, the night manager, and Freida, the bookkeeper, deliberately failed to record payments by several customers. Robert entered the store with a knife and demanded that Walt give him a free soda.

Mr. Jones has committed _____.
(larceny/robbery/theft by false pretenses)

Daniel and Freida have committed_____.
(larceny/embezzlement/robbery)

Mr. Jones' son has committed _____.
(larceny/robbery/embezzlement)

Robert has committed _____.
(theft by false pretenses/robbery/burglary)

True-False Questions

1.   In a criminal trial, the defendant has burden of proof with regard to a defense. _____

2.   Voluntary intoxication is a complete defense to a crime. _____

3.   The duty of a grand jury is a complete defense to a crime. _____

4.   In order to convict a defendant, the prosecution must prove only that the defendant performed a prohibited act. _____

5.   In most states, an element of burglary is breaking and entering. _____

6.   Children between the ages of seven and fourteen are presumed capable of committing a crime. _____

7.   The judge decides whether a case is a felony or a misdemeanor. _____

8.   In a civil case, the victim is the plaintiff; in a criminal case, the government is the plaintiff. _____

9.   A speeding ticket is an example of a felony. _____

10.   Mistake of law is never a defense to a crime. _____

11.   Theft of property may be accomplished by computer alteration of inventory records. _____

12.   Destruction of computer data can easily be prosecuted under current larceny statutes. _____

Multiple-Choice Questions

1.   Cindy has a $45,000 debt. Her only asset is a condominium in Colorado. Cindy sells the condo to her brother Ralph for a price of $50 and she declares bankruptcy. Cindy has committed which of the following bankruptcy crimes?

      a.   Scam bankruptcy

b.   Fraudulent transfer of property
c.   False claims of creditors
d.   Embezzlement

2.   Which of the following statements is <u>false</u>?

a.   In civil law, a fine may be imposed against the defendant.
b.   Criminal law is primarily statutory law.
c.   In criminal law, a wrong is committed against society as a whole.
d.   In civil law, the burden of proof is by a preponderance of the evidence.

3.   Sammy enters Mrs. Smith's house planning to steal her television set. Mrs. Smith's large dog meets Sammy in the living room and he runs away without taking anything. Sammy has committed:

a.   robbery.
b.   burglary.
c.   larceny.
d.   no crime, because he didn't take the television set.

4.   The formal charge issued by a grand jury in a felony case is an:

a.   information.
b.   incrimination.
c.   indisposition.
d.   indictment.

5.   In order for a magistrate to issue an arrest warrant, he must believe:

a.   beyond a reasonable doubt that the accused committed the crime.
b.   by a preponderance of the evidence that the accused committed the crime.
c.   that there is probable cause to arrest the accused.
d.   that it is more likely than not that the accused committed the crime.

6.   Mary attends a Christmas party where a fellow guest had "spiked" the punch. Mary did not know that liquor had been added to the punch. She drank several glasses and then committed a misdemeanor on the way home from the party. Mary's best defense would be:

a.   voluntary intoxication.
b.   involuntary intoxication.
c.   mistake of law.
d.   immunity.

7.   Which of the following defenses is usually connected with plea bargaining?

a.   Mistake of law

b.   Mistake of fact
c.   Immunity
d.   Entrapment

8.   Which of the following "legal" definitions of insanity is hardest for the defendant to meet?

     a.   The M'Naghten test
     b.   Irresistible impulse
     c.   Model Penal Code
     d.   None of the above

9.   Which of the following facts constitute forgery?

     a.   Lucy deliberately alters her age on her marriage license.
     b.   Roberts steals Allen's checkbook and writes a check to his accountant.
     c.   Sidney knows that his wife has "doctored" the amounts on an insurance claim form, but he submits it to his insurance company for payment.
     d.   All of the above constitute forgery.

10.   Pete enters Bill's house, grabs Bill's new power drill and is jumping over the fence into the alley when Bill sees him and shoots him. If <u>Bill</u> is prosecuted, he:

     a.   will be found not guilty if he pleads self-defense.
     b.   will be found not guilty if he pleads defense of property.
     c.   will not be found guilty because he did not commit a crime.
     d.   will be found guilty.

11.   In Question 10, Pete has committed:

     a.   larceny.
     b.   robbery.
     c.   burglary.
     d.   theft by false pretenses.

12.   As Robert is leaving a restaurant, he picks up a hat from the rack in the front of the restaurant. Later in the day, he discovers that he has taken someone else's hat although his hat looks exactly like the one he took. Robert has committed:

     a.   larceny but he has a good defense if he pleads mistake of fact.
     b.   larceny but he has a good defense if he pleads mistake of law.
     c.   larceny and he has no defense.
     d.   robbery and he has no defense.

13.   Which of the following statements about computer crime is <u>false</u>?

a. Computer crime is one of the crimes which is prosecuted least often.
b. In some states, computer crime is not larceny, because software is not "property" as defined in the larceny statute.
c. Computer crime is one of the crimes which is punished most severely.
d. Victims of computer crime are often corporations whose officers usually let the case be plea bargained.

14. RICO has:

a. criminal remedies only.
b. civil remedies only.
c. civil and criminal remedies.
d. been repealed by the U.S. Congress

15. In a scam bankruptcy, the crime is committed by:

a. debtors only.
b. creditors only.
c. debtors and creditors.
d. debtors, creditors and government officials.

16. Roger enters a bank, pulls out a gun, and forces the teller to fill a bag with money and to steal the bank president's car. The teller's best defense to a charge of larceny would be:

a. self-defense.
b. duress.
c. entrapment.
d. duress to a charge of stealing of money but she has no defense to stealing the bank president's car.

17. Roger, a building contractor, submits a bid to the City of Midville for construction of a new jail. He offers two city councilmen 5 percent of the profits if he is awarded the contract. The city councilmen refuse the money and vote to give the contract to Dennis. Roger has committed:

a. commercial bribery.
b. bribery of a public official.
c. no crime because the councilmen did not take the money.
d. no crime because he was not awarded the contract.

18. If a defendant tries to plead entrapment as a defense to a crime, he or she must show:

a. that a private person suggested that the crime be committed and that the private person persuaded him or her to commit the crime.
b. that a public officer suggested that the crime be committed and that the public officer persuaded him or her to commit the crime.

c.   that a public official told the defendant that his actions were not a crime.

d.   that another person forced him or her to commit the crime.

19.   The following crimes are listed in order from most to least serious. Which is correct?

a.   Misdemeanors, petty offenses, felonies
b.   Felonies, misdemeanors, petty offenses
c.   Misdemeanors, felonies, petty offenses
d.   Felonies, petty offenses, misdemeanors

20.   Consent, if proven, would be a proper defense to which of the following crimes?

a.   Bribery
b.   Forgery
c.   Theft
d.   Bankruptcy fraud

21.   Allen has supplied credit for several years to Ace Drilling Co. When the price of oil drops, Allen learns that Ace is about the declare bankruptcy. Although Ace owes Allen $20,000, Allen files a claim form in bankruptcy court showing that $40,000 is owed. Which crime has been committed?

a.   Scam bankruptcy
b.   Fraudulent claims of creditors
c.   Receipt of stolen property
d.   Embezzlement

22.   Plasma Labs, Inc. offers Dr. Schlock a 4% return on any blood test or X-ray ordered by Dr. Schlock and performed by Plasma. Plasma's offer is an example of:

a.   embezzlement.
b.   receipt of stolen property.
c.   commercial bribery.
d.   forgery.

23.   Which of the following determines if a particular crime is a felony or a misdemeanor?

a.   The judge
b.   The prosecuting attorney
c.   The jury
d.   The legislature

24.   Tort law differs from criminal law because in tort law, the defendant:

a.   may pay a fine but will not receive a prison sentence.
b.   may pay compensation to the victim but will not receive a prison sentence.
c.   may pay a fine and may receive a prison sentence.
d.   may pay compensation to the victim and may receive a prison sentence.

25.   When a police officer arrests a suspect, he must:

a.   have probable cause to believe that the suspect committed the crime.
b.   believe beyond a reasonable doubt that the suspect committed the crime.
c.   neither of the above, an arrest warrant must be issued before a police officer can arrest a suspect.
d.   none of the above, the grand jury must issue an indictment before a police officer can arrest an suspect.

Answers to Study Questions

Fill-in-the-Blank Questions

Mr. Jones has committed theft by false pretenses; by writing a check, he represented to Walt that he had a current bank account. Daniel and Freida have committed embezzlement. Mr. Jones' son has committed larceny; he has not committed robbery because he did not use force or fear when he took the comic book. Robert has committed robbery and larceny; a robbery always includes larceny.

True-False Questions

1.   T.

2.   F. Voluntary intoxication may lessen the degree of the charge; involuntary intoxication is a complete defense.

3.   F. The duty of the grand jury is to decide if there is enough evidence to hold the defendant for trial.

4.   F. The prosecution must also prove that the defendant possessed the required state of mind.

5.   F. Most states have eliminated this requirement.

6.   F. They are presumed incapable but the prosecution can prove otherwise.

7.   F. The legislation decides when it passes a statute.

8.   T.

9.   F. It is an example of a petty offense.

10.   F. It is a mistake if the law has not been published or widely circulated or if the defendant relies on the advice of a government official such as an attorney general.

11.   T.

12.   F. Most larceny statutes do not cover computer crimes because computer data is an intangible product.

Multiple-Choice Questions

1.	b	10.	d	18.	b
2.	a	11.	c	19.	b
3.	b	12.	a	20.	c
4.	d	13.	c	21.	b
5.	c	14.	c	22.	c
6.	b	15.	a	23.	d
7.	c	16.	b	24.	b
8.	a	17.	b	25.	a
9.	d				

CHAPTER

6

Ethics and Social Responsibility

General Principles

Ethics represents the shared beliefs of a society on moral issues. Ethical values may change over time as a society changes. Law often reflects ethical values, but it is not synonymous.

Business ethics usually require a choice between alternatives: a tradeoff. Corporation's and other businesses try to achieve a balance between the conflicting goals of profit maximization, consumer protection, and societal pressures. Ethical tradeoffs in the business world can involve an employee's right to privacy, protection of an employee's religious practices and dealing with foreign governments.

Chapter Summary

I.   Nature of Ethical Issues--Ethics involves moral values and are based on the beliefs of a group at a certain point in time. Therefore, a group's ethical or moral values may change over a period of time.

II.   Ethics and Law--Ethics and law are not the same although they are connected. General legal rules are known collectively as positive law or black letter law. These rules represent the basic ethics of a society. In other words, there is enough agreement about the moral implications of an action to pass a law about it. However, ethics and law are not identical. An act may be legal but unethical.

There is a philosophical debate over whether law shapes ethics or whether ethics shapes law. In business law, the latter is probably more appropriate because business law is based on custom.

III.   Tradeoffs and Ethical Decision Making

    A.   Definition--A tradeoff is a choice between goals; it occurs because not all actions are 100 percent beneficial to 100 percent of the people.

    B.   Application--A product may help society as a whole but may also injure a smaller group of people. The tradeoff is between producing the product and risking harm to a few people or foregoing production and eliminating all risk of harm. However, under the second choice, society as a whole may give up a benefit.

    C.   Statistical Vocabulary--A "Type I" error is a harmful result of an action based on positive action. In the example above, a Type I error would occur if the product were to be produced. A "Type II" error is a harmful result of an action based on inaction. An error of this type would occur in the example above if the product were not produced.

IV.   Corporate Social Responsibility--Should the corporation dedicate its allegiance to its shareholders, its employees, consumers or to the general public or should it try to find a compromise? The duty to each group is explained below.

    A.   Duty to Shareholders--Shareholders are investors in and the owners of a corporation. According to one view, the directors of the corporation are entrusted with the shareholders' money and the duty is to maximize profit. Persons holding this view also argue that a corporation should not make ethical decisions; they claim that society as a whole should determine values through the political process.

    B.   Duty to the Consumers--The question here is not whether there is a duty but how much of a duty is owed. How far does the corporation have to go to protect the consumer? If the consumer is negligent, then the answer is fairly simple. However, a question may be raised as to the morality of making a product at all. Although consumers may think otherwise, they can influence corporate decision-making through purchasing power.

    C.   Duty to Society--The decision whether or not to make a potentially dangerous product, as addressed in the section above, is an example of the view that a corporation may owe a duty to society. Proponents of this view argue that this duty has come to rest on business because business controls a good deal of the wealth in a society. Most corporations do contribute to or create charities. However, the concept of social investing goes a bit further. Social investors argue that corporations will be forced to fulfill their duty to society if investors choose to purchase products and stocks from socially responsible companies.

D.   Balancing Interests--Tradeoffs are almost always involved. Any decision to spend money, whether on charitable contributions or on employee salaries, will reduce shareholders' dividends, at least in the short run. The law regulates some decisions (e.g. labor law) but the law represents the minimum duty owed to each group, not necessarily the ethically proper duty. It is difficult to evaluate corporate social responsibility because of the balancing of interests, and sometimes, because of the lack of information about the corporation.

V.   The Right to Privacy--This right is not spelled out in the U.S. Constitution, but the Supreme Court has implied that certain amendments when read together, give an individual a right to privacy from governmental intrusion. Also, invasion of privacy is recognized as a tort and acts as protection against intrusion by non-governmental parties. The right to privacy has become more important with the advent of computers and the access to private information by computer.

A.   Legislation--Federal laws protect an individual from some invasions of privacy. The Privacy Act of 1974 regulates government use of personal information.   Other statutes, such as the Freedom of Information Act and the Fair Credit Reporting Act, allow a person access to information in his or her file. Specific statutes deal with computer use in banking transactions, educational records, and cable-service operations.

B.   Privacy in Employment Matters--In the 1980s, legislation and rules have been enacted to protect the privacy of the employee. Some examples of the issues involved follow:

(1)   Drug Testing--Involves the Fourth Amendment right against unreasonable search and seizure.   The probable cause requirement for a warrantless search is also involved. A tradeoff is required between an individual employee's privacy rights and protection of the public from the actions of an unsafe employee.   The courts have tended to side with employers in cases involving government employees, but the decisions are split when private industry is involved. For the most part, private industry is regulated by state law and most states have not passed drug-testing statutes.

(2)   Lie-Detector Tests--The polygraph measures physical responses to questions administered to an employee or potential employee. The test is the polygram. Given to detect employee theft and to screen job applicants. Before federal legislation, labor agreements and state legislation curbed the use of lie detectors.

Employee Polygraph Protection Act--Most employers cannot administer lie detector tests to screen job applicants, to ask about testing results, or to threaten sanctions against employees based on their refusal to take the tests or upon results of tests. More leniency is granted when investigating theft. Governmental entities, security service firms and companies dealing in controlled substances are usually exempt from the legislation and can administer the tests.

(3)   <u>Monitoring Job Performance</u>--Can be done electronically by computer or by telephone eavesdropping. There are no clear-cut guidelines, but an employee has the option of suing for invasion of privacy.

VI.   <u>Ethics and Religion (Free Exercise Clause)</u>--First Amendment to the U.S. Constitution states that there can be no law prohibiting the free exercise of religion. This applies in the workplace when workers are asked to perform certain tasks or to work on certain days. The courts have held that the employer must make <u>reasonable accommodations</u> for an employee's religious practice. Usually decided on a case-by-case basis. An employee who is genuinely "forced to resign" because of interference with religion may collect unemployment benefits. A tradeoff is involved if other employees resent the "special treatment" given to the employee asking to exercise his or her religious beliefs; disgruntled employees v. free exercise of religion for one employee.

VII.   <u>Foreign Corrupt Practices Act</u>--Passed in 1977 by the U.S. Congress. Designed to prevent bribery of foreign officials. The law prohibits a corporation from giving value (money or otherwise) to an official of another government if the purpose is to <u>get</u> business for the company. However, "grease" payments, given in order to speed up legally owed services, are allowed. Furthermore, the law regulates corporate record-keeping so that bribes cannot be disguised. Penalties include corporate fines and imprisonment or personal fines for directors and officers. 1982 amendments relaxed reporting requirements somewhat because American corporations were not able to compete effectively overseas, where such "payments" are common.

<u>Study Questions</u>

<u>Fill-in-the-Blank Questions</u>

Phil is applying for a job at Central Grocery. The manager of Central Grocery asks Phil to take a lie detector test. Phil does so reluctantly and is hired. Later, after $4,000 cash is found missing from a register, all the employees are asked to take a lie-detector test and a drug test.

The manager's request for a lie-detector test as a condition of employment is _____ under federal law.
(legal/illegal)

The manager's request for a lie-detector test while investigating a theft is probably _____ under federal law.

       (legal/illegal)

Assuming no state legislation has been passed, the grocery business _____ a proper industry for the initiation for drug testing.

      (is/is not)

True-False Questions

1. In business law, customs and ethical concerns affect the operation of law. _____

2. Federal law does not regulate an employee's right to privacy. _____

3. A "Type I" error is committed when a company chooses to manufacture an antidepressant drug which may cause convulsions in some people. _____

4. The Foreign Corrupt Practices Act has been made more stringent in recent years. _____

5. In terms of an employee's right to privacy, a tradeoff is required between public safety and an employee's Fourth Amendment rights. _____

6. Social investing is a factor in influencing corporate social responsibility. _____

7. The probable cause requirement of the U.S. Constitution determines whether an employee's right to practice his or her religion has been violated. _____

8. Most states have passed laws regulating employees drug- testing. _____

9. Positive law is a synonym for statutory law. _____

10. Governmental employers are exempt from the Employee Polygraph Protection Act. _____

Multiple-Choice Questions

1. The basic social ethic on a topic is defined as:

    a.   the U.S. Constitution.
    b.   social responsibility.
    c.   black-letter law.
    d.   consensus morality.

2. An employee who quits a job because he or she was forced to compromise religious principles:

a.   is entitled to unemployment benefits under federal legislation.
b.   is entitled to unemployment benefits under recent Supreme Court decisions.
c.   is not entitled to unemployment benefits.

3.   Which of the following statements is <u>false</u>?

a.   Ethical questions ask what is fair, not what is legal.
b.   The ethics of a society may change over time.
c.   Some experts believe that law is a guiding force in society.
d.   Law and ethics are identical.

4.   It can be argued that a corporation owes a duty to each of the following groups <u>except</u>:

a.   shareholders.
b.   officers.
c.   employees.
d.   consumers.

5.   A corporation's social responsibility to its shareholders is best defined as duty to:

a.   maximize profits.
b.   produce safe products.
c.   support charitable causes.
d.   provide a safe working environment.

6.   The right to privacy:

a.   is stated explicitly in the U.S. Constitution.
b.   has been implied by U.S. Supreme Court decisions.
c.   does not exist in the workplace.
d.   does not involve tradeoffs with public safety.

7.   Which of the following is <u>not</u> involved in a right to privacy case?

a.   Free Exercise clause
b.   Fourth Amendment
c.   Probable cause requirements
d.   Federal polygraph legislation

8.   Job works for a manufacturing company that operates seven days per week. Employees are expected to work six days per week, including Saturdays or Sundays. Job objects to working on Saturday because it is his religious Sabbath. Which of the following best describes Job's rights?

a.   Job can refuse to work on Saturday.
b.   Job must work on Saturday if his employer asks.

c.   Job's employer must make reasonable accommodations for Job's religious practice.

d.   Job may exercise his religion only if no tradeoff with other employees is required.

9.   Job's right to practice his religion is found in the:

a.   First Amendment of the U.S. Constitution.
b.   Fourth Amendment of the U.S. Constitution.
c.   Federal legislation.

10.   Alpha Manufacturing is considering marketing a new "diet" food. The product does not contain sugar, but it does contain a chemical which may cause addiction in some people. Alpha decides to delay introduction of the food while researching a substitute for the potentially harmful chemical. Alpha has committed:

a.   a Type I error.
b.   a Type II error.
c.   no error.
d.   both Type I and Type II errors.

11.   In the above question, which statement best describes the tradeoffs implied in Alpha's decision?

a.   The immediate impact of the decision favors consumers and harms employees.

b.   The immediate impact of the decision favors shareholders and harms consumers.

c.   The immediate impact of the decision favors consumers but shareholders, through social investing, may benefit in the long term.

d.   No tradeoff is involved.

12.   Jane, a shareholder of Alpha, threatens to withdraw her support if Alpha produces the diet food. This is an example of:

a.   social investing.
b.   consumer buying power.
c.   free exercise clause.
d.   Fourth Amendment rights.

13.   Which of the following is not an argument made concerning a corporation's social responsibility to society?

a.   Corporations control a lot of the country's wealth and they have a duty to act ethically.

b.   Corporations have no duty, as long as they don't break the law.

c.   Corporations should not use their wealth to make political decisions; the voters should have this responsibility.

d.   Corporations should try to balance responsibility to shareholders, consumers and to society.

14.   The Foreign Corrupt Practices Act:

a.   prohibits bribes to foreign officials in order to obtain international business.
b.   requires corporations to keep records accounting for payments to foreign governments.
c.   both a & b.
d.   neither a nor b.

15.   Omega International, a multinational corporation, has established a factory in the country of Oz. The corporation is having trouble obtaining electrical service and Oz's minister of public services informs Omega that it will be some months before service can be connected. Omega's president pays a sum of money to the minister so that service can be connected immediately. The action of Omega's president is:

a.   "grease" and is not illegal.
b.   "grease" and is illegal.
c.   a bribe and is illegal.
d.   a bribe and is not illegal.

16.   Which of the following does not involve an employee's right to privacy in the workplace?

a.   Monitoring job performance by computer
b.   Listening in on employee telephone conversations
c.   Drug testing
d.   All of the above raise the issue of an employee's right to privacy.

17.   Which of the following best describes current law regarding drug testing of employees?

a.   Most states have passed legislation on this issue.
b.   The right to conduct drug tests depends on the nature of the employee's work.
c.   All random drug testing is prohibited.
d.   The U.S. Supreme Court has not heard cases on this issue.

18.   Which of the following is not prohibited by the Employee Polygraph Protection Act?

a.   Asking all job applicants to take a lie-detector test.
b.   Administering lie-detector tests when employee theft is suspected.
c.   Asking government employees to take lie detector tests.
d.   Threatening demotion or dismissal if an employee refuses to take the test.

19.   Which of the following is an example of a legal but ethically questionable act of a corporation?

a.   Donating funds to charity
b.   Producing products abroad to avoid high labor costs
c.   Distributing potentially dangerous products overseas because their distribution has been banned in this country
d.   Giving each employee a "religious" holiday choice

20.   Ethics is most closely related to:

a.   civil law.
b.   criminal law.
c.   social standards.
d.   legislation

21.   Which of the following is not an example of corporate social responsibility?

a.   Donating corporate funds to charity
b.   Refusing to deal with governments who support apartheid
c.   Complying with regulations of the Environmental Protection Agency
d.   Creating job-training programs for employees

22.   An example of law acting as a guiding social force is:

a.   court decisions prohibiting discrimination.
b.   legislation banning most lie-detector tests.
c.   amendments to the Foreign Corrupt Practices Act.

23.   A society's ethical values:

a.   are based on a collection of shared beliefs.
b.   are created by law.
c.   are identical to a society's laws.

24.   A synonym for a lie-detector test is a:

a.   polymer.
b.   polygram
c.   polyester.
d.   tradeoff.

25.   The U.S. Congress:

a.   has not passed legislation dealing with computer information and the right to privacy.
b.   has passed this type of legislation, but only with regard to financial transactions.
c.   has passed general and industry-specific legislation dealing with the

        use of computer information.
    d.   has passed laws prohibiting improper use of computer information but an individual has no right under federal law to learn about information in his or her file.

Answers to Study Questions

Fill-in-the-Blank Questions

The manager's request is illegal under the federal Employee Polygraph Protection Act. A grocery business is not likely to be an industry which is exempted from the law. However, once employee theft is suspected, the manager has a good reason for administering the test and his actions are probably legal. In considering whether the drug test was proper, a court might balance the risk to public safety against violation of the employee's privacy. In this case, a court might conclude that the risk is too indirect to warrant violating individuals' rights.

True-False Questions

1.   T

2.   F. Several laws and the U.S. Constitution deal with an employee's right to privacy.

3.   T.

4.   F. The reporting requirements are now more lenient.

5.   T.

6.   T.

7.   F. The probable cause requirement deals with a right to privacy. The free exercise clause determines an employee's right to practice his or her religion.

8.   F. Some states have, but most have not.

9.   F. Positive law is a synonym for black-letter law.

10.   T.

Multiple-Choice Questions

1.	c	10.	b	18.	c
2.	b	11.	c	19.	c
3.	d	12.	a	20.	c
4.	b	13.	b	21.	c
5.	a	14.	c	22.	a
6.	b	15.	a	23.	a
7.	a	16.	d	24.	b
8.	c	17.	b	25.	c
9.	a				

7

Nature and Classificaton

General Principles

A contract is a legal obligation to perform an act or to refrain from performing an act. The legal obligation is based on a promise. When the promise isn't kept, the result is a suit for breach of contract. When a person sues for breach of contract he or she must prove the following facts:

1.   A valid contract was formed. The requirements are listed below.

2.   The defendant has no legal excuse (if the defendant asserts that he or she does). The most common defenses are listed below.

3.   The contract was breached. The defendant failed to perform as promised.

4.   The plaintiff has suffered injury. Even if a contract was made and breached, the plaintiff cannot recover unless he or she can prove injury.

Chapter Summary

I.   Basic Requirements for Formation of a Contract

      A.   Agreement--One party must make a valid offer to perform and the other party must accept the offer.

      B.   Consideration--Each party must be willing to do an act or to refrain from doing an act.

      C.   Contractual Capacity--Each party must have the legal ability to make a contract. Minors, insane persons, and intoxicated persons are protected by law

D.   Legality--The subject matter of the contract must be lawful. A court will not enforce an illegal contract.

In addition, it must be shown that the defendant has no defense against payment (if the defendant asserts a defense against payment). The most common defenses include:

E.   Reality of Assent--The defendant must consent to the agreement. No mistake, fraud, duress, or undue influence.

F.   Form--Some contracts must be in writing.

II.   Types of Contracts

A.   Bilateral v. Unilateral

(1)   Bilateral--Promise in exchange for another promise. Most common.

(2)   Unilateral--Promise in exchange for an act. The best example is a contest.

It is often difficult to distinguish between the two. Ask yourself if the person making the first promise (the offeror) will be satisfied with a promise to perform from the other party (offeree). If a promise is insufficient, then the contract is unilateral.

EX: A disk jockey promises a free album to the 9th caller. The disk jockey would not be satisfied with your promise to be the 9th caller. You must be the 9th caller. The contract is unilateral.

In a unilateral contract, the offeror cannot revoke the offer if the offeree has started performing. It would be unfair for the disk jockey to take back his promise once you have begun dialing.

B.   Express v. Implied Contract

(1)   Express--Terms are stated; need not be written.

(2)   Implied--Contract is implied from the conduct of the parties. It is an objective test. Ask yourself how a reasonable person would have interpreted the conduct.

Proof of an implied-in-fact contract:

1.   One person furnished some service or property.
2.   That person expected to be paid for his trouble and a reasonable person would have realized that payment was expected.

3.   The other person had a chance to reject the offer but did not do so.

The party furnishing the service is usually the plaintiff; the recipient is usually the defendant.

C.   Contract Implied in Law or Quasi Contract

Implied in Law (Quasi Contract)--Not a true contract because one or more elements are missing but one party (plaintiff) has performed and it would be unfair to let the defendant receive something for nothing.

Proof of a Contract Implied in Law:

1.   The plaintiff did an act that benefitted the defendant.
2.   The defendant was unjustly enriched. (The defendant got something for nothing.)
3.   The plaintiff was not negligent or dishonest.

D.   Formal v. Informal Contracts

(1)   Formal--Requires a special format or a special procedure to execute them. A contract under seal requires a special seal to be placed on the document. A recognizance (surety bond), a negotiable instrument, and a letter of credit require certain formalities.

(2)   Informal--All other contracts.

E.   Executed v. Executory

(1)   Executed--Has been performed by both parties.

(2)   Executory--An agreement has been reached but neither party has performed. A contract can be executory on one side and executed on the other.

F.   Valid, Void, Voidable and Unenforceable Contracts

(1)   Valid--Meets all the requirements for formation listed above and no defense to performance exists.

(2)   Void--No contract and neither side can enforce its terms. Illegal contracts are usually void.

(3)   Voidable--A valid contract, but one or both parties can choose to cancel the contract. Usually occurs with a minor or when there are problems with genuineness of assent.

(4)   <u>Unenforceable</u>--Meets the requirements of formation but a defense exists and the plaintiff cannot sue the defendant for failure to perform.

Study Questions

Fill-in-the-Blank Questions

Tom offers in writing to sell his TV to Bridget for $50. Bridget accepts the offer in writing and promises to pay Tom on Tuesday. On Tuesday, Tom hands Bridget the TV set but Bridget refuses to pay.

The contract between Tom and Bridget is _____.
                                          (bilateral/unilateral)

The contract is _____.
                   (formal/informal)

The contract is _____.
                   (express/implied in fact)

True-False Questions

1.   Quasi contract is another name for a contract implied in fact. _____

2.   A bilateral contract consists of a promise given in exchange for another promise. _____

3.   A voidable contract may be canceled by one or both of the parties. _____

4.   An express contract must be written. _____

5.   Fraud is a defense to enforcement of a contract. _____

6.   Consideration is required for formation of a contract. _____

7.   An implied-in-fact contract is formed by the conduct of the parties. _____

8.   A letter of credit is an example of a formal contract. _____

9.   The defendant in a suit based on quasi contract is the party who received the goods or services. _____

10.   Contractual capacity is one requirement for formation of a contract.

Multiple-Choice Questions

1. Nancy enters Lucy's Cafeteria and places an order of fried chicken and a salad on her tray. The cashier hands Nancy a ticket showing the cost of the meal. The contract between Nancy and Lucy's is:

    a. implied in law and Nancy must pay for the meal.
    b. implied in fact and Nancy must pay for the meal.
    c. express and Nancy must pay for the meal.
    d. unenforceable because Nancy did not agree to pay.

2. Burger Queen restaurant is sponsoring a promotion to introduce its new "Topper" hamburger. Burger Queen promises to give a T-shirt to the first 20 customers who order a "Topper". Ned is the 15th customer. Burger Queen:

    a. is the offeror and the contract is bilateral.
    b. is the offeror and the contract is unilateral.
    c. is the offeree and the contract is bilateral.
    d. is the offeree and the contract is unilateral.

3. The contract between Ned and Burger Queen is:

    a. implied in law and unenforceable.
    b. implied in fact and unenforceable.
    c. express and unenforceable.
    d. express and enforceable.

4. Sol hires Benjy to rake his lawn and to burn the dry grass and leaves. A city ordinance prohibits burning trash, leaves, and grass. The contract between Benjy and Sol is:

    a. valid.
    b. voidable.
    c. void.
    d. unenforceable.

5. Beverly takes her silk blouse to the dry cleaners and asks them to clean it. Anne leaves an identical blouse at the same store. She asks the owner to clean it and to replace the buttons. The owner scrambles the order and replaces the buttons on Beverly's blouse. Although Beverly likes the new buttons, she refuses to pay for them. The owner sues Beverly on which of the following theories?

    a. Implied-in-fact contract
    b. Implied-in-law contract
    c. Express contract
    d. Informal contract

6. The owner will be:

a.   successful because Beverly was unjustly enriched.
b.   successful because the owner furnished the buttons.
c.   unsuccessful because the owner was negligent.
d.   successful because a reasonable person would have paid for the buttons.

7.   Bill offers to walk Cindy's dogs every day next week at a rate of $2 per day. Cindy agrees to pay him $10 after the Friday walk. The contract between Bill and Cindy is:

a.   unilateral and implied in fact.
b.   unilateral and express.
c.   bilateral and express.
d.   bilateral and implied in law.

8.   On Friday, after the walk. but before Cindy pays, the contract is:

a.   executed on Bill's side and executory on Cindy's side.
b.   executed on Cindy's side and executory on Bill's side.
c.   executed on both sides.
d.   executory on both sides.

9.   Which of the following is not required for formation of a contract but is a defense to enforcement of the contract?

a.   Agreement
b.   Form
c.   Consideration
d.   Legality

10.   Which of the following is not a formal contract?

a.   A sales contract
b.   A negotiable instrument
c.   A surety bond
d.   A letter of credit

11.   Mary, age ten, buys a yo-yo from the toy store. Because Mary is a minor, she can cancel the contract at any time. The contract between Mary and the store is:

a.   void.
b.   voidable.
c.   valid.
d.   invalid.

12.   Linda is shopping at Al's Grocery. She fills her cart and gets in line at the cash register. After the cashier has rung up the purchases, Mary writes a check to pay for the goods. The next day Mary stops payment on the check,

returns the groceries and tells Al that she was only kidding. She would never buy groceries from him. The contract between Linda and Al:

    a.   is enforceable because of the objective theory of contracts.
    b.   is unenforceable because Mary didn't really intend to make a contract.
    c.   is unenforceable because the contract is implied and not express.
    d.   is unenforceable because it is unilateral and not bilateral.

13.   Alice rents an apartment from Oscar. State law requires that all leases be in writing. The contract between Alice and Oscar is:

    a.   void.
    b.   voidable.
    c.   valid.
    d.   unenforceable.

14.   Andrew tells Ted that he will pay Ted $100 if Ted will find Andrew's lost dog. The contract between Ted and Andrew is:

    a.   bilateral and formal.
    b.   bilateral and informal.
    c.   unilateral and formal.
    d.   unilateral and informal.

15.   Aunt Becky tells Tom that she will pay him $4 if he will paint her fence. After Tom has painted part of the fence, Aunt Becky tells Tom that she has decided to hire a professional painter. Aunt Becky:

    a.   can revoke her offer because Tom has not accepted.
    b.   can revoke her offer because the contract is informal.
    c.   cannot revoke her offer because Tom has begun performance.
    d.   cannot revoke her offer because the contract is bilateral.

Answers to Study Questions

Fill-in-the-Blank Questions

The contract is bilateral. Tom promises to sell and Bridget promised to buy. The contract is informal. It does not matter that the contract is written; it is not a letter of credit, recognizance, and does not require a seal. The contract is express; the terms are stated.

True-False Questions

1.   F. Quasi contract is a synonym for a contract implied in law.

2.   T.

3.   T.

4.   F. An express contract is one whose terms have been stated; it may be oral.

5.   T. Remember genuineness of assent.

6.   T.

7.   T.

8.   T.

9.   T.

10.   T

Multiple-Choice Questions

1.	b		9.	b
2.	b		10.	a
3.	d		11.	b
4.	c		12.	a
5.	b		13.	d
6.	c		14.	d
7.	c		15.	c
8.	a			

Agreement and Consideration

General Principles

The first requirement for a valid contract is agreement between the parties: an offer by one party that is accepted by the other party. The offeror is the "master" of the offer; he or she establishes the terms of the agreement. The offeree can accept these terms or propose new ones. When the offeree accepts, there is agreement, and the first condition for a contract is satisfied.

Consideration is another requirement for an enforceable contract. Each party to a contract must make a commitment or give up a legal right. In most contracts, one party promises to pay money and the other promises to provide goods or services, but consideration need not be money. If only one party provides consideration, a gift, not a contract, exists.

Chapter Summary

I.   Agreement--Occurs when there is an offer and an acceptance of that offer. If all details of the contract are not clearly stated, the objective theory of contracts (based on the reasonable interpretation of a party's actions) will be used to determine if a contract has been made. When in doubt, the court will find that there is a contract. In a contract for the sale of goods, if some terms of the contract are missing, but it is clear that a contract is intended the Uniform Commercial Code provides rules for filling in the missing terms.

II.   Requirements of the Offer--An offer expresses a serious intent to be bound to a contract. It must be reasonably definite so that the court could order a remedy if one party should breach. The offer must be communicated to the offeree.

        A.   Intention--An offer creates the power in the offeree to accept and conclude a binding agreement that the offeror must be willing to perform. Do not confuse performance with intention to be bound. A legal contract is formed when the parties agree although performance may not take place immediately.

(1)   Seriousness--A statement made in anger, frustration, or as a joke is not an offer. The effect of the statement is measured by what a reasonable person would think if he or she heard it. This is the objective theory of contracts.

(2)   Present Intent to be Bound

(a)   Distinguish an invitation for offers from a genuine offer. Ads, auctions, price lists, and solicitation for bids are not true offers. Remember that a true offer would allow everyone who saw the ad or submitted a bid to accept and the offeror would be obligated to fill numerous contracts. An invitation to offer requires three steps to agreement instead of the usual offer and acceptance: 1) invitation to offer; 2) offer; 3) acceptance.

Example: Auctioneer asks for bids (invitation for offers); bidders propose prices (offers); the auctioneer drops the hammer and says "Sold" (acceptance)

Exception: Occasionally an advertisement can be considered an offer. If the contract is unilateral and the ad is very specific, the courts may rule that it is an offer.

(b)   Distinguish an expression of intention from a true offer. Equivocal language such as, "I plan to" or "I intend to" are insufficient.

(3)   Statements of Opinion--Distinguish a prediction from a promise.

B.   Definiteness--Also an indication of intent to be bound. If many terms are left blank, it is reasonable to assume that the parties are still negotiating. In a contract for the sale of goods, the UCC will allow the courts to fill in several blanks using reasonable terms or industry customs. Ask yourself: If one party breached, would a court be able to determine the obligations of each party. If so, the contract is sufficiently definite.

C.   Communication--Only the intended offeree has the power to accept; a bystander cannot. An offeree cannot accept an offer if he has not received it.

III.   Termination of the Offer

A.   Acts of the Parties

(1)   Revocation--As a general rule, the offeror can revoke the offer at any time prior to acceptance. The revocation is effective when it is received by the offeree. An offer can be revoked directly (when the offeror tells the offeree) or indirectly (the offeree learns from someone else).

There are three exceptions to this rule: 1) an option contract where the offeree pays the offeror to hold the option open; 2) action by the offeree due to reliance on the offer; 3) a firm offer for a sale of goods by a merchant.

(2)   Rejection--If the offeree expressly indicates that he or she will not accept the terms proposed, the offer is terminated.

(3)   Counteroffer--If the offeree makes a new proposal, a counteroffer is created. It is treated as a new offer and the offeree becomes the offeror. In non-sales contracts, any variance from the original offer becomes a counteroffer (mirror-image rule).

In sales contracts, if the important terms are agreed on by the parties, a contract may exist even though the details are not settled. This situation usually occurs when the offeree uses a different form to respond to an offer (battle of the forms). The new terms may become a part of the contract depending on the sophistication of the parties.

(a)   Non-Merchants (one or both parties)--The new terms proposed by the offeree do not become a part of the contract.

(b)   Merchants--Because merchants deal with contracts routinely, new terms may become a part of the contract unless the new terms include important or material changes, the offeror insisted on a "take it or leave it" acceptance, or the offeror refuses the new terms within a reasonable time.

B.   Operation of Law

(1)   Lapse of Time--If the offer is not accepted within a reasonable time, it expires. Reasonableness may depend on the subject matter of the contract.

(2)   Destruction of the Subject Matter

(3)   Death or Incompetency of a Party--Notice is not required. Some option contracts may be binding on the heirs of a party.

(4)   Supervening Illegality--The offer was legal when made but the laws changed and it is now illegal.

IV.   Acceptance

A.   Offeree--Can only be the person to whom the offer was made. Third party cannot accept.

B.   Unequivocal--Requires the same definite commitment as the offer.

Silence--Usually not sufficient unless the offeree's actions show a willingness to go through with the contract. Distinguish prior dealings between parties and the continuation of performance under a long-term contract.

Example: Many book and record clubs will send a member a monthly selection unless notice is received. Remember that the contract was formed when the member joined the club. The monthly offerings are performance of the contract.

C.   Communication--Unless specified by the offeror, communication is not necessary. However, if the offeror does not receive an answer, the offer may lapse.

D.   Mode--Unless specified by the offeror, any reasonable method of acceptance is acceptable. Mail is normally adequate.

E.   Time of Effect--An acceptance is effective when it is sent (mailbox rule). An offeror should not make an offer unless he or she is willing for another party to accept. If the acceptance is lost in the mail due to the negligence of the offeree, it is not effective until it is received. An offer can expressly require receipt of acceptance.

F.   Acceptance and Rejection--If the offeree sends both an acceptance and a rejection, the first communication to be received is effective. It is immaterial which was sent first. Examine the rule from the offeror's point of view; he or she does not know that a second communication has been sent and should be able to rely on a response when it is received.

V.   Consideration--Its Requirements--Consideration is a bargained-for exchange between the parties. Each party must promise to do something that he or she is not legally obligated to do or each party must give up a legal right (forbearance).

A.   Adequacy of Consideration--The monetary value exchanged need not be equal or equivalent. If the contract is extremely one-sided, a court may cancel on the grounds of unconscionability.

B.   Pre-Existing Duty Rule--Occurs with modification of contracts. If a contract is modified, then each party must provide new consideration. The rule was created to prevent blackmail.

EX: Paul's Plumbing agrees to install a new shower at a cost of $600. When Paul is halfway done, he informs the homeowner that he will walk off the job if the owner does not pay an extra $400. The owner reluctantly agrees. There is no consideration for the owner's promise to pay $400.

It is unenforceable even though he has agreed.

Paul	Homeowner
install shower	$600
+	+
_____	$400

Exceptions:

(1)   Unforeseen Difficulties--If Paul had experienced difficulties which a reasonable plumber would not have predicted, his extra work is consideration for the extra money.

(2)   Rescission and New Contract--If both parties willingly agree to give up rights under the old contract, they have given up legal rights and the new contract is enforceable.

D.   Past Consideration--The parties must agree to the exchange at the time the contract is formed. An act performed in the past before the promise is made is not valid consideration.

IV.   Problems Concerning Consideration

A.   Uncertain Performance--Ask if one party has given up something of value or if it only appears so.

(1)   Requirements Contracts--Usually made between a large seller and a small buyer. The buyer promises to buy all the seller's goods that he or she needs. The buyer gives up the right to buy from anyone else; the seller promises to fulfill the buyer's needs before selling to others. Must be expressed in terms of needs and not desires.

(2)   Output Contracts--The opposite of a requirements contract and

involves a large buyer and small seller. The seller promises to sell all his production to the buyer and gives up the right to sell to others. The buyer agrees to buy all the seller's goods before purchasing from another.

(3)   Option-to-Cancel Clauses--An option to cancel at any time with no notice is an illusory promise because the party can back out at any time. However, if notice must be given in advance, usually a certain number of days in advance, the clause will be legal. It is not necessary that both parties have this option in order for the clause to be enforced.

B.   Settlement of Claims

(1)   Accord and Satisfaction--A debtor offers to pay a creditor less than the total amount due. The accord is the new agreement; the satisfaction is the performance of the new agreement. A settlement will be enforceable if the amount is genuinely in dispute (unliquidated). If the amount is predetermined and the only quarrel is a refusal to pay, then settlement for less than the full amount is not adequate consideration.

EX: Mary purchases a washing machine from AAA Appliances. She agrees to pay $400 a month for 2 months. The washer breaks down and Mary sends AAA a check for $1 marked "paid in full."

Creditor	Debtor
gives up $799	_____

If Mary had given up the right to sue for breach of contract, then the accord and satisfaction would be enforceable.

(2)   Release--Usually occurs as settlement of a lawsuit or other unliquidated claim. Each party gives up the right to prove the actual damages and the release is enforceable. Some states require that a release be executed in writing.

(3)   Covenant Not to Sue--Resembles an accord and satisfaction. A promise not to sue by one party is based on another's promise to pay for damages. If payment is not forthcoming, the substituted performance fails and the injured party may sue for breach of contract.

C.   Promissory Estoppel (Detrimental Reliance)--An equitable remedy which may be used to enforce a contract if all the following elements are present:

(1)   The defendant made a promise to the plaintiff.

(2)   The plaintiff justifiably (reasonably) relied on the promise.

(3)   The plaintiff suffered substantial detriment as a result of the reliance.

(4)   It is fairer to enforce the contract than not to enforce it.

Study Questions

Fill-in-the-Blank Questions

John puts an ad in the paper, "1968 Cadillac for sale. Vintage condition. $2000." Rob reads the ad, calls John and says, "I'll take it".

John has made an _____.
                        (offer/invitation to offer)

Rob has made an _____.
                        (offer/acceptance)

There _____ a valid agreement between Rob and John.
            (is/is not)

True-False Questions

1.   If the offeree makes a counteroffer, the original offer is terminated. _____

2.   A covenant not to sue is another term for a release. _____

3.   In an auction contract, acceptance is made when the auctioneer says "Sold". _____

4.   A requirements contract is an exception to the pre-existing duty rule. _____

5.   In non-sales contracts, an acceptance must agree to the offer as stated and any change will be considered a counteroffer. _____

6.   A properly executed accord and satisfaction will discharge a liquidated debt. _____

7.   An option contract is an irrevocable offer. _____

8.   If the price is omitted from a sales contract, the contract cannot be enforced.
_____

9.   An offer may be terminated if the subject matter of the contract is destroyed.
_____

10.   The seriousness of an offer is measured by the subjective intent of the offeror. _____

Multiple-Choice Questions

1.   Sandra writes to Paula and offers to sell her 10-speed bicycle for $200. Sandra mails the offer on Monday and it is received on Wednesday. Paula calls Sandra on Thursday and tells Sandra she will buy the bicycle. She mails a check to Sandra on Friday. Sandra receives the check on Saturday. Paula's acceptance is effective on:

   a.   Wednesday.
   b.   Thursday.
   c.   Friday.
   d.   Saturday.

2.   Sandra could have revoked the offer legally on:

   a.   Monday.
   b.   Thursday, after Sandra's call.
   c.   Friday.
   d.   none of the above; Sandra has no right to revoke an offer.

3.   Bobby sees a dog wandering on the street. He reads the dog's tags and returns the dog to its owner, Susan. When Bobby returns home, he reads the evening paper and discovers that Susan is offering a reward for the return of her dog.

   a.   Bobby can collect the reward because he provided consideration by returning the dog.
   b.   Bobby can collect the reward because Susan's ad in the newspaper was an offer and Bobby accepted when he returned the dog.
   c.   Bobby cannot collect the reward because Susan has not provided consideration.
   d.   Bobby cannot collect the reward because Bobby did not know of the offer when he returned the dog.

4.   Mrs. Evans worked as a secretary for Big M Corporation for 25 years. When she retired, the board of directors of Big M passed a resolution which promised to pay Mrs. Evans $200 per month for the rest of her life "in consideration of her loyalty to Big M Corporation." Mrs. Evans received the money for 2 years, during which she refused job offers to work for a Big M competitor, but when a new board was elected, it refused to pay. Mrs. Evans sued the board and Big M.

a.   Mrs. Evans will win because she provided consideration to the company by working for 25 years.

b.   Mrs. Evans will win because she accepted the payments.

c.   Mrs. Evans will win because she relied on the promise made by Big M's board.

d.   Mrs. Evans will lose because the board's declaration was not an offer.

5.   Phineas Pharmaceuticals offers to sell Dr. Smock a case of its newest creation, "Mega-Multi Vitamin". The offer is received by Dr. Smock but before he can respond, the Food and Drug Administration bans the sale of the vitamin. Dr. Smock is unaware of the ban.

a.   Phineas must revoke the offer before Dr. Smock accepts.

b.   The offer will terminate only if Dr. Smock does not accept.

c.   The offer terminated automatically when the vitamin was banned and Phineas does not have to revoke the offer.

d.   The offer has not been terminated.

6.   Vern's Wholesale Vegetables offers to sell Sizemore Supermarkets 20 cartons of frozen peas for $100 per carton. The president of Sizemore writes to Vern and states, "Please send 20 cartons of peas and include 2 boxes of your new Gourmet Carrots". Sizemore's president:

a.   has rejected Vern's offer.

b.   has accepted Vern's offer for 20 cartons of peas.

c.   has made a counteroffer.

7.   E-Z Auto Finance sells a used car to Mrs. Smith for $4,000. Mrs. Smith soon discovers that the car has engine trouble and is only worth $400.

a.   The contract between Mrs. Smith and E-Z is invalid because she provided more consideration than E-Z.

b.   The contract is invalid because Mrs. Smith did not accept E-Z's offer.

c.   The contract is invalid because E-Z has provided no consideration.

d.   Both parties have provided consideration and a valid contract has been formed, but a court might cancel the contract on other grounds.

8.   Rose belongs to the Bargain Book Club. The club agreement states that Rose will receive a book each month unless she notifies the club in writing. Rose received a book in the mail last week but refuses to pay.

a.   Rose does not have to pay because silence is never acceptance.

b.   Rose does not have to pay because the book club did not make an offer.

c.   Rose must pay for the book because she accepted the terms of the agreement when she joined the club.

d.   Rose does not have to pay for the book because she has not accepted it

9. Linda buys a stereo from AAA Appliances. She pays $50 down and agrees to pay $50 per month for 6 months. The stereo quits working after the first month. Linda sends AAA a check for $1 with the notation "payment in full". AAA cashes the check.

    a. AAA can sue Linda for the remaining amount due because the debt is liquidated.
    b. AAA can sue Linda for the remaining amount because the debt is unliquidated.
    c. AAA cannot sue Linda because there has been an accord and satisfaction and the debt is liquidated.
    d. AAA cannot sue Linda because there has been an accord and satisfaction and the debt is unliquidated.

10. Paul writes to Pete and offers to sell his bicycle to him for $30. Pete does not want the bicycle but Pete's roommate, Tony, sees the letter. Tony writes Paul and promises to pay him $30.

    a. There is a contract between Paul and Tony because Tony accepted Paul's offer.
    b. There is a contract between Paul and Tony because Tony provided consideration by promising to send $40.
    c. There is no contract between Paul and Tony because Tony did not receive an offer.
    d. There is no contract between Paul and Tony because a promise to pay $30 is not valid consideration.

11. Oliver writes to Sidney and offers to sell him his house. Sidney receives the offer on Monday. He mails an acceptance on Tuesday but has second thoughts and sends a telegram on Thursday rejecting the offer. The rejection is received on Thursday; the acceptance is received on Friday.

    a. There is a contract because the acceptance was sent before the rejection.
    b. There is a contract because the acceptance was effective on Tuesday and Sidney cannot change his mind.
    c. There is not a contract because Sidney sent the rejection after the acceptance.
    d. There is not a contract because the rejection arrived before the acceptance.

12. Paul's Painting offers to paint Sally's house for $500. Sally agrees. After beginning work, Paul refuses to complete the job unless Sally pays an additional $200. Sally reluctantly agrees but later refuses to pay.

    a. Sally is within her rights because she accepted Paul's original offer.
    b. Sally is within her rights because of the pre-existing duty rule.
    c. Sally must pay the extra $200 because she promises Paul that she would.

d.   Sally must pay the extra $200 because Paul has the right to modify the contract.

13.   Mrs. Foster's dog escapes from her backyard and tramples the neighbor's garden. Mrs. Foster offers to pay the neighbor $50 for the damage and the neighbor accepts. Mrs. Foster writes him a check for $50. He signs a statement that the $50 is accepted for all damages. Three days later, the neighbor tells Mrs. Foster that his actual damages were $150 and he intends to sue her for the difference.

a.   The neighbor will not succeed because he has signed a valid release.
b.   The neighbor will not succeed because he has signed a valid covenant not to sue.
c.   The neighbor will not succeed because he has signed a valid accord and satisfaction.
d.   The neighbor will succeed.

14.   Which of the following is an exception to the pre-existing duty rule?

a.   Past consideration
b.   Price change due to inflation
c.   Unilateral contract
d.   Rescission and new contract

15.   McRonald's Restaurant contracts with Farmer Brown to buy all the eggs Brown's chickens can produce for $.60 per dozen. The agreement between McRonald's and Farmer Brown:

a.   is invalid because it is indefinite.
b.   is invalid because Farmer Brown has not provided consideration.
c.   is a valid requirements contract.
d.   is a valid output contract.

16.   Which of the following is not a requirement for promissory estoppel?

a.   Justifiable reliance by the promisee
b.   A promise by the promisor
c.   Substantial action or forbearance by the promisee
d.   A promise by the promisee

17.   Bill writes to Sandy and offers to mow her lawn for $25 per week. Sandy calls Bill on the phone and accepts.

a.   There is no contract because Sandy did not accept by using the same mode used by Bill to send the offer.
b.   There is no contract because an oral acceptance is never effective.
c.   There is no contract because Bill did not make an offer.
d.   There is a contract between Sandy and Bill.

18.   Marge sees a chair she likes at a garage sale. She does not promise to buy the chair but tells the owner she will come back later in the day with the money for the chair. When Marge returns, she discovers that the chair has been sold. If Marge sues the seller, she will:

       a.   succeed because she accepted an offer to buy the chair.
       b.   succeed because the seller had no right to revoke the offer.
       c.   succeed because the seller accepted her offer to buy.
       d.   not succeed.

19.   Fine China, Inc. places an ad in the local paper which states the Rosebud silver pattern is on sale for $50 per setting. Bob reads the ad and drives to Fine China's store. When he arrives, he offers to buy 10 settings but the manager tells him that they have sold all the Rosebud settings. In a breach of contract suit, Bob will:

       a.   succeed because he accepted their offer to buy the silverware.
       b.   not succeed because his promise to buy 10 settings is not valid consideration.
       c.   not succeed because the ad was not an offer.
       d.   succeed because Fine China revoked its offer to sell.

20.   Which of the following is an irrevocable offer?

       a.   A bid at an auction
       b.   An option contract
       c.   An advertisement in a newspaper
       d.   An accord

21.   Susan tells her friend David that she is planning to sell her TV. She tells him, "I should get about $200." Dave says, "I'll take it".

       a.   Susan's statement was an offer.
       b.   Susan's statement was not an offer.
       c.   Dave's statement was an acceptance.
       d.   Dave's statement was a counteroffer.

22.   George tells Louise he will paint her house for $1500. Louise says, "OK, but only if you also paint the shed in the backyard."

       a.   Louise has accepted George's offer.
       b.   Louise has rejected George's offer and has not made a counteroffer.
       c.   Louise has made a counteroffer.
       d.   George did not make an offer.

23.   George tells Louise he will paint her house for $1500 using AAA paint. Louise tells George that the price is right but that she wants him to use Coverall brand paint

a.   Louise's statement is a counteroffer.
b.   Louise's statement is an acceptance, but George can use AAA paint.
c.   Louise's statement is an acceptance, but George must use Coverall paint.
d.   Louise's statement is revocable.

24.   Which of the following is <u>not</u> an example of termination of an offer by operation of law?

a.   Death of the offeror
b.   Revocation
c.   Supervening illegality
d.   Lapse of time

25.   Jimmy accidentally drives his car through his cousin's garage door. Jimmy promises to pay for the door if the cousin will not sue. The cousin agrees but Jimmy's check bounces and he refuses to pay.

a.   The agreement between Jimmy and his cousin was a covenant not to sue and the cousin cannot sue because he agreed not to do so.
b.   The agreement between Jimmy and his cousin was a covenant not to sue and the cousin can sue because Jimmy breached the covenant.
c.   The agreement between Jimmy and his cousin was a valid release and the cousin cannot sue.
d.   The agreement between Jimmy and his cousin was an accord and satisfaction and Jimmy did not complete the satisfaction and the cousin can sue.

Answers to Study Questions

Fill-in-the-Blank Questions

John has made an invitation to offer. An ad is an invitation to offer unless it is very specific and is part of a unilateral contract. Rob has made the offer. Because there has been no acceptance, there is not a valid agreement between Rob and John.

True-False Questions

1.   T.

2.   F. A covenant not to sue is a promise not to sue made in exchange for another party's promise to pay damages. If payment is not made, suit is possible. In a release, each party gives up the opportunity to prove the actual amount of damages and another law suit is not possible.

3.   T.

4.   F. A requirements contract exists when a buyer promises to purchase all the

goods he or she needs from one seller.

5.   T.

6.   F. It will discharge an unliquidated debt.

7.   T.

8.   F. The court will imply a reasonable price <u>if</u> there is other evidence to show that the parties intended to make a contract.

9.   T.

10.   F. It is measured by what a reasonable person would have thought. This is an objective test.

<u>Multiple-Choice Questions</u>

1.	b		14.	d
2.	a		15.	d
3.	d		16.	d
4.	c		17.	d
5.	c		18.	d
6.	b		19.	c
7.	d		20.	b
8.	c		21.	b
9.	a		22.	c
10.	c		23.	a
11.	d		24.	b
12.	b		25.	b
13.	a			

Capacity and Legality

General Principles

The public welfare sometimes overrides the legal obligation to complete a contract. The law protects certain types of people from the legal obligations of a contract. The law also prohibits illegal contracts and prevents them from being enforced. The law tries to balance the need for protection with the general duty to fulfill contracts.

Minors, mentally incompetent and intoxicated persons are given the option of completing or canceling a contract. If they choose to cancel the contract, they must return any benefits they have received from the contract. Nevertheless, these people may be responsible for paying for basic necessities or if they have deceived the other party to the contract.

Contracts to perform illegal acts are void. The law may also prohibit contracts which threaten public safety or free enterprise. A court may choose to enforce part of the contract or it may regard the whole contract as void. People will be discouraged from attempting to make illegal contracts if they cannot enforce them.

Chapter Summary

I.   <u>Minors</u>--Defined by law but usually persons under the age of 18. A minor can usually cancel or disaffirm a contract, although there are some exceptions. An adult who contracts with a minor does not have this right. The contract is said to be <u>voidable</u> at the option of the minor.

     A.   <u>Disaffirmance--General Rules</u>--A minor's right to set aside or "get out of" a contract. This right continues until the minor turns 18 and for a reasonable time thereafter. Minor must disaffirm the entire contract; he or she cannot decide to avoid some parts of a contract and agree to other parts.

B.   <u>Duty of Restoration</u>--This is the duty of the minor to return what he has received under the contract. The other party is required to return the minor's consideration. In most states, it is irrelevant if the goods received by the minor have been damaged or destroyed; it is sufficient if he or she restores what is available. In a few states, the minor owes a duty of restitution, which requires the minor to repair the damage before returning the goods. In these cases, the other party is entitled to a "full refund."

C.   <u>Effect of Misrepresentation of a Minor's Age</u>-- Courts disagree on an appropriate remedy when a minor lies about his or her age. Some states have passed laws which prevent the minor from disaffirming the contract. In other states, the courts require a duty of restoration or allow the minor to disaffirm the contract but hold him or her liable for the tort of misrepresentation. These rules apply only if the misrepresentation was believable.

D.   <u>Liability for Necessaries</u>

(1)   <u>Definition</u>--Any item or service which is essential such as clothing, food, and shelter. Insurance is not usually a necessary but some states allow enforcement of contracts for health or life insurance. Loans are not necessaries unless the lender controls the funds and ensures that food, clothing, or shelter is purchased.

(2)   The contract is enforceable only for the reasonable value of the goods or services. The law encourages merchants to sell to minors by allowing the merchants to collect a fair price.

E.   <u>Ratification</u>--The contract becomes enforceable against the minor. A minor can decide to ratify or enforce a contract only after he or she reaches the age of majority. Ratification can be express or can be implied from conduct. Can be assumed if a contract is not disaffirmed within a reasonable time after the minor gains contractual capacity.

F.   <u>Liability for Torts</u>--Minors are responsible for their torts. In some cases, where the minor does a malicious act or acts under the direction of his or her parents, the parents may be responsible for the minor's torts.

II.   <u>Intoxicated Persons</u>--An intoxicated person who makes a contract can later disaffirm the contract if there is proof that he or she was too inebriated to understand the legal consequences of making a contract. The intoxication may be voluntary. The intoxicated party must disaffirm the contract within a reasonable time after becoming sober.

III.   Mentally Incompetent Persons--A person who has been officially declared mentally incompetent by a court of law cannot make a contract. Any attempt to make the contract is void. A guardian appointed by the court makes all legal decisions for the incompetent. A person who is mentally incompetent but has not been declared mentally incompetent is treated in the same manner as an intoxicated person, i.e. the test is whether the mentally incompetent person understood the nature of his or her actions.

V.   Illegality--State or federal statutes may determine the legality of some contracts. Other contracts are detrimental to the public welfare and are outlawed even though no specific rule states that they are illegal.

A.   Contracts Contrary to Statute

(1)   Usury--Loans made above the maximum rate of interest. Exceptions for small loans or loans to corporations. In some states revolving credit card charges, which allow monthly payments, are exempt from usury laws.

Legal rate of interest is the rate established by the state and is used in contracts where the interest rate is not stated.

Judgment rate of interest is the amount accruing on an award of money at the conclusion of a lawsuit. If the loser doesn't pay immediately, the money earns interest.

If a loan is usurious, the court may void the entire contract, but this is rare. Most states allow the lender to collect the principal of the loan or the principal plus the maximum rate of interest.

(2)   Gambling Contracts--Prohibited in most states. Includes any situation where a person pays money or other consideration for a chance to receive property. The element of chance is the crucial factor. For this reason, lotteries are illegal in some states.

An insurance contract can be considered a gambling contract if the purchaser has no legitimate interest in the subject matter of the contract. You cannot purchase a life insurance contract on the life of another person. A person to whom money is owed and who has a lien on property to secure payment of the loan does have a legitimate (insurable) interest in the property and may purchase insurance. Commodity futures contracts are also exempt from gambling laws.

(3)   Sabbath Laws--Prohibits contracts made on Sunday. The most common type is the "blue law" which prohibits the sale of certain goods on Sunday. Even so, contracts for necessities and

fully executed contracts are usually enforceable. These laws have been declared unconstitutional in some states.

    (4)   <u>Licensing Statutes</u>--A contract entered into with an unlicensed person may or may not be enforceable depending on the purpose of the licensing statute. If the purpose of the statute is to protect the public from fraudulent experts and a competency test is required to obtain the license, then the contract will be unenforceable. Contracts with doctors, lawyers, dentists, and realtors fall into this category. If the purpose of the statute is merely to raise revenue, then the contract will be enforceable.

B.   <u>Contracts Contrary to Public Policy</u>--These contracts may or may not be the subject of a specific statute. If not, a court may decide that they are illegal according to common law.

    (1)   <u>Contracts to Commit an Immoral Act</u>--Contracts prohibiting marriage or contracts for the sale of children.

    (2)   <u>Contracts in Restraint of Trade</u>--Illegal only if they unreasonably restrain trade. Exclusive distributorships and franchises may be reasonable if they are not too restrictive.

          <u>Covenants Not to Compete</u>--Legal only if the following requirements are met:

          (a)   part of an employment contract or sale of a business
          (b)   reasonable in time
          (c)   reasonable in geographic scope (depends on type of business)

    (3)   <u>Unconscionability</u>--A contract may be illegal if parts of it are so unfair that the court's sense of right and wrong is shocked. Procedural unconscionability is based on legalese, fine print, and methods of negotiating the agreement. Substantive unconscionability relates to terms of the contract (e.g. payment, repossession). UCC and UCCC have provisions dealing with this subject.

    (4)   <u>Exculpatory Clauses</u>--Clauses that release a party from liability if damage or injury occurs, no matter who is at faul. A court may choose not to enforce this type of clause if the parties have unequal bargaining power. For example, employers and public utilities are usually barred from using exculpatory clauses.

VI.   <u>Effect of Illegality</u>--The court may enforce the entire contract, part of the contract or it may void the whole contract. The court may choose to "rewrite" an unreasonable covenant not to compete. The general rule is that neither party can enforce the contract in the hope that few people will make these types of contracts.

Exceptions--A court may enforce an illegal contract if one party is relatively innocent. This category may include incidental parties, who were unaware of the illegality, or parties given special protection by statute (e.g. investors), parties who withdraw from the contract before illegal activity is performed, or parties who were wrongfully induced to enter the contract.

Study Questions

Fill-in-the-Blank Questions

Tom, age seventeen, rents a garage apartment from Mrs. Murphy. He signs a six-month lease and agrees to pay $250 per month. Mrs. Murphy is aware of Tom's age but thinks that he is a responsible young man. After two months, Tom finds a cheaper apartment and moves. He refuses to pay the remainder of the rent. Similar apartments rent for $200-300 per month.

In general, Tom _____ have contractual capacity.
                              (does/does not)

The apartment _____ a necessary.
                          (is/is not)

Tom has tried to _____ the lease.
                      (ratify/disaffirm)

The lease contract _____ enforceable.
                          (is/is not)

True-False Questions

1.   A minor may ratify a contract while he or she is still under age. _____

2.   Loans to corporations are usually exempt from usury laws. _____

3.   A party may ratify a contract by words or by conduct. _____

4.   A covenant not to compete is illegal unless it is part of a sale of a business or an employment contract. _____

5.   Sporting equipment is considered a necessary. _____

6.   An exculpatory clause gives a minor the right to disaffirm a contract. _____

7.   A person who becomes intoxicated voluntarily cannot disaffirm a contract. _____

8.   A person who has been declared mentally incompetent in a court of law can make a valid contract. _____

9.   A contract which contains fine print is an example of a contract which may be unconscionable. _____

10.   A lottery is an example of a gambling contract. _____

Multiple-Choice Questions

1.   Barry attends a party and drinks too much. He offers to sell his mixed-breed dog to Sam for $25. The next day when Sam comes to collect the dog, Barry claims he doesn't remember making the offer.

       a.   Sam can enforce the contract if a reasonable person would have believed that the offer was genuine.
       b.   Sam cannot enforce the contract if a reasonable person would have realized that Barry was intoxicated when he made the offer.
       c.   Sam cannot enforce the contract because Barry cannot remember making the offer.
       d.   Sam can enforce the contract even if he knew Barry was too drunk to know what he was saying.

Use the following facts to answer questions 2-5. John, seventeen, and Sandy, fifteen, purchase stereos from AAA Appliances. Both pay one-third down and agree to pay $35 per month for twelve months. John told the salesman that he was nineteen. Sandy said nothing. Two months later, when John and Sandy's mother discovers the stereos, she orders them to return the stereos and to collect the money they have paid.

2.   a.   The contract is enforceable against John because he lied about his age.
       b.   The contract is not enforceable against John but he may be liable in tort because he lied about his age.
       c.   The contract is enforceable against Sandy.
       d.   John can return the stereo but AAA can keep his down payment

3.   a.   Sandy cannot return the stereo because he kept the stereo for two months.
       b.   Sandy can return the stereo but he cannot recover his down payment.
       c.   Sandy can recover his down payment but he does not have to return the stereo.
       d.   Sandy can recover his down payment but he must return the stereo.

4. a. Sandy and John have ratified the contracts.
    b. John has ratified the contract but Sandy has not.
    c. Sandy has disaffirmed the contract, but John has not.
    d. Sandy and John have disaffirmed the contracts.

5. a. The contracts with AAA are void.
    b. The contracts with AAA are valid.
    c. The contracts with AAA are voidable at the option of John and Sandy.
    d. The contracts with AAA are voidable at the option of AAA.

6. Melinda, an aspiring fashion model, contracts with Orville, an orthodontist, to straighten her teeth. Orville straightens Melinda's teeth and sends her a bill for $4,000. Melinda then discovers that Orville has never been licensed to practice by the state.

    a. Melinda must pay the bill but if she is not satisfied with Orville's work, she can sue him.
    b. Melinda must pay Orville only if she is satisfied with his work.
    c. Melinda does not have to pay regardless of the quality of Orville's work.
    d. Melinda does not have to pay because $4,000 is an unreasonable charge for Orville's services.

7. A "blue law" is:

    a. a contract in restraint of trade.
    b. an example of a Sabbath law.
    c. an example of a law contrary to public policy.
    d. an example of a gambling contract.

8. Which of the following types of contracts may be exempt from usury laws?

    a. Lotteries
    b. Loans to corporations
    c. Licensing statutes
    d. Covenants not to compete

9. Mary sues John for injuries she received in an automobile accident. The court awards Mary $15,000 in damages. If John does not pay immediately, the $15,000:

    a. will earn interest at the legal rate.
    b. will earn interest at the judgment rate.
    c. will earn interest at the maximum rate of interest allowed in Mary's state.
    d. will not earn interest.

10. Sid is celebrating his new promotion and has too much to drink. While he is in this state, a magazine salesman sells him a 10-year subscription to Today's

Executive. Sid receives the magazine for 6 months and then decides to disaffirm the contract. Today's Executive refuses to cancel.

    a.   Sid can disaffirm because he was intoxicated when he made the contract.

    b.   Sid cannot disaffirm because he drank voluntarily.

    c.   Sid cannot disaffirm because he has ratified the contract.

    d.   Sid has not ratified the contract.

11.   Jerry has been declared mentally incompetent by a court of law and Bill is appointed as his guardian. Jerry orders a set of golf clubs from the pro shop. The guardian discovers the clubs and tries to return them. The contract between Jerry and the pro-shop:

    a.   is valid.

    b.   is voidable at the option of Jerry.

    c.   is voidable at the option of the pro shop.

    d.   is void.

12.   When the guardian attempts to return the clubs, he will be:

    a.   successful because Jerry had no contractual capacity.

    b.   successful only if Jerry appeared insane to a reasonable person.

    c.   unsuccessful because Jerry ratified the contract when he kept the clubs.

    d.   unsuccessful because the contract is voidable at the pro shop's option.

13.   Mary, age sixteen, buys a car from Paul's Pontiac. The next day Mary wrecks the car and attempts to return it. In Mary's state, Mary can return the car but she must pay for the damage. Mary's obligation is:

    a.   the duty of restoration.

    b.   the duty of ratification.

    c.   the duty of restitution.

    d.   the duty of cancellation.

14.   Cindy and Joe purchase a house and sign a mortgage with First Bank. Which of the following parties can purchase fire insurance on the house?

    a.   Cindy only

    b.   Joe only

    c.   Cindy and Joe only

    d.   Cindy, Joe and First Bank

15.   Allen is in desperate need of money and borrows $10,000 from Don Corleone. Corleone charges 35 percent interest. The maximum legal rate is 21 percent. When Allen refuses to pay, Corleone sues. The Court:

    a.   may cancel the entire contract.

    b.   may allow Corleone to collect the principal only.

    c.   may allow Corleone to collect the principal and 21 percent interest.

    d.   may choose any of the above.

16.   Which of the following is least likely to be considered a necessary?

    a.   A winter coat

    b.   An apartment lease

    c.   A can of tomato soup

    d.   Auto insurance

17.   Which of the following is an example of an exculpatory clause?

    a.   Seller reserves the right to cancel at any time.

    b.   Seller is not responsible for personal injury or property damage regardless of the cause of the injury.

    c.   Buyer agrees to pay any costs of collection.

    d.   Buyer agrees to notify seller of any change in address.

18.   Abel Attorney signs an employment contract with Crook & Low, Attorneys at Law. The contract contains the following clause, "Employee promises not to practice law in this state for 8 months following termination of employment". The clause:

    a.   is unenforceable because it is unreasonable in time.

    b.   is unenforceable because it is unreasonable in geographic in scope.

    c.   is unenforceable because the contract is not for the sale of a business.

    d.   is enforceable.

19.   Jim, age seventeen, purchases a computer from Harold's Hardware. Jim pays $1,000 down and promises to pay $50 per month for twenty-four months. Jim pays for eighteen months then the computer breaks down. Jim attempts to disaffirm the contract and collect the payments he has made. Harold claims that Jim has ratified the contract.

    a.   Jim will be successful because he did not expressly agree to ratify the contract when he turned 18.

    b.   Jim will be successful because he made the contract when he was a minor and he retains the right to disaffirm forever.

    c.   Jim will be unsuccessful because he should have disaffirmed before he turned 18.

    d.   Jim will be unsuccessful because he made several payments on the computer after he turned 18.

20.   A state law makes it illegal to sell a car without a written statement from the seller that the odometer has not been turned back. Ed buys a car from Susan but no statement is signed.

    a.   The contract is voidable at Susan's option.

b.   The contract is voidable at Ed's option.
c.   The contract is voidable at the option of Ed or Susan.
d.   The contract is valid.

21.   Patti suffers from manic-depressive illness. She takes medication for her illness and acts rationally most of the time. She purchases a $40 pair of tennis shoes from Sneaker Emporium.

a.   Patti can disaffirm the contract and collect her $40.
b.   Patti can disaffirm the contract but will be liable in quasi-contract for the sneakers.
c.   Patti can disaffirm the contract but she will be liable for any damage to the sneakers.
d.   Patti cannot disaffirm the contract if she understood that she was buying sneakers.

22.   The city of Woodside collects an annual license fee from all restaurants which serve alcohol. Bob, a patron of the Too Far Bar, learns that the bar has not paid the fee for several years. Bob orders $25 worth of drinks and then refuses to pay the bill.

a.   Bob can refuse to pay the bill because the contract for the drinks was illegal.
b.   Bob can refuse to pay the bill because the bar was not licensed to sell alcohol.
c.   Bob can refuse to pay the bill because the drinks were sold in violation of the licensing statute.
d.   Bob cannot refuse to pay the bill.

23.   A contract most likely will be declared unconscionable if:

a.   it is unfair to one party.
b.   it contains a cancellation clause.
c.   it shocks a court's sense of right and wrong.
d.   it is signed by a minor.

24.   Which of the following is an exception to the general rule that illegal contracts cannot be enforced by either party?

a.   One party is a minor
b.   One party is insane
c.   One party is induced to enter the contract through fraud
d.   One party is in violation of a revenue-raising licensing statute

25.   Randy is the owner of the only dry cleaners in Midtown. He learns that Howard is planning to open a dry cleaning shop in the next block. Randy offers to pay Howard $5,000 if Howard will not open a shop within 2 miles of Randy's shop. Howard agrees. The contract between Howard and Randy:

a.   is legal because it is reasonable in geographic scope.
b.   is legal because it contains no time limit.
c.   is illegal because it contains no time limit.
d.   is illegal because it is not part of a sale of Randy's business.

Answers to Study Questions

Fill-in-the-Blank Questions

Tom, a minor, lacks contractual capacity. The apartment is a necessary. Tom has tried to disaffirm the lease. The contract is enforceable because the apartment is a necessary and because it was rented at a reasonable rate.

True-False Questions

1.   F.   A minor must have reached the age of majority before he or she can ratify.

2.   T.

3.   T.

4.   T.

5.   F.   Food, clothing, and shelter are necessaries.

6.   F.   An exculpatory clause relieves one party from suit caused by negligence.

7.   F.   In contract law, it makes no difference whether the intoxication is voluntarily or involuntarily.

8.   F.   A person who is judged mentally incompetent cannot make contracts; only his or her guardian can.

9.   T.

10.   T.

Multiple-Choice Questions

1.	b	10.	c	19.	d	
2.	b	11.	d	20.	b	
3.	d	12.	a	21.	d	
4.	d	13.	c	22.	d	
5.	c	14.	d	23.	c	
6.	c	15.	d	24.	d	
7.	b	16.	d	25.	d	
8.	b	17.	b			
9.	b	18.	b			

CHAPTER

10

Genuiness of Assent

<u>General Principles</u>

Chapters 8 & 9 explained the necessary elements of a contract: agreement, consideration, legality, and contractual capacity. This chapter discusses one defense to enforcement of a contract. The contract may have been validly formed but it may not be enforceable.

Genuineness of assent relates directly to agreement. If a party is mistaken as to the nature of the contract or is fraudulently induced to enter a contract, then he or she has not agreed to the true terms of the contract, he or she has not consented willingly. These defenses are simple in theory but difficult to prove.

<u>Chapter Summary</u>

I.   <u>Mistakes</u>

     A.   <u>Unilateral Mistake</u>--Error is made by only one party. The contract is usually enforceable. The only exceptions reinforce obligations of good faith. If the non-mistaken party should have known that a mistake has been made, he or she is not allowed to take advantage of it. Similarly, if a mathematical error has been made, the mistaken party may be entitled to relief, but only if he or she has not been careless or grossly negligent.

     B.   <u>Bilateral (Mutual) Mistake</u>--Both parties must be mistaken about an important (material) fact; either party can rescind or cancel the contract. If the mistake concerns value, then the contract stands. It is sometimes difficult to tell the difference but ask yourself if both parties knew that they were taking a risk. If so, the mistake is probably one of value and the contract is enforceable.

111

II.   Fraudulent Misrepresentation--All of the elements below must be proven. The deceived party has the choice of rescinding the contract or suing for the damages he or she has suffered.

       A.   Misrepresentation Must Occur--Misrepresentation of a material or important fact must occur. An opinion is insufficient unless the plaintiff is able to prove that he or she is naive and the other party is an expert in the field. Misrepresentation of law is not usually grounds for canceling a contract, unless one of the parties has superior knowledge.

          Misrepresentation can occur by words or by conduct. As a general rule, silence is not misrepresentation because the parties are assumed to be dealing at arms' length and a cautious person would verify the facts. Exceptions: serious defect could not be discovered by reasonable inspection, the parties are in a fiduciary relationship or one party is asked a direct question which he or she does not answer.

       B.   Intent to Deceive (Scienter)--May be inferred by showing that the guilty party had knowledge of a fact and lied about it.

       C.   Justifiable Reliance--The defrauded party must show that it was reasonable to rely on the facts as presented by the other party.

       D.   Injury--If the innocent party chooses to sue for damages, he or she must prove injury. Exemplary or punitive damages are often awarded in fraud cases.

III.   Undue Influence--Occurs when someone in a position of trust influences a weaker party to agree to a contract with a third party. Some relationships automatically fall into this category (fiduciary): doctor-patient, attorney-client, guardian-ward, trustee-beneficiary, and husband-wife.

IV.   Duress--A party is forced into a contract by threats or blackmail. A threat to settle a contractual suit by suing for breach of contract does not constitute duress. Economic pressure is usually insufficient to prove duress.

V.   Plain-Language Laws--Created by state and federal laws. Under federal law, written warranties must be written in simple language. State laws follow this pattern; some limit the number of words in a sentence and the use of "legalese" and complex words.

Study Questions

Fill-in-the-Blank Questions

Paula purchases a new computer from Future Graphics, Inc. Paula asks the salesman how much memory the machine has and he responds, "10 megabytes". Paula does not ask if a joystick can be used with the machine, but she assumes that it can. She does not ask for a demonstration. When Paula uses the computer for the first time, she notices that the machine has 5 megabytes of memory and that it does not have a joystick adaptation.

Paula wants to sue Future Graphics for misrepresentation. Paula will be successful if her suit is based on _____.
(size of the memory/joystick/either)

The salesman _____ have a duty to tell Paula about the
(did/did not)
joystick options.

Paula _____ rescind the contract.
(can/cannot)

True-False Questions

1.   Silence is not usually considered misrepresentation. _____

2.   A unilateral mistake occurs when only one party is mistaken as to the essence of a contract. _____

3.   A mutual mistake in the value of the contract allows either party to cancel the contract. _____

4.   An attorney-client relationship is an example of a fiduciary relationship.
_____

5.   In order for a plaintiff to recover damages in a misrepresentation suit, he or she must prove injury. _____

6.   Scienter is a synonym for duress. _____

7.   Unilateral mistake is never a defense to enforcement of a contract. _____

8.   A party who is forced to sign a contract under threat of blackmail will be allowed to rescind the contract. _____

9.   Genuineness of assent is required for enforcement of a contract. _____

10.   Misrepresentation of law is usually grounds for rescission of a contract.
_____

Multiple-Choice Questions

Use the following facts to answer questions 1-3.

1.   Sally is shopping for a new car. A salesman at Midland Motors shows her the new Delight model. He describes it as very dependable and tells Sally that it will get 35 miles to the gallon in town. Sally and the salesman sign a sales contract for $12,000, payable in 36 installments. The car breaks down after 2 weeks. Sally:

      a.   can sue the salesman for misrepresentation because he told her the car was very dependable.
      b.   can rescind the contract on the basis of mutual mistake because neither the salesman nor Sally knew that the car would break down.
      c.   cannot sue for misrepresentation because she signed a written contract.
      d.   cannot sue for misrepresentation because "very dependable" is not a factual description of the car.

2.   If Sally discovers that the car gets only 18 miles to the gallon in town, she:

      a.   can sue because a material fact was misrepresented.
      b.   cannot sue because it is unreasonable to believe that a car could get 35 miles to the gallon.
      c.   cannot sue because she signed a written contract.
      d.   cannot sue because the average miles per gallon is statement of opinion, not fact.

3.   On the basis of the incorrect mileage statement, Sally can:

      a.   rescind the contract but she cannot sue for damages.
      b.   sue for damages but cannot rescind the contract.
      c.   rescind the contract or sue for damages.
      d.   rescind the contract and sue for damages.

4.   Allen finds a shiny blue rock while he is walking in the woods. He shows the rock to Herman, who agrees to buy it for $30. Herman shows the rock to a geologist friend who tells him that the rock is worth $700. When Herman tells Allen, Allen claims that he never would have sold the rock if he had known its true worth.

      a.   Allen can rescind the contract on the grounds of unilateral mistake.
      b.   Allen can rescind the contract on the grounds of bilateral mistake.
      c.   Allen can rescind the contract on the grounds of misrepresentation.
      d.   Allen cannot rescind the contract.

5.   Herman:

    a.   cannot enforce the contract because there was no written contract and the value of the rock is $700.

    b.   cannot enforce the contract because there was no written contract and the price of the rock is $30.

    c.   can enforce the contract because the price of the rock is $30.

    d.   can enforce the contract because a unilateral mistake was made.

6.   Exemplary damages:

    a.   are awarded to punish a wrongdoer.

    b.   are based on the amount of money lost in a breach of contract suit.

    c.   are awarded only in duress cases.

    d.   can never be rewarded if a contract suit is brought.

7.   Which of the following is not a fiduciary relationship?

    a.   Lawyer-client

    b.   Husband-wife

    c.   Buyer-seller

    d.   Doctor-patient

8.   Sandra realizes that she has charged too many purchases on her credit card. She visits E-Z Finance Co. where a loan officer proposes a bill consolidation loan of $7500 at the legal rate of 19 percent interest. Sandra feels that she will have to declare bankruptcy and reluctantly agrees to E-Z's terms.

    a.   The contract is voidable at Sandra's option.

    b.   The contract is voidable at E-Z's option.

    c.   The contract is void.

    d.   The contract is valid.

9.   Sandra:

    a.   can rescind the contract on the basis of duress.

    b.   can rescind the contract on the basis of unilateral mistake.

    c.   can rescind the contract on the basis of undue influence.

    d.   cannot rescind the contract.

10.   Which of the following is an example of bilateral mistake?

    a.   Paul sells Renee a dog which both think is purebred. The dog is not a purebred.

    b.   Paul sells Renee a dog which he knows is not purebred, but Renee thinks that the dog is a purebred.

    c.   Paul tells Renee that she should buy the dog or he will sue her for breach of contract.

    d.   Renee knows that the dog is a purebred but Paul does not.

11.   A fiduciary relationship is required for which of the following?

    a.   Unilateral mistake
    b.   Bilateral mistake
    c.   Undue influence
    d.   Duress

12.   "Puffing" is a synonym for:

    a.   scienter.
    b.   undue influence.
    c.   sales talk.
    d.   detrimental reliance.

13.   Lacey wants to sell a motorcycle to Shanna. Lacey tells Shanna that this dirt bike can be driven in town, on the street. In fact, it is illegal to drive the dirt bike on a public street. Shanna buys the bike but then wants to rescind the contract.

    a.   Shanna can rescind the contract because a mistake of law has occurred.
    b.   Shanna can rescind the contract because duress has occurred.
    c.   Shanna cannot rescind the contract because a mistake of law has occurred.
    d.   Shanna cannot rescind the contract because only economic duress has occurred.

14.   Which of the following would most likely support a case for misrepresentation? A salesman tells a potential customer that:

    a.   a house has three bedrooms, when it only has two bedrooms.
    b.   a house is "comfortable" when it would be too cramped for the customer's family.
    c.   a house is located in a good neighborhood, and a bank robber lives next door.
    d.   the backyard is fenced, when the fence is in disrepair.

15.   Paula is Mrs. Williams' lawyer. Paula induces Mrs. Williams to sell some assets for much less than their fair market value to Paula's friend. If Mrs. Williams' family wants to sue Paula, the most successful suit would be based on:

    a.   misrepresentation.
    b.   undue influence.
    c.   bilateral mistake.
    d.   duress.

16.   "Punitive" damages is a synonym for:

a. exemplary damages.
b. quasi-contract damages.
c. damages for negligence.
d. damages caused by duress.

17. Bettina is contemplating plastic surgery. Her doctor, Paul, tells her that acupuncture is much less expensive and that he will refer her to Abe, a specialist. Abe and Paul tell Bettina that she will "look twenty again". Bettina agrees to a series of ten treatments but has second thoughts. Bettina:

a. can rescind the contract on the grounds of duress.
b. can rescind the contract on the grounds of undue influence.
c. can rescind the contract on the grounds of fraudulent misrepresentation.
d. cannot rescind the contract.

18. Peggy agrees to sell her prize German Shepard to Tammy. Peggy draws up a written contract for $300 but mistakenly omits a zero. She sends the contract to Tammy who accepts immediately. When Tammy comes to collect the dog, she shows Peggy the contract and refuses to pay more than $30. Peggy:

a. can rescind the contract because Tammy should have known that the price was incorrect.
b. can rescind the contract because of mutual mistake.
c. cannot rescind the contract because it is written.
d. cannot rescind the contract because unilateral mistake is never a defense to enforcement of a contract.

19. Paul orally agrees to represent Dora in a divorce case. He tells Dora that his fee will be $5000. Paul makes several threats and Dora reluctantly signs the contract. Which of the following is not an example of duress sufficient to allow rescission of the fee agreement?

a. Threatening to publish false and damaging rumors
b. Threatening to publish true and damaging facts
c. Threat of criminal prosecution for adultery
d. All of the above are sufficient to allow rescission

20. In a case of misrepresentation, a plaintiff must prove all of the following except:

a. a material fact was misrepresented.
b. justifiable reliance on the misrepresentation.
c. intent to deceive.
d. a fiduciary relationship.

Answers to Study Questions

Fill-in-the-Blank Questions

Paula has a misrepresentation suit based on the size of the memory. The salesman misrepresented an important fact. Paula did not ask about the joystick and the salesman was not obligated to tell her; silence is not usually considered to be misrepresentation. Paula can rescind the contract.

True-False Questions

1.   T.

2.   T.

3.   F. A mutual mistake as to the <u>identity or subject matter</u> allows rescission.

4.   T.

5.   T.

6.   F. Scienter means guilty knowledge.

7.   F. It is a defense if the non-mistaken party should have known that a mistake had been made. Also, if an arithmetic error has been made and gross negligence is not shown, the mistaken party can rescind.

8.   T.

9.   T.

10.   F. Misrepresentation of <u>fact</u> is usually grounds for rescission.

Multiple-Choice Questions

1.	d		11.	c
2.	a		12.	c
3.	c		13.	c
4.	d		14.	a
5.	c		15.	b
6.	a		16.	a
7.	c		17.	b
8.	d		18.	a
9.	d		19.	d
10.	a		20.	d

Writing and Form

General Principles

Most laymen think that all contracts need to be written, but only a few categories of contracts require a writing. A written contract is the best proof of an agreement. The formality of a writing serves another purpose; it gives the parties a chance to reflect on the legal commitments they are about to undertake. Most contracts which require a writing involve significant expenditures of time or money.

If a writing is necessary, then the next question is how much of a writing is required? A contract need not be several pages long. If a writing shows the basic terms of the agreement, it is sufficient. If there is a written contract, it should reflect the entire agreement of the parties. If it does not, and a dispute arises, a court may hear testimony to explain or supplement the writing.

Chapter Summary

I.   The Statute of Frauds--Requirement of a Writing--A written contract is the best evidence of an agreement between two parties. If there is no written agreement and a dispute arises and results in litigation, the only proof of the contract is the testimony of the parties and their versions may differ. The law requires some contracts to be written; this law is known as the Statute of Frauds. A contract is "within" the statute if it needs to be written.

A.   Sale of Land--Land includes fixtures (personal property attached to the land), minerals, buildings, and crops. Land is considered an important "product", therefore contracts for its sale must be in writing.

Exception: Buyer has moved onto the land, begun substantial improvements and has paid part of the purchase price. The actions are evidence that a contract was made.

Other Interests--It may also include life estates and easements (the right to use another's land) unless the easement is obviously necessary, e.g. a house situated on a land-locked piece of property.

B.   One-Year Rule--Must not be possible of being performed in a year or less. The formula below should held in "close cases". List:

(a)   Date contract is formed.

(b)   Day after (a), which is the date the time begins to run.

(c)   Date performance starts.

(d)   Earliest date performance can possibly end.

Compare (b) and (d), if more than one year, the contract must be in writing.

C.   Collateral Promises--"Collateral" means "on the side". A collateral promise is made by someone other than the original parties to a contract. Most collateral promises involve a promise by a third party to pay the debt of another party who cannot or will not pay. There are always three parties: a debtor, a creditor, and a third party who offers to pay. The definition of a collateral promise has three elements:

(1)   Promise between debtor and creditor

(2)   Promise between third party and creditor

(3)   Third party promise to pay if debtor doesn't or won't

The main purpose rule is an exception. If the third party is making the promise for his own benefit, the promise can be oral.

D.   Promises Made in Consideration of Marriage--Includes pre-nuptial agreements and situations where one party is paid to marry another.

E.   Sale of Goods--Price (not value) of $500 or more. 3 exceptions (all show proof of a contract):

(1)   Custom-made goods when performance by the seller has begun

(2)   Admission under oath by the party against whom enforcement is sought that a contract existed

(3)   Partial performance--Buyer has paid for or received some of the goods. Contract is enforceable only to extent the buyer has performed.

E. **Promissory Estoppel**--First discussed as an exception to a requirement of consideration, it may also be used to enforce an oral contract that was required to be in writing. Purpose is to honor an oral contract, when one party has reasonably relied on another's promise. Its use in this area is in dispute.

II. **Statute of Frauds--Sufficiency of the Writing**--Need show only the essence of the contract. Different rules for sales contracts.

   A. **Sales Contracts**--Quantity and signature of the party to be charged (defendant).

   If a contract is formed between two merchants, it may be enforceable if only one of the parties signs the contract. If one party signs the contract, sends it to the other, and the second party does not object within ten days, the contract is enforceable by and against both parties. Generally, it is easier to hold a merchant to a contract.

   B. **Non-Sales Contracts**--Parties, subject matter, consideration, and quantity. Land contracts usually must have a description of the land so that it can be identified.

III. **The Parol Evidence Rule**--Applies only if there is a written contract. Evidence given in court of the parties' prior negotiations or agreements or contemporaneous oral agreements cannot contradict the writing. Ask yourself whether the parties would have included the term in the writing. If so, evidence on that subject will not be allowed. The exceptions listed below concern situations where the parties might not have thought to include the disputed term.

   (1) **Subsequent Modification**--Change after signing would not have been included in the contract so evidence is allowed, if the modification itself is not required to be in writing.

   (2) **Void/Voidable**--Can introduce evidence to show a contract was never formed.

   (3) **Ambiguous**--Oral evidence is allowed to explain unclear terms.

   (4) **Incomplete**--If contract is obviously incomplete, oral evidence is allowed to fill in blanks.

   (5) **Prior Transactions/Trade Usage**--Applies to sales contracts only. Can show prior dealings between the same parties or general customs of the trade if the contract doesn't address the problem specifically.

   (6) **Conditional Contract**--Agreement based on a condition that never comes about. Only proof of the condition is allowed,

(7)   <u>Clerical Error</u>--Must be obvious from the fact of the contract. Evidence is allowed to show correct terms.

IV.   <u>Interpretation</u>--The goal is to enforce the contract that the parties made, not to remake it. General rule is to rely on the expressed terms of the contract as much as possible. As a part of this philosophy, separately negotiated terms and handwritten terms in a standardized contract will be given more weight. Other rules which help to determine the parties' intent:

A.   <u>Plain Meaning Rule</u>--Use plain meaning of the words that are already in the contract. Don't bring in outside (extrinsic) evidence to define a term which is already clear. If there is ambiguity:

B.   <u>Other Rules</u>--Contract will be presumed legal and ambiguous terms will be interpreted to make the contract legal. All parts of the contract will be read together. Course of performance, course of dealing and trade usage will be used (in that order) only if needed to interpret ambiguous terms. Ambiguous terms will be construed <u>against</u> the person who wrote the contract because the author had a chance to make his or her intention clearer.

Study Questions

Fill-in-the-Blank Questions

Abel Attorney orders two electric typewriters from Office Products, Inc. The salesman fills out a receipt for the typewriters which shows that Abel ordered two Model Z typewriters at a price of $400 each on January 3, 1988. The salesman places his initials on the receipt.

The contract between Abel and Office Products _____
require a written contract.   (does/does not)

The receipt _____ sufficient to prove a contract.
                        (is/is not)

The contract _____ enforceable against Office Products.
                        (is/is not)

At trial, Abel wants to testify that the price of the typewriters was $350 each. Abel
_____ be allowed to testify about the price.
              (will/will not)

True-False Questions

1.   If a contract is "within" the Statute of Frauds, it must be in writing in order to be enforced. _____

2. A change made after a contract has been signed is an exception to the parol evidence rule. _____

3. The collateral promise rule involves two parties: a debtor and a creditor. _____

4. If a contract contains ambiguous terms, a court will usually refuse to enforce it. _____

5. One of the essential terms required for enforcement of a non-sales contract is an expression of consideration. _____

6. In order to be enforceable, a sales contract must show the price of the goods. _____

7. An easement is an synonym for a mortgage. _____

8. In order to be enforceable, a sales contract between two merchants must be signed by both of them. _____

9. All leases of real property must be in writing. _____

10. The main purpose rule is an exception to the requirement that sales contracts must be in writing. _____

Multiple-Choice Questions

Use the following facts for questions 1-3.

1. Sally is shopping for a new car. A salesman at Midland Motors shows her the new Delight model. He describes it as very dependable and tells Sally that it will get 35 miles to the gallon in town. Sally and the salesman sign a sales contract for $12,000, payable in 36 installments. The contract between Sally and the salesman:

    a. must be written in order to be enforced.
    b. need not be written in order to be enforced.
    c. is enforceable only by Sally because she is not a merchant.

2. The contract between Sally and the salesman must contain:

    a. the price of the car.
    b. the signature of Sally if she sues the salesman for breach of contract.
    c. the signature of the salesman if Sally sues for breach of contract.
    d. the number of installment payments required.

3. If the case goes to trial, which of the following will <u>not</u> be barred by the parol evidence rule.

a.   Testimony that the price of the car was really $10,000
b.   Testimony that the salesman misrepresented the gas mileage
c.   Testimony that Sally agreed to buy a different model
d.   Testimony that she agreed to make 48 monthly payments

4.   Written evidence of a contract which is not a part of the contract is referred to as:

a.   parol evidence.
b.   trade usage evidence.
c.   collateral promise evidence.
d.   extrinsic evidence.

5.   The rule of contract interpretation which states that words in a contract will be given their normal meaning is the _____ rule.

a.   plain meaning
b.   parol evidence
c.   extrinsic evidence
d.   statute of frauds

6.   Best Publishing orally hires Peter to write a textbook on the law of contracts. They agree that Peter will have 15 months to complete the book. After Peter begins work on the book, Best tells him that they have hired another author for less money. The contract between Best and Peter:

a.   is unenforceable because it is oral and cannot be completed within one year.
b.   is unenforceable now but will be enforceable if Peter can complete the book in less than one year.
c.   is enforceable because Peter could complete the book in one year.
d.   is enforceable but Peter can collect only for the work which he has performed and Best can cancel the rest of the contract.

7.   Which of the following would least likely be within the Statute of Frauds?

a.   Contract to sell two lakefront lots
b.   Contract to sell cabins on the lakefront lots
c.   Contract to sell seller's canoes tied to the dock of the lakefront lots
d.   Contract to mortgage two lakefront lots

8.   Which of the following best describes an exception to the rule that all real estate contracts must be in writing?

a.   Seller has posted his house for sale.
b.   Buyer has moved in and made improvements to the land.
c.   A house is being sold by a merchant.
d.   The land costs less than $500.

9.   The main purpose rule is an exception to the:

       a.   parol evidence rule.
       b.   plain meaning rule.
       c.   rule that collateral promises must be in writing.
       d.   rule that contracts for the sale of land must be in writing.

10.   Which of the following is not an exception to the rule that a contract for the sale of goods over $500 must be in writing:

       a.   The seller has shipped the goods.
       b.   The buyer has paid for the goods.
       c.   The buyer has ordered custom-made goods and the seller has begun performance.
       d.   The seller has admitted in court that a contract exists.

11.   Jerry, an auto salesman, orders a shipment of plywood from Larry's Lumberyard. The written order form, which is initialed by Larry, states that Jerry will pay $850 for the lumber which is to be delivered on June 1. When the lumber arrives, Larry refuses to deliver until Jerry pays cash. Jerry refuses and Larry sues. At trial, which of the following oral evidence will be admitted as an exception to the parol evidence rule?

       a.   Jerry's testimony that he has always charged on account.
       b.   Larry's testimony that the shipment was not due until July 1.
       c.   Larry's testimony that the price of the lumber was $950.

12.   The order form is:

       a.   sufficient to prove a contract if Larry is the defendant.
       b.   sufficient to prove a contract if Jerry is the defendant.
       c.   sufficient to prove a contract if either Jerry or Larry is defendant.
       d.   insufficient to prove a contract.

13.   Sally, a newly licensed beautician, orders $300 worth of beauty supplies from Pretty Hair, Inc. The manager of the beauty supply store does not know Sally and asks Ron, an established hair dresser, to guarantee payment and Ron agrees.

       a.   Ron's promise to pay if Sally doesn't is a primary promise.
       b.   Ron's promise to pay if Sally doesn't is a secondary promise.
       c.   Sally's order is a collateral promise.
       d.   Ron is a co-signer.

14.   Which of the promises in problem 13 must be in writing?

       a.   Sally's order
       b.   Ron's promise to the manager of Pretty Hair
       c.   Both Sally and Ron's promises

d.   Neither Sally's nor Ron's promise

15.   Which of the following real estate contracts must be in writing?

a.   A 10-year lease
b.   A sale of a house
c.   A mortgage
d.   All of the above

16.   Bob places a telephone order for 2000 widgets from Widget World; the widgets are priced at $1 each. Bob sends a check for $400 as a down payment. When the first 400 widgets arrive, Bob keeps them but refuses to pay and asks Widget World to refund his down payment. The contract between Widget World and Bob is:

a.   unenforceable because the contract is oral and Widget World must refund the down payment.
b.   enforceable and Bob must pay $1600.
c.   enforceable to the extent of 400 widgets.
d.   unenforceable because of the parol evidence rule.

17.   Which of the following is not an exception to the parol evidence rule?

a.   Modifications made after the written contract has been signed.
b.   Modifications made before the written contract had been signed.
c.   Evidence of fraud or undue influence.
d.   Evidence of a conditional contract.

18.   A written contract for a non-sales transaction is sufficient if it shows:

a.   the parties and the consideration.
b.   the parties and the subject matter.
c.   the parties, the subject matter, and the consideration.
d.   the consideration and the subject mater.

19.   On May 1, 1988, Nancy, a college professor, orally agrees to teach a business law class during the 1988-9 academic year. Classes begin on August 25, 1988 and end on June 2, 1989. On August 1, 1988, the college notifies Nancy that it will no longer need her services. Nancy sues to enforce the contract. Nancy:

a.   will win because she will teach for less than 10 months.
b.   will win because the college waited until August to cancel the contract.
c.   will lose because the contract cannot be performed in less than one year.
d.   will lose but only if the college agreed to pay her more than $500.

20.   The dates used to measure the length of the contract in problem 19 are:

a.   May 1, 1988 to June 2, 1989.
b.   August 25, 1988 to June 2, 1989.
c.   August 1, 1988 to June 2, 1989.
d.   May 1, 1988 to August 25, 1988.

21.   U.S. Bus Lines is badly in need of qualified drivers. Ron, the personnel director, hires Al to drive the Phoenix to Dallas route. U.S. Bus Lines requires all employees to pay for their uniforms and to wear uniforms on the job. Al orders $200 worth of uniforms from a local store. The store telephones Ron and asks him to pay if Al cannot. U.S. Lines agrees. Al quits after two weeks and leaves town. The uniform supplier sues Ron for the cost of the uniforms. Ron claims that the contract must be in writing:

a.   Ron is incorrect because the cost of the uniforms is less than $500.
b.   Ron is incorrect because he is the primary debtor.
c.   Ron is incorrect because the main purpose rule applies.
d.   Ron is correct.

22.   Mary agrees to sell Tom, age 17, her washing machine and dryer for $500. Tom tells her that he will buy them if he determines that he has the proper electrical hook-ups at his apartment. Mary and Tom write up the contract but fail to mention the electrical hook-up. Tom later learns that he does not have proper wiring and does not wish to purchase the appliances. If Mary sues Tom for breach of contract:

a.   Mary will succeed because the contract is in writing.
b.   Mary will succeed because Tom agreed and forgot to put the condition in writing.
c.   Tom will succeed if he can prove that the contract was conditional.
d.   Tom will succeed because the contract did not need to be in writing.

23.   Tom:

a.   will be able to testify about the condition regarding the wiring.
b.   will not be able to testify about the condition regarding the wiring.
c.   will be able to testify that the price was really $450.
d.   will not be able to testify that he is a minor.

24.   Which of the following rules concerning interpretation of a contract is false?

a.   Handwritten terms are given more weight than printed terms.
b.   All clauses of a contract will be construed together if possible.
c.   An ambiguous term will be construed against the party who wrote the contract.
d.   Extrinsic evidence will be allowed if the terms of the contract are clearly expressed.

25.   The parol evidence rule states that:

a.   a collateral promise must be in writing.
b.   intent to deceive can be proven by the action of the parties.
c.   evidence of prior negotiations or agreements or contemporaneous oral agreements will not be admitted to contradict terms of a written contract.
d.   an oral contract for the sale of land is valid if it is shown that the buyer has moved on the land, has made a down payment, and has made improvements to the property.

Answers to Study Questions

Fill-in-the-Blank Questions

The contract must be in writing because the price of the typewriters is $800 and a contract for the sale of goods for $500 or more must be in writing. The receipt is sufficient to prove a contract against Office Products only. A sales contract requires only the quantity and the signature of the party to be charged (defendant). Abel will not be allowed to testify about the price of the typewriters because the $350 price contradicts the receipt and Abel's testimony would be a violation of the parol evidence rule.

True-False Questions

1.   T.

2.   T.

3.   F.   It also involves a third party.

4.   F.   The court will hear extrinsic evidence to interpret ambiguous terms.

5.   T.

6.   F.   Price is not necessary.

7.   F.   An easement is a right to use someone else's land.

8.   F.   Only one need sign it if it is sent to the other and the recipient does not object within ten days.

9.   F.   Most states permit oral short-term leases (usually of a year or less) to be enforceable.

10.   F.   The main purpose rule is an exception to the requirement that a collateral promise must be in writing to be enforceable.

Multiple-Choice Questions

1.	a		14.	b
2.	c		15.	d
3.	b		16.	c
4.	d		17.	b
5.	a		18.	c
6.	c		19.	c
7.	c		20.	a
8.	b		21.	c
9.	c		22.	c
10.	a		23.	a
11.	a		24.	d
12.	a		25.	c
13.	b			

12

Third Party Rights and Discharge

General Principles

Each party to a contract receives a benefit and is obligated to perform a duty. As a general rule, the benefit and the duty can be transferred to a third party. They can be transferred separately or together. If the transfer would cause hardship to one party, the transfer may be prohibited.

A contract between two parties may affect a third party. If the contract was made with the intent to benefit the third party, then he or she acquires rights in the contract and may sue to enforce these rights. If the effect on the third party is coincidental, then no rights are acquired and the third party cannot sue.

The last half of this chapter deals with performance of the contract. The level of performance may vary greatly; it may be perfect, contain minor or major flaws, or be absent altogether. The seriousness of the error or breach determines the rights of the other party. As a general rule, the law favors the enforcement of contracts and a minor flaw may not allow cancellation of the contract but it may allow money damages to correct the error. Cancellation is permitted only in the most serious cases. Also, contractual obligations can be discharged by an agreement to call off the contract or to modify it.

Chapter Summary

I.   <u>Assignment of Rights and Delegation of Duties</u>--A transfer of rights or benefits under a contract is an assignment. A transfer of obligations or duties is a delegation.

A.   Assignment--The transferor is the assignor-obligee; the transferee (third party) is the assignee. The obligor is the party who contracted originally with the assignor. After the assignment and notice, the obligor will perform for the assignee. All contracts can be assigned except those listed below.

(1)   Exceptions

(a)   A statute prohibits transfer. The most common examples are laws which forbid the assignment of wages, employee benefits or child support payments.

(b)   The contract states that the rights cannot be assigned.

(c)   The rights acquired are personal. An obligation to pay money is not personal.

(d)   The obligor's duty is substantially changed or enlarged. This exception often goes hand-in-hand with (c); if the right is personal, it is likely that the obligor's duty will have changed.

(2)   Notice--An assignment is effective without notice. However, if notice is given and the same right is assigned to two different people, a dispute can arise between the two assignees. Usually, the first assignee wins, but in a few states, the first assignee to give notice, wins. Until the obligor receives notice, he or she can fulfill the contractual obligation by giving performance to the assignor, the original party to the contract.

B.   Delegation--The opposite of assignment; a party's duty under a contract is transferred. The transferor is the delegator-obligor; the transferee is the delegatee. The obligee is the person entitled to performance who originally contracted with the delegator. As with assignments, almost all duties can be delegated. The exceptions are similar to those noted above.

(1)   Exceptions

(a)   The contract requires the personal talents of the delegator, the original party. An artistic project, design, or professional service usually requires individual performance.

(b)   There is a trust relationship between the original parties to the contract.

(c)   Performance by a third party would differ greatly from the original service. Usually occurs with (a).

(d)   The contract expressly prohibits delegation.

(2)   <u>Liability of Parties</u>--If the delegation is legal, the obligee must accept substitute performance. If the delegatee fails to perform, most states hold that both the delegatee and the delegator can be sued.

II.   <u>Third-Party Beneficiaries</u>--A party may sue to have an agreement enforced if he or she has rights under the contract (standing to sue). The original parties who have reached an agreement with each other have privity of contract; they are bound together by the agreement and have the right to sue if something goes wrong. A third party may acquire similar rights if he or she was <u>intended</u> to benefit from the contract.

A.   <u>Intended Beneficiaries</u>--Can enforce the contract. Ask if the contract between the original parties was made with the third party in mind. There are two basic categories of intended beneficiaries:

(1)   <u>Creditor Beneficiary</u>--Owed a duty (usually money) by one of the parties to the contract. The most common example is the sale of an item on which the seller owes money to a creditor. If the buyer agrees to take over the payments, the creditor of the seller is a third party beneficiary of the sales contract between the buyer and the seller.

(2)   <u>Donee Beneficiary</u>--Receives a gift or free benefit as a result of the contract between the original parties.

B.   <u>Incidental Beneficiary</u>--Happens to benefit from the contract between the original parties. Cannot sue to have the contract enforced. Ask if the contract was made with the third party in mind. If not, he or she is incidental.

C.   <u>Vesting of Rights</u>--A third-party has standing to sue if he or she is an intended beneficiary <u>and</u> the contract is finalized. The contract normally becomes final when the third party makes commitments relying on the benefits to be received. If the original contract specifies that the parties have the right to cancel or alter the agreement, the third party's rights may never vest.

III.   <u>Conditions of Performance</u>--Most contracts contain the implied condition that one party will perform only if the other also performs. Some contracts are more explicit and a stated condition must be satisfied before performance is due. Remember to separate the validity of a contract from its performance. A contract may be valid but a condition may cancel the duty to perform.

A.   <u>Conditions Precedent</u>--The duty to perform does not occur until a condition is satisfied. If the condition is not met, there is no duty to perform and neither party can sue for breach of contract. Fulfillment of the condition precedes the duty to perform.

B.   Conditions Subsequent--The duty to perform is absolute unless a condition relieves a party of this obligation. The condition follows the duty to perform.

C.   Concurrent Conditions--The parties are obligated to perform at the same time. The only difference between concurrent conditions and implied conditions is that the former is expressly stated in the contract. Before a party can sue, he or she must show that he or she is ready to act (tender of performance).

IV.   Discharge--Most contracts are terminated when both sides perform. However, the parties may agree to cancel the contract, to transfer the contract to others, or performance may become impossible.

A.   Performance--When performance is incomplete or unsatisfactory, the non-breaching party acquires certain rights. These rights depend on the severity of the mistake and the specificity of the contract.

(1)   Strict (Complete) Performance--Requires absolute compliance with the terms of agreement or the non-breaching party can cancel. Because this rule can be abused, the agreement must specifically state that only perfect execution will do. An express condition, only strict performance, will allow cancellation; a constructive condition will not.

(2)   Substantial Performance--Requires satisfaction of the major provisions of the contracts. The non-breaching party must carry out his or her side of the bargain but may sue for any damages as a result of incomplete or unsatisfactory performance.

(3)   Material Breach--Serious errors. The non-breaching party loses the benefits of the contract and is excused from performance.

(4)   Personal Satisfaction--If expressly stated, performance must meet the standards of a designated person. May be seen as a condition precedent to payment or as a promise which could be satisfied by substantial compliance. If the non-breaching party is being picky only to avoid payment, the contract will be enforceable. If the contract is personal, satisfaction must occur. This rule does not apply to mechanical performance.

(5)   Anticipatory Repudiation--Performance is not due until time stated in the contract and no right to sue accrues until that time. However, if one party tells the other that he or she intends to breach, the innocent party can sue immediately or can make plans for substitute performance.

B.   Discharge by Agreement--The parties can agree to cancel the contract or to change the terms.

(1)   Rescission--An agreement to cancel the contract. Requires offer, acceptance, and consideration on both sides. The consideration is satisfied if each party agrees to give up rights under the contract. If one party has performed, he or she must receive some consideration, usually payment or a refund of money. Rescission need not be in writing unless the contract or other law so specifies.

(2)   Novation--Similar to assignment or delegation but all three parties agree to a new contract. When a proper novation is executed, the original contract is canceled and a new one is formed. The original obligor is no longer liable in contrast to the rule outlined above with respect to delegation of duties.

(3)   Accord and Satisfaction--Parties agree to substitute performance. The accord is the new agreement and the satisfaction is the performance of the new agreement.

NOTE: Can occur when one party is paying for a faulty performance or bad service and tries to cancel the debt by sending payment for less than the full amount. If the creditor accepts the partial payment, he may be accused of agreeing to the accord. The test is whether the amount of the debt is liquidated or in genuine dispute. If the debt is liquidated, partial payment will not be considered an accord and satisfaction. A second way to understand this problem is to examine the consideration required to support the accord or new contract. If the creditor accepts less than full payment, he is giving up his right to full payment. The debtor is providing no consideration, therefore the accord is invalid.

(4)   Discharge by Impossibility of Performance--An unforeseeable event occurs between the time the contract is formed and the time for performance. The courts will cancel the contract if performance becomes objectively impossible (no one could do it).

Automatic discharge when a party to a personal service contract dies or a change in law would make performance illegal. If the subject matter of the contract is destroyed, the contract may be canceled if the subject matter was specifically stated and is not available from other sources. However, if the subject matter is described generally, discharge may not be allowed.

Commercial impracticability is a new application of the impossibility rule. Courts may excuse a party from contractual obligations if a change in conditions makes performance more difficult and the change was unforeseeable. If the change was brought about by a normal risk of doing business (e.g.

inflation) the court will enforce the contract.

Study Questions

Fill-in-the-Blank Questions

Penny purchases a 1986 VW on the installment plan. She owes twenty-four installments of $200 each when she decides to sell the car to Tom. Tom agrees to pay $500 cash and to assume the payments.

With regard to the loan agreement between Penny and Tom, Penny is the
_____.
(assignor/assignee)

The bank is the _____.
(delegatee/obligee)

Tom is the _____.
(delegator/obligor)

The bank is an _____ beneficiary.
(intended/incidental)

True-False Questions

1.   A duty cannot be delegated if the original contract called for the personal skill of the obligor. _____

2.   A condition precedent excuses one party from performance until the condition is satisfied. _____

3.   If one party complies substantially with the terms of the contract, the other party does not have to perform. _____

4.   A novation usually requires three parties. _____

5.   Impossibility of performance is a method of discharging a contract. _____

6.   Rescission occurs when two parties agree to substitute a new contract for the original contract. _____

7.   A creditor beneficiary is an intended beneficiary. _____

8.   An assignor is a third party to whom contract rights are transferred. _____

9.   If a delegatee fails to perform a contractual duty, the party to whom performance is due can sue the delegatee and the delegator _____

10.   The beneficiary of a life insurance policy is an example of an incidental beneficiary. _____

Multiple-Choice Questions

1.   Joe is re-roofing Alice's house. Joe and Alice agree that instead of paying Joe, Alice will send the payment to Joe's banker, Sid. Sid is:

    a.   the assignee of Joe's right.
    b.   the assignor of Joe's right.
    c.   the delegator of Joe's right.
    d.   the delegatee of Joe's duty.

2.   Alice is:

    a.   the delegator.
    b.   the assignor.
    c.   the assignee.
    d.   the obligor.

3.   Bobby agrees to mow Terry's lawn for ten weeks at $25 per week. Terry decides that her lawn needs to be mowed only five times, and she assigns her rights to Mary. She tells Joe that he should mow Mary's lawn every other week. The assignment is:

    a   invalid because Terry has not notified Mary.
    b.   invalid because Mary is not paying Joe.
    c.   valid only if Joe agrees.
    d.   valid only if Joe's duty is not increased significantly.

4.   Farmer Brown has ten apple orchards. He contracts with Paul's Produce to deliver three bushels of apples per week. Two of Farmer Brown's orchards are destroyed by fire. The contract between Farmer Brown and Paul's is:

    a.   discharged due to impossibility of performance.
    b.   discharged due to accord and satisfaction.
    c.   not discharged because Farmer Brown can deliver apples from the remaining eight orchards.
    d.   not discharged because the contract was conditioned on good weather.

5.   Which of the following duties cannot be delegated:

    a.   Designing a wedding gown
    b.   Paying money to a bank
    c.   Delivering television sets
    d.   Selling television sets

6.   Allen agrees to sell ten typewriters to Sally at a 10 percent discount if he can buy them at the wholesale price from Tim. The contract between Allen and

Sally has:

a.   a condition precedent.
b.   a condition subsequent.
c.   concurrent conditions.
d.   no conditions.

7.   If Tim refuses to sell the typewriters to Allen:

a.   Sally can sue Allen for material breach.
b.   Sally cannot sue Allen because the contract was discharged due to accord and satisfaction.
c.   Sally cannot sue Allen, because Allen has substantially performed.
d.   Sally cannot sue Allen, because Allen's promise was conditional.

8.   Bob hires Susan the Snake Charmer to dance at Dave's birthday party. Susan refuses to perform at the last minute. Bob, Dave, and the guests are upset and threaten to sue. Which of the following parties can sue Susan?

a.   Bob only
b.   Bob or Dave
c.   Bob, Dave, or the guests
d.   Dave only

9.   Dave is:

a.   an incidental beneficiary.
b.   a creditor beneficiary.
c.   a donee beneficiary.
d.   as assignor.

10.   The guests are:

a.   incidental beneficiaries.
b.   intended beneficiaries.
c.   obligors.
d.   assignors.

11.   Ross agrees to sell Kathleen a Model X washer for $450. Ross then discovers that Model X is out of stock and he offers to sell Kathleen a Model Y for $400. Kathleen agrees. The agreement between Ross and Kathleen is:

a.   a novation.
b.   an accord and satisfaction.
c.   rescission.
d.   an assignment.

12.   Paul borrows money from First Bank to build an apartment complex. He tells his tenants to send their rent to First Bank. Paul is:

      a.   the assignee.
      b.   the delegator.
      c.   the incidental beneficiary.
      d.   the assignor.

13.   Larry, a new tenant, is not told about the payment arrangements and sends his rent to Paul. Larry:

      a.   has discharged his duty to pay the rent by sending the money to Paul, because he did not receive notice of the assignment.
      b.   has not discharged his duty to pay the rent, because the assignment states that he must pay First Bank.
      c.   has discharged his duty to pay rent, because he did not agree to the assignment.
      d.   has discharged his duty to pay rent because the assignment was invalid.

14.   The bank is:

      a.   a creditor beneficiary of the lease agreement between Larry and Paul.
      b.   an incidental beneficiary of the lease agreement between Larry and Paul.
      c.   a delegatee.
      d.   a delegator.

15.   Margaret is building a new home. She requests that her contractor use a bathroom tile made by the Trane Co. The contractor is unable to obtain the tile from Trane and uses similar tile made by Tilex Co. Margaret:

      a.   does not have to pay the contractor because he used the wrong tile.
      b.   must pay the contractor but can recover damages for the difference in the two brands.
      c.   does not have to pay the contractor because of anticipatory breach by the contractor.
      d.   must accept the new tile and cannot sue for damages.

16.   Failure to give strict or complete performance by one party will discharge the other party only if:

      a.   the contract expressly requires strict performance.
      b.   the contract constructively requires strict performance.
      c.   only strict performance can discharge the promise.
      d.   the contract is substantially performed.

17.   Glenda hires Will to build a monument to her great-grand-father Thomas Jefferson Lee, a Civil War hero. The contract specifically states that Glenda has approval of all details and that she must be satisfied before payment is due. When the statue is complete, Glenda refuses to pay on the grounds that she is dissatisfied with the project. Will sues for breach of contract. Which of the following statements is true?

a.   Glenda must pay if a reasonable person would be satisfied with the statue.

b.   Glenda must pay if a court determines that Glenda is acting in bad faith and trying to avoid payment.

c.   Glenda must pay because Will has substantially performed.

d.   Glenda will not have to pay under any circumstances.

18.   Mrs. Richards has worked for XYZ Company for 25 years. As a retirement gift, the president of the company has his stock dividends assigned to her. Mrs. Richards thanks him for the present and tells him that she can now afford an expensive 4-bedroom condo. Mrs. Richards' rights to the dividends:

a.   vested when the president assigned the stock.

b.   vested when she retired.

c.   vested when she signed the agreement to buy the condo.

d.   can never vest because she is a donee beneficiary.

19.   Regan's department store contracts with Narrow Shirts for an order of 200 white T-shirts to be delivered March 1. In February, Narrow tells Regan that it will be unable to deliver the shirts.

a.   Regan can sue immediately because of anticipatory breach.

b.   Regan cannot sue until March 1 because Narrow has until that date to perform.

c.   Regan cannot sue because the contract was discharged be accord and satisfaction.

d.   Regan cannot sue because the contract was discharged by rescission.

20.   Peter agrees to paint Art's house. Peter is overworked and asks Art if John can complete the work. Art agrees and a new contract is drawn up. If John does not paint Art's house, Art can sue:

a.   Peter only.

b.   Peter or John, but not both.

c.   John only.

d.   Peter and John.

21.   Perry orders fifteen rolls of film from Photon Photography. The contract states that Perry will pay when the film is delivered and Photon will deliver the film when Perry pays. This contract is an example of:

a.   a condition precedent.

b.   a condition subsequent.

c.   concurrent conditions.

d.   strict compliance.

22.   If Photon refuses to deliver the film:

a.   Perry can sue immediately without further action.

b.   Perry can sue only if he pays first.

c.   Perry can sue only if he pays or shows that he is willing to pay for the film.

d.   Perry can sue because Photon is excused from performance.

23.   Melinda makes an appointment with Dr. Spock. When Melinda arrives, she discovers that Dr. Spock has been called out on an emergency and that Dr. Cure is taking his calls. Melinda:

a.   must see Dr. Cure or she will be in breach of contract.

b.   has no duty to see Dr. Cure, because she was given no notice of the delegation.

c.   has no duty to see Dr. Cure, because a doctor's services are personal and cannot be assigned.

d.   must see Dr. Cure because Dr. Spock is excused from performance.

24.   Bob's Barbecue agrees to cater the refreshments for the Pecos rodeo. As he is driving to the rodeo, he learns that the rodeo has been canceled due to a stampede of Brahma Bulls. Bob:

a.   can sue the rodeo officials for material breach.

b.   can sue the rodeo officials for anticipatory breach.

c.   cannot sue the rodeo officials because the contract was discharged by impossibility of performance.

d.   cannot sue the rodeo officials because the contract was discharged by rescission.

25.   Which of the following is least likely to result in discharge of a contract by commercial impracticability?

a.   A war between the U.S. and Mexico

b.   Inflation

c.   A computer failure

d.   A trucker's strike

26.   Larry is having money problems. In order to get a loan, he assigns his rights to a royalty payment to Shark Finance. Shark does not notify the payor of the royalty payments. The next week, Larry assigns the same rights to his brother. In most states:

a.   Larry's brother is entitled to the royalties.

b.   Shark Finance is entitled to the royalties.

c.   Larry is entitled to keep the royalties.

d.   The payor must pay both Larry's brother and Shark Finance.

Answers to Study Questions

Fill-in-the-Blank Questions

Penny is the assignor. The bank is the obligee. Tom is the obligor. The bank is an intended (creditor) beneficiary.

True-False Questions

1.   T.

2.   T.

3.   F.   The other party must perform but may receive damages for any injuries received.

4.   T.

5.   T

6.   F.   This is the definition of accord and satisfaction.

7.   T.

8.   F.   An assignor is the person who transfers the rights.

9.   T.

10.   F.   It is an example of an intended beneficiary.

Multiple-Choice Questions

1.	a		14.	a
2.	d		15.	b
3.	d		16.	a
4.	c		17.	b
5.	a		18.	c
6.	a		19.	a
7.	d		20.	c
8.	b		21.	c
9.	c		22.	c
10.	a		23.	c
11.	b		24.	c
12.	d		25.	b
13.	a		26.	b

Breach and Remedies

General Principles

Once it has been determined that a valid contract exists and that one party has breached the agreement, the next step is to determine the remedy of the non-breaching party. There are two general types of remedies: legal and equitable.

Legal remedies are monetary awards or damages. Contract law will award the non-breaching party money only for injuries that can be proven. The non-breaching party can recover funds equal to the benefit of the bargain so that he or she is in the same position as if the contract has been performed.

Equitable remedies usually do not involve money and are only awarded when money is an inadequate remedy. The plaintiff must show not only that substitute performance cannot be obtained elsewhere but also that he or she has acted in good faith and is entitled to this special remedy.

Chapter Summary

I.   Remedies at Law versus Remedies in Equity--Although an equitable remedy may involve the transfer of money, it is usually not granted if money damages would compensate the plaintiff. A plaintiff seeking equity must act timely and in good faith.

    A.   Historical Background--In England, courts of equity were developed to assist injured parties who wanted a remedy other than land, property or money. The courts of law were allowed to give only those remedies. In the past, remedies at law and remedies in equity were made by different courts. In the United States today, most courts can give both legal and equitable remedies.

B.   Equitable Principles and Maxims--Still relied on by courts in deciding whether to grant an equitable remedy. The idea of equity is based on fairness. Therefore, a plaintiff usually cannot recover unless he or she has acted justly and in good faith. One of the most common equitable principles is the doctrine of laches. This rule is similar to a statute of limitations and requires that a plaintiff bring a lawsuit while the evidence is fresh. In most states, the doctrine of laches has been replaced by a statute of limitations which sets an absolute limit on the time in which to file a lawsuit.

II.   Damages

A.   Types of Damages

(1)   Compensatory Damages--The non-breaching party receives money lost due to the breach but any money saved must be subtracted to determined the final amount. The formula used starts with the amount of performance promised in the contract. Then you must subtract the value of the consideration received and any money saved. This equation plus additional expenses and lost profits is an accurate measure of actual losses suffered.

(a)   Service Contracts--The extra cost, if any, of replacement services less money saved.

(b)   Sale of Goods--The difference between the contract price and the market price. If the goods are custom-made, the seller can sue for lost profits and costs incurred in manufacture.

(c)   Sale of Land--If the buyer breaches, the seller receives the difference between the contract price and the market price. If the seller breaches, the buyer can sue for the equitable remedy of specific performance or is entitled to the refund of any down payment. A few states also award the buyers money spent in performing the contract, e.g. title searches, appraisers' and attorneys' fees.

(d)   Construction Contracts--If the homeowner breaches, the contractor is entitled to lost profits + labor used + material used. If the contractor breached, the homeowner is entitled to the difference between the value if the contract had not been breached and the value as performed or the cost of repair, whichever is less. If the breach occurs during construction, the homeowner is entitled to the cost of finishing. The homeowner also may be able to sue for expenses incurred because of a delay in construction.

        (2)   <u>Consequential Damages</u>--Occur as a result of the breach, usually lost profits. Must be foreseeable or the breaching party must have reason to know that additional damages would be incurred. Can be eliminated if stated in the contract.

        (3)   <u>Punitive Damages</u>--Designed to punish the breaching party and are not available in a contract suit. May be available in some contract suits which also involve a tort, such as misrepresentation. Awarded on a showing of bad faith or intentional wrongdoing.

        (4)   <u>Nominal Damages</u>--A small monetary amount, usually one dollar. Occurs when there is a breach but the non-breaching party suffers no financial loss.

    B.   <u>Mitigation of Damages</u>--Because contract law only awards damages for actual losses, the non-breaching party has a duty to lessen or mitigate damages. He or she cannot maliciously allow the damages to accumulate.

    C.   <u>Liquidated Damages v. Penalties</u>--A pre-set amount of damages agreed on by the parties. Must be distinguished from an illegal penalty which punishes the breaching party. Ask yourself if damages would be difficult to estimate (i.e., if the contract was not performed on time) and if so, are the liquidated damages a reasonable estimate of the loss to be suffered. If the answers to both questions are yes, the liquidated damages are enforceable.

III.   <u>Rescission and Restitution</u>--Rescission is cancellation of the contract. Restitution returns the parties to the position they were in <u>before</u> the contract. (Compare damages which tries to put the parties in the same positions as if the contract had been performed.) If money has changed hands, it must be returned. The exact goods must be returned if possible (in specie) or the money equivalent. Usually granted if the plaintiff has decided to cancel the contract and does not want substitute performance.

IV.   <u>Specific Performance</u>--Breaching party is ordered by the court to perform the contract. Rarely granted because this remedy must be supervised and enforced by the court. Usually occurs in cases involving the sale of land or unique items. Never allowed for enforcement of personal service contracts.

V.   <u>Reformation</u>--Correction of a contract. Occurs when an error has been made in drafting the final contract and the parties do not want to cancel the agreement.

VI.   <u>Quasi-Contract (Contract Implied in Law)</u>--Used when the contract between the parties is unenforceable and one party has already performed. The other party would get a free ride, so equity will pay the performing party for the work he or she has done (not the contract price). A plaintiff must show:

(1)   The defendant received a benefit.
(2)   The defendant should have known that he or she was expected to pay.
(3)   The plaintiff performed expecting to be paid.
(4)   The defendant is receiving something without paying for it (unjust enrichment).

VII.   Election of Remedies--The non-breaching party may choose between available remedies but cannot choose more than one. If damages are granted, then specific performance is unavailable because the non-breaching party would be getting twice the benefits.

VIII.   Waiver of Breach--The innocent party may intentionally or accidentally overlook a breach. He or she can still sue for consequential damages. If a breach is overlooked several times, the innocent party may give up the right to complain about a similar breach in the future.

IX.   Limitation of Remedies--Most will be allowed if the court determines that the parties willingly agreed to the terms. Exculpatory clauses usually allowed only if the parties are of equal bargaining power.

UCC Provisions

(1)   Limit on Amount Recoverable--Permissible to set liquidated damages.

(2)   Limit on Types of Damages--Permissible to deny consequential damages, if not unconscionable. Damages due to negligence may also be denied if parties are on equal footing. Cannot restrict damages for personal injury or intentional wrongs.

(3)   Limit on Type of Remedy--In sales contracts, recovery can be limited to repair or replacement. If a remedy fails, then the limitation clause does not apply.

Study Questions

Fill-in-the-Blank Questions

Yum-Yum Bakery orders 4 dozen jars of cinnamon-flavored heart-shaped candy from Sweet Nothings Confectioners. The candy is to be delivered on January 25, in time for Yum-Yum to use them for Valentine Day specials. The jars cost $25 per dozen. On January 26, Sweet Nothings informs Yum-Yum that it will be unable to deliver the hearts and offers no explanation. Yum-Yum buys replacement candy from Ken's Kandy Shoppe at a price of $29 per dozen and has to pay freight charges of $50. Sweet Nothings' delivery charge was $10. Assume that Yum-Yum has not paid Sweet Nothings.

Yum-Yum should sue for _____ damages.
                              (compensatory/punitive)

Excluding freight and shipping costs, Yum-Yum's damages are

_____.
($16/$4/$116)

Yum-Yum should _____ Ken's freight charges to the total
above.   (add/subtract)

Yum-Yum should _____ the delivery charges from
Sweet Nothings.   (add/subtract/ignore)

Yum-Yum's total damages are _____.
($16/$56/$66/$156)

True-False Questions

1.   Specific performance is usually granted if a personal service contract is breached. _____

2.   Nominal damages may be awarded if the plaintiff has not suffered economic loss. _____

3.   Liquidated damages are always illegal. _____

4.   An exculpatory clause which denies recovery for personal injury is illegal. _____

5.   Specific performance would be an appropriate remedy if a seller breached a contract for the sale of a Picasso painting. _____

6.   Consequential damages are awarded to punish the defendant. _____

7.   Mitigation of damages is the duty of the breaching party to lessen damages. _____

8.   Reformation would be appropriate remedy if a party wants to correct a description of land in a real estate sales contract. _____

9.   Quasi-contract is an equitable remedy. _____

10.   In a suit based on quasi-contract, the plaintiff must show that he or she performed with the expectation of being paid. _____

11.   In the past, courts who awarded money and property were distinguished from courts that could award other remedies. _____

12.   The doctrine of laches is a synonym for the duty of the restitution. _____

Multiple-Choice Questions

1.   Sally buys a used car from Midville Motors. The salesman tells Sally that the car has never been involved in an accident. Sally then discovers that the salesman is lying. Sally can:

   a.   sue for misrepresentation and collect damages.
   b.   sue for breach of contract and collect damages.
   c.   sue for rescission and recover her payments.
   d.   sue for breach of contract, rescission or misrepresentation.

2.   If Sally sues for breach of contract, she can collect:

   a.   compensatory damages.
   b.   punitive damages.
   c.   nominal damages.
   d.   compensatory and punitive damages.

3.   Ron buys a watch from Clockex Inc. The contract states, "Buyer's remedy is limited to repair or replacement." The clause is:

   a.   illegal because it limits damage and Ron can cancel the contract.
   b.   enforceable if the watch can be repaired or replaced.
   c.   unenforceable and Ron can sue for damages.
   d.   enforceable even if the watch cannot be repaired or replaced.

4.   Cecil Cosgrove, a famous conductor, agrees to speak to the advanced music class at State University for a fee of $2000. He also agrees to sell a rare copy of "Brahms Lullaby" to the university library for $10,000. Cecil is a temperamental artist and refuses to honor any part of the contract. With regard to the speech, the university:

   a.   can sue Cecil for specific performance.
   b.   cannot sue Cecil for specific performance, but may sue for damages.
   c.   can sue Cecil for specific performance, but cannot sue for damages.
   d.   can sue Cecil for specific performance or for damages.

5.   With regard to the sheet music, the university:

   a.   can sue Cecil for specific performance.
   b.   cannot sue Cecil for specific performance, but may sue for damages.
   c.   can sue Cecil for specific performance, but cannot sue for damages.
   d.   can sue Cecil for specific performance or for damages.

6.   Cindy purchases an automobile insurance policy from AAA Liability Co. After Cindy has paid the first premium, she discovers that the policy describes her automobile as a Suburban when in fact she owns a Subaru. The premiums for a Suburban are substantially higher than those for a Subaru. Cindy does not want to cancel the policy but she does want to correct the contract. She should sue for:

a.   rescission.
b.   reformation.
c.   quasi-contract.
d.   punitive damages.

7.   Mrs. O'Leary faints while shopping in the supermarket. Dr. Jones administers first aid and calls an ambulance. When Mrs. O'Leary regains consciousness, she refuses to pay the ambulance bill. The ambulance company should sue for:

a.   breach of contract and compensatory damages.
b.   reformation.
c.   rescission.
d.   quasi-contract.

8.   Bob agrees to buy a house from Sid and signs an earnest-money contract. Sid agrees to take his house off the market for 30 days. The contract states that if Bob decides not to buy the house, he must pay damages of $500. The damages clause is:

a.   an illegal penalty and is unenforceable.
b.   a legal liquidated damages clause because Sid suffers damages when he removes his house from the market and the damages would be difficult to estimate.
c.   a legal liquidated damages clause because Bob agreed to its terms.
d.   a legal penalty and is enforceable.

9.   Halloween Heaven, a costume and novelty store, orders twenty vampire costumes from Count Dracula Supplies. The costumes cost $30 each and are scheduled to arrive by October 15. Count Dracula informs Halloween Heaven that it will be unable to ship the costumes in time for Halloween. The costume shop immediately orders from another supplier but is only able to buy fifteen costumes at a price of $40 each. As a result, the costume shop must turn away five customers. The costume shop sues for the extra price of the costumes and for the loss of business. The lost profits are:

a.   compensatory damages.
b.   nominal damages.
c.   consequential damages.
d.   punitive damages.

10.   The extra price of the costumes would be classified as:

a.   compensatory damages.
b.   nominal damages.
c.   consequential damages.
d.   punitive damages.

11.   Assuming that Count Dracula had not been paid, Halloween Heaven's damages would be:

a. $750 + lost profits.
b. $600 + lost profits.
c. $150 + lost profits.
d.   lost profits only.

12.   Millie takes her pet poodle to Doggie Do's for grooming services. She asks the groomer to shampoo and clip her dog. On the same day, Connie brings her dog to the shop and requests the deluxe treatment including toenail painting and matching bows. The groomer scrambles the orders and Millie's dog is given the deluxe treatment. When Millie collects her dog, she refuses to pay the higher amount. The groomer sues in quasi-contract. The groomer:

a.   will be successful because Millie was unjustly enriched.
b.   will be successful because he did the work and should be paid.
c.   will be unsuccessful because Millie was unjustly enriched.
d.   will be unsuccessful because he was negligent.

13.   Ollie's Orange Juice has a long-standing contract with Farmer Brown to deliver three carloads of oranges on the first day of every month. In January, the truckers go on strike and the oranges are not delivered until January 10th. Ollie is grateful for any deliveries during the strike and accepts the late oranges. Ollie:

a.   has waived the right to complain about the January shipment but has not waived his right to complain about other late shipments.
b.   has waived his right to complain about the January shipment and also has waived his right to complain about future late shipments.
c.   has not waived his right to complain about the late January shipment because he must notify Farmer Brown that he does not intend to sue.
d.   has not waived his right to complain about the late January shipment because he must sign a written waiver.

14.   Bright Lights disco purchases a stereo system from Sound Sensations. The contract states that Sound will not be responsible for any property damage resulting from malfunction of the stereo or lost profits. Sound has tried to disclaim:

a.   compensatory damages.
b.   nominal damages.
c.   consequential damages.
d.   compensatory and consequential damages.

15.   The stereo breaks down immediately and Bright Lights is forced to close for 3 days while it is being repaired. According to the contract between the parties, Bright Lights can sue for:

a.   the cost of repairing the stereo and profits lost during closing.
b.   the cost of repairing the stereo only.
c.   the lost profits only.
d.   neither the lost profits nor the repair costs.

16.   Mr. Jones contracts with Top-Notch Housing for the construction of a five bedroom house. Before Top-Notch begins work, Jones suffers financial setbacks and cancels the contract. Top-Notch's damages will equal:

    a.   the cost of the house.
    b.   Top-Notch's profits + labor + materials used.
    c.   Top-Notch's profits + labor only.
    d.   Top-Notch's profits only.

17.   Assume that Jones had breached after Top-Notch had started construction, Top-Notch's damages will equal:

    a.   the cost of the house.
    b.   Top-Notch's profits + labor used + materials used.
    c.   labor used + materials used.
    d.   Top-Notch's profits only.

18.   Aaron agrees to sell his land to Sid. After the contract is signed, Aaron finds someone who is willing to pay more and tells Sid that he will not sell. If Sid sues, he:

    a.   can seek specific performance, refund of the purchase price, and expenses.
    b.   can seek specific performance or the refund of the purchase price.
    c.   can seek refunds of the purchase price only because specific performance is not available.
    d.   can seek specific performance only because damages are not available.

19.   Mobile Home Manufacturing orders 3,000 custom-made fiber glass shower doors from Glassworks, Inc. Glassworks has completed one-third of the order when the manufacturing company cancels. Glassworks can recover:

    a.   lost profits only.
    b.   the cost of the doors completed only.
    c.   lost profits and the cost of the completed doors.
    d.   the entire contract price.

20.   McBurger Restaurant orders 400,000 bushels of potatoes from Wholesale Vegetables, Inc. At the time of the order, the potatoes are selling for $15 per bushel. Due to falling crop prices, at the time of the contract, potatoes are selling at $10 per bushel. If Wholesale breaches and McBurger sues, it will be entitled to:

    a.   nominal damages only.
    b.   nominal damage and compensatory damages.
    c.   compensatory damages.
    d.   punitive damages.

21.   Ron's Car Wash has posted the following sign at the entrance to the car wash: "Not responsible for loose chrome, antennas, property damage caused by

accidental, negligent, or intentional acts of the owner or its employees. Damages for personal injury are limited to $5,000 per person." Which of the clauses, if any, are unenforceable?

a.   The entire disclaimer is enforceable.
b.   The disclaimer is enforceable with the exception of the limited on personal injury damages.
c.   The disclaimer is enforceable with the exception of the limits on personal injury damages and damages suffered by intentional acts of Ron's employees.
d.   The entire disclaimer is unenforceable.

22.   Dr. Denton contracts with Home Nursing Services to provide care for his patients for one year at a cost of $200 per month per patient. After two months, Home cancels. Dr. Denton waits ten months and sues. He did not hire a replacement nursing service. Dr. Denton:

a.   can sue for the cost of 10 months nursing care.
b.   can sue for the cost of 10 months nursing care less the cost of a replacement service because he had the duty to mitigate damages.
c.   cannot sue because he had the duty to mitigate damages.
d.   can sue for punitive damages.

23.   Susan contracts with Home Builders, Inc. to build a new office for her silk-flower business. After the building is completed, Susan discovers that the workroom is two feet shorter than the contract specifications. Susan:

a.   can refuse to pay until Home Builders rebuilds the workroom.
b.   can sue Home Builders for the cost of enlarging the workroom regardless of the cost.
c.   can sue for the difference between the value of the building as specified or the cost of repair, whichever is less.
d.   cannot sue because the breach is minor.

24.   Merlin the magnificent, a magician, performs at birthday parties. Sarah hires him to perform at her son's birthday party. The contract price is $60. The day before the party, Sarah cancels. Merlin is lucky enough to find other work at a bar mitzvah but it pays only $45. Merlin:

a.   can recover $60 from Sarah.
b.   can recover $15 from Sarah.
c.   can recover $15 and punitive damages from Sarah.
d.   cannot recover from Sarah because he found other work.

25.   Assuming that Merlin was unable to find other work on such short notice, he:

a.   can recover $60 from Sarah.
b.   can recover $60 and punitive damages from Sarah.
c.   can recover in specific performance.
d.   can recover punitive damages.

26.   Which of the following is <u>not</u> an equitable maxim?

      a.   Equity aids the vigilant.
      b.   Where there is equal equity, a case must be dismissed.
      c.   Whoever seeks equity must do equity.
      d.   Equity regards substance rather than form.

Answers to Study Questions

Fill-in-the-Blank Questions

Yum-Yum can only sue for compensatory damages. Punitive damages are not allowed for breach of contract. Excluding freight and shipping (incidental) damages, Yum-Yum's damages are the difference in the price between Sweet Nothings and Ken's. $4 per dozen ($29 - $25) multiplied by the number of dozen ordered (4) or $16. Ken's freight charges should be added. Yum-Yum should subtract Sweet Nothings' delivery charge because it saved that amount. Yum-Yum's total damages are the cost of the replacement candy ($16) + the cost of extra freight ($50) less any savings ($10) or $56.

True-False Questions

1.   F.   The court will not force a person to perform a service contract.

2.   T.

3.   F.   Liquidated damages are legal; a penalty is illegal.

4.   T.

5.   T.

6.   F.   They are awarded to compensate the plaintiff for loss which occurs as a result of the breach.

7.   F.   It is the duty of the non-breaching party.

8.   T.

9.   T.

10.   T.

11.   T.

12.   F.   The doctrine of laches is an equitable principle similar to a statute of limitation.

Multiple-Choice Questions

1.	d		14.	c
2.	a		15.	b
3.	b		16.	d
4.	b		17.	b
5.	d		18.	b
6.	b		19.	c
7.	d		20.	a
8.	b		21.	c
9.	c		22.	b
10.	a		23.	c
11.	c		24.	b
12.	d		25.	a
13.	a		26.	b

Introduction to Sales Contracts and Their Formation

14

General Principles

The UCC (Uniform Commercial Code) establishes the rules for contracts involving the sales of goods. In Chapter 7, you learned that sales contracts sometimes followed different guidelines than those of non-sales contracts. In general, the UCC has fewer formal requirements. This chapter reviews the essential elements for formation of a contract but addresses only sales contracts.

You should also keep in mind that if one or both parties to a contract are merchants, the rules change yet again. It is assumed that merchants are familiar with the business world; their contracts are less rigid.

Chapter Summary

I.   The Sale of Goods

      A.   Sale--Passage of title or formal ownership in exchange for consideration. A gift does not involve an exchange of consideration. A lease does not involve a transfer of ownership. The UCC has added a new article on leases.

      B.   Goods--Goods are tangible (can be touched) and movable.

            (1)   Tangible--Money, stock certificates, accounts receivables, and checks represent a legal right but they are not tangible. For example, a stock certificate represents ownership in a corporation.

(2)   <u>Movable</u>--Real estate is not movable and sales of land are not covered by the UCC. If goods are attached to the land, the items will still be considered goods if they can be removed without material injury to the land.

Crops and timber, which are grown in order to be sold, are always goods, even before they are removed from the ground. Oil, gas, and other minerals are goods if the seller removes them and fixtures if the buyer removes them.

(3)   <u>Goods v. Services</u>--Some transactions such as a permanent given by a beautician or a blood transfusion combine goods and services. The UCC does not specify and leaves the decision to the courts with one exception: the sale of food by a restaurant, regardless of whether it is eaten on the premises, delivered, or carried out <u>is</u> a sale of goods.

C.   <u>Who is a Merchant?</u>--Although the UCC offers three different definitions of a merchant, he or she is someone who has experience or expertise in a particular area. A person who is a merchant of one product is not necessarily a merchant for another type of product. A person who hires a broker or a specialist to conduct the sale is also a merchant. As the text indicates, the courts have split on whether a farmer is a merchant.

II.   <u>The Sales Contract</u>--Usual test of an offer and an acceptance is not strictly applicable; there may be a contract even if the exact moment of formation is unclear.

A.   <u>The Offer</u>

(1)   <u>Open Terms</u>--If other evidence shows that the parties intended to make a contract, the following terms can be left open. Keep in mind that the more open terms, the less likely a court is to find that the parties did intend to make a contract. The contract must always specify the <u>quantity</u> of goods. The contract is not enforceable beyond the quantity stated.

(a)   <u>Price</u>--Reasonable price at the time of delivery.

(b)   <u>Payment terms</u>--Payment on delivery is presumed.

(c)   <u>Delivery terms</u>--Buyer takes delivery at seller's unless a third location is indicated. If the contract indicates that the goods are to be shipped, the seller can make reasonable arrangements.

(d)   <u>Cancellation of ongoing contract</u>--Each party has the right to cancel within the bounds of good faith and commercial practice.

(e)   Performance--Buyer chooses the assortment of goods, if not specified in the contract. The seller makes the shipping arrangements unless the contract provides otherwise.

(2)   Firm Offer--A merchant who makes a written, signed offer and promises to hold it open cannot revoke it for the period stated in the offer or if no time period is stated, for a reasonable time. Three months is the maximum length of time. An option contract, with a down payment, is not required.

B.   Acceptance

(1)   Methods of Acceptance--Any reasonable means is satisfactory. If the offer specifies a particular form of acceptance and that form is not used by the offeree, the acceptance is still effective if it reaches the offeror by the time set out in the offer. An offer to buy can be accepted by a promise or by shipment. A promise to ship is effective when sent.

Acceptance by Shipment--No notice of shipment is necessary unless the shipment will be delayed. If the seller ships goods that do not meet contract specifications (non-conforming), the acceptance is still valid, but the seller has breached the contract. If the seller ships non-conforming goods, but specifies that they are shipped only as an accommodation, the accommodation is a counteroffer and the buyer can either reject or accept the goods. An accommodation may occur if the seller is out of stock of the goods requested but ships more expensive goods at the same price or ships similar goods at a discounted price.

(2)   Additional Terms (Acceptance or Counteroffer)--The mirror-image rule does not apply. If the offeree accepts but includes minor different or additional terms, there is a contract. If the offeree conditions acceptance on the new terms, he or she has made a counteroffer.

If the offeree has accepted, the next question is which terms control: the offeror's or the offeree's. If either of the parties is a non-merchant, the original terms control. If both parties are merchants, the new terms proposed by the offeree control unless:

(1)   the original offer was a "take it or leave it" proposition, or;

       (2)   the new terms materially (greatly) alter the original offer, or;

       (3)   the offeror objects within a reasonable time.

This rule allows merchants to include new terms in the contract without additional communication. Note that the new terms cannot be forced on the offeror; he or she need only object.

C.   Consideration--An exception to the pre-existing duty rule. (See Chapter 7.) A modification, proposed in good faith, is binding without additional consideration. Note that if a modification causes the price to change to $500 or more, a written contract is required.

D.   Ethical Standards--Implied in the following situations; does not need to be stated in the contract.

       (1)   Good Faith--Honesty in fact; applies to all contracts for the sale of goods.

       (2)   Commercial Reasonableness--Obligation to perform according to reasonable business practices and allows cancellation if circumstances would make performance unreasonable. Applies to merchants only.

E.   Writing (Statute of Frauds)--Required if price of goods is $500 or more; must be signed by the party who is being held to the contract (the defendant in a breach of contract suit). If the contract involves two merchants, the writing requirement is relaxed. If one merchant sends a signed copy of the contract to the other party, who must also be a merchant, the writing is treated as being signed by both of them unless the recipient objects within 10 days of receipt. This rule applies only if the recipient had reason to know that the memo contains the terms of the contract. The exceptions listed below provide evidence that a contract does exist.

       (1)   Admissions by a party in court documents.

       (2)   Custom-made goods, if they cannot be sold elsewhere and the seller has made a significant start.

       (3)   Partial performance to the extent that the buyer has accepted or paid for the goods.

F.   The Parol Evidence Rule--Remember that the parol evidence rule is designed to prevent parties from testifying in court that the written contract conflicts with the terms of an earlier agreement or contemporaneous oral agreement. However, if the testimony explains the contract, it will be allowed. The following types of evidence, as long as they do not contradict the written contract, are admissible:

(1)   Explanation of ambiguous terms by testimony regarding additional terms that do not differ from the written contract.

(2)   Commercial practices between the parties, including the course of performance under the present contract, the course of dealing under several contracts, trade usage in the industry.

If there is a conflict between the commercial practices, the most specific controls: express terms, course of performance, course of dealing and finally, trade usage, in this order.

G.   Unconscionability--Blatantly unfair contracts may be canceled in whole or in part by the court, which also has the option to restrict the enforcement of harsh terms.

Study Questions

Fill-in-the-Blank Questions

Leather Loafers, Inc., a shoe manufacturer, offers to manufacture 5,000 pairs of custom-made tennis shoes for Walkin' Tall, a nation-wide retailer. Leather Loafers, Inc. proposes a price of $20 per pair, delivery in 6 months, with a WT logo on the toe of every pair. The manager of Walkin' Tall sends the following oral reply: "We will gladly accept your offer, please place logo on the heel of each pair." Leather has begun production when it learns that Walkin' Tall will breach.

Walkin' Tall's reply is a(n) _____.
                          (counteroffer/acceptance)

The logo must be placed on the _____.
                               (heel/toe)

The contract _____ unenforceable because it is oral.
            (is/is not)

The contract does not specify a delivery or shipment terms.   It   is
_____.
    (enforceable/unenforceable)

Because the contract does not specify shipment terms, _____ can make them.
        (Walkin' Tall/Leather Loafers)

True-False Questions

1.   The parol evidence rule states that no consideration is necessary to modify a contract for the sale of goods. _____

2.   An offer to buy can be accepted by a promise to ship goods or by a shipment of goods. _____

3.   The time limit for a merchant's firm offer is two months. _____

4.   The mirror-image rule of offer and acceptance applies to service contracts but it does not apply to a contract for a sale of goods. _____

5.   Trade usage is a synonym for industry custom. _____

6.   A contract for the sale of goods which specifies more than 500 items must be in writing. _____

7.   Food purchased in a restaurant and eaten in the restaurant is a sale, not a service. _____

8.   A business law teacher, who raises hamsters for sale in her spare time, is a merchant with regard to hamsters. _____

9.   If an offer for the sale of goods specifies a particular means of acceptance, a reply received within the time limits of the offer will be an acceptance, even if the offeree used a different means of acceptance. _____

10.   If a court determines that a contract is unconscionable, it can eliminate the unconscionable terms but it cannot prevent enforcement of the contract. _____

Multiple-Choice Questions

1.   Which of the following is most likely to be considered a good?

      a.   A built-in bookcase
      b.   A 40 year-old oak tree
      c.   A microwave oven sitting on a counter
      d.   A central air conditioning system

2.   Susan's Sewing Supply offers to buy 300 spools of "Royal Blue" thread from Martin's Mills at a price of $.02 per spool. Martin ships "Peasant Blue" thread instead at the same price. Martin gives no notice of the change.

      a.   There is no contract between Martin and Susan because Martin sent the wrong color of thread.
      b.   There is no contract between Martin and Susan because Martin never

                promised to ship the thread.

    c.   There is a contract between Martin and Susan but Martin has breached the contract.

    d.   There is a contract between Martin and Susan and Martin has not breached the contract if he reasonably believed that Susan would accept the substitution.

3.   Same facts as above, except that Martin sends a notice to Susan telling her that his stock of "Royal Blue" is temporarily depleted and he hopes that she will accept the substitution.

    a.   There is no contract between Martin and Susan because Martin sent the wrong color of thread.

    b.   There is no contract between Martin and Susan because Martin never promises to ship the thread.

    c.   There is a contract between Martin and Susan but Martin has breached the contract.

    d.   There is a contract between Martin and Susan and Martin has not breached the contract.

4.   Ozzie's Office Machines writes to Crook & Low, Attorneys at Law, and offers to sell them a used personal computer for $1000. The letter states that the offer will remain open for five days. On the fourth day, Crook & Low try to accept but Ozzie tells them that he has sold the computer to someone else.

    a.   Ozzie has breached the contract because he promised to keep the offer open.

    b.   Ozzie has not breached the contract because Crook & Low should have made a down payment.

    c.   Ozzie has not breached the contract because Crook & Low are not merchants with regard to computers.

    d.   Ozzie has not breached the contract because he revoked before Crook & Low tried to accept the offer.

5.   Bennie orders four books from Literary Times, a used book dealer, for a total of $50. The order blank says nothing about payment terms.

    a.   Bennie will have to pay for the books when he receives them.

    b.   Bennie will have a reasonable time to pay for the books.

    c.   There is no contract because payment terms were not specified.

    d.   Bennie will have thirty days to pay for the books.

6.   Farmer Brown, who owns an orchard, offers to sell thirty truckloads of oranges to Sweet Juice, Inc. for $1,000 per truckload. A trucker's strike makes delivery by truck impossible so Brown telephones Sweet Juice and proposed to send the oranges by train, even though Sweet will have to pay $50 more per truckload. Sweet Juice agrees but later refuses to pay the extra money.

    a   Sweet Juice is within its rights because of the pre-existing duty rule.

b.   Sweet Juice is not within its rights because Farmer Brown is not considered a merchant.

c.   Sweet Juice is not within its rights because the change in shipping terms was made in good faith.

d.   Sweet Juice is within its rights because Farmer Brown has provided no consideration for the extra shipping costs charged to Sweet.

7.   Which of the following is <u>not</u> a sale of goods?

a.   Sale of lumber to be cut by the seller
b.   Sale of lumber to be cut by the buyer
c.   Sale of a "hamburger to go" by McDonald's
d.   Sale of stock in a corporation

8.   Sylvia is negotiating a sale of her dogs, three golden retrievers, to Brad. Brad and Sylvia have lunch and agree on a price of $200 per dog and that Sylvia will deliver them to Brad's house next week. Sylvia scribbles the following items on a paper napkin, "3 goldens, $200 each, send to Brad next week". Sylvia asks Brad to sign the "contract". Brad feels silly but does so; Sylvia does not sign the contract.

a.   The contract is enforceable against Brad only.
b.   The contract is enforceable against Sylvia only.
c.   The contract is enforceable against Brad and Sylvia.
d.   The contract is not enforceable; the napkin is not a writing.

9.   Using the same facts in Question 8, answer the following question. Assume that Brad refuses to buy the dogs. The napkin is admitted as evidence at trial when Sylvia sues him for breach of contract. Which of the following testimony would <u>not</u> be allowed by the parol evidence rule?

a.   Testimony that "goldens" refers to golden retrievers
b.   Testimony that the price was $200 total
c.   Testimony that the sale of a dog usually includes a copy of the animal's vaccination record
d.   Testimony that Sylvia promised to groom the dogs before she sold them to Brad.

10.   Mary, an insurance saleswoman and Pete, a doctor, are neighbors. Mary offers to sell her car to Pete for $1500. Pete says, "That's a great price. I accept at $1500 for the car and the fuzzy dice hanging from the rear-view mirror".

a.   Mary and Pete do not have a contract, because Pete made a counteroffer.
b.   Mary and Pete have a contract, but it does not include the fuzzy dice.
c.   Mary and Pete have a contract and it does include the fuzzy dice.
d.   Mary and Pete do not have a contract, because the mirror-image rule applies.

11.   Same facts as above, but Mary sells used cars for a living.

   a.   Mary and Pete do not have a contract, because Pete made a counteroffer.
   b.   Mary and Pete have a contract, but it does not include the fuzzy dice.
   c.   Mary and Pete have a contract and it does include the fuzzy dice.
   d.   Mary and Pete do not have a contract because the mirror-image rule applies.

12.   Which of the following is (are) merchants?

   a.   Betty, a lawyer, who hires Donald, a horse breeder, to sell her Appaloosa mare
   b.   Boy Scouts selling candy as a one-time fundraiser
   c.   Both Betty and the Boy Scouts are merchants
   d.   Neither Betty nor the Boy scouts are merchants

13.   Karen's Cosmetics places a telephone order for five cartons of eyeshadow, twenty cartons of lipstick and eighteen cartons of mascara from Color Me, Inc., a wholesaler of cosmetics. The cost of the order is $800. Color Me's shipping department sends Karen a copy of the order which contains the following information: Karen's name and address, the quantity of each item, the price per item and the initials of the clerk who took the order. Karen receives the copy of the order, and one month later, she decides to cancel the contract.

   a.   Karen is within her rights because the order does not contain enough information to show a contract.
   b.   Karen is within her rights because she never signed a written contract
   c.   Karen is not within her rights because the contract did not have to be in writing
   d.   Karen is not within her rights because a representative of Color Me signed the order and Karen failed to object.

14.   If a contract for the sale of goods fails to state a price:

   a.   the contract will be unenforceable unless both parties are merchants.
   b.   the contract will be unenforceable regardless of whether parties are merchants.
   c.   the contract will be enforceable and the court will use a reasonable price at the time of delivery.
   d.   the contract will be enforceable and the court will use a reasonable price at the time the contract was formed.

15.   Merlin's Party Shop telephones Nancy and tells her that it has a set of reindeer antlers in stock for $15, if Nancy can pick them up by the end of the week. Nancy agrees to think about the offer and she comes in the next afternoon. She discovers that the reindeer antlers have been sold to someone else. Nancy tells the manager of Merlin's that it was obligated to sell the

antlers to her.

a.   Nancy is correct because Merlin is a merchant.
b.   Nancy is correct because Merlin promised.
c.   Nancy is incorrect because both parties must be merchants.
d.   Nancy is incorrect because Merlin did not make its promise in writing.

16.   If a contract for the sale of goods fails to specify a place for delivery and shipment is <u>not</u> expected, delivery takes place:

a.   at the seller's place of business.
b.   at the buyer's place of business.
c.   at neither location; the contract is too indefinite to be enforced.

17.   Strong Brothers Department Store orders 500 pairs of assorted gloves to be delivered in ten installments. The price of the entire contract is $1000.

a.   The contract must be in writing because 50 pairs of gloves were ordered.
b.   The contract need not be in writing because each shipment of gloves contains only 100 pairs.
c.   The contract must be in writing, but if it is not, Strong is responsible for any gloves it accepts.
d.   The contract must be in writing, and if it is not, Strong can cancel the contract and send back any gloves that have been delivered.

18.   Which of the following terms <u>cannot</u> be omitted from a contract for the sale of goods?

a.   The price
b.   The quantity
c.   The shipment terms
d.   None of the above, all must be included

19.   The customary practice of parties under one installment contract is:

a.   trade usage.
b.   course of performance.
c.   course of dealing.
d.   admission.

20.   Rod's Sporting Goods offers to sell Herman a stationary bicycle for $400. Herman tells the salesman, "It sounds good. I'll take it if you can deliver it by tonight."

a.   Herman and Rod's have a contract, but Rod's is not obligated to deliver the bike tonight.
b.   Herman and Rod's have a contract and Rod's is obligated to deliver the bike tonight.

c.   Herman and Rod do not have a contract because Herman changed the terms of Rod's offer.

d.   Herman and Rod do not have a contract because Herman's response was conditional and was a counteroffer.

21.   Which of the following is most likely to be considered a merchant?

a.   A mother having a garage sale
b.   A university bookstore selling spiral notebooks
c.   A car salesman selling his boat
d.   A farmer selling a used fishing rod

22.   Gardenscape Nursery orally offers to sell Mrs. Jones fifteen tomato plants at a price of $1.50 per plant. She accepts and tells Gardenscape that she will pick them up this afternoon. When Mrs. Jones arrives, the plants have been sold to someone else. Mrs. Jones threatens to sue for breach of contract.

a.   Mrs. Jones will win because the contract did not need to be in writing.
b.   Mrs. Jones will lose because Gardenscape's offer was not in writing.
c.   Mrs. Jones will lose because although there was an offer and an acceptance, the contract should have been in writing.
d.   Mrs. Jones will lose because she is not a merchant.

23.   General Motors offers to sell AAA Auto Parts five clutches for $50 each. General Motors' offer specifies that all acceptances must be sent by mail and postmarked no later than January 15, 1988. AAA sends a telegram, which arrives on January 2.

a.   There is no contract because AAA did not accept by mail as specified in the offer.
b.   There is no contract because it needed to be in writing, and the telegram is not in "writing".
c.   There is a contract because AAA accepted by the deadline.
d.   There is no contract because even though the contract did not need to be in writing, AAA's acceptance by telegram was ineffective.

24.   Mr. Brown buys a lawnmower from Draper Hardware. The terms of the contract state, "Draper is not responsible for personal injury received as a result of use, regardless of the negligence of Draper and/or its retailers." If a court finds that the clause is unconscionable, which of the following modifications could be enforced by the court?

a.   The court could cancel the contract.
b.   The court could extend Draper's liability and hold it responsible for personal injury damages caused by Draper's negligence.
c.   Either of the above.
d.   Neither of the above; a contract cannot change the terms of a contract.

25.   If a court agrees to hear parol evidence to help interpret a contract, and if all of the following testimony is offered and is in conflict, which terms will control?

a.   Course of dealing
b.   Course of performance
c.   Trade usage
d.   Industry custom

Answers to Study Questions

Fill-in-the-Blank Questions

Walkin' Tall's reply is an acceptance. Its response clearly expressed an intent to make a contract, was not conditional, and did not contain a <u>material</u> difference from the offer. Because both parties are merchants and because Leather Loafers did not object, the new terms control. The logo must be placed on the heel of each shoe. The contract is enforceable if Leather Loafers has made a substantial commitment towards the manufacturer. This is true because the goods are custom-made. Delivery and shipment terms may be left open; the contract is enforceable without them. Leather Loafers is the seller and he can make the shipping arrangements, as long as the arrangements are reasonable.

True-False Questions

1.   F.   The parol evidence rule deals with extrinsic evidence concerning a written contract.

2.   T.

3.   F.   It is three months or a date specified in the offer, whichever is less.

4.   T.

5.   T.

6.   F.   It must be in writing if the price is $500 or more.

7.   T.

8.   T.   She has expertise in raising hamsters and holds herself out as having that knowledge.

9.   T.

10.   F.   A court can do either if it determines that a contract is
unconscionable.

<u>Multiple-Choice Questions</u>

1.	c	11.	b	21.	b
2.	c	12.	a	22.	a
3.	a	13.	d	23.	c
4.	a	14.	c	24.	c
5.	a	15.	d	25.	b
6.	c	16.	a		
7.	d	17.	c		
8.	a	18.	b		
9.	b	19.	b		
10.	b	20.	d		

CHAPTER 15

Title and Risk of Loss

General Principles

This chapter focuses on a common problem in sales contracts: destruction or damage to goods after they have been completed but before the buyer has received actual delivery of the goods. The problem can arise while the goods are being stored at the seller's warehouse or at an intermediate destination or while the goods are in transit. Obviously, one party to the contract must bear the loss. If the seller bears the loss, then the buyer has the right to cancel unless the seller provides replacement goods. If the buyer bears the loss, he or she must pay regardless of whether the goods have been delivered as promised.

Pre-UCC law allocated loss based on which party had title or technical ownership of the goods. It was difficult to determine the exact moment when title passed and the court decisions were confusing. The UCC separates risk of loss from title. Generally, if a party has breached the contract, he or she will bear the risk of loss. If neither party has breached, then the party with control over the goods is more likely to bear the risk of loss. Insurance coverage may also affect the distribution of loss.

Chapter Summary

I. Identification of the Goods--Identification is the designation of the goods. The goods then "belong" to a particular contract between buyer and seller and cannot be sold to another. Goods must be identified before title or risk of loss can pass.

    A. Sale or Contract to Sell--Title and risk of loss cannot pass until a sale has taken place. A sale occurs when the goods contracted for are in existence and the goods have been identified to the contract between the buyer and the seller. Before this time, there is only a contract to sell the goods (future goods) and a sale has not occurred.

B.   <u>Process of Identification</u>--May depend on the type of goods to be sold.

    (1)   <u>Agreement of the Parties</u>--Always controls if there is a specific provision in the contract.

    (2)   <u>General Rule</u>--Marked or otherwise noted by the seller. This can include a notation on an invoice or physical separation of the goods. Separation must take place if the goods are part of a larger group. If the goods are separated at the time the contract is made, then identification occurs when the contract is formed.

    (3)   <u>Fungible Goods</u>--Usually commodities stored in a silo or other container and impossible to distinguish except by separation (e.g. grains, liquids). In most cases, several sellers that share storage containers are called "owners in common." Identification takes place when the buyer replaces the seller as the owner in common.

    (4)   <u>Farm Products</u>--Contract for animals to be born or crops to be harvested within twelve months of the contract date are identified when the animals are conceived or when the crops begin to grow.

C.   <u>Passage of Title</u>--Formal passage of ownership. Identification must have occurred.

    (1)   <u>General Rule</u>--Parties can agree on time of passage. If they do not, title changes when the seller makes physical delivery of the goods. "Physical delivery" is a legal term and may depend on the type of contract as outlined below.

    (2)   <u>Shipment and Destination Contracts (Carrier Cases)</u>--Applies when the goods are moved. Under a <u>shipment</u> contract, title passes when the seller delivers the goods to the carrier and arranges for transportation. Under a <u>destination</u> contract, title passes when the seller tenders or tries to deliver the goods at a location designated in the contract. Note that physical delivery to the buyer's place of business is <u>not</u> always required.

    (3)   <u>Delivery Without Movement of the Goods</u>--The goods remain in one place. Sometimes documents of title (bills of lading or warehouse receipts) are used to represent the documents and the documents are sent from buyer to seller. Documents of title are used when a bailee or third party is storing or holding the goods. If the buyer is to pick up the goods from the seller, at the seller's place of business, a document of title usually is not used.

    (1)   <u>Document of title</u>--Title passes when and where the <u>document</u> is delivered.

    (2)   <u>No document</u>--If the buyer picks up the goods, title passes when the goods are identified. If the goods are identified prior to the contract, title passes when the contract is formed.

II.   <u>Risk of Loss</u>--The UCC attempts to distribute loss between buyer and seller only. In most cases, a carrier or an insurance company may be liable in the end. May or may not coincide with the time that title passes. Determine first if the contract distributes risk of loss.

    A.   <u>Carrier Cases</u>--(Delivery with movement of goods)

        (1)   The rules are the same as for passage of title. Under a <u>shipment</u> contract, the risk passes when the seller delivers the goods to a carrier. Under a <u>destination</u> contract, the risk passes when the seller tenders or tries to deliver the goods at a specified location. In the absence of shipping terms, the UCC presumes a <u>shipment</u> contract.

        (2)   <u>Contract Terms</u>--Some affect price only; for risk of loss purposes, the question remains whether the contract is a shipment or destination contract.

            (a)   <u>F.O.B. (free on board)</u>--A destination contract which requires the seller to ship the goods at his or her cost to a specific location. Note that the location may be in seller's city. "Destination" does not necessarily means the buyer's city or place of business.

            (b)   <u>F.A.S. (free alongside)</u>--Usually a shipment contract where the seller is required to deliver the goods to the vessel and make arrangements for shipment.

            (c)   <u>CIF or C&F (cost, insurance, freight or cost and freight)</u>--A shipment contract. These terms relate to the cost of the goods, not the seller's duty to deliver.

            (d)   <u>Delivery ex-ship (from the carrying vessel)</u>--A destination contract. The seller bears the risk until the goods are properly unloaded.

    B.   <u>Delivery Without Movement of the Goods</u>--Remember the goods don't move, but documents (bill of lading or warehouse receipt) will.

        (1)   <u>Goods Held by Seller</u>--If the seller is a merchant, the risk passes when the buyer physically picks up the goods. If the

seller is not a merchant, the risk passes when the seller tenders or is ready to part with the goods. Note that a merchant seller is much more likely to have insurance covering the goods than is a non-merchant seller.

(2)   Bailee Cases--When the goods are held by a third party, risk of loss passes when the bailee acknowledges the right of the buyer to the goods or when one of the following events occurs. If documents of title (document showing ownership) are involved, the answer depends on the type of document. If the document is negotiable, the risk passes when the buyer receives the document. If the document is non-negotiable, the risk passes when the buyer receives the document and has had a reasonable time to present it to the bailee and to take possession of the goods.

C.   Sale on Approval or Sale on Return Contracts

(1)   Sale on Approval--Seller makes only an offer to sell the goods and allows the buyer to take possession on a trial basis. Because no sale has occurred, the risk stays on the seller (unless the loss is caused by action of the buyer). If the buyer keeps the goods beyond the trial period or acts as owner, the risk shifts. A sale on approval, as opposed to a sale or return, is presumed if the buyer is to use the goods in his business (equipment).

(2)   Sale or Return--Seller delivers goods to buyer but the buyer can return or keep all or part of the goods. The risk shifts to the buyer when the buyer receives possession. If the buyer chooses to return some goods, the risk shifts back to the seller when the goods are returned. A sale or return is presumed if the buyer intends to sell the goods (inventory).

Consignment--The owner (consignor) delivers goods to be sold by another (consignee). The goods can be returned if they are not sold. A consignment is a sale or return and the consignee bears the risk of loss.

D.   Breached Contracts--Risk of loss usually rests on the breaching party.

(1)   Seller Breaches--Risk stays on seller if he or she ships goods which do not conform to the contract and would give the buyer a right to reject them. (This rule refers to a buyer's right to reject discussed in Chapter 16). If the buyer accepts the goods, in spite of defects, risk of loss passes on acceptance. If the buyer discovers a hidden defect, acceptance can be revoked and the risk shifts back to the seller but only to the extent that the buyer's insurance does not cover the loss.

(2)   Buyer Breaches--Risk automatically shifts to the buyer if the seller has identified the goods to the contract. Even so, the buyer is only responsible for a reasonable time after the seller learns of the breach. The seller must make arrangements to reclaim the goods. In addition, the buyer is only responsible for damages not covered by the seller's insurance.

III.   Insurable Interest--A buyer or seller can purchase insurance on goods only if he or she has an interest in the goods. It is possible for both the buyer and the seller to have an interest in the goods. If this concept is difficult to understand, think of buying a car on time. The buyer has insurance but so does the bank or the seller until the final payment is made.

  A.   Buyer--Acquires an insurable interest when the goods are identified to the contract.

  B.   Seller--Has an insurable interest until title passes. Can have an insurable interest until payment is received to secure payment (security interest).

IV.   Bulk Transfers--Sale of a major part of equipment or inventory used in seller's business. Does not cover usual sales made by seller. Designed to protect the seller's creditors. Unless the buyer and seller follow the rules listed below, the seller's creditors have claim on the goods for six months after the sale. In order for the buyer to obtain a clear title:

  A.   The seller must furnish under oath a list of his creditors;

  B.   The buyer and seller must list property to be transferred;

  C.   The buyer must keep the list for 6 months and make it available to the seller's creditors;

  D.   The buyer must send notice of the transfer to the seller's creditors at least 10 days before payment or possession by the buyer.

The rules dealing with bulk transfers are being revised. It is felt that the old rule placed a heavy burden on the buyers. New rules apply only to transactions which involve more than $10,000 and less than $25 million. Instead of (D) above, the new rules provide for public notice if the seller has more than 200 creditors and the notification period is extended to forty-five days. The time period in (C) is extended to one year.

V.   Sales by Non-Owners--This is not so much a question of when title passes as if title passes. Usually causes problems when a seller (manufacturer) has title problems, but sells to a buyer (retailer) and a buyer sells to a third party.

  A.   Void Title--No title at all. Occurs when the goods have been stolen. The thief and anyone who obtains the goods after him has no title and the true owner can reclaim them.

B.   Voidable Title--Although the seller's title may be rescinded by the true owner, the seller has the power to pass good title to others who pay for them and do not know of the seller's title problems. (The person who buys the goods from the seller must act in good faith and pay value for the goods). Occurs when the seller obtained the goods from a minor or by fraud or payment with a bad check. Can also occur if the seller was insolvent when he or she bought them.

C.   Entrustment--Occurs with bailments when the true owner delivers the goods to a merchant for repair. The merchant can pass good title to a third party who buys the goods from him or her. The true owner can then sue the merchant-seller.

Study Questions

Fill-in-the-Blank Questions

Video Visions, a New York manufacturer of television sets, receives an order for 300 Model XX television sets from Shopper's Universe, a retailer. The contract calls for delivery F.O.B. Shopper's warehouse in Chicago. Video's foreman prepares the order, places the 300 sets on the loading dock and marks them for shipment. Before the sets can be loaded onto a delivery truck a fire destroys all of the television sets.

At the time of the fire, _____ has title to the television sets.   (Video Visions/Shoppers Universe)

At the time of the fire, the risk of loss is on _____
_____.
(Video Visions/Shopper's Universe)

Video Visions and Shopper's Universe have a _____
contract.   (destination/shipment)

True-False Questions

1.   It is possible for a buyer and seller of goods to have an insurable interest in the same property at the same time. _____

2.   If goods are to be shipped delivery ex-ship, the buyer is responsible for the goods when the seller leaves them with the carrier. _____

3.   If the seller breaches the contract, the risk of loss does not shift to the buyer until the buyer accepts the goods. _____

4.   Goods must be identified to the contract before risk of loss can pass from the seller to the buyer. _____

5.   Identification of fungible goods can take place only after the goods have been separated. _____

6.   The purpose of the bulk transfer rules is to protect the seller from revocation by the buyer. _____

7.   Transfer of title to goods and risk of loss always pass to the buyer at the same time. _____

8.   A contract which calls for delivery CIF is a destination contract. _____

9.   When a contract calls for the sale of crops to be harvested, identification takes place when the crops are harvested. _____

10. The parties can agree to change the point at which the risk of loss passes from seller to buyer. _____

Multiple-Choice Questions

1.   Under the law existing before the Uniform Commercial Code, risk of loss passed from seller to buyer when:

   a.   the goods were identified to the contract.
   b.   the buyer acquired title to the goods.
   c.   the goods were delivered to the buyer's business.
   d.   the seller transferred the goods to a carrier.

2.   REV, an automobile manufacturer, receives an order from the Texas State Police for fifty patrol cars. REV records the serial numbers of the cars for shipment to Texas. At this time:

   a.   the cars have been identified to the contract because the serial numbers have been recorded.
   b.   the cars have been identified to the contract because REV has filled the order.
   c.   the cars have not been identified to the contract, because they have not been separated from other cars.
   d.   the cars have not been identified to the contract, because they have not been shipped to Texas.

3.   Needlepoint Notions, a manufacturer, ships fifty needlepoint kits to the Yarn Barn, a retailer. Needlepoint and Yarn have agreed that Yarn may select any or all of the kits for resale to its customers. Any unsold kits are to be returned to Needlepoint within six weeks. The contract between Needlepoint and Yarn Barn is:

a.   a sale or return.
b.   a sale on approval.
c.   a contract to sell, no sale has taken place.
d.   a final sale.

4.   If a fire destroys the kits two weeks after they are received and while they are stored at the Yarn Barn, who will bear the risk of loss?

a.   Needlepoint, because the sale to Yarn Barn is not final.
b.   Needlepoint, because Yarn Barn has not accepted the kits.
c.   Yarn Barn, because it has accepted the kits.
d.   Yarn Barn, because title and risk of loss have passed to it.

5.   Future Electronics, a retailer, orders fifty transistor radios from Audiotronics. Payment is due within sixty days. The day after the goods are received, but before Future pays Audiotronics, Future sells one of the radios to Mrs. Murphy. One week later, Future sends a check to Audiotronics, but the check bounces. Who has title to the radio purchased by Mrs. Murphy?

a.   Audiotronics, because Future did not pay for the radio which was sold to Mrs. Murphy.
b.   Mrs. Murphy, because she paid for the radio in good faith.
c.   Audiotronics, because Mrs. Murphy received voidable title.
d.   Future, because Mrs. Murphy received voidable title.

6.   Mr. Smith is having a garage sale. Susan sees a desk that she likes and asks Mr. Smith to hold the desk for her until she can arrange for transportation. Before Susan can return, another shopper at the garage sale carelessly backs over the desk with her car. Between Susan and Mr. Smith, who will bear the loss?

a.   Mr. Smith, because he had possession of the desk when it was destroyed.
b.   Mr. Smith, because the risk does not pass until the desk is received by Susan.
c.   Susan, because the risk shifted when the contract was made.
d.   Susan, because the risk shifted when Mr. Smith tendered delivery.

7.   At the time the desk was destroyed, who had title to the desk?

a.   Mr. Smith, because he had possession of the desk.
b.   Mr. Smith, because Susan had not paid for the desk.
c.   Susan, because title passed when the contract was made.
d.   Susan, because Mr. Smith is not a merchant.

8.   Printed Word, a publishing company, contracts with Mystery Bookstore for the sale of fifty copies of the latest best seller. The books are to be shipped F.O.B. Mystery Bookstore. The seller marks the books for shipment and then

receives a phone call from the manager of Mystery Bookstore. The manager informs Printed Word that he will not honor the contract. The next day, the books are destroyed when the seller's warehouse is demolished by a storm. Who bears the risk of loss to the books?

    a.   Mystery Bookstore must bear the total loss because it breached the contract.

    b.   Mystery Bookstore must bear the loss but only to the extent that Printed Word's insurance does not cover the loss.

    c.   Printed Word must bear the total loss because the books had not been shipped.

    d.   Printed Word must bear the total loss only if Mystery Bookstore's insurance will cover the loss.

9.   In a bulk transfer of assets, the <u>seller</u> must:

    a.   swear to his or her creditors that either the seller or the buyer will pay existing debts.

    b.   notify each creditor of the sale.

    c.   give the buyer a list of creditors.

    d.   file the list of creditors in a designated public office.

10.   The entrustment rule:

    a.   applies to risk of loss in breached contracts.

    b.   applies to passage of title.

    c.   applies to bulk transfers of goods.

    d.   applies to identification of goods.

11.   If goods are to be shipped "F.A.S.":

    a.   a shipment contract exists and the seller will bear the cost of shipping to the buyer's place of business.

    b.   a shipment contract exists and the buyer will bear the cost of shipping.

    c.   a destination contract exists and the seller will bear the cost of shipping to the buyer's place of business.

    d.   a destination contract exists and the buyer will bear the cost of shipping.

12.   Farmer Jones has stored his wheat crop in a silo in the Midwest. He is an owner in common with other farmers who also store their wheat crops in the silo. He contracts with Breakfast Foods, a cereal manufacturer, for the sale of the wheat. Identification of the wheat to the contract will occur when:

    a.   the contract is made between Farmer Jones and Breakfast Foods.

    b.   the wheat is removed from the silo.

    c.   Breakfast Foods pays for the wheat.

    d.   the wheat is removed from the silo and shipped to Breakfast Foods.

13.   Assuming a negotiable document of title is required, title to the wheat will pass when:

    a.   the document of title is sent by the seller.
    b.   the document of title is received by the buyer.
    c.   the document of title is presented to the owner of the silo.
    d.   the contract is made between Farmer Jones and Breakfast Foods.

14.   Assuming a negotiable document of title is required, risk of loss to the wheat will pass when:

    a.   the document of title is sent by the seller.
    b.   the document of title is received by the buyer.
    c.   the document of title is presented to the owner of the silo.
    d.   the contract is made between Farmer Jones and Breakfast Foods.

15.   Computer Country delivers a personal computer to L. Eagle, Attorney at Law. Eagle has agreed to try the computer for one week. Two days after the computer is delivered, a fire destroys Eagle's office. Who will be responsible for the loss of the computer?

    a.   Eagle, because this contract is a sale or return and the risk of loss is on the buyer.
    b.   Computer Country, because this contract is a sale on approval and the risk of loss is on the seller.
    c.   Computer Country, because this contract is a sale or return and the risk of loss is on the buyer.
    d.   Eagle, because this contract is a sale on approval and the risk of loss is on the buyer.

16.   Martin's Mills, a shirt manufacturer, receives an order from Carter Clothing, a retailer. The contract calls for shipment of 200 cotton shirts F.O.B. Martin's Mills. The shirts are destroyed in transit. The contract between Martin's Mills and Carter Clothing is:

    a.   a destination contract and Martin is responsible for the loss.
    b.   a shipment contract and Martin is responsible for the loss.
    c.   a destination contract and Carter is responsible for the loss.
    d.   a shipment contract and Carter is responsible for the loss.

17.   Cindy buys a prom dress from Fine Fashions and leaves the dress for alteration. The dress is accidentally sold to Matilda, another prom-goer. To whom does the dress belong?

    a.   Cindy, because Fine Fashions had no title to the dress.
    b.   Cindy, because Matilda has voidable title.
    c.   Matilda, because Fine Fashions has void title.
    d.   Matilda, because Fine Fashions was entrusted with Cindy's dress.

18. Walter purchases a new couch from Fred's Furniture. Walter makes arrangements to pick up the couch on Wednesday. Fred's warehouse and Walter's couch are destroyed by flood on Tuesday. Who will bear the loss of the couch?

    a. Walter, because he has paid for the goods and Fred tendered delivery.
    b. Walter, but only to the extent that Fred's insurance won't cover the loss.
    c. Fred, because Walter has not taken delivery of the couch.
    d. Fred, but only if Walter's insurance doesn't cover the loss.

19. Verdant Veggies, a wholesale distributor of canned foods, contracts to sell Sunshine Market six cases of green beans. The manager of Verdant Veggies tells his shipping foreman to reserve six cases for Sunshine. The foreman forgets to fill Verdant's order. Before the goods can be shipped, a fire destroys Verdant's warehouse. Who will bear the loss of the green beans?

    a. Verdant, because the goods have not been identified to the contract.
    b. Verdant, because although the goods have been identified to the contract, they have not been shipped.
    c. Sunshine, because the goods have been identified to the contract.
    d. Sunshine, because the goods have been identified to the contract and it has an insurable interest in the goods.

20. "Delivery ex-ship" means:

    a. the seller must deliver the goods alongside the vessel or carrier.
    b. the seller must deliver the goods to the carrier and the seller will pay the freight costs.
    c. the seller must deliver the goods to a particular destination and the seller will pay the freight.
    d. the seller bears the risk of loss until the goods leave the carrier and are unloaded properly.

21. Lawn and Garden Supply orders 200 leaf rakes from Green Thumb Manufacturer's. The contract calls for the goods to be shipped F.O.B. Lawn and Garden Supply. When the goods arrive, the manager of Lawn and Garden Supply discovers that grass rakes have been sent by mistake. Lawn stores the rakes in its storeroom until it can arrange for shipment to the manufacturer. The rakes are destroyed accidentally. Who will bear the risk of loss?

    a. Lawn and Garden, because the rakes were in its possession.
    b. Lawn and Garden, because the rakes were identified to the contract.
    c. Green Thumb, because this is a destination contract.
    d. Green Thumb, because it is in breach.

22. Dr. Burns orders an X-ray machine from Orton's Medical Equipment. A shipping charge appears on the bill and Dr. Burns' address appears on the box but no other shipping terms are noted in the contract or on the merchandise.

If the goods are destroyed in transit, who will be responsible for the loss?

    a.   Dr. Burns, because in the absence of express terms, a destination contract is presumed.

    b.   Dr. Burns, because in the absence of express terms, a shipment contract is presumed.

    c.   Orton, because in the absence of express terms, a destination contract is presumed.

    d.   Orton, because in the absence of express terms, a shipment contract is presumed.

23.   Which of the following would not be subject to the bulk transfer rules?

    a.   Sale by a computer manufacturer of its entire stock of computers.

    b.   Sale by a doctor of his practice to another doctor.

    c.   Sale by a clothing store of all its inventory except accessories.

    d.   Sale by a university bookstore of all textbooks and school supplies.

24.   Dyer's Drugstore purchases an insurance policy which covers all goods in which Dyer has an interest or title. Dyer orders forty cases of aspirin from Cure-All Pharmaceuticals. The aspirins are destroyed on the manufacturer's loading dock and Dyer files a claim with his insurance.

    a.   Dyer's claim will be denied because the goods had not been identified to the contract.

    b.   Dyer's claim will be denied because he did not have an insurable interest in the aspirin.

    c.   Dyer's claim will be denied because he did not have title to the aspirin.

    d.   Dyer's claim will be allowed because he had an insurable interest in the aspirin.

25.   Texas Wines, Inc., a bottler in Dallas, agrees to buy 2,000 gallons of wine from Vicon Vineyards, which is located in Lubbock. The wine is stored in a vat in Lubbock. The storage facilities are owned by Commodity Storage, Inc. In order to take possession of the wine, a party must present a receipt of ownership to Commodity's manager. Texas Wines receives a non-negotiable receipt from Vicon and plans to withdraw 200 gallons. Between Texas Wines and Vicon, who will bear the loss of the wine if it is destroyed before shipment?

    a.   Vicon, because Texas had not withdrawn any wine.

    b.   Vicon, but only if Texas had not had a reasonable time to withdraw the wine.

    c.   Texas Wines, because it had title to the wine.

    d.   Texas Wines, because it had an insurable interest in the wine.

Answers to Study Questions

Fill-in-the-Blank Questions

At the time of the fire, the goods have been identified to the contract, because Video Visions' foreman segregated them. Because the goods are to be moved, the rules involving carriers apply. Title passes when the goods are moved, therefore title remains in Video Visions. The risk of loss is also on Video Visions. Shopper's Universe does have an insurable interest in the goods; an insurable interest arises when the goods are identified to the contract. This is a destination contract; Video Visions has the responsibility for shipping goods to Shopper's warehouse.

True-False Questions

1. T.

2. F.   The seller bears the risk until the goods are properly unloaded at their destination.

3. T.

4. T.

5. F.   If the goods are stored in a silo or other facility, the buyer can replace the seller as an owner in common of the fungible goods.

6. F.   The purpose of the bulk transfer rules is to protect the creditors of the seller by giving them notice of the proposed sale of assets.

7. F.   The rules are different.

8. F.   It is a shipment contract. CIF relates to cost of shipment only.

9. F.   Identification takes place when the crops begin to grow.

10. T.

Multiple-Choice Questions

1.	b		14.	b
2.	a		15.	b
3.	a		16.	c
4.	d		17.	d
5.	b		18.	c
6.	d		19.	a
7.	c		20.	d
8.	b		21.	d
9.	c		22.	b
10.	b		23.	b
11.	b		24.	d
12.	a		25.	b
13.	b			

CHAPTER
16

Performance and Breach

General Principles

As you learned in Chapter 13, if one party fails to complete a contractual duty, breach results. The first part of this chapter defines the duties of the parties to a sales contract. In general, the seller has the duty to provide the exact goods promised at the time and place set out in the contract. The buyer has the duty to pay for the goods according to the terms of the agreement. The UCC also imposes a duty on the buyer to inform the seller of any defect in the goods, so that if possible, the seller can correct the error.

The second half of this chapter deals with the remedies available to the parties once a breach has been established. Although a buyer or seller may have several options, some choices are available only in specific cases. Note also that some remedies involve monetary compensation while others provide for possession of the goods.

Chapter Summary

I.   Good Faith and Commercial Reasonableness--Both the buyer and the seller have the duty to comply with the following standards.

     A.   Good Faith--This is an obligation to act fairly and honestly and is implied in every contract for the sale of goods.

     B.   Commercial Reasonableness--Merchants are held to a higher standard. They must not only act honestly but their conduct must conform to reasonable business standards. Note the many places in this chapter where "reasonableness" is the test for performance.

II.   Performance of a Sales Contract--A seller's obligation is to transfer the goods to an agreed location and to deliver goods which match the description in the contract (conforming goods). A buyer's obligation is to accept and pay for goods which do conform to the contract.

III.   Seller's Obligations

    A.   Tender of Delivery--Tender is the duty to be ready, willing, and able to perform the contract. The seller has the duty to provide conforming (goods which meet contract specifications) goods at the time specified in the contract. If the buyer is to take delivery, the seller must notify the buyer and give the buyer a reasonable time to collect the goods.

    B.   Place of Delivery--Usually specified in the contract. If not, the circumstances may indicate a place. In the absence of these guides, use the rules below.

        (1)   Presumption--Buyer picks up the goods at the seller's place of business or at the seller's home if the seller has no established place of business.

        (2)   Agreed Location--If identified goods are stored at a warehouse or grain elevator, delivery takes place at that location.

        (3)   Carrier Cases--Under a shipment contract, the seller has the duty to deliver the goods to a carrier, to make the contract for delivery, and to notify the buyer of the shipment. If a document such as a bill of lading is required to obtain the goods, the seller must forward it to the buyer.

            Under a destination contract, the seller has the responsibility of transporting the goods to an agreed location and to notify the buyer of their arrival. Notice must be given at a reasonable hour and the buyer must have a reasonable time to collect the goods.

    C.   The Perfect Tender Rule--States that the goods tendered by the seller must conform to the contract in every detail; they must be perfect. If the goods are not perfect, the buyer has the right to reject; there is no substantial performance rule. Because a buyer who wishes to get out of a contract might be able to do so by seizing on trivial errors, the UCC lists several exceptions to the perfect tender rule. The exceptions include:

        (1)   Agreement of the Parties--If the contract makes allowances for imperfect tender, the buyer must adhere to the provisions of the contract.

        (2)   Cure--This is the seller's right to correct mistakes. The buyer has the duty to inform the seller of problems (mitigation of

damages). If the buyer does not do so, he or she loses the right to reject the goods, <u>if</u> the mistake could have been remedied.

The seller has the right to cure if the time for performance has not passed. Even if the deadline has passed, the seller can cure if there is reason to believe that the goods shipped would have been an acceptable substitute (e.g. a more expensive model at the same price).

(3) <u>Substitution of Carriers</u>--When the goods cannot be shipped in the manner specified in the contract, and the seller is not at fault, he or she can make other reasonable arrangements for transport.

(4) <u>Installment Contracts</u>--Basically a substantial performance requirement. The buyer may reject an installment only if the value of that installment is substantially impaired and cannot be remedied. The buyer can cancel the <u>entire</u> contract (all installments) only if the value of the whole contract is seriously damaged.

(5) <u>Commercial Impracticability</u>--Same rule as non-sales contracts. The seller is relieved of contractual duties if an unforeseeable event beyond his or her control makes performance impracticable. If only part of the contract is affected, the seller must apportion the remaining goods among the buyers and each buyer has the right to accept or to reject the apportionment.

(6) <u>Destruction of Identified Goods</u>--Same rule as non-sales contracts, if the seller still bears the risk of loss. If the buyer bears the risk when the goods are destroyed, then the seller has performed and the buyer must pay. The buyer has the option to accept damaged goods at a reduced price.

IV. <u>Buyer's Obligations</u>

A. Furnish a place for the goods to be stored.

B. Pay for the goods at the time and at the place the goods are delivered. Note that delivery occurs when the seller has completed his or her responsibility and may have nothing to do with the physical location of the goods.

C. The buyer accepts goods by words or conduct. Failure to complain after a reasonable opportunity to inspect is acceptance. If the buyer uses the goods or in any way acts as the owner of the goods, acceptance has occurred. Partial acceptance is proper if made in commercial lots.

D. The buyer has a right and duty of inspection if he or she is obligated to pick up the goods. Payment constitutes acceptance. Therefore, if the goods are to be delivered C.O.D. or before the buyer has a chance to inspect them, the buyer retains a right to revoke acceptance of non-conforming goods. Similarly, in cases where a document of title is used, payment is due at the time the document is transferred.

E. Revocation of Acceptance--Because the buyer has the duty to inspect the goods, the right to revoke acceptance is limited. It is available only if the buyer had reason to believe that the seller was performing as agreed. The value of the goods must be substantially impaired and one of the following events must occur.

   (1) The buyer notified the seller of the problem; the buyer reasonably expects the seller to cure and the seller has not done so.

   (2) The defect is hidden.

   (3) The seller assured the buyer that the goods were acceptable and the buyer, relying on the seller's promise, did not inspect the goods.

V. Anticipatory Repudiation--If either party has notice of breach before the delivery date, the non-breaching party can (1) pursue any of the remedies available when a contract is breached; (2) wait for a reasonable time to see if the breaching party will perform (note that if the waiting period is unreasonable, the non-breaching party has not mitigated damages); (3) stop performance.

VI. Remedies of the Seller

A. Withhold delivery

B. Stop goods on their way to the buyer. Must notify the carrier in time to stop delivery and give substitute instructions. The seller is responsible for any additional cost. Must be at least a carload or larger.

C. If the buyer is insolvent, the seller can demand cash for the goods or withhold delivery. The seller may also reclaim goods in possession of a bankrupt buyer if the seller acts within ten days of delivery. This time limit does not apply if the buyer misrepresented his or her financial condition in writing within three months before delivery.

D. Resell the goods at a commercially reasonable, but not necessarily public, sale. The seller must inform the buyer of the sale unless the goods are perishable and losing value and the delay would result in further decline. The seller can then sue the buyer for any deficiency including the expense of the sale.

The seller can use this remedy even if at the time of the contract, the goods have not been identified to the contract (set aside for the buyer). The seller can identify the goods before sale. In the case of partially manufactured goods, the seller can cease production and sell the goods for scrap or complete the goods and sell them. The decision must be reasonable.

E.   The seller can sue for the <u>entire purchase price</u> and expenses only under extraordinary circumstances (usually when the goods are not available for resale).

    (1)   When the buyer has accepted the goods and has not paid.

    (2)   When conforming goods have been lost or damaged and the risk of loss is on the buyer.

    (3)   When the goods have been identified to the contract and the seller cannot resell (custom-made goods).

F.   If the seller can show that the traditional damages outlined above do not compensate for the loss which has occurred, he or she may sue for wrongful repudiation of the contract. The damages include lost profits and incidental expenses. Usually available with high-price, low-volume items such as airplanes.

VII.   <u>Remedies of the Buyer</u>

A.   The buyer can always reject nonconforming goods but remember that the buyer must notify the seller of the problem. A merchant buyer must make adequate provisions for storing the goods or reshipping them to the seller. If the goods are perishable, the merchant buyer can sell them and send the proceeds to the seller less the expenses of the sale.

B.   If the seller is insolvent at the time of payment or becomes insolvent within ten days, the buyer has the right to possession of any identified goods.

C.   Specific performance if unique goods are involved.

D.   If the buyer can show that substitute goods are not available, he or she may also be able to replevy the goods or to recover the goods if the goods have been identified to the contract. The buyer cannot force the seller to manufacture or to identify the goods.

E.   A buyer who has paid for the goods or incurs expenses with regard to them, receives a security interest to enforce payment. If the goods remain in the buyer's possession after rejection, the buyer can use any of the seller's options including resale of the goods to other buyers. Excess monies must be remitted to the seller.

F.   Cancel the contract in whole or in part. Notice must be sent to the seller.

G.   The most popular remedy is cover or the buyer's right to buy substitute goods. Cover corresponds to the seller's right of resale. The buyer can sue the seller for the extra cost of the goods and expenses. (The latter are incidental damages.) The buyer may also sue for losses which are foreseeable as a result of the breach (consequential damages).

H.   If the buyer decides not to purchase substitute goods, the seller may be sued for breach of contract. The damages are the difference between the contract price and the time the buyer learned of the breach. The buyer may also recover incidental and consequential damages.

I.   If the buyer decides to keep the damaged goods, the seller may be sued for the difference between the value of the goods promised and the value of the goods received if the suit is for breach of warranty. In other cases, the buyer can sue for foreseeable losses. The buyer can deduct the losses from the purchase price owed to the seller.

VIII.   Statute of Limitations--Unless the contract specifies otherwise, the statute of limitations provided in the Uniform Commercial Code is four years from the date that the seller tenders (offers to release) the goods. The parties may agree to shorten a warranty, but it may not be less than one year. A buyer suing under non-UCC theory, such as breach of contract, follows the statute of limitations for that kind of suit.

IX.   Limitation of Remedies--Generally permitted unless a consumer is involved or the only remedy offered cannot be used.

A.   Changing Remedies--Additional remedies are always acceptable. Remedies can be limited, but any remedies mentioned in the contract are considered as additions, not limitations, unless the contract clearly states otherwise.

B.   Exclusive Remedies--Parties can designate one remedy and one remedy only. This clause will be enforceable as long as the remedy designated can be used.

C.   Consequential Damages--These are damages which flow from the breach and are reasonably foreseeable. An example would be lost profits, if a plant had to shut down because it purchased defective machinery.   Most of these clauses are enforceable between businessmen, especially if the loss is property or profits. However, a consumer cannot be deprived of the right to sue for consequential <u>personal</u> injury.

Study Questions

Fill-in-the-Blank Questions

Holiday Cards, Inc., a manufacturer of greeting cards, contracted with Sam's Stationery Shoppe to deliver 100 boxes of Christmas cards at a price of $2 per box. Sam specified delivery by November 15. The cards arrived on November 7th but due to a mix-up on the loading dock, Hanukkah cards were sent. Sam opened the cards when they arrived and chose not to notify Holiday. Instead, he purchased substitute cards from Creative Cards at $2.15 per box. Sam shipped Holiday's cards back to them after the first of the year.

At the time of the breach, November 7th, Holiday _____ have a right to cure. 	(did/did not)

If the cards had arrived on November 15th, Holiday _____ a right to cure. 	(would have had/would not have had)

Sam's purchase of substitute cards is _____. 	(cover/reclamation)

True-False Questions

1.   A merchant must always act in a commercially reasonable manner, regardless of whether he or she breached the contract. _____

2.   Anticipatory repudiation is the buyer's right to purchase substitute goods. _____

3.   If no place of delivery is stated in the contract, delivery takes place at the buyer's place of business. _____

4.   Replevin is the right of the buyer to take possession of specific goods in the seller's possession. _____

5.   The perfect tender rule cannot be altered by an agreement between the parties. _____

6.   If a buyer receives damaged goods, he or she may keep them and sue for breach of warranty. _____

7   If the buyer breaches the contract after the seller has begun production of the goods, the seller has the option of finishing the goods or ceasing manufacture

and selling the partially finished goods for scrap._____

8.   A seller may sue for the entire contract price if the goods have been identified to the contract. _____

9.   Commercial impracticability is an exception to the perfect tender rule. _____

10.   If the goods are destroyed while the buyer bears the risk of loss, the contract is canceled. _____

Multiple-Choice Questions

1.   Sleep-Easy Mattress Co. delivers fifty mattresses to the Good Night Sleep Shop. When Good Night receives the mattresses, it sends Sleep-Easy notice that it is filing for bankruptcy and it cannot pay. Sleep-Easy:

   a.   can reclaim the goods within ten days of delivery.
   b.   can reclaim the goods within three months of delivery.
   c.   cannot reclaim the goods but can sue for damages.
   d.   cannot reclaim the goods and cannot sue for damages.

2.   Tender of delivery occurs when:

   a.   the goods are placed in the hands of the buyer.
   b.   the seller notifies the buyer that the goods are ready.
   c.   the buyer pays for the goods.
   d.   the buyer accepts the goods.

3.   Houndog Pet Food and Herman's Feed Store have a shipment contract for the sale of fifty bags of dog food at $7 per bag. Houndog's duty with regard to transportation of the dog food is:

   a.   placement with a carrier.
   b.   notice to Herman.
   c.   neither of the above.
   d.   both of the above.

4.   If the goods are destroyed in transit, after the risk has passed to Herman, Houndog:

   a.   cannot sue Herman for the price of the goods because Herman never received them, but Houndog is not obligated to replace the destroyed goods.
   b.   cannot sue Herman for the price of the goods because Herman never received them and Houndog must replace the goods.
   c.   can sue Herman for the price of the goods.
   d.   can sue Herman for the cost of the goods.

5. Bernard's Grocery orders 500 cases of liquid dishwasher soap from Kleen Products, Inc. Delivery is to take place in ten installments of fifty cases on the fifteenth of each month. In the fourth month, Bernard opens the shipment and discovers that all the bottles of soap have leaked.

    a.   Bernard can cancel the remaining portions of the contract and sue for breach of contract.
    b.   Bernard can reject the fourth shipment and cancel the rest of the contract.
    c.   Bernard can reject the fourth shipment only.
    d.   Bernard cannot reject the fourth shipment but he can sue for damages.

6. Parsons Manufacturing orders a widget-maker from Miscellaneous Parts, Inc. Parsons inspects the machine and pays for it. Two days later, when the machine has been in use for twenty-four hours, Parsons discovers a defect. Parsons:

    a.   has not accepted the machine.
    b.   cannot revoke his acceptance because he paid for the machine.
    c.   cannot revoke his acceptance because he inspected the machine.
    d.   can revoke his acceptance of the machine because the defect was not apparent.

7. Initially Yours, a monogram shop, contracts with Central University, for the sale of thirty-five sweaters with the college's logo. A week before the date of delivery, Central informs Initially Yours that due to budget cuts, it will not pay for the sweaters. Initially Yours:

    a.   can wait for Central to perform or sue immediately.
    b.   must wait for the delivery date and sue.
    c.   must sue immediately.
    d.   must cancel the contract.

8. In which of the following cases, can the seller sue for the <u>purchase price</u> of the goods?

    a.   The buyer refuses payment and the goods can be resold at a loss.
    b.   The buyer refuses payment and the goods cannot be resold.
    c.   The buyer refuses payment and revokes acceptance.
    d.   The buyer refuses payment and the goods are destroyed at the seller's warehouse.

9. Unless otherwise specified in the contract, the buyer must pay for the goods:

    a.   when the goods are physically in the buyer's hands.
    b.   when the goods are delivered to the buyer under the terms of the contract, regardless of the physical location of the goods.
    c.   within ten day of delivery.
    d.   within twenty-four hours of delivery.

10.   The buyer's right of inspection:

   a.   applies even if the shipment is C.O.D.
   b.   cannot be waived by the buyer.
   c.   may affect the buyer's right to sue if the goods are plainly defective.
   d.   does not prevent the seller from suing for payment.

11.   The seller can stop goods in transit:

   a.   only if the buyer is insolvent.
   b.   only if the buyer has given notice of intent to reject.
   c.   only if the contract is a shipment contract.
   d.   only if the carrier is given reasonable notice.

12.   Fine Furniture Co. manufacturers chairs, tables and other household items. A fire destroys the warehouse and only one-tenth of the goods are salvaged. Fine has twenty-five customers to whom it owes furniture.

   a.   Fine can cancel all the contracts.
   b.   Fine can apportion the remaining furniture and the buyers must accept the goods if Fine's decision is reasonable.
   c.   Fine can apportion the remaining furniture but the buyers have the right to accept or to reject the remaining goods.
   d.   Fine must fulfill all the contracts or be liable for breach of contract.

13.   Paul's Produce contracts with Taco Town to deliver fifty heads of iceberg lettuce per week. Last week Paul accidentally delivered romaine lettuce. Taco purchases replacement lettuce for a price of ten cents more per head and sells the romaine lettuce to Posh Eatery for ten cents less than the contract price.

   a.   Taco can sue Paul for the following damages: the extra cost of the iceberg lettuce, the expenses of procuring the iceberg lettuce, and the expenses of the sale of the iceberg lettuce less the sale price of the romaine lettuce.
   b.   Taco can sue Paul for the following damages: the extra cost of the iceberg lettuce and the expenses in procuring it, but Taco cannot sue for anything connected with the sale to Posh Restaurant because Taco had no right to sell the romaine lettuce.
   c.   Taco cannot sue Paul because it had no right to sell the romaine lettuce but Paul cannot sue Taco because it breached the contract.
   d.   Taco cannot sue Paul but Paul can sue Taco for wrongfully selling the romaine lettuce.

14.   The duty of good faith applies:

   a.   to both parties, regardless of breach.
   b.   to breaching parties only.

    c.   to merchants only.

    d.   to non-breaching parties only.

15.   Which of the following is <u>not</u> a remedy of the seller:

    a.   Cancellation

    b.   Withhold delivery

    c.   Specific performance

    d.   Sue for the contract price

16.   Leather Products, Inc. ships fourteen briefcases to Executive Luggage, a retailer. Although payment is due upon receipt, after two weeks, Leather has received nothing from Executive. Leather:

    a.   can assume that Executive has accepted the briefcases and can sue for the contract price.

    b.   can assume that Executive has accepted the briefcases but must give Executive a reasonable time to pay.

    c.   cannot assume that Executive has accepted the briefcases because Leather must demand that Executive inspect the briefcases.

    d.   cannot assume that Executive has accepted the briefcases because Executive must give notice of acceptance.

17.   Patsy orders a ceramic cookie jar from Kitchen Kuties. The order form calls for delivery by OPS overnight service. Kitchen fills Patsy's order but then discovers that due to mechanical failure, OPS will not deliver for two days. Kitchen arranges for transportation by Fast Express Trucking Service.

    a.   Patsy can reject the cookie jar if it arrives before the delivery date.

    b.   Patsy can reject the cookie jar regardless of the date of delivery because of the perfect tender rule.

    c.   Patsy cannot reject the cookie jar because Patsy's substitution of carriers was reasonable.

    d.   Patsy cannot sue because she received the goods.

18.   AAA Appliance orders fifty autumn gold refrigerators from Kold, Inc. Two weeks before the order is due, AAA cancels wrongfully. Kold, who has not previously filled AAA's order, identified the refrigerators to the contract and sells them to BB's at a slightly lower price and sues AAA for the difference. Is Kold within its rights?

    a.   Yes, because it had a right to identify the goods to the contract and resell them.

    b.   No, because it had no right to identify the goods to the contract.

    c.   No, because it had no right to sell the goods to BB's.

    d.   No, because although it had a right to sell the refrigerators, it cannot sue AAA for the loss.

19.   Same facts as above, but assume BB's is owned by the son-in-law of Kold's president. The sale was not announced to the public.

        a.   The sale is automatically invalid because it was made to an insider.
        b.   The sale is invalid because it was not announced to the public.
        c.   The sale is valid if it was made in a commercially reasonable manner.
        d.   The sale is invalid, because Kold had no right to resell the goods.

20.   Peter and Abel had a long-standing agreement. On the first of each month, Peter ships Abel ten boxes of floppy diskettes. Abel pays on delivery. Peter has not received payment for the last four shipments. Peter may.

        a.   cancel the contract and sue for damages.
        b.   withhold delivery of further shipments until payment is received.
        c.   sue for breach of contract.
        d.   do all of the above.

21.   Cindy orders a set of towels from a linen supply store. The store promises to deliver on or before July 13. On July 15, Cindy has not received the towels. The towels arrive on July 16. Cindy:

        a.   can reject the towels because of the perfect tender rule.
        b.   cannot reject the towels because the linen supply has substantially performed.
        c.   cannot reject the towels because late shipments are an exception to the perfect tender rule.
        d.   can reject the towels only if they do not conform to the contract.

22.   Omega is a manufacturer of television sets. It contracts with X Mart for the delivery of forty Model 100 sets. Delivery is to occur on the sixteenth of the month. The sets arrive on the due date but X Mart discovers that Omega has shipped the more expensive Model 200 sets with a note that says "we are temporarily out of stock of Model 100, you can have these for the same price." X Mart:

        a.   can cancel the contract immediately because Omega shipped nonconforming goods.
        b.   can cancel the contract because Omega's right to cure expired on the 16th.
        c.   cannot cancel the contract because Omega has substantially performed and X Mart must accept the substitution.
        d.   cannot cancel the contract because Omega retains the right to cure for a reasonable time after the 16th.

23.   The same week, X Mart received a shipment of sixty cartons of toothpaste from Dental Products. X Mart discovers that 1 carton of toothpaste is defective. X Mart:

        a.   can accept the defective toothpaste and sue for breach of contract.

b.   can accept the toothpaste and deduct the cost of the defective toothpaste.

c.   can choose either remedy.

d.   must reject the defective goods or pay full price.

24.   Which of the following is an exception to the perfect tender rule?

a.   Commercial impracticability

b.   Destruction of the goods after the risk has passed to the buyer

c.   Substantial performance

d.   Substitution of merchandise

25.   Replevin is an appropriate remedy when:

a.   the seller cannot resell the goods.

b.   the buyer cannot cover.

c.   the seller has shipped defective goods.

d.   the buyer has accepted defective goods.

Answers to Study Questions

Fill-in-the-Blank Questions

Holiday did have the right to cure on November 7th but not on November 15th. The seller has an absolute right to cure before the date performance is due. After the deadline, the seller has the right to cure only if he or she had reason to believe that the substitute goods would be accepted. Hanukkah cards are not an acceptable substitute for Christmas cards. Sam's purchase of substitute goods is cover; reclamation is a seller's remedy.

True-False Questions

1.   T.

2.   F.   Anticipatory repudiation is a party's notice that he or she does not intend to honor the contract.

3.   F.   It is at the seller's place of business.

4.   T.

5.   F.   The contract controls.

6.   T.

7.   T.

8.   F.   Other requirements must be satisfied. This remedy is proper only if the buyer is in possession of the goods or if the risk has passed to the buyer.

9.   T.

10.   F.   The buyer must still pay for the goods.

Multiple-Choice Questions

1.	a		14.	a
2.	b		15.	c
3.	d		16.	a
4.	c		17.	c
5.	c		18.	a
6.	d		19.	c
7.	a		20.	d
8.	b		21.	a
9.	b		22.	d
10.	c		23.	c
11.	d		24.	a
12.	c		25.	b
13.	a			

Warranties and Product Liability

General Principles

A warranty is a promise by a seller. Under the UCC, there are warranties of ownership (title) and warranties of quality. A seller does not have to give a warranty; if the goods are unsuitable, the buyer can sue for breach of contract. Any warranty given may also be disclaimed or canceled. To determine if the plaintiff has a good cause of action, you should ask yourself the following questions:

(1) Was a warranty made?
(2) Was a disclaimer made?
(3) Is the disclaimer proper (effective)?
(4) Was the warranty breached?
(5) Was the breach the proximate cause of the plaintiff's injury?

Product liability is the general term for suits by users or consumers against manufacturers and retailers. In addition to suits for breach of warranty, the plaintiff may also have a suit for negligence or strict liability.

Chapter Summary

I.   Warranties of Title--Relates to ownership rights.

A.   Good Title--This is an implied warranty which attaches automatically to any sale of goods. The seller promises that he or she owns the goods. If the warranty is breached, (i.e. the seller has no title), the true owner can reclaim the goods and the buyer can sue the seller.

B.   No Liens--An implied warranty. Problems may arise with used goods. The seller promises that no one else, usually a creditor, has an interest in the goods. When expensive goods are bought on credit, the seller-creditor usually retains the right to repossess the goods if payment is not made. If the buyer sells the goods to a third party and does not mention the creditor's lien, the warranty is breached. If the original seller decides to repossess, the third party can sue his or her seller, the original buyer. If the original buyer is a merchant and the sale to the third party in the ordinary course of business, the third party (second buyer) is protected.

C.   No Infringement--The seller promises that any goods transferred do not violate copyright, trademark, or patent regulations. If an infringement suit is brought against the buyer, the seller has a right to defend it. The buyer must notify the seller and allow the seller to defend the suit before the buyer can sue for breach of warranty.

D.   Disclaimer--Can be disclaimed only by specific words on the contract. Look for phrases like "only the seller's right, title and interest".

II.   Express Warranties--The elements are:

A.   Oral or written statements by the defendant; model or sample is also sufficient

B.   Statement must be one of fact; puffing or an opinion is insufficient unless the seller is an expert and plaintiff shows reasonable reliance

C.   Statement must be an important factor in the purchase (basis of the bargain)

D.   Product did not perform as promised (breach)

III.   Implied Warranties

A.   Implied Warranty of Merchantability

(1) Seller is a merchant

(2)   Product is not fit for the ordinary purpose for which it is used (breach)

(3)   If defects are obvious, there is no breach

(4)   Proximate cause

B.   Implied Warranty of Fitness for a Particular Purpose - Quality

(1)   Seller does not have to be a merchant

(2)   Seller has reason to known the buyer's particular reason for the purchase

(3)   Buyer relies on the seller's judgment

(4)   Proximate cause

IV.   Other Implied Warranties--A party's course of performance, course of dealing, or trade usage in the industry can give rise to an implied warranty.

V.   Overlapping Warranties--Warranties accumulate unless they are inconsistent with each other; a plaintiff may be able to sue under several theories. When warranties do conflict, the most specific prevails. Express warranties and warranties for a particular purpose override warranties of merchantability. Samples and specifications control rather than general descriptions.

VI.   Buyer's Refusal to Inspect--If the buyer refuses to inspect the goods, any defect which would have been revealed by a reasonable inspection cannot be raised as a breach of warranty. The seller must demand that the buyer inspect the goods.

VII.   Unconscionability--No specific provisions related to warranties, but courts may look at the overall provisions of the contract.

VIII.   Third-Party Beneficiaries (Who Can Sue?)--A breach of contract suit can be brought by a party to the contract. This requirement is "privity of contract". The UCC gives state legislatures three choices. Under one option, family members are covered; in another, anyone who would reasonably be expected to use the product can sue.

IX.   Warranty Disclaimers

A.   Express Warranty--If no statements are made by the seller, no warranty has been made. In addition, most written contracts contain a disclaimer of oral promises. Look for phrases like "all warranties made appear in this writing" or "no other promises have been made."

B.   Implied Warranties

(1)   Implied Warranty of Merchantability--Can be oral or written, but if written, must be conspicuous. A writing is conspicuous if it is different from the rest of the writing; the difference can be in color, case, type, or size. "As is" or "with all faults" is sufficient; otherwise the disclaimer must mention merchantability.

(2)   Implied Warranty of Fitness for a Particular Purpose--Must be conspicuously written. "As is" or "with all faults" is sufficient. Need not mention fitness.

X.   Magnuson-Moss Warranty Act--Consumer protection act enacted by the Congress. Enforced by the Federal Trade Commission, an attorney general, or the consumer. Applies only if a written warranty is given.

A.   Creation--Affects express written warranties where the purchaser is a consumer. If the cost of the item is more than $15, the language of the warranty must be easy to understand and list the name and address of the manufacturer and the specifics of the warranty.

B.   Full v. Limited Warranty--When the cost of the item is more than $10, the warranty must state whether it is "full" or "limited". A full warranty must promise to repair or replace any defective part if it fails and the failure is not the fault of the consumer. If repair is not possible, the consumer can choose a refund or replacement. A limit on consequential damages (which flow from the breach of warranty) must be printed conspicuously. A full warranty need not specify a time limit but if it does, it must be stated. A limited warranty lacks some or all of the provisions of a full warranty.

C.   Effect on UCC Warranties--Although implied warranties are not covered under the Magnuson-Moss Act, if an express warranty is made, a seller cannot disclaim or modify the UCC implied warranties. Sellers can put a time limit on the implied warranties but they must be the same as the time limit of any express warranty.

XI.   Liability Based on Negligence

A.   Elements

(1)   Duty owed by defendant to plaintiff--Assumed in product liability cases.

(2)   Breach of Duty--Plaintiff must show that the defendant was careless. Can be proven by showing improper testing, warnings, product design.

(3)   Cause in Fact--Breach must have been the physical cause of the injury.

(4)   Proximate Cause--Bystanders and non-purchasers can sue if injury to them is foreseeable. Privity of contract is not required.

The advantages of a negligence suit are possibly higher damages and non-purchasers can sue (no privity of contract). The primary disadvantage is the plaintiff must prove that the defendant was careless (breach of duty). No showing of negligence is necessary under breach of warranty.

B.   Misrepresentation

(1)   Seller makes factual statement

      (2)   Statement is false

      (3)   Scienter (Guilty Knowledge)--This element is not required for innocent misrepresentation.

      (4)   Fact was important (basis of the bargain)

      (5)   Reasonable reliance by the plaintiff

      (6)   Injury related to misrepresentation

XI.   Strict Liability

A.   Elements

      (1)   Merchant Seller

      (2)   Product is defective--can be defective due to improper manufacture, improper labeling or inadequate warnings

      (3)   Product is unreasonably dangerous

      (4)   Proximate cause--Defect must be related to the injury

      (5)   Goods must be in the same condition at the time of the sale and at the time of the injury. If a retailer changes the product, manufacturer is not liable. If plaintiff makes changes in the product, neither the manufacturer nor the retailer is liable.

             Advantages to this theory are obvious; non-purchasers can sue (bystanders are specifically covered) and the plaintiff need not prove carelessness. The primary disadvantage is that a product may be defective but may not be unreasonably dangerous.

B.   Defenses

      (1)   Assumption of Risk--Plaintiff knows that the product is defective but voluntarily continues to use it.

      (2)   Product Misuse--Plaintiff uses the product for an unexpected and dangerous use. The misuse must be unforeseeable; if the misuse is foreseeable, the defendant will be liable.

      (3)   Contributory/Comparative Negligence--If the plaintiff is careless, recovery in negligence may be defeated in whole or in part. Although this defense usually does not apply to strict liability, some courts apportion the fault between the plaintiff and the defendant.

C.   <u>Strict Liability to Bystanders</u>--The courts will allow a bystander to sue, if his or her injury was reasonably foreseeable. In other words, this type of plaintiff must satisfy the proximate cause element.

D.   <u>Other Applications of Strict Liability</u>--Manufacturers and retailers are the usual defendants in product liability suits. However, manufacturers of parts and lessors may also be found liable.

Study Questions

Fill-in-the-Blank Questions

Rhonda is shopping for a television set. She talks to a salesman at Video World. She tells him that she needs a set that is "cable-ready". The salesman tells her that she needs Model 21-A. The written sales contract signed by Rhonda describes the set as a Model 21-A and contains the following language in red ink. "This contract contains the only representations by the seller. No other promises have been made." After Rhonda purchases the set, she discovers that the set is not "cable-ready" and that she will have to purchase an expensive adapter from the cable television company.

An express warranty _____ made by the salesman.
                                   (was/was not)

The implied warranty of merchantability _____ breached.
                                                      (was/was not)

The implied warranty of fitness for a particular purpose _____ been disclaimed.
                                                                        (has/has not)

Rhonda can sue for _____.
                        (breach of express warranty/misrepresentation)

True-False Questions

1.   The implied warranty of merchantability can be disclaimed. _____

2.   The Magnuson-Moss Warranty act requires a written warranty if the price of the item is more than $15. _____

3.   The warranty of no infringement is a warranty of quality. _____

4.   The implied warranty of fitness for a particular purpose applies to merchants only. _____

5. Assumption of risk is a defense to negligence but it is not a defense to product liability. _____

6. In a strict liability case, the plaintiff must prove that the product is unreasonably dangerous. _____

7. Privity of contract applies to contract cases, but does not apply to negligence suits. _____

8. An advantage of a negligence suit is that punitive damages may be recovered. _____

9. A limited warranty is warranty which has an outside time limit of one year. _____

10. An express warranty may be made by showing a representative sample to the buyer. _____

Multiple-Choice Questions

1. Mrs. Curtis purchased a "New Woman" home hair-bleaching kit from Serv-U Drug Stores. The saleswoman told her that it would make her hair look "very nice" and the box described the product as "safe for all types of hair." Mrs. Curtis followed the directions on the package. Her hair and scalp were badly burned. In an action against Serv-U for misrepresentation Mrs. Curtis will:

    a. succeed because the saleswoman told Mrs. Curtis that her hair would look "very nice".
    b. succeed because Mrs. Curtis relied on the saleswoman's opinion.
    c. not succeed because the saleswoman's statement was an opinion.
    d. not succeed because Mrs. Curtis's injury was not related to the saleswoman's promise.

2. If Mrs. Curtis sues Serv-U for breach of the implied warranty of merchantability, she will:

    a. succeed because she relied on the saleswoman's statement and Serv-U is a merchant.
    b. succeed because Serv-U is a merchant and the product was not fit for the ordinary purpose of curling hair.
    c. not succeed because Serv-U made no factual representations about the product.
    d. not succeed because Serv-U is not the manufacturer.

3. If Mrs. Curtis sues New Woman for breach of express warranty, she will:

    a. succeed because the writing on the package promised that the product was safe.

b.   succeed because the product was not fit for the ordinary purpose of curling hair.

c.   not succeed because the writing on the package did not constitute an express warranty.

d.   not succeed because there was no breach of the warranty.

4.   If Mrs. Curtis sues New Woman on the theory of strict liability, she will:

a.   succeed if she can prove that New Woman was careless in its testing of home permanents.

b.   succeed if she can prove that the product was unreasonably dangerous.

c.   succeed if she can prove that the statement on the package was a statement of fact.

d.   succeed if she can prove that New Woman knew the reason Mrs. Curtis purchased the product.

5.   If Mrs. Curtis sues New Woman for negligence, she will:

a.   succeed if she can prove that New Woman was careless in its testing of home permanents.

b.   succeed if she can prove that the product was unreasonably dangerous.

c.   succeed if she can prove that the statement on the package was a statement of fact.

d.   succeed if she can prove that New Woman knew the reason Mrs. Curtis purchased the product.

6.   Susan steals Roger's bike and sells it to Sid for $100. When Roger sees Sid with his bike, he demands that Sid return it. Sid refuses. Is Sid within his rights?

a.   Yes, because he did not know the bike was stolen.

b.   Yes, because Roger must sue Susan.

c.   No, because Roger is the true owner and Sid must sue Susan.

d.   No, because Roger is the true owner and Sid has no recourse against Susan.

7.   Susan:

a.   has breached the warranty of good title.

b.   has breached the warranty of merchantability.

c.   has not breached the warranty of good title because the warranty does not apply to used goods.

d.   has not breached the warranty of title because Susan did not tell Sid that the bike was hers.

8.   Mrs. Jones purchased a steam iron for $45 from AAA Appliance. The package inserts gave a description of the iron but made no warranties. The iron malfunctions and Mrs. Jones sues AAA under the Magnuson-Moss Warranty Act. Mrs. Jones will:

a.   succeed because a written warranty is required on all products with a price of $15 or more.
b.   succeed because the act requires AAA to give a refund or replacement.
c.   not succeed because the iron cost less than $50.
d.   not succeed because no warranty was made.

9.   If Mrs. Jones sues AAA, under which theories will she succeed?

a.   Magnuson-Moss Warranty Act and implied warranty of merchantability.
b.   Magnuson-Moss Warranty Act and express warranty.
c.   Express warranty and implied warranty of merchantability.
d.   Implied warranty of merchantability and breach of contract.

10. Crook & Low, Attorneys at Law, purchase a copier from Reproduction Masters, Inc. The salesman tells Mr. Crook that the copier will make 2,000 copies before a new ink cartridge is needed. The sales contract contains the following language: "THE ENTIRE AGREEMENT OF THE PARTIES IS CONTAINED IN THIS WRITING. NO OTHER PROMISES WRITTEN OR ORAL HAVE BEEN MADE. THE SELLER MAKES NO WARRANTIES AS TO THE MERCHANTABILITY OF THIS PRODUCT OR AS TO ITS FITNESS FOR ANY PARTICULAR PURPOSE." Mr. Crook has to purchase a new ink cartridge after 1,000 copies. Which of the following warranties have been disclaimed properly?

a.   Implied warranties of merchantability and fitness for a particular purpose
b.   Express warranty and the implied warranty of merchantability
c.   Express warranty and the implied warranties of merchantability and fitness for a particular purpose
d.   None, disclaimers are illegal

11. If Mr. Crook sues Reproduction Masters, Inc., he will succeed under which of the following theories?

a.   Misrepresentation
b.   Breach of express warranty
c.   Breach of implied warranty of merchantability
d.   Breach of implied warranty of fitness for a particular purpose

12. Tommy is moving to Arizona and holds a garage sale. He sells his refrigerator to Susan. Susan does not know that Tommy has used the refrigerator as security for a loan from E-Z Finance Co. Tommy:

a.   has breached the warranty of no infringements.
b.   has breached the warranty of good title.
c.   has breached the warranty of no liens.
d.   has breached no warranties.

13.   Which of the following statements correctly describes the difference between a suit for strict liability and a suit for breach of implied warranty of merchantability?

    a.   In a suit for strict liability, the plaintiff need not prove that the seller is a merchant.
    b.   In a suit for strict liability, bystanders are always proper parties to sue but in a warranty case, bystanders may not be able to sue.
    c.   In both suits, the plaintiff must prove that the product is unreasonably dangerous.
    d.   In a suit for breach of implied warranty of merchantability, the plaintiff must prove that the seller is negligent.

14.   Mrs. Green purchases a carving knife by mail from A-1 Products. When she uses the knife for the first time, she notices that the blades are loose. She continues to use the knife and is seriously injured while carving a turkey. The evidence at trial shows that the socket for the blades is too shallow. If Mrs. Green sues A-1 for negligence, A-1 could raise which of the following defenses?

    a.   Product misuse and assumption of risk
    b.   Contributory negligence and assumption of risk
    c.   Product misuse and contributory negligence
    d.   Assumption of risk and no breach of duty

15.   Mrs. Smith is shopping for a new washing machine. She tells the salesman that she needs a washing machine with a pump guard because her husband is always leaving coins and paper clips in his pockets. The salesman tells her that she needs to purchase the Deluxe Model because it has a pump guard and not every washer is so equipped. Mrs. Smith purchases the washing machine. The first time she uses it, a dime slips into the motor and ruins the machine. Mrs. Smith then discovers that the washer has no pump guard and decides to sue the seller. On which of the following theories will Mrs. Smith succeed?

    a.   Breach of express warranty only
    b.   Breach of express warranty and breach of implied warranty of merchantability
    c.   Breach of express warranty and breach of implied warranty of fitness for a particular purpose
    d.   Breach of express warranty and breach of both implied warranties

16.   Same facts as above but Mrs. Smith purchases a washer from her neighbor, Flo. Assume that Flo made the same statements as the salesman. On which of the following theories will Mrs. Smith succeed?

    a.   Breach of express warranty only
    b.   Breach of express warranty and breach of implied warranty of merchantability

c.   Breach of express warranty and breach of implied warranty of fitness for a particular purpose

d.   Breach of express warranty and breach of both implied warranties

17.   Ron purchases a new watch from Clockex, Inc. for $75. The package contains the following statement.   "THE SELLER WARRANTS THAT THIS PRODUCT IS FREE FROM DEFECTS. IF THIS PRODUCT FAILS TO FUNCTION PROPERLY, THE MANUFACTURER AGREES TO REPLACE OR REPAIR THE PRODUCT AT NO COST TO THE CONSUMER FOR A PERIOD OF ONE (1) YEAR. THIS WARRANTY DOES NOT APPLY TO MALFUNCTION CAUSED BY ABUSE BY THE PURCHASER."

a.   The Magnuson-Moss Warranty applies and the warranty is satisfactory as written.

b.   The Magnuson-Moss Warranty does not apply but the warranty must be labeled as "full" or "limited".

c.   The Magnuson-Moss Warranty applies but the warranty must be labeled as "full" or "limited".

d.   The Magnuson-Moss Warranty does not apply.

18.   Which of the following are proper plaintiffs (can sue) under the Magnuson-Moss Warranty Act?

a.   Federal Trade Commission only

b.   Federal Trade Commission and a state's attorney general only

c.   Federal Trade Commission and the consumer only

d.   Federal Trade Commission, a state's attorney general and the consumer

19.   Mr. Roberts purchases a stuffed bear manufactured by Unbearably Unique. The bear's eyes are made of small bits of hard plastic. A warning on the package states, "Not suitable for children under six years." Mr. Roberts gives the toy to his three year-old son, who chews on the toy, swallows one of the eyes and is severely injured. Mr. Roberts sues Unbearable on a strict liability theory. Unbearable raises the defense of product misuse.

a.   Unbearably will succeed on the product misuse theory only if it can prove that it was unforeseeable that the toy would have been given to a child under six years.

b.   Unbearably will succeed on the product misuse theory because a warning was given.

c.   Unbearably will succeed because the product was not defective.

d.   Unbearably will succeed because the proximate cause element was not satisfied.

20.   Cure-All Pharmaceuticals manufactures "Sneez-Away", a cold remedy. The package insert mentions that the product can cause drowsiness but does not mention that it should not be taken with aspirin. Mrs. Miller purchases a bottle of "Sneez-Away" and takes it with aspirin. She breaks out in hives and

suffers from blurred vision. If Mrs. Miller sues Cure-All for negligence and strict liability, she will:

a.   succeed on the strict liability theory only because Cure-All was not negligent.
b.   succeed on the negligence theory only because the product was not unreasonably dangerous.
c.   succeed on either theory.
d.   not succeed on either theory.

21.   Ron purchased a new saw from Abe's Hardware. Abe tells Ron that he has used a similar saw but that he can't vouch for its merchantability. Which of the following warranties have been disclaimed properly?

a.   Implied warranty of fitness for a particular purpose only
b.   Implied warranty of merchantability only
c.   Both implied warranties have been disclaimed
d.   Neither warranty has been disclaimed

22.   Which of the following is not a warranty of quality?

a.   Implied warranty of merchantability
b.   Implied warranty of fitness for a particular purpose
c.   Express warranty
d.   Warranty of no infringement

23.   Which of the following is not required for a suit in strict liability?

a.   Seller is a merchant
b.   Proximate cause
c.   A promise by the seller
d.   Defective product

24.   For which of the following is proximate cause not required?

a.   Negligence
b.   Strict liability
c.   Misrepresentation
d.   Breach of express warranty

25.   Mary purchases a leash from Pet Emporium. She tells the salesman that she needs a leash which will be suitable for a Great Dane. The salesman, who honestly believes that a metal leash will be sufficient, sells her the top of the line metal leash. Mary's Great Dane snaps the leash on his first walk. On which theories will Mary be successful?

a.   Fraudulent misrepresentation and breach of warranty of fitness for a particular purpose
b.   Breach of implied warranty of merchantability and breach of implied

<ul>
<li>warranty of fitness for a particular purpose</li>
</ul>

c.   Breach of express warranty and breach of implied warranty of fitness for a particular purpose

d.   Breach of express warranty and fraudulent misrepresentation

Answers to Study Questions

Fill-in-the-Blank Questions

The salesman did make an express warranty when he told Rhonda that she needed to buy Model 21-A because he was stating that Model 21-A was cable-ready. The implied warranty of merchantability has <u>not</u> been breached because the television functions properly. The implied warranty of fitness for a particular purpose has been disclaimed. The writing in red type is conspicuous. Rhonda can sue for misrepresentation. She cannot sue for breach of express warranty because the express warranty made by the salesman was disclaimed.

True-False Questions

1.   T.

2.   F.   The Magnuson-Moss Act does not require the seller to make a written warranty, but if a written warranty is made, certain disclosures are required.

3.   F.   It is a warranty of title.

4.   F.   It applies to any seller.

5.   F.   It is a defense to both.

6.   T.

7.   T.

8.   T.

9.   F.   A limited warranty is one which promises less than free replacement or repair. The time element is irrelevant.

10.   T.

Multiple-Choice Questions

1.	c		14.	b
2.	b		15.	c
3.	a		16.	c
4.	b		17.	c
5.	a		18.	d
6.	c		19.	a
7.	a		20.	c
8.	d		21.	b
9.	d		22.	d
10.	c		23.	c
11.	a		24.	c
12.	c		25.	c
13.	b			

CHAPTER
18

Commerical Paper--
Introduction
Negotiability, and
Transferability

General Principles

In order for checks and other commercial paper to be an acceptable substitute for money, banks and merchants must be willing to accept them. The law of negotiable instruments outlined in the UCC is designed to lessen the risks associated with commercial paper. As you review, remember that the requirements of negotiability are designed to reduce these risks.

A negotiable instrument is transferred by indorsement and/or delivery. An indorser may incur liability and some forms of indorsement lessen liability and the risk of transfer.

Commercial paper is any instrument that operates as a substitute for money. Checks and notes are the most common examples of commercial paper. You may write a check instead of paying cash. In order for commercial paper to be an acceptable substitute for money, its transfer must be relatively risk-free. People who receive a check or note must have some protection against forgery, alteration, and other problems. This concept is essential to an understanding of the subject and is the basis for the rules outlined in the articles 3 and 4 of the Uniform Commercial Code.

When you read the following chapters, it may help to think of the process of writing and cashing a check. The check may pass through several banks before it is finally paid.

Chapter Summary

I.   The Functions of Commercial Paper

A. Definition--Commercial paper is a written promise or order to pay a sum of money. A promissory note is an example of a promise to pay; a check is an example of an order to pay.

B. Purpose--Commercial paper is a convenient alternative to cash. A secondary function of commercial paper is to lend money. A ninety-day promissory note allows the borrower to use someone else's money for ninety days.

II. Types of Commercial Paper--There are four basic forms of commercial paper or instruments.

A. Drafts and Checks--Drafts and checks are orders from one person (a drawer) to another person (the drawee). The order is to pay money to a third person (the payee). There are always three parties involved. For example, if you write a check to the grocery store for milk, you would be the drawer and the store would be the payee. Your bank is the drawee. By writing the check, you are telling the bank to pay money from your account to the store.

(1) Draft--A draft is an unconditional order to pay money. It may be payable on a certain date (time draft) or when it is presented to the drawee (sight draft).

A trade acceptance is a special kind of draft used by a buyer and seller. The seller is both the drawer (who orders payment) and the payee. The order is directed to the buyer, who is the drawee. When the buyer agrees to pay the trade acceptance, he signs his name. The seller can then sell the trade acceptance to a bank for immediate cash.

(2) Check--A check is a special type of draft, which is payable on demand. The drawee of a check is always a bank.

B. Promissory Notes and CD's--Promissory notes and certificates of deposit (CD's) involve two parties: the maker, who promises to pay money, and a payee, who receives the money.

(1) Note--The maker borrows the money and the promise is to repay the payee. Sometimes the payee may demand property as security to make certain that the maker will pay. If the security is real estate, the note is a mortgage note; if the security is personal property, the note is a collateral note.

(2) CD--A CD is a written acknowledgement of receipt of funds and a promise to repay the money. The bank (maker) receives money from a customer (payee) and promises to repay the money with interest at a later date.

III.   Letter of Credit--A letter of credit is <u>not</u> a type of commercial paper; it is a financing arrangement using a note and a draft. The three parties are the buyer, the seller, and the buyer's bank. The buyer makes a note to his bank; his bank issues a letter of credit, which promises to pay any draft ordered by the buyer. The seller presents the draft and any supporting documents to the buyer's bank for payment. The seller is assured of payment and the buyer can receive his goods immediately.

IV.   Other Ways of Classifying Commercial Paper--All types of commercial paper fall into the categories listed below. Each category has two options; an instrument must fall under one of these options.

A.   Demand v. Time Instruments--An instrument is either payable at a certain time, or it is payable when presented to someone for payment (on demand). Drafts can be either time or demand instruments; a check is always a demand instrument. A sight draft is payable when presented and is a demand instrument.

B.   Order to Pay v. Promise to Pay--Checks and drafts are orders to pay; notes and CD's are promises to pay.

C.   Negotiable v. Nonnegotiable--A negotiable instrument must meet all of the requirements listed in the following sections. If one element is missing, the instrument is not negotiable. This classification is important because different laws apply to negotiable and non-negotiable instruments. A negotiable instrument is governed by the rules of Article 3 of the UCC. A nonnegotiable instrument is governed by the rules of general contract law.

V.   What Is a Negotiable Instrument?--These rules apply only to the face or front of the instrument and when it is first issued.

A.   Writing--A negotiable instrument must be in writing on a permanent and easily transferable substance.

B.   Signature--A negotiable instrument must be signed by the maker or the drawer. It does not have to be signed by the drawee or payee. Any writing that is intended as a signature, such as a rubber stamp, is acceptable. The signature may appear anywhere on the document.

D.   Promise or Order to Pay--A negotiable instrument must contain an affirmative order or promise to pay. For this reason, an I.O.U., which merely acknowledges a debt, but does not promise to repay it, is insufficient and is not negotiable.

D.   The Promise or Order Must Be Unconditional--A negotiable instrument must promise or order absolute payment. If payment is conditioned on the occurrence of an outside event or on the provisions of another document, the instrument is nonnegotiable.   A memorandum or reference to an outside document will not destroy negotiability unless payment is conditioned on or made "subject to" the terms of that document. A "memo" line on a check, which shows the reason for payment, is valid.

E.   Sum Certain in Money--A negotiable instrument must specify an exact amount of money to be paid or the amount must be easily calculated from the face of the instrument. An instrument which carries a stated rate of interest or specifies monthly payments is satisfactory. An instrument payable at the prime rate or other variable rate is not negotiable. An instrument which is payable at the "judgment" or "legal" rate is negotiable.

A negotiable instrument must also be payable in money or currency. If an instrument were payable in goods or services, the value of those goods or services, and the value of the instrument could vary from day to day. Payment in currency of another country is allowed.

F.   Payable on Demand or at a Definite Time--A negotiable instrument must be payable at a definite time, a time that can be calculated from the face of the instrument, or payable when presented to the drawee or maker (payable on demand or on sight).

Many notes contain acceleration or extension clauses. An acceleration clause allows the holder to call the note due if a payment is late. A note with an acceleration clause is negotiable. An extension clause extends time for payment. If the maker or drawer has the option to extend, the extension must be for a stated period of time. If the holder has the option to extend, a definite period of time need not be specified.

G.   Payable to Order or to Bearer--A negotiable instrument must be payable to the order of a specified person (order paper) or payable to anyone with possession (bearer paper). A check payable to "the order of John Jones" is order paper; a check payable to "cash" is a bearer instrument. An order instrument can name more than one payee or designate the payee by title so long as the payee can be identified with certainty.

VI.   Factors Not Affecting Negotiability--If an instrument meets all of the requirements listed above, it is negotiable. Questions sometimes arise in the situations listed below but these details do not determine whether or not the instrument is negotiable.

A.   Date--Not required unless a date is necessary to determine a time for payment. For example, a time draft, payable 30 days from the date it is issued must contain a date; a check need not.

An instrument may be payable before the date on which it is issued (antedated) or after the date on which it is issued (postdated).

B. Conflict in Terms--The most specific terms control because they are better indications of the true intent of the parties. Therefore, typewritten terms outweigh printed terms and handwritten terms outweigh both.

If there is a conflict in the amount payable because the numerals and the words do not match, the words control, unless the words in and of themselves are ambiguous.

C. Interest Rates--An interest rate can affect the amount to be paid and therefore, the "sum certain" requirement. To avoid problems, if the instrument does not specify an interest rate, the judgment rate of interest applies.

VII. Transfer by Assignment and Negotiation--Initial determination is made by determining if the instrument is negotiable. The person with possession of the instrument is going to transfer his rights to another party. Negotiability determines which rights will be transferred.

A. Assignment--The assignee or transferee only receives the rights that his transferor had. This is crucial because any defense against payment that was good against the transferor will also be good against the assignee.

B. Negotiable--If the instrument is transferred properly, the transferee becomes a holder. Under the rules of commercial paper, a holder can receive more rights than the transferor. This type of transferee is a holder in due course. The rules for proper transfer depend on the status of the instrument.

(1) Negotiating Order Paper--Order paper names a specific payee or indorsee. In order to transfer order paper, the party named must sign and voluntarily deliver to the holder.

(2) Negotiating Bearer Paper--Bearer paper does not name a specific payee and can be transferred without indorsement; voluntary delivery is the only requirement.

(3) The status of an instrument can be changed from order paper to bearer paper and vice versa, by naming or not naming a specific transferee.

VIII. Indorsements--An indorsement is a signature found usually on the back of an instrument. In commercial paper, a signature implies liability. Some indorsements lessen the risk of transfer by placing conditions on the transfer.

All indorsements have the following characteristics: blank or special, qualified or unqualified, and restrictive or unrestricted.

A.   Blank or Special Indorsement--A blank indorsement is simply the signature of the payee or an indorser.

An indorser can cause the instrument to become order or bearer paper depending on the type of indorsement. A blank indorsement causes the instrument to be bearer paper and anyone with possession of the instrument can transfer it. A special indorsement contains the signature of the indorser and the name of the indorsee. A special indorsement causes the instrument to be order paper and only the indorsee can transfer or cash it.

B.   Qualified or Unqualified Indorsement--A qualified indorsement, denoted by the words "without recourse", limits to some extent the liability of the signer. An unqualified indorsement does not contain these words.

C.   Restrictive or Unrestricted Indorsement--A restrictive indorsement gives directions to the indorsee regarding further transfer of the instrument.   The indorsee must follow these instructions.   An unrestricted indorsement contains no special instructions.

1.   Conditional Indorsement--An indorsement may condition payment on the happening of a specific event. A holder who receives the instrument after the condition has been imposed has no right to payment until the condition is satisfied. (An exception applies to intermediary banks who receive the instrument as it is being processed for collection.) If the condition is on the face of the instrument, the instrument is nonnegotiable.

2.   Indorsements for deposit or collection--An indorsement which contains the words "for deposit only" is commonly used when an instrument is transferred from a customer to his bank. This indorsement does not prohibit further transfer but the immediate transferee (usually the payee's bank) must obey the instructions and transfer the money to the depositor's account. "Pay any bank" is a collection indorsement used between banks.

3.   Agency or Trust Indorsement--This indorsement is made by an agent or a trustee acting on behalf of a third person.

D.   Unauthorized Signatures--An unauthorized signature is one made without the permission of the person whose name was used. A negotiable instrument may pass through several owners or holders and an unauthorized signature may not be detected until the instrument is presented for payment. At that time, if the guilty party cannot be found, someone must absorb the loss. The general rule is that the person who was in the best position to notice or to prevent the wrongdoing is responsible.

Forged Indorsement--Liability usually rests on the party who took the instrument directly from the forger. Two exceptions to this rule are the "fictitious payee" and the "imposter" rules.

E.   Imposter--The wrongdoer poses as another and induces the maker or drawer to make an instrument payable to name used by the imposter. The imposter forges the "payee's" indorsement but again, it was the drawer or maker who could have determined the scheme most easily and therefore the maker or drawer will be responsible.

F.   "Fictitious Payee"--An employee "pads the payroll" with a fake payee. The dishonest employee then forges the name of the phony payee, indorses the instrument to himself and collects the cash. Although the "payee's" indorsement has been forged, the drawer was in the best position to spot the wrongdoing. The drawer could have supervised his employee or determined that the payee did exist.

G.   Correction of Name--Sometimes the name of the indorsee or payee is misspelled. The misspelling does not affect the negotiability of an instrument. An indorsement is effective whether the correct or incorrect spelling is used.

Study Questions

Fill-in-the-Blank Questions

> July 3, 1990
>
> Thirty days from date, I, _____,
> promise to pay County Bank the sum of $1,000.
> The maker reserves the right to extend the due
> date until September 3, 1990. This agreement
> is subject to the terms of a sales contract
> between the maker and Artie's Antiques.

This instrument is a _____   _____.
                   (draft, note, check, CD)

It is _____ .
(negotiable/nonnegotiable)

Wilma's signature is _____ .
(valid/invalid)

Wilma's promise to pay is _____ .
(conditional/unconditional)

The maker's right to pay on September 3 is an _____
clause.   (extension/acceleration)

August 1, 1990

60 days from date, pay to the order of B. Law
Teacher the sum of $1,000.

_____

To: C. Student, Sr.

This instrument is a _____ .
B. Law Teacher is the _____ .
C. Student, Sr. is the _____ .
C. Student, Jr. is the _____ .

April 2, 1991

On December 2, 1991 I promise to pay B. Law
Teacher the sum of $500.

_____

This instrument is a _____ .
B. Law Teacher is the _____ .
B. Student is the _____ .

True-False Questions

1.   A note payable "on the death of my uncle John" is not negotiable. _____

2.   An instrument indorsed "for deposit only" is an example of an instrument with a conditional indorsement. _____

3.   A note is nonnegotiable if it is payable to Bob and Mary Lamb. _____

4.   "Pay any bank" followed by the indorsee's signature is a restrictive indorsement. _____

5.   "Pay to the order of Cindy" followed by the indorsee's signature is a special, unrestricted, unconditional indorsement. _____

6.   John steals a check payable to bearer. John is a holder of the check. _____

7.   A draft ordering payment of 3,000 French francs is negotiable in the United States. _____

8.   A nonnegotiable note can be assigned but it cannot be negotiated. _____

9.   A check written on a paper napkin is nonnegotiable. _____

10.   The maker of a certificate of deposit is a bank or other financial institution. _____

11.   A draft has two original parties. _____

12.   All checks are drafts but not all drafts are checks. _____

13.   The drawee of a check is a bank. _____

14.   A payee of a check becomes an indorser when he or she signs the back of the instrument. _____

15.   The drawee of a trade acceptance is usually a seller of goods. _____

16.   A letter of credit is a form of commercial paper. _____

17.   Mary finds a signed check for $200. The space for the payee's name is left blank. Mary is a holder of the check. _____

Multiple-Choice Questions

Use the following facts to answer questions 1-5.

Edna indorses her paycheck with her name only and gives it to her landlord as payment for her rent. The landlord signs his name on the back of the check and writes "for deposit only, Acme Apartments, by Leonard Landlord, manager."

1.   The landlord:

    a.   is a holder of the check.
    b.   is not a holder of the check.
    c.   is an indorsee.
    d.   is the drawee.

2.   The landlord's indorsement:

    a.   is unrestricted and blank.
    b.   is unrestricted and special.
    c.   is restrictive and blank.
    d.   is restrictive and special.

3.   The check:

    a.   is order paper when Edna's employer issues it.
    b.   is bearer paper after the landlord indorses it.
    c.   is order paper after Edna indorses it.
    d.   is bearer paper when Edna's employer issues it.

4.   Edna's indorsement:

    a.   is blank and restrictive.
    b.   is special and restrictive.
    c.   is blank and conditional.
    d.   is blank and unconditional.

5.   Paul writes a check for $45.00 payable to the order of Ron's Repair service. The face of the check states that it is payable only if Paul's TV works properly. The check:

    a.   is nonnegotiable because it is not payable at a definite time.
    b.   is nonnegotiable because it does not state an exact sum of money to be paid.
    c.   is nonnegotiable because it contains a conditional order.
    d.   is negotiable.

6.   Sally receives a birthday check from her aunt Linda. Sally signs her name on the back of the check and cashes it at her aunt's bank. Sally's indorsement is:

a.   blank, restrictive, and unconditional.
b.   special, restrictive, and unconditional.
c.   special, unrestricted, and unconditional.
d.   blank, unrestricted, and unconditional.

7.   Which of the following is (are) holder(s) of the instrument?

a.   Sally
b.   The bank
c.   Both Sally and the bank
d.   Sally, Sally's aunt and the bank

8.   On March 23, 1990, Michael makes a note which is payable to First State Bank in forty-eight monthly installments of $100.00. The note contains a clause which allows the bank to collect the entire amount immediately if Michael misses a payment. The note:

a.   is nonnegotiable because it is not payable at a definite date.
b.   is nonnegotiable because it fails to state a certain sum of money.
c.   is nonnegotiable because it fails to name a payee.
d.   is negotiable.

9.   The clause which allows the bank to collect the entire amount immediately is:

a.   an extension clause.
b.   an acceleration clause.
c.   a conditional indorsement.
d.   a restrictive indorsement.

10.   Ralph, posing as Mr. Brown, a high school bank director, receives a donation check from Mrs. Black, a new teacher. Ralph cashes the check and disappears. When the scheme is discovered, who will be responsible?

a.   Mr. Brown
b.   Mrs. Black
c.   The bank which cashed the check
d.   The high school bank

11.   Nancy writes a check to Sam's Supermarket in payment for groceries. She writes "weekly groceries" on the memo line of the check. Sam turns the check over and writes "Payable to Wanda's Wholesalers, if a shipment of oranges is received by next week" and signs his name. Sam's indorsement is:

a.   special, restrictive and conditional.
b.   special, unrestricted and conditional.
c.   special, restrictive and unconditional.
d.   blank, unrestricted and conditional.

12.   The check:

    a.   is nonnegotiable because of the notation on the memo line.
    b.   is nonnegotiable because of Sam's indorsement.
    c.   is nonnegotiable because the check is not payable at a definite time.
    d.   is negotiable.

13.   Donna writes a check payable to the order of "Cash." The check:

    a.   is a negotiable order instrument.
    b.   is a negotiable bearer instrument.
    c.   is a nonnegotiable order instrument.
    d.   is a nonnegotiable bearer instrument.

14.   Anita, a legal secretary, asks her employer to write a check payable to Ozzie's Office Supplies, Inc. as payment for typewriter ribbons. In fact, Anita did not buy ribbons from Ozzie. Anita forges Ozzie's signature and cashes the check at First Bank. If Anita cannot be found, who will be responsible?

    a.   Anita's employer
    b.   Ozzies's Office Supplies
    c.   First Bank
    d.   None of the above

15.   Harold signs a note payable to Second State Bank to purchase a new car. The note, payable in twenty-four monthly installments of $300.00, states that Harold has also signed a security agreement and if Harold does not pay, the bank has the right to repossess the car. The note:

    a.   is nonnegotiable because it contains a conditional promise.
    b.   is nonnegotiable because it fails to state a sum certain.
    c.   is nonnegotiable because it fails to name a payee.
    d.   is negotiable.

16.   Cathy issues a draft payable to Felicia. On the back of the draft, Felicia writes "payable to Mona," signs her name, and gives it to Mona. In Mona's possession,

    a.   the draft is order paper and Mona must indorse it before she can negotiate it.
    b.   the draft is order paper and Mona can negotiate it by delivery alone.
    c.   the draft is bearer paper and Mona can negotiate it by delivery alone.
    d.   the draft is bearer paper and Mona must indorse it before she can negotiate it.

17.   Jim makes a note payable to Second National Bank. The note contains the following clause: "The maker or the holder retains the right to extend the time for payment indefinitely." The note;

a.   is nonnegotiable because Second National Bank has the right to extend payment for an unspecified time.
b.   is nonnegotiable because Jim has the right to extend payment for an unspecified time.
c.   is nonnegotiable because a maker never has the right to extend the time for payment.
d.   is negotiable.

18.   Which of the following clauses in a draft would make it nonnegotiable?

a.   The draft is payable to Sally and Sid Morrow
b.   The draft is payable when delivered to the drawee for payment but no other date is specified
c.   The draft is payable in dollars, German marks or diamonds
d.   None of the clauses would destroy negotiability

19.   Fine Fashions accepts a check from Harriet Housewife as payment for a dress. Sylvia, the president of Fine Fashions, indorses the check and writes "payable to Rodney's Real Estate, without recourse." Sylvia's indorsement is:

a.   is conditional, qualified and special.
b.   is unconditional, qualified and special.
c.   is conditional, qualified and blank.
d.   is unconditional, unqualified and blank.

20.   Roger paints Donna's house and receives a check from Donna in the amount of $2300.00 as payment for his services. Roger writes "Pay to Helen Smith" and signs his name. Roger loses the check and Vinnie finds it. Vinnie forges Helen's name and cashes the check at Helen's bank. Helen's bank transfers the check to Donna's bank, which pays the check and takes the money from Donna's account. Who will be ultimately responsible for payment of the check if Vinnie cannot be found?

a.   Roger
b.   Helen's bank
c.   Donna's bank
d.   Donna

21.   Roger's indorsement:

a.   is special and unqualified.
b.   is blank and unqualified.
c.   is special and restrictive.
d.   is special and conditional.

22.   On January 13, 1988, Valerie borrows $10,000 from County Bank in order to buy a new car. The note states that it is payable in thirty-six monthly installments at an interest rate of thirteen percent per year. The note:

a.   is nonnegotiable because the amount of each monthly payment is not specified.

b.   is nonnegotiable because the note does not promise to pay an exact sum of money.

c.   is nonnegotiable because it is not payable at a specific time.

d.   is negotiable.

23.   Sally Student signs a note to borrow money in order to buy a new car. Sally is:

a.   the drawee.
b.   the maker.
c.   the accommodation party.
d.   the indorsee.

24.   Bob writes a check to Gary's Grocery to pay for mushroom soup. Gary indorses the check. Gary is:

a.   the payee.
b.   the indorser.
c.   neither the payee nor the indorser.
d.   both the payee and the indorser.

25.   Bob is:

a.   the drawee.
b.   the drawer.
c.   the indorser.
d.   the indorsee.

26.   Sam writes a check for $75.00 to Tom's TV Repair. Tom goes to Sam's bank, indorses the check, and delivers it to the bank. The bank gives Tom $75.00 cash. The bank becomes an acceptor of the check when:

a.   Sam writes the check.
b.   Tom accepts the check.
c.   Tom indorses the check.
d.   Sam's bank cashes the check.

27.   Sam's bank is:

a.   the drawee.
b.   the indorser.
c.   the drawer.
d.   the payee.

28.   Connie borrows money from First Bank in order to buy a computer. The instrument Connie will sign is a:

  a.   CD.
  b.   note.
  c.   draft.
  d.   trade acceptance.

29.   First Bank is the:

  a.   maker.
  b.   payee.
  c.   drawer.
  d.   drawee.

Answers to Study Questions

Fill-in-the-Blank Questions

The first instrument is a note. It is nonnegotiable. Wilma's signature is valid; the signature can appear anywhere on the document. Wilma's promise to pay is conditional because it is subject to the terms of the sales contract. The maker's right to pay on September 3 is an extension clause.

The second instrument is a draft; an order to pay but the drawee is not a bank. B. Law Teacher is the payee. C. Student, Sr. is the drawee. C. Student, Jr. is the drawer.

The third instrument is a note. B. Law Teacher is the payee. B. Student is the maker.

True-False Questions

1.   T.

2.   F.   It is an example of a restrictive indorsement.

3.   F.   A negotiable instrument may be payable to 2 or more payees.

4.   T.

5.   T.

6.   F.   John is not a holder because the transfer was not voluntary.

7.   T.

8.   T.

9.   F.   It is negotiable because it is in writing on a portable and permanent

substance. However, it is probably not very marketable.

10.   T.

11.   F. It has three original parties.

12.   T.

13.   T.

14.   T.

15.   F. The buyer is a drawee; the seller is the payee and drawer.

16.   F. It is a financing arrangement consisting of a note and a draft.

17.   T.

Multiple-Choice Questions

1.	a	11.	a	21.	a
2.	d	12.	d	22.	d
3.	a	13.	b	23.	b
4.	d	14.	a	24.	d
5.	c	15.	d	25.	b
6.	d	16.	a	26.	d
7.	c	17.	b	27.	a
8.	d	18.	c	28.	b
9.	b	19.	b	29.	b
10.	b	20.	b		

Commericial Paper--Holder in Due Course, Liability, and Defenses

General Principles

This chapter discusses the obligations of parties if a dispute arises concerning payment of a negotiable instrument. If payment of the instrument is refused, the holder can sue the maker or drawer of the instrument or he or she can sue the chain of people who transferred the instrument (payee and indorsers). The holder's success depends on four factors:

1. Is the person seeking payment as holder in due course or merely a holder?

2. Has the defendant (indorser) signed the instrument?

3. Has the defendant (indorser) breached warranties made when he or she transferred the instrument or presented it for payment?

4. Does the maker or drawer have a valid defense against payment?

Remember that the lawsuit will focus on the transfer of the instrument and not on the underlying contract. The UCC attempts to shift liability back to the person who was in the best position to prevent the wrongdoing.

Chapter Summary

I.   Holder v. Holder in Due Course

  A.   Holder--A holder is a person in possession of an instrument who is entitled to payment. If the instrument is order paper, a holder is the payee or an indorsee. If the instrument is bearer paper, a holder is anyone with legal possession of the instrument.

B.   Holder in Due Course (HDC)--A holder in due course is a holder who also meets the following requirements: 1) he or she must have paid value in exchange for the instrument; 2) he or she must have acted honestly with regard to the instrument; and 3) he or she must receive the instrument without knowledge of a defect in the instrument or its transfer.

C.   Difference in Status--When a maker or drawer refuses to pay or honor an instrument, litigation results. An HDC will be entitled to payment regardless of most problems or defenses claimed by the maker or drawer. A holder does not enjoy the same protection. He or she has to defend against all claims and defenses of other parties. A holder is in the same position as an assignee of a contract; he or she can have no more rights than the person who transferred the instrument.

II.   Requirements for HDC Status--An HDC must meet all of the following tests in order to quality for protected status.

A.   Value--An HDC must give value in exchange for the instrument. Value can be money, services performed or another negotiable instrument. A bank can give value by clearing the instrument. A holder can also give value by taking an instrument in payment of a previous debt owed to him or her or taking an instrument as collateral for payment of a prior or current debt owed him or her. A promise to perform in the future is not good value. Partial value is acceptable but the holder is an HDC only to the extent that actual value has been received.

B.   Good Faith--An HDC must act honestly. It does not matter that he received the instrument from a wrongdoer.

C.   Without Notice--An HDC must receive the instrument without notice of any defect in the instrument. Some defects such as crude forgeries, alterations and overdue payments are obvious. The test is whether a reasonable person would have been put on notice and would have investigated the irregularity.

D.   Payee as HDC--Can qualify if meets the above requirements.

III.   Holder Through a Holder in Due Course (Shelter Principle)--A holder who does not qualify as an HDC may still receive protected status if a previous holder is an HDC. However, a holder cannot receive HDC status if he recycles or launders the instrument through an HDC.

IV.   Signature Liability--A holder who indorses an instrument impliedly promises to pay the instrument when it comes due. This obligation is extremely important because a holder seeking payment can sue previous indorsers as well as the maker or drawer. An indorser who signs "without recourse" has no signature liability although he or she may have warranty liability.

    A.   Signature--A signature is any symbol used to validate a writing. It need not be handwritten.

    B.   Authority to Sign (Agents' Signatures)--A party is only responsible for a signature if he or she authorizes it or ratifies it after the fact. An agent will be personally liable for a signature only if it fails to show agency status or a named principal. Parol evidence may be admitted to show authorization if the signature shows an agency but fails to name a principal or if two names are shown but it is unclear which party is the principal.

    C.   Primary Liability--Absolutely and immediately liable. A maker and an acceptor are primarily and absolutely liable. The only exception to the maker's liability is a real defense (discussed below). A drawee has no liability to a holder requesting payment until he or she accepts the instrument. Some instruments require the holder to present the instrument to the acceptor before payment is due.

    D.   Secondary Liability--All other parties to an instrument are secondarily liable and will be required to pay only if the drawee or maker refuses to do so. A drawer of a check must pay unless his bank has become insolvent.

    E.   Presentment--A holder requesting payment of an instrument must follow the steps outlined below.

        (1)   Proper Presentment--If not presented to the correct party or if presented late, an indorser's liability may be discharged. Checks and drafts are presented to the drawee for payment; CDs and notes are presented to makers. Presentment can be made in person, by mail, or by sending the instrument through a clearing system (e.g. depositing a check). Instruments must be presented on the date specified or, if no date is specified, within a reasonable time.

        (2)   Proper Notice--Notice must be given to an indorser or other secondary party if the primary party refuses to pay. Notice may be made in any reasonable manner. Notice deadlines vary on the status of the indorser. If the recipient or party giving notice is a bank, notice must be given by midnight of the next banking day after receipt. Other parties have until midnight of the third banking day after receipt.

(3)   <u>Accommodation Party</u>--An accommodation party is anyone who signs an instrument in order to let his name be used as security for payment. An accommodation party is liable in the capacity under which he or she signed. That is, an accommodation maker is primarily liable; an accommodation indorser is secondarily liable.

V.   <u>Warranty Liability</u>--A party to a negotiable instrument may also be liable on the basis of implied warranties made by transferring the instrument. A transfer warranty is made <u>by</u> a holder <u>to</u> another holder. A presentment warranty is made <u>by</u> a holder <u>to</u> a party responsible for payment such as a maker, drawer, or drawee.

A.   <u>Transfer Warranties</u>--A holder promises that:

1.   he or she has good title to the instrument.

2.   all signatures are authorized or genuine (no forgeries).

3.   the instrument has not been materially altered.

4.   no party has a defense against payment to the holder.

5.   if an instrument has been refused, the holder does not know that the maker, drawer or acceptor is bankrupt.

Generally, these warranties operate to protect anyone who takes the instrument after the holder. If the holder has not indorsed the instrument, he or she makes the promises only to the party next in line (his immediate transferee). An indorser who signs "without recourse" changes the fourth warranty. The promise is only that the holder has <u>no knowledge</u> of a defense.

B.   <u>Presentment Warranties</u>--A holder presenting the instrument for final payment, as opposed to a simple transfer, promises that:

1.   he or she has good title to the instrument.

2.   he or she has no knowledge that the signature of the <u>maker or drawer</u> is unauthorized.

3.   The instrument has not been materially altered.

If an HDC is presenting the instrument to the maker or drawer, he or she does not make the second and third promises because the maker or drawer should recognize his own signature and the instrument.

VI.   Defenses to Payment--If the maker or drawer of the instrument is sued, the holder must determine if there is a valid defense against payment. At this point, the status of the holder becomes very important. A limited number of real defenses are good against an HDC. Other, more common, personal defenses are good against a holder but not against a holder in due course.

A.   Real Defenses--Forgery, material alteration, fraud in the execution, discharge of the debt in bankruptcy, minority, extreme duress, illegality, or mental incapacity that causes the instrument to be void.

B.   Personal Defenses--Breach of contract, payment, fraud in the inducement, unauthorized completion of the instrument, mental incapacity or illegality that causes the instrument to be voidable.

C.   FTC Rule--The FTC Rule was issued by the Federal Trade Commission after the UCC went into effect. The FTC Rule applies to consumer credit transactions only. In these cases, an HDC is not protected because anyone who buys a consumer note is subject to all defenses (real and personal) of the maker.

VII.   Discharge--Discharge is a broad term that covers all release of liability on an instrument. Discharge normally occurs when the instrument is finally paid and taken out of circulation. Discharge can also occur if the instrument has been materially altered. If a party reacquires an instrument, everyone between the first and second possessions is automatically discharged.

Study Questions

Fill-in-the-Blank Questions

Barton Barrister, Attorney at Law, purchases a copier from Once-Owned Office Equipment, Inc. Barrister pays for the copier by making a sixty-day promissory note in the amount of $1,200.00 payable to Once-Owned. Once-Owned is in need of cash to buy more inventory so it sells the note to its bank. The copier does not work and when the bank presents the note to Barrister, he refuses to pay. The bank (holder) sues Barrister (maker-defendant).

The bank _____ an HDC.
                    (is/is not)

Barrister has a _____ defense.
                        (real/personal)

The bank _____ prevail in the suit.
                    (will/will not)

Assume that Barrister is bankrupt and that a court has relieved him of liability for the note. The bank sues Once-Owned for the money. Once-Owned _____ breached the transfer warranty.   (has/has not)

Once-Owned _____ signature liability.
                        (has/has no)

True-False Questions

1.   The FTC rules apply to all consumer transactions involving a negotiable instrument. _____

2.   A holder who promises to pay a note next week has given good value. _____

3.   A rubber stamp can be a valid signature. _____

4.   An agent who signs a company check in his own name will always be personally liable for the check. _____

5.   Fraud in the execution is a real defense. _____

6.   An indorser who signs "without recourse" has no signature liability. _____

7.   A holder who transfers a bearer instrument has no warranty liability. _____

8.   A presentment warranty is made to an indorser. _____

9.   The shelter principle protects holders in due course. _____

10.   A check may be presented for payment by depositing it in the payee's bank account. _____

Multiple-Choice Questions

1.   Alice receives a check from her grandmother as a birthday present.

      a.   Alice is a holder.
      b.   Alice is an HDC.
      c.   Alice is a holder through a holder in due course.
      d.   Alice is not a holder.

2.   Alice indorses the check and deposits it in her bank account. Alice's bank forwards the check to grandmother's bank for payment.

    a.   Grandmother is a holder, but not an HDC.
    b.   Alice's bank is a holder, but not an HDC.
    c.   Alice's bank is an HDC.
    d.   Grandmother is an HDC.

3.   Tom finds a check payable to Simple Simon. Tom forges Simon's signature and deposits the check in his bank account. Tom's bank stamps "Pay any bank" on the back of the check and forwards it through a clearinghouse to Simon's bank for payment.

    a.   Tom's bank has breached the transfer warranty.
    b.   Tom's bank has breached the presentment warranty.
    c.   Tom's bank is not an HDC.
    d.   Tom's bank has no signature liability.

4.   Tom:

    a.   has breached the transfer warranty.
    b.   has not breached the transfer warranty.
    c.   is an HDC.
    d.   is the payee of the check.

5.   Melinda buys a car from Lemon Limos and signs a four-year $12,000 installment note payable to Lemon. Lemon discounts the note to First Bank and receives $10,500 cash. Lemon knows that the car is a bomb. After two months, the car malfunctions and Melinda stops paying on the note.

    a.   Melinda is a holder.
    b.   Lemon is a holder.
    c.   First Bank is a holder but not an HDC.
    d.   Lemon is an HDC.

6.   Lemon:

    a.   has signature liability only.
    b.   has warranty liability only.
    c.   has both signature and warranty liability.
    d.   has no liability to First Bank.

7.   If First Bank sues Melinda:

    a.   Melinda will win because First Bank is not an HDC.
    b.   Melinda will win because the FTC rule applies.
    c.   First Bank will win because it is an HDC.
    d.   First Bank will win because the FTC rules applies.

8.   An indorser who signs "without recourse":

a.   has no signature liability.
b.   has no warranty liability.
c.   has both signature and warranty liability.
d.   has no liability.

9.   Sam Salesman works for Investment Realty, Inc. and is authorized to spend $5,000 without prior approval. He draws a draft in the amount of $1,000 and Investment is named as drawee. Sam signs the draft, "Sam Salesman for Investment Realty, Inc."

a.   Sam is personally liable as a drawer.
b.   Sam is personally liable as a drawee.
c.   Investment Realty is liable as a drawer.
d.   Investment Realty is not liable as a drawer.

10.   If the signer intends to validate a negotiable instrument, which of the following is (are) acceptable as a signature?

a.   Rubber stamp
b.   Typewritten name
c.   Printed Name
d.   All of the above are acceptable.

11.   Gary's Grocery places a $7,500 order with the Wholesale Fruit Co. and sends them a check for the entire amount. Wholesale cashes the check but sends only half the order. Wholesale promises to send the remainder in two weeks. At the time that Wholesale cashes the check, it is:

a.   a holder but not an HDC.
b.   an HDC for $7,500.
c.   an HDC for $3,750.
d.   not a holder.

12.   Wholesale's bank deposits the check in Wholesale's bank account and forwards it to Gary's bank for payment.

a.   Gary's bank is a holder, but not an HDC.
b.   Gary's bank is an HDC for $7,500.
c.   Gary's bank is an HDC for $3,750.
d.   Gary's bank is not a holder.

13.   Freddie Forger receives his $1,000 paycheck and skillfully raises the amount of the check to $10,000. He transfers the check to AAA Autos as payment for a car. AAA indorses the check and deposits it in its bank account.

a.   AAA has breached the transfer warranty.
b.   AAA has not breached the transfer warranty.
c.   AAA is not an HDC.

      d.   AAA has no signature liability.

14.   John sells his automobile to Tony who is sixteen years old. Tony pays $100 down and promises to pay $25 a month for twelve months. John sells the note to E-Z Finance Co. and receives cash. Tony makes only two payments. E-Z sues Tony:

      a.   Tony will lose because he has a personal defense.
      b.   Tony will lose because he has a real defense.
      c.   Tony will win because he has a personal defense.
      d.   Tony will win because he has a real defense.

15.   Assume E-Z sues John.

      a.   John will win because he is an HDC.
      b.   John has no signature liability.
      c.   E-Z will win because John has breached the transfer warranty.
      d.   John will win because E-Z is not an HDC.

16.   Penny sells her dog and receives a check for $200 from Cathy. Penny indorses the check to her mother. Which of the following persons, if any, have secondary liability on the instrument?

      a.   Penny
      b.   Penny and Penny's mother
      c.   Cathy, Penny and Penny's mother
      d.   Cathy's bank

17.   George writes a check payable to "cash" and delivers the check to Sally. Sally delivers the check without indorsement to Ron. Ron indorses the check and deposits it in his bank account. If George and his bank refuse to honor the check:

      a.   Ron's bank can sue Ron but not Sally.
      b.   Ron's bank can sue both Ron and Sally.
      c.   Ron's bank can sue Sally only.
      d.   Ron's bank cannot sue.

18.   Sally:

      a.   has signature liability.
      b.   has transfer liability to Ron and his bank.
      c.   has transfer liability to Ron.
      d.   has no liability to Ron or his bank.

19.   Pixie makes a note to Mouse Trailers, Inc. in the amount of $500. Pixie signs the note by typing, "Pixie, Dixie" on the signature line.

a. Pixie is personally liable on the instrument unless he can show that he was Dixie's agent.
b. Pixie is not personally liable on the instrument regardless of proof.
c. Dixie is not liable on the instrument regardless of proof.
d. Neither Pixie nor Dixie is liable because the signature is improper.

20. On August 1, 1990, Rhett makes a sixty-day $400 note payable to Scarlett's Souvenir Shop. On October 15, 1990, the shop discounts the note to the Bank of Georgia for $375 cash. The bank:

a. is not an HDC because it did not give value.
b. is not an HDC because the note is overdue.
c. is not an HDC because it acted in bad faith.
d. is an HDC.

21. Sam owes $300 to Flamingo Factory. Sam receives his paycheck and indorses it to Flamingo.

a. Flamingo is not an HDC because it did not give value.
b. Flamingo is not an HDC because it did not take the check in good faith.
c. Sam is not an HDC because he did not give value.
d. Flamingo and Sam are HDCs.

22. Abel Attorney receives a check for $400 in payment of a legal fee. Abel gives the check to his daughter for a graduation present. The daughter deposits the check in her bank account. Abel's daughter:

a. is an HDC.
b. is a holder only and cannot claim HDC protection.
c. is a holder through a holder in due course and can claim HDC protection.
d. is a holder through a holder in due course but cannot claim HDC protection.

23. Which of the following is a real defense?

a. The instrument has been paid
b. Breach of contract
c. Fraud in the inducement
d. Material alteration of the instrument

24. Walker Shoes hires Rumpole Roofing to repair the roof of its store. Walker gives Rumpole a sixty-day $750 note. Rumpole sells the note to Second Bank. Rumpole never completes the repairs and is declared bankrupt.

a. Second Bank will be successful in a suit against Walker because Walker has a personal defense.

      b.   Second Bank will be unsuccessful in a suit against Walker because the FTC rule applies.

      c.   Second Bank will be unsuccessful in a suit against Walker because Walker has a real defense.

      d.   Second Bank will be unsuccessful in a suit against Walker because Second Bank is not an HDC.

25.   Assume that Second Bank sues Rumpole.

      a.   Second Bank will be unsuccessful because the FTC rule applies.

      b.   Second Bank will be unsuccessful because Rumpole has a real defense.

      c.   Second Bank will be successful because the FTC rule does not apply.

      d.   Second Bank will be successful because Rumpole has a personal defense.

Answers to Study Questions

Fill-in-the-Blank Questions

The Bank is an HDC. It gave value for the instrument by paying cash to Once-Owned. Did the bank act honestly? Yes. Did the bank buy the instrument without notice that Barrister's machine was faulty? Yes, unless Once-Owned told the bank, which is unlikely.

Barrister has a personal defense. His plea is breach of contract or possible fraud in the inducement. These are personal defenses and are not good against an HDC.

The bank wins in a suit against Barrister. Barrister will have to sue Once-Owned to recoup his losses.

Once-Owned has breached the transfer warranty. It promised that no defense of any party was good against him. Bankruptcy is a real defense and is good against Once-Owned. He must pay the bank. Once-Owned also has signature liability because he indorsed the note as the payee.

Remember that the bank as an HDC has several options. It can and should sue Barrister because as the maker he has primary liability. The bank can also sue Once-Owned by tracing back the line of transfer. As a transferor of the instrument, Once-Owned incurred signature and warranty liability.

True-False Questions

1.   F.   The FTC rule applies to consumer <u>credit</u> transactions. It does not apply if the consumer uses a check to pay for goods or services.

2.   F.   Value must actually be received; a promise to pay is insufficient.

3.   T.

4.   F.   Because the check is on a company account, the agent may be able to prove his status by parol evidence.

5.   T.

6.   T.

7.   F.   The holder has transfer liability to his immediate transferee only.

8.   F.   It is made to a maker, a drawer or a drawee.

9.   F.   It protects holders who do not qualify as HDCs.

10.   T.   The banking system is a proper method of presentment.

Multiple-Choice Questions

1.	a		14.	d
2.	c		15.	c
3.	a		16.	c
4.	a		17.	a
5.	b		18.	c
6.	c		19.	a
7.	b		20.	b
8.	a		21.	d
9.	c		22.	c
10.	d		23.	d
11.	c		24.	a
12.	b		25.	b
13.	a			

Commerical Paper-- Checks and the Banking System

General Principles

This chapter highlights the most common form of commercial paper: the check. There are three parties to a check: the drawer who orders payment, the drawee who pays according to the drawer's orders, and the payee. The rules outlined in previous chapters regarding indorsement, liability and holder in due course apply to checks. It may help to visualize the path of a check as it is deposited in the payee's bank and makes its way through the banking system to the drawee bank. The banks are transferees or holders of the check.

Article 4 of the UCC regulates the contractual relationship between a bank and its customer. The bank has a duty to follow the instructions of its customer; the customer has a duty to keep sufficient funds in his account and to examine bank statements for error.

Chapter Summary

I.   Types of Checks

      A.   Cashier's Checks--A bank is the drawer <u>and</u> the drawee on a cashier's check. A customer purchases the check from the bank and is named as payee. A cashier's check is more acceptable than an ordinary check because it is presumed that the bank has sufficient funds to insure payment.

      B.   Traveler's Check--The drawer and drawee are the same person, usually a financial institution but not necessarily a bank. As protection against forgery, the purchaser must sign the check twice, once when he or she receives it and again when he or she transfers it.

C.   <u>Certified Check</u>--A certified check is a check that has been formally accepted by the bank. Because the bank has accepted the check, the holder is assured that sufficient funds are available to pay the check. If the drawer requests certification, he or she remains secondarily liable. If a holder requests certification, anyone who has signed the check before certification (drawer and previous indorsers) is discharged from liability.

        The bank is liable for the amount of the check at the time of certification. If the check is altered after certification, the bank is not liable for the additional amount.

II.   <u>The Bank-Customer Relationship</u>--The bank acts as its customer's agent in processing checks; it credits and debits the customer's account according to the instruments received. The bank owes a general duty to the customer to follow his or her orders. The bank may be liable to its customer if it does not. The customer owes a duty to keep sufficient funds on hand to pay incoming checks and to act responsibly. The bank may be able to shift liability to the customer if the customer acts negligently.

III.   <u>Honoring Checks</u>--The bank has a duty to honor only those checks which are "properly payable." Altered checks or checks with forged indorsements are not properly payable.

A.   <u>Stale Checks</u>--An uncertified check presented more than six months after its date is stale and the bank has no obligation to pay it. If the bank pays the check in good faith, it may charge the customer's account.

B.   <u>Missing Indorsements</u>--The bank is the customer's agent and can supply the customer's indorsement unless the instrument requires personal indorsement (e.g. government checks).

C.   <u>Death or Incompetence of a Customer</u>--A bank is not responsible for mispayment until notified. If the drawer dies, the bank can still pay checks for ten days after death unless an heir of the deceased customer objects.

D.   <u>Stop-Payment Orders</u>--If the customer issues a stop-payment order in a reasonable manner and within a reasonable time for the bank to act, the bank must follow the customer's instructions. A written stop-payment order is valid for six months; an oral stop-payment order (if permitted) is valid for fourteen days.

        The bank will be liable if it fails to follow proper instructions. However, if the customer had no legal right to stop payment, the bank may recoup its losses from the customer. A stop-payment order does not automatically relieve the customer from liability to the holder or payee. That question must be litigated separately. The outcome will depend on the type of defense presented by the drawer and whether the holder is an HDC.

E.   Overdrafts--A bank may, if it chooses, pay incoming checks even if there are insufficient funds in the customer's account. The bank is then entitled to recoup its losses from the customer. A bank that routinely pays overdrafts may be liable to the customer if it changes policy without notifying the customer.

If the bank chooses not to honor the overdraft, the holder can demand payment from the drawer directly or resubmit the check. A "bounced" check has been dishonored and the holder must notify a previous indorser or lose the right to collect payment from him or her.

F.   Forged Drawer's Signature--The bank is responsible for recognizing its customer's signature and will be liable unless it can prove that the customer was negligent. The customer has a duty to examine his or her bank statement and to report forgeries to the bank within fourteen days after the statement is received. If the customer fails to report within the time limit and similar forgeries occur, the customer will be responsible for the forgeries which would have been prevented by reporting promptly.

G.   Forged Indorsement--The bank is liable to its customer for checks paid over a forged indorsement. The bank can then recover from the person who presented the check for payment because the presenter has breached a warranty. The customer must report a forged indorsement within three years in order to hold the bank liable.

H.   Altered Check--The bank is responsible for the difference between the check as written and as altered. The bank will be able to recover the extra amount from the person who presented the check because a presentment warranty has been broken. If the check is presented to someone who should know the original amount (e.g. drawer, maker, acceptor), then that party is responsible. The bank may be able to shift the loss back to its customer if it can prove that he or she was negligent.

IV.   Accepting Deposits--The bank's duty is to credit deposits to the customer's account and initiate collection process. A bank may have different responsibilities and liabilities depending on its position in the collection chain.

A.   The Collection Process--The first bank to receive the check is the depositary bank. The final bank in the chain, the bank which will pay the check, is the drawee or payor bank. An intermediary bank is any bank in the chain except the depositary or payor bank. A collecting bank is one which forwards the instrument for collection and includes the depositary bank and all intermediary banks.

B.   Restrictive Indorsements--A bank in the collection chain is required to follow only the restrictive indorsement from its immediate transferee. The depositary bank must credit the funds to the customer's account if the customer requests. "Pay any bank" is a restrictive indorsement used by banks in the collection process. It specifies that the next holder in the collection chain must be a bank.

C.   Check Collection--The depositary and each collecting bank must forward the check for collection by midnight of the next banking day following its receipt of the check (midnight deadline). As the check travels through the banking system, each bank gives and receives a provisional credit for the amount of the check. When the payor bank receives the check, it must pay or dishonor the check by its midnight deadline. When the depositary bank and the payor bank are the same, the time limit is the opening of the second banking day. This is an "on-us" item.

Unless the payor bank dishonors the check, the provisional credits become final and the payor bank is responsible. If the payor bank and the depositary bank are different, then the payor bank has until midnight of the next banking day to pay or dishonor the check.

The time limit for payment or forwarding is so short that the UCC allows a bank receiving a check after a certain time (usually 2 p.m.) to delay formal receipt until the next day. This process is called deferred posting and gives the bank an extra day to forward or pay a check.

D.   The Expedited Funds Availability Act--Designed to allow depositors to draw on funds deposited in the bank. Before this act, a bank could hold a check deposited with it and prevent the payee (its depositor) from using the money. Reduced time limits for holding a check, indicated in (1), became effective in 1990.

(1)   Outside limit--Local checks: one day. Nonlocal checks: four days.

(2)   Next Business Day--"Safer" instruments such as cashier's checks, certified checks, government checks, wire transfers, and first $100 of any check. The latter is increased by $400 on the following business day.

(3)   Automated Teller Machines--If not owned by the depository bank, six day maximum hold on all deposits.

V.   Electronic Fund Transfer System (EFTS)--This system provides for the transfer of funds without using checks or other written instruments.

A.   System Components

(1)   Automated Teller Machines--An automated teller machine is connected to the bank by a computer. The customer uses an access or debit card and a personal identification number (PIN) to withdraw money, make deposits and complete other banking transactions.

(2)   Pay-by-Telephone--Consumer has access to bank's computer via the telephone.

(3)   Direct Deposits and Withdrawals (Automated Clearinghouse)-- Federal Reserve banks and other collecting banks move funds using electronic pulses instead of checks.

(4)   Point-of-Sale System--A merchant's store maintains a computer hook-up with the customer's bank. The customer uses his PIN card to make payments instead of writing a check.

B.   Consumer Transfers
(Responsibilities and Liabilities)

(1)   If the customer's access card is used without permission, the customer is liable for only $50. However, the customer must inform the bank within two days of the loss or liability increases to $500. The customer can be liable for more than $500 if he or she fails to examine the bank statement and report the loss within sixty days.

(2)   If the customer reports an error within sixty days after he or she receives a bank statement, the bank has ten days to investigate. If the investigation exceeds ten days, the bank must recredit the amount to the customer's account until the dispute is resolved.

(3)   The bank must provide a receipt for each transaction and each transfer must be reported on the bank statement.

(4)   If the customer uses a prepayment system for paying utility bills or insurance premiums, he or she can cancel the transaction three days before the transfer is scheduled.

C.   Advantages and Disadvantages of EFTS

(1)   Advantages--The EFTS is more convenient than writing checks because the automatic teller machines are located in shopping centers, grocery stores, etc. The customer can order automatic payment of bills. EFTS also reduces the vast amount of paperwork needed to collect checks.

(2)   Disadvantages--EFT transactions occur immediately and so it

is difficult to issue stop payment orders. Also, the "float" or the time between writing a check and its payment is eliminated. Although the bank is required to provide a record of EFT transactions, these records are not as complete as those provided by canceled checks. Finally, it is easier to tamper with EFT records and the customer's privacy may be reduced.

VI.   Commercial Wire Transfers--Funds can be transferred between accounts by using public or private services. Loss from an unauthorized transfer rests on victim unless thief can be found. Disputes now resolved under contract and tort law but UCC has drafted new article on this.

Study Questions

Fill-in-the-Blank Questions

Aunt Lillie, who lives in New York City, writes a check payable to her niece Beth and mails the check to Beth, who lives in Carmel, California. Beth receives the check and deposits it in her bank account. Beth's bank forwards the check to the Federal Reserve Bank of Los Angeles, which forwards it to the Federal Reserve Bank of New York, which presents the check for payment at Aunt Lillie's bank.

Beth's bank is a(n) _____ bank.
                            (depositary/intermediary)

Aunt Lillie's bank is a _____ bank.
                            (payor/collecting)

The Federal Reserve Bank of New York is a _____ bank.
                            (collecting/depositary)

The Federal Reserve Bank of Los Angeles is a(n) _____ bank.
                            (intermediary/payor)

True-False Questions

1.   An EFTS transaction is processed more quickly than a written check. _____

2.   A check is considered stale if it has not been cashed within four months of the date it was issued. _____

3.   A cashier's check is a check which has been accepted by the drawee bank. _____

4.   A drawee bank is the same as a payor bank. _____

5. A bank which pays a check with a forged indorsement must re-credit its customer's account if the customer discovers and reports the error within three years._____

6. A traveler's check is a draft. _____

7. An oral stop-payment order is valid in every state._____

8. A collecting bank must pay a check or dishonor it before midnight of the next banking day. _____

9. A bank has the right to pay a customer's overdrafts and charge the amount to the customer's account. _____

10. When the drawer of a check asks the bank to certify the check and the bank does so, the drawer is no longer liable on the instrument. _____

11. Liability for unauthorized wire transfers is decided under common law. _____

Multiple-Choice Questions

1. Mary issues a written stop-payment order to her bank. Four months later, the bank pays the check. In a suit between Mary and her bank:

    a. Mary will win because the stop-payment order is valid for six months.
    b. The bank will win because the stop-payment order is valid for fourteen days.
    c. The bank will win because the check is stale.
    d. The bank will win because it has the right to refuse payment of any check.

2. Tony steals his mother's checkbook and writes a check to Ralph's Records for $26. Ralph deposits the check in his bank account. Ralph's bank credits his account and sends the check to mother's bank. In a suit between the two banks:

    a. Ralph's bank will lose because it violated the transfer warranty.
    b. Ralph's bank will lose because it violated the presentment warranty.
    c. Ralph's bank will win because the transfer warranty was not breached.
    d. Ralph's bank will win because the presentment warranty was not breached.

3. Tony's mother receives her bank statement three weeks later. She immediately notifies the bank of the forgery. In a suit between Tony's mother and the bank:

a.   The bank will win because mother waited three weeks to report the forgery.

b.   Mother will win because she has three years to report the forgery.

c.   Mother would win even without notification because her bank should recognize her signature.

d.   Mother will win because she notified the bank of the forgery within two weeks of receiving her bank statement.

4.   Linda writes a $500 check to her landlord Mabel. Mabel indorses the check and transfers it to Pete's Plumbing as payment for maintenance. Pete takes the check to Linda's bank and asks the bank to certify it. The bank agrees. When the bank certifies the check:

a.   Linda and Mabel are no longer liable.

b.   Mabel is no longer liable but Linda is.

c.   Linda is no longer liable but Mabel is.

d.   Linda and Mabel are liable but Pete cashes the check.

5.   Business Law Teacher asks her aide to buy some supplies at Campus Bookstore. She gives the aide a signed check made out to Campus Bookstore but fails to fill in the amount. The aide fills in the check for $100 more than the cost of the supplies and leaves town.

a.   Business Law Teacher is only responsible for the lesser amount because she authorized payment for supplies only.

b.   Business Law Teacher is responsible for the entire amount because she was negligent in filing out the check.

c.   The bank is responsible for the entire amount because it should have checked with Business Law Teacher before paying the check.

d.   The bookstore is responsible because it should have checked with Business Law Teacher before paying the check.

6.   Penny writes a check to Sam's Grocery on Tuesday morning. Sam deposits the check in his bank account on Wednesday morning. Assuming that Sam and Penny do not use the same bank, Sam's bank:

a.   must forward the check by midnight Wednesday.

b.   must forward the check by midnight Thursday.

c.   must forward the check by midnight Friday.

d.   has no duty to forward the check.

7.   If Sam and Penny use the same bank, the bank:

a.   must forward the check by midnight Wednesday.

b.   must forward the check by midnight Thursday.

c.   must dishonor or pay the check by midnight Wednesday.

d.   must dishonor or pay the check by midnight Thursday.

8.   Which of the following are parts of an EFT system?

a. Automated teller machines
b. Point-of-sale systems
c. Automated clearinghouses
d. All of the above

9. Mary has a telephone number which gives her access to a store's credit department which is linked to her bank. She pays her bill by transferring funds to the proper account. Mary is using:

a. an automated teller machine.
b. a point-of-sale system.
c. an automated clearinghouse.
d. a telephone payment system.

10. Cindy is mugged and the thief takes her wallet. He uses her EFT card to withdraw $1,000 from her bank account. Cindy immediately notifies her bank. Cindy is responsible for:

a. $0.
b. $50.
c. $500.
d. $1,000.

11. If Cindy had waited two weeks to report the loss, she would be responsible for:

a. $0.
b. $50.
c. $500.
d. $1,000.

12. Susan writes a check to Betty's Boutique. Betty indorses the check and takes it to Susan's bank. Susan's bank refuses to cash the check.

a. Betty can sue Susan's bank only if Susan had sufficient funds in the bank to pay the check.
b. Betty can sue Susan's bank regardless of the amount of money in Susan's account.
c. Betty cannot sue Susan's bank because Betty should have deposited the check and let it clear through the banking system.
d. Betty presented the check in a proper manner but she cannot sue Susan's bank.

13. Susan:

a. can sue her bank if she had sufficient funds in her account to pay the check.
b. can sue her bank regardless of the amount of money in her account because a bank must honor its customer's overdrafts.

c.   cannot sue the bank because Betty did not present the check in a proper manner.

d.   cannot sue her bank because the bank owes no duty to Susan.

14.   On a cashier's check:

a.   the bank is both drawee and payee.
b.   the bank is both drawee and drawer.
c.   the bank is both payee and drawer.
d.   the bank is payee, drawee and payee.

15.   Bill receives a $10,000 check as a down payment for his sports car. Bill asks the buyer's bank to certify the check. Bill then transfers the check to his bank, where a teller skillfully raises the amount to $100,000. Bill's bank presents the altered check to the buyer's bank for payment.

a.   The buyer's bank is responsible for $100,000 because it certified the check.
b.   The buyer's bank is responsible for $10,000 because $10,000 was the amount of the check when the bank certified it.
c.   The buyer's bank is not responsible for any amount because the check has been altered.
d.   Bill is liable for the additional $90,000.

16.   Cindy deposits her paycheck in the bank but forgets to indorse it.

a.   The bank cannot collect the check because Cindy's indorsement is missing.
b.   The bank can supply Cindy's indorsement if the check does not expressly require her signature.
c.   The bank can supply Cindy's signature on any check because the bank is her agent.
d.   The bank can never supply a customer's indorsement.

17.   Ron buys a microwave oven from AAA Appliance and writes a check for $450. Ron changes his mind when he sees the same oven on sale for $350 at another store. Ron stops payment on the check. When AAA presents the check for payment, Ron's bank refuses to pay.

a.   AAA can sue the bank because it refused to honor the check and it can sue Ron for wrongfully issuing a stop-payment order.
b.   AAA can sue the bank but not Ron.
c.   AAA can sue Ron but not the bank.
d.   AAA cannot sue Ron or the bank.

18.   Bob steals his employer's checkbook and forges five checks on the following dates: March 1, March 8, March 15, April 15, and April 30. Bob takes the money and moves to Switzerland. The employer receives his March bank statement on April 8 and the checks forged in March appear on the statement.

The employer notifies the bank of the forgeries on April 16.

a.   Bob's employer is responsible for all the checks.
b.   The bank is responsible for all the checks.
c.   Bob's employer is responsible for the March checks and the April 15 check.
d.   Bob's employer is responsible only for the April 30 check.

19.   Assume that Bob's employer did not report the forgeries:

a.   Bob's employer is responsible for all the checks.
b.   The bank is responsible for all the checks.
c.   Bob's employer is responsible for the March checks and the April 15 check.
d.   Bob's employer is responsible only for the April 30 check.

20.   Sally gives her EFT card and her PIN number to her friend Fred and tells him to withdraw $40 from her bank account. Fred withdraws $440 from one automatic teller and $100 from another. He returns the card to Sally and says nothing about the extra withdrawal. When Sally receives the bank statement the following month, she discovers the extra withdrawal and tells the bank she will pay only $40.

a.   Sally is responsible for $40 only because she reported the mistake promptly.
b.   Sally is responsible for $540 ($500+$40) because she did not report the loss within two days.
c.   Sally is responsible for $90 ($50+$40) because her liability is limited to $50 for unauthorized use.
d.   Sally is responsible for $540 ($500+$40) because she allowed Fred to use her card.

21.   A bank which receives checks after 2 p.m. can postpone recording the transaction until the next day. This process is:

a.   deferred collection.
b.   deferred clearing.
c.   deferred posting.
d.   deferred payment.

22.   Phil has an account with 1st Bank. Phil is killed in a plane crash on March 30. The bank learns of Phil's death on June 2. The bank pays several checks which were written by Phil before his death. The checks were received by the bank on March 30, June 1, June 2 and June 12. The bank has received no notice from a representative of Phil's estate. The bank has the authority to pay which of the following checks?

a.   The check received on May 30 only
b.   The checks received on May 30 and June 1

c.   None of the checks
d.   All of the checks

23.   Mary has a checking account with State Bank. The bank-customer contract states that the bank will pay overdrafts which total less than $200. The amount of the overdraft and a service fee will be deducted from the customer's account. Mary writes a check for $50 and has only $22 in her account. The bank dishonors or "bounces" the $50 check.

a.   Mary can sue the bank because a bank must always honor its customer's overdrafts.
b.   Mary cannot sue the bank because a bank can always choose not to honor an overdraft.
c.   Mary can sue the bank because the bank promised to honor small overdrafts.
d.   Mary and the payee of the check can sue the bank because the bank promised to honor small overdrafts.

24.   Sandra receives a check from her brother. She indorses the check "for deposit only" and transfers it to her bank. Sandra's bank forwards the check immediately to her brother's bank.

a.   Sandra's bank cannot forward the check because it is marked "for deposit only".
b.   Sandra's bank can forward the check but only if it credits Sandra's account with the money.
c.   The brother's bank cannot pay the check because it is marked "for deposit only".
d.   Sandra's bank can cash the check but cannot deposit it in her account.

25.   The brother's bank is:

a.   a collecting bank and the depositary bank.
b.   a collecting bank and the payor bank.
c.   an intermediary bank and the payor bank.
d.   the drawee bank and the payor bank.

Answers to Study Questions

Fill-in-the-Blank Questions

Beth's bank is a depository bank. Aunt Lillie's bank is a payor bank. The Federal Reserve Bank of New York is a collecting bank. The Federal Reserve Bank of Los Angeles is an intermediary bank.

True-False Questions

1.   T.

2.   F.   It is considered stale if it has not been cashed within six months of its date.

3.   F.   A certified check has been accepted by the drawee bank. On a cashier's check the drawer and the drawee are the same bank.

4.   T.

5.   T.

6.   T.

7.   F.

8.   F.   A payor bank must pay or dishonor a check before midnight of the next business day. A collecting bank must forward the check for payment within the deadline.

9.   T.

10.   F.   The drawer is relieved only when the drawee bank pays the check.

11.   T.

Multiple-Choice Questions

1.	a		14.	b
2.	d		15.	b
3.	d		16.	b
4.	a		17.	c
5.	b		18.	b
6.	b		19.	d
7.	d		20.	d
8.	d		21.	c
9.	d		22.	d
10.	b		23.	c
11.	c		24.	b
12.	d		25.	d
13.	a			

CHAPTER

21

Secured
Transactions

<u>General Principles</u>

A secured transaction is a loan where payment is guaranteed by some property of the borrower or debtor. The lender can seize the property if the debtor does not repay the debt. Most car loans are secured transactions. An unsecured loan is not backed by specific property of the debtor. Most minor purchases on a credit card are unsecured loans.

A lender, or secured party, has two primary interests: 1) the right to collect the property securing the loan, and 2) priority if the debtor should be unable to pay several of his or her creditors. The rules attempt to simplify the lending process by granting preferences to lenders and by providing a notice system so that a lender will not advance money to an over-extended debtor. As you review, it may help to think of two types of common secured transactions: the car loan mentioned earlier and the financing of a retail business.

<u>Chapter Summary</u>

I. <u>Scope of Article 9 of the UCC</u>--Article 9 of the Uniform Commercial Code applies to any transaction where money is loaned and payment is assured by personal property. It does not apply to real estate mortgages, liens by contractors (mechanics) or landlords, or debts arising from litigation.

II. <u>Terminology</u>

    A. <u>Parties</u>--The borrower is the debtor; the lender is the secured party.

    B. <u>Transaction</u>--The lender is given a security interest in the property or collateral. The contract which creates the lender's interest is a security agreement.

C.   <u>Property</u>--The property which secures the debt is called collateral.

III.   <u>Creating a Security Interest</u>--Creation of a security interest is called attachment. Establishes rights between the debtor and the secured party; third parties are not affected. The three steps below must occur before the security interest <u>attaches</u> to the collateral (before the creditor has a right to a specific piece of property).

A.   A written security agreement signed by the debtor must contain a reasonably definite description of the collateral. The written agreement is unnecessary if the secured party takes physical possession of the collateral.

B.   The secured party must give value which is usually accomplished by advancing money, promising to do so, or by selling goods on credit. Can apply to loans made in the past (antecedent debt).

C.   The debtor must have the right to possession or ownership of the collateral.

IV.   <u>Purchase-Money Security Interest (PMSI)</u>--Includes any security interest where the debtor uses the borrowed funds used to <u>buy</u> collateral. The secured party can be the seller or a bank. An example of a PMSI in consumer goods is the purchase of a washer and dryer on an installment plan. A PMSI lender (a financier of purchases) is usually in a preferred position with regard to other creditors of the debtor, at least in property he has financed.

V.   <u>Perfecting a Security Interest</u>--Enforcement of a security interest in collateral against other creditors who also may have any interest in the same collateral. Designed to give notice so that creditors will not be misled and will not extend more funds to a debtor who has already borrowed. The method of perfection depends on the classification of the collateral.

A.   <u>Physical transfer</u>--Called a pledge. This is the only way to perfect an interest in financial instruments. Note that if the lender has possession of the document, the debtor cannot show it to another lender to obtain more credit.

B.   <u>PMSI in Consumer Goods</u>--Perfects automatically once the security interest has attached. Rules are less strict because it is not likely that another creditor would lend money using consumer goods as collateral. In some states, less expensive farm equipment is also automatically perfected. <u>Note:</u> There are different rules for fixtures and automobiles, even though they may have been purchased by a consumer.

C.   <u>Filing</u>--The most common method is to file a financing statement in a public records office. The financing statement must include the signature of the debtor, the addresses of the secured party and the debtor, and a description of the collateral. The statement is filed with the county clerk or the secretary of state, depending on the type of collateral and state law. In general, financing statements for fixtures, farm products, and consumer goods are filed locally.

D.   Property--Collateral is classified according to its use by the debtor. Classification is extremely important because the perfection rules differ depending upon the type of collateral.

   (1)   Goods--Tangible items which are movable at the time acquired by the debtor.   Goods are further classified into five categories.

      (a)   Consumer goods are used for household or personal purposes.

      (b)   Inventory consists of goods held for resale or raw materials used in the manufacturing process.

      (c)   Fixtures are goods which become attached to real estate.

      (d)   Farm products (owned only by a farmer) are crops, livestock and supplies used in farming.

      (e)   Equipment consists of goods used to produce goods or carry on a business. This is a catchall category; if the collateral is a good and does not fall into another category, it is classified as equipment.

   (2)   Indispensable Paper--Documents which show an ownership or security interest.

      (a)   Chattel paper includes documents which show both a loan and a security interest, e.g. a car note.

      (b)   Documents of title are warehouse receipts, bills of lading and any other documents which show a party's right to possession of goods.

      (c)   Instruments include negotiable instruments, stock certificates and non-negotiable instruments.

   (3)   Intangibles--Accounts are accounts receivable or any contract which promises repayment other than those noted above.

D.   Time Limits--A financing statement is valid for five years. Continuation statements may be filed as many times as necessary. Can file up to six months before expiration.

VI.   <u>Scope of a Security Interest (The Floating Lien)</u>--When you review these rules, it may help to think of a retail business which has a line of credit with a bank. The bank extends credit so that the retailer can purchase inventory and equipment and pay employees. If the business is successful, the retailer will sell the original inventory, take in cash, checks or accounts receivable. The floating lien allows the <u>original</u> security interest to cover new property acquired by the debtor and to advance funds without making a new agreement. It floats over the debtor's assets. The following clauses are often found in such agreements.

   A.   <u>Proceeds</u>--Covers whatever the debtor receives when he or she sells or disposes of collateral. Necessary in inventory financing or the lender's collateral would evaporate. Because it is difficult to keep track of proceeds, the lender's interest is limited by the following perfection rules.

   The lender's interest is automatically perfected for ten days. After that time the interest becomes unperfected unless one of the following occurred:

   (1)   the proceeds are identifiable cash (e.g. separate bank account).

   (2)   lender perfects an interest in the proceeds (before the ten days expire).

   (3)   original financing statement covers the type of proceeds received (e.g. accounts or chattel paper).

   B.   <u>After-Acquired Property</u>--The security interest attaches to any property acquired by the debtor after the original agreement is made. This is necessary in inventory financing, otherwise as the retailer sold the goods, the lender's collateral would disappear. Limit on consumer goods: debtor must get rights within ten days of the agreement or a new agreement must be signed.

   C.   <u>Future Advances</u>--Used with a line or letter of credit. The lender agrees to advance a sum of money when needed by the debtor. The debtor may not use all the money at once; interest is paid only when the funds are used. A future advance clause allows the lender to give out the funds without creating a new agreement. Each advance of funds dates back to the time of the original agreement.

   D.   <u>Movement of Collateral to Another Jurisdiction</u>--If the collateral is mobile, and the debtor moves it to another state, the original financial statement is valid only for four months or the expiration date, whichever is earlier. The secured party can refile in the new state. Perfection can be lost earlier with an automobile if a certificate of title without notation of the security interest is acquired.

VII.   <u>Priorities</u>--Used to resolve disputes between creditors and between creditors and purchasers of collateral.

    A.   <u>Disputes Between Secured Creditors</u>--Generally first in time is first in right. A perfected interest always prevails over an unperfected interest. Between perfected parties, the first to file wins. If neither party is perfected, the first to attach wins. The following are exceptions and are designed to prevent one creditor from obtaining complete control of the debtor's business.

        (1)   <u>Purchase-Money Security Interest</u>--Second in time wins if the following steps are followed:

            (a)   <u>Inventory</u>--Lender perfects before or at the time debtor takes possession and written notice is given to previous creditors on record.

            (b)   <u>Other</u>--Lender perfects within ten days after debtor gets possession. No notice required.

        (2)   <u>Crops</u>--Lender who gives new value within three months of planting has priority over a creditor to whom repayment is six months overdue.

    B.   <u>Disputes Between Secured and Unsecured Creditors</u>-A perfected secured creditor prevails over all unsecured creditors. (Some states may give priority to contractors under mechanic's and materialmen's liens.) If the secured party is unperfected, he or she loses to anyone with a lien. In order to obtain a lien, a party generally must have established the debt in a court proceeding, received a judgment, and filed a lien in the public records.

    C.   <u>Disputes Between Secured Creditors and Buyers</u>

        (1)   <u>Buyer in the Ordinary Course</u>--Prevails over a secured party if the purchase was part of the debtor's regular business. Buyer wins even if he or she knows that the property is subject to a security interest. The most common example is a sale to a consumer by a seller who is financed by a bank.

        (2)   <u>Consumer Goods</u>--Consumer seller sells his or her consumer goods to another consumer. The buyer pays value and has no knowledge of the security interest. The buyer will win <u>unless</u> the secured party has filed a financing statement.

        (3)   <u>Chattel Paper</u>--Purchaser wins over secured party if the purchaser gives new value, takes possession in the ordinary course of business and had no actual knowledge of secured party's perfection. Can occur if a retailer sells on credit and

then sells his buyer's note to a third party.

(4)   <u>Purchasers of Other Documents</u>--Purchaser of negotiable instruments, document of title and securities prevails over secured party. Secured party should have possession of the document and if he or she doesn't, the buyer wins.

VIII.   <u>General Rights and Duties of Debtors and Creditors</u>

A.   <u>Information Requests</u>--The office which keeps financing statement records must give creditors information on other secured transactions entered into by the debtor. A secured party who files is entitled to a file-marked copy of the financing statement.

The debtor is entitled to find out the status of the debt at any time. The information is free every six months; the secured party can charge for additional requests. The lender must comply within two weeks or may be liable to the debtor for any loss caused by a refusal to give the information.

B.   <u>Assignment, Amendment and Termination</u>--Secured party can assign his interest to another; assignee is protected if he or she files notice with or on the financing statement. Amendments must be signed by both the debtor and the secured party.

When the debt is paid, the lender has the obligation to file a termination statement in the appropriate public office or send it to the debtor. Must be filed within one month for consumer goods or ten days after written request by the debtor for all collateral including consumer goods. Failure to do so will subject the lender to $100 payment and any loss caused to the debtor by failure to file the termination statement.

C.   <u>Care of Collateral</u>--The lender has the general duty to take reasonable care of the collateral if it is in his or her possession. The debtor is responsible for costs of care. If the collateral increases in value, the lender can keep increase as security unless it is in the form of money (e.g. a contract obligation is paid). Money must be sent to the debtor or used to reduce the debt.

IX.   <u>Default</u>--One advantage of a secured transaction is the lender's right to repossess the collateral if the debtor fails to repay. The secured party has several options. Written notice of the secured party's decisions must be given to the debtor unless the debtor waives this right <u>after</u> default.

A.   <u>Judgment, Levy and Execution</u>--If the collateral has declined in value and the debtor has other valuable property, the lender may decide to sue. Once judgment is received, a public officer will seize property of the debtor, sell it at a public sale and remit the proceeds to the lender.

The lender may also choose this option if repossession would be difficult.

B. Retention of the Collateral--Secured party may decide to keep the collateral as payment of the debt. Notice must be sent to the debtor and other secured parties who file a written notice of claim. If a written objection is filed, the secured party must sell the collateral. With consumer goods, notice to the debtor is sufficient.

C. Sale--Public or private sale as long as the sale is commercially reasonable. With consumer goods, a sale is required if the debtor has paid at least 60 percent of the purchase price unless the debtor waives this right in writing and after default. Notification must be sent to other secured parties who have filed a written notice of claim.

When the collateral is sold, the proceeds from the sale are applied first to reasonable expenses of repossession, storage and sale. Then the secured party and other creditors with an interest in the property are paid. If any funds remain, they are sent to the debtor. Unless otherwise agreed, if the sale does not bring enough money to pay the debt, the secured party can sue the debtor for the remainder (deficiency judgment). The debtor and any other secured party with an interest in the property have the right to redeem the property before sale if the debt and expenses are paid.

D. Repossession--If the lender keeps the collateral or sells it, he or she must first repossess it. The lender can repossess the collateral, if repossession can be accomplished without breaching the peace. In general, the lender cannot enter the debtor's house or garage without permission. If the lender breaches the peace, he or she may be liable to the debtor in tort.

Study Questions

Fill-in-the-Blank Questions

Linda purchases a microwave oven for her home from AAA Appliance. She pays $50 down and agrees to pay $25 per month for one year. Linda signs a security agreement but AAA does not file a financing statement. After two months, Linda needs cash and sells the oven to her brother, who does not know of AAA's security interest.

The oven is classified as _____.
(equipment/consumer good/inventory)

AAA _____ a perfected security interest.
(has/does not have)

If a dispute arises, _____ has priority in the oven.
                         (AAA/Linda's brother)

If Linda had purchased the oven for use in her restaurant, it would have been classified
as _____.
            (equipment/consumer good/inventory)

True-False Questions

1.   If a debtor does not repay a loan, a secured party may repossess the collateral.

        _____

2.   A lender perfects a security interest in a negotiable instrument by filing a financing statement. _____

3.   Before a security agreement can attach, the debtor must have physical possession of the collateral. _____

4.   A purchase-money security interest is created when a bank lends money and the money is used to purchase a car. _____

5.   An unperfected security agreement will always have priority over an unsecured creditor. _____

6.   If the debtor makes a written request, the secured party must file a termination statement when the debt is repaid. _____

7.   The debtor has the right to request the status of the debt or amount owed at any time and the secured party is obligated to fulfill this request. _____

8.   A "proceeds clause" usually is used in inventory financing. _____

9.   Attachment governs rights between competing creditors. _____

10.   A financing statement must be signed by both the debtor and the creditor.

        _____

Multiple-Choice Questions

1.   When a secured party repossesses collateral and sells it, the proceeds are applied to debts and expenses. Which of the following is the correct order of disposition?

        a.   Expenses of the sale, secured party who conducted the sale, debtor, other secured parties
        b.   Expenses of the sale, all secured parties in a ratio of proceeds to debt, debtor

c.   Secured party who conducted the sale, expenses of the sale, other secured parties, debtor

d.   Expenses of the sale, secured party who conducted the sale, other secured parties, debtor

2.   Ronald borrows $200,000 from First Bank to finance his shoe factory. Ronald purchases leather to use in manufacturing the shoes. The leather is classified as:

a.   equipment.
b.   inventory.
c.   general intangible.
d.   consumer goods.

3.   Connie, who operates a retail card shop, borrows $10,000 from State Bank. She uses the money to purchase birthday cards, candles and other items for sale in the shop. Connie signs a security agreement and State Bank files a financing statement which covers inventory, equipment, fixtures and any property later acquired by Connie. Two months later, Connie borrows $5,000 from her father to purchase a computer for use in her business. A security agreement is signed and a financing statement covering the equipment is filed. Connie receives the computer five days later.

a.   Connie's father and State Bank have security interests in the computer.
b.   Connie's father only has a security interest in the computer.
c.   State Bank only has a security interest in the computer.
d.   Neither State Bank nor Connie's father has a security interest in the computer.

4.   In a priority dispute between Connie's father and State Bank over the rights in the computer:

a.   Connie's father has priority because he has a properly perfected security interest.
b.   the bank has priority because it did not receive notice of the security interest held by Connie's father.
c.   the bank has priority because it filed first.
d.   Connie's father has priority because the computer is a consumer good.

5.   Which of the following are necessary for attachment of a security interest?

a.   The debtor must have rights in the collateral.
b.   The lender must file a financing statement.
b.   The lender must have a floating lien.
d.   The debtor must have physical possession of the collateral.

6.   In order to perfect a purchase money interest in consumer goods, which of the following is required?

a.   A financing statement filed with the secretary of state
b.   A financing statement filed with the county clerk
c.   A pledge
d.   None of the above; the interest is perfected when the security interest attaches.

7.   If a secured party repossesses equipment collateral and decides to retain possession, which of the following is required?

a.   Written notice to the debtor unless the debtor waived this right in the security agreement
b.   Written notice to the debtor and creditors who send written notice of a claim in the collateral
c.   Written notice to the debtor, unless the debtor waived this right after default, and to creditors who send written notice of a claim in the collateral
d.   Written notice to the debtor and all creditors

8.   Second Bank has a perfected floating lien on the inventory, equipment, fixtures and accounts of Tim's Sporting Goods. The security agreement contains an after-acquired property clause and a proceeds clause. John, a customer of Tim's, purchases a snowmobile for his personal use in exchange for a sled, $50 down payment and a note of $300. Tim takes a security interest in the snowmobile. Two weeks after the sale, Second Bank has a perfected security interest in which of the following proceeds of the sale to John?

a.   The sled only
b.   The sled and the note signed by John
c.   The sled, the note and the $50
d.   The sled, the note and the $50, but the security interest is perfected in the $50 only if it is identifiable as the $50 received from John

9.   Tim sells John's note to City Bank, who knew nothing of Second Bank's floating lien. If a priority dispute arises between Second Bank and City Bank over the note, who will prevail?

a.   Second Bank because it filed first
b.   Second Bank because the proceeds clause included the note
c.   City Bank, because Second Bank's interest in the note expired
d.   City Bank, because it bought the note without knowledge of Second Bank's interest

10. Regina borrows $2,000 from her sister and gives her sister a diamond ring to hold as collateral. The sister takes possession of the ring.

a.   Regina's sister has a perfected security interest in the ring.
b.   Regina's sister has a security interest in the ring but it is not perfected because no financing statement was filed.

c. Regina's sister does not have a security interest in the ring, because Regina did not sign a security agreement.

d. Regina's sister has a purchase-money security interest in the ring.

11. Which of the following are obligations of a secured party?

a. The secured party must file a termination statement when the debt is paid, if the debtor requests in writing.

b. The secured party must take reasonable care of collateral in its possession.

c. The secured party must sell repossessed consumer goods if the debtor has paid at least 60 percent of the purchase price.

d. All of the above.

12. Which of the following would be classified as inventory?

a. Law books owned by West Publishing

b. Law books owned by attorney

c. Blender owned by a housewife

d. Bicycle owned by delivery service

13. If the sale of repossessed collateral is less than the debt owed, the secured party generally has the right to sue the debtor for the remaining money owed. This is the right to:

a. proceeds.

b. after-acquired property.

c. a deficiency judgment.

d. redemption.

14. Susan, a resident of New Mexico, borrows $4,000 from E-Z Finance Co. in order to buy a cash register for her business. A security-agreement is signed and E-Z files a financing statement on July 1, 1989. Susan moves to Texas on October 1, 1989. Assuming that Susan does not use the collateral for a new loan, when does E-Z's security interest expire?

a. October 1, 1989

b. November 1, 1989

c. October 1, 1994

d. February 1, 1990

15. Edna owns and operates an exotic fashion business. The following events occur. On June 15, 1988, Edna discusses a line of credit for $50,000 with City Bank. The bank files a financing statement covering equipment, inventory, proceeds and after-acquired property on June 16, 1988. On June 17, the bank promises to give Edna her line of credit and Edna signs a security agreement. On June 18, Edna purchases $5,000 of inventory from Safari Supplies. The security agreement attached to the inventory on:

a.   June 15.
b.   June 16.
c.   June 17.
d.   June 18.

16.   On August 1, 1988, Edna buys $5,000 inventory from African Collectibles on credit. Edna signs a security agreement and African files a financing statement. The new inventory is delivered on August 2, 1988. If a priority dispute arises between African Collectibles and City Bank regarding the inventory purchased from African Collectibles:

a.   African Collectibles and City Bank have interests in the inventory but City Bank's interest has priority because it filed first.
b.   African Collectibles and City Bank have interests in the inventory but African Collectible's interest has priority because it is a purchase-money security interest.
c.   City Bank has no interest in the inventory supplied by African Collectibles.
d.   African Collectibles has no security interest because it failed to notify City Bank of its interest.

17.   On September 8, 1988, Cindy purchases an item of inventory supplied by African Collectibles. Who has priority to the item purchased by Cindy?

a.   City Bank
b.   African Collectibles
c.   Edna
d.   Cindy

18.   Which of the following is not a purchase-money security interest?

a.   Washing machine purchased on credit from retailer
b.   Washing machine purchased using proceeds of bank loan
c.   Equipment owned by retailer to secure loan for remodeling
d.   Equipment owned by retailer and purchased under a line of credit

19.   If the collateral is not moved to another jurisdiction a financing statement is valid for:

a.   four months.
b.   five months.
c.   five years.
d.   indefinitely; there is no expiration date.

20.   Which of the following types of collateral would be classified as an account?

a.   A copyright
b.   A negotiable promissory note
c.   A written contract promising to pay for services rendered

d.   All of the above

21.   Which of the following will not prevail over an unperfected secured party?

a.   Secured creditor
b.   Judgment creditor without a lien
c.   Judgment creditor with a lien
d.   None of the above; all will prevail over an unperfected secured creditor

22.   Which of the following are required for proper sale of repossessed consumer goods?

a.   Secured party must sell to the highest bidder at a public sale.
b.   Secured party must give notice of the sale to other creditors.
c.   The debtor must receive notice of the sale.
d.   Secured party must give notice of the sale to the debtor unless this right is waived after default.

23.   Tom purchases a bicycle for his delivery service from Wheels Unlimited. He pays $50 down and agrees to pay $20 per month for ten months. A security agreement is filed but no financing statement is filed. Wheels does not know that First Bank has a perfected floating lien on all property owned or acquired by Tom.

a.   Wheels Unlimited's interest in the bicycle has not attached and is not perfected.
b.   Wheels Unlimited's interest in the bicycle has attached but it is not perfected.
c.   Wheels Unlimited's interest in the bicycle has attached and is perfected.
d.   First Bank's interest in the bicycle has attached but it is not perfected.

24.   In a priority dispute between Wheels Unlimited and First Bank with regard to the bicycle:

a.   First Bank has priority because it has a perfected security interest in the bank.
b.   Wheels Unlimited has priority because the bike is a consumer good.
c.   Wheels Unlimited has priority because it has a perfected security interest.
d.   First Bank has priority because Wheels Unlimited's security interest did not attach to the bicycle.

25.   Tom also owes money to his attorney, who filed suit against Tom. The attorney prevailed and has levied a lien on Tom's bicycle and other assets of the delivery business. Between Wheels Unlimited and the attorney, who will prevail?

a.   The attorney, because Wheels Unlimited's security interest did not attach to the bicycle.
b.   The attorney, because Wheels Unlimited's security interest in the bicycle was not perfected.
c.   Wheels Unlimited because the attorney is an unsecured creditor.
d.   Wheels Unlimited if its interest attached before the attorney's interest attached.

Answers to Study Questions

Fill-in-the-Blank Questions

The oven is classified as a consumer good because Linda is going to use the oven for personal use; the use by the debtor is the deciding factor. AAA does have a perfected security interest when Linda owns the oven. This is a purchase-money transaction in consumer goods; no filing is necessary. Linda's brother has priority. A consumer-to-consumer transaction in used goods cuts off the interest of the secured party unless a financing statement has been recorded. If Linda had purchased the oven for use in a restaurant, it would have been classified as equipment.

True-False Questions

1.   T.

2.   F.   Perfection of a negotiable instrument can be accomplished only by possession.

3.   F.   The debtor must have rights in the collateral; physical possession is not necessary.

4.   T.

5.   F.   A judgment creditor with a lien will prevail over an unperfected secured party.

6.   T.

7.   T.

8.   T.

9.   F.   Attachment governs the rights between the debtor and the creditor; perfection governs the rights between third parties.

10.   F.   It need only be signed by the debtor.

Multiple-Choice Questions

1.	d		14.	d
2.	b		15.	d
3.	a		16.	b
4.	a		17.	d
5.	a		18.	c
6.	d		19.	c
7.	c		20.	c
8.	d		21.	b
9.	d		22.	d
10.	a		23.	b
11.	d		24.	a
12.	a		25.	b
13.	c			

22 Creditors' Rights and Bankruptcy

General Principles

Not all creditors are secured parties within the scope of Article 9 of the Uniform Commercial Code. However, these creditors are not without remedies. State law outlines the procedures to be followed in collecting a debt. Many states give priority to claims by laborers and contractors. The debtor is also protected by homestead laws; certain assets are exempt from seizure by most creditors. Keep in mind that the law tries to strike a balance between the rights of creditors and protection of debtors.

Bankruptcy is an available form of relief for over-extended debtors. In a typical straight bankruptcy, the assets of the debtor are gathered and distributed to the creditors. Other forms of bankruptcy attempt to establish a plan under which the debtor can continue in business and pay all or part of the money owed. Note that certain debts are given priority in payment and that some debts must be paid regardless of bankruptcy.

Chapter Summary

I. Laws Assisting Creditors

    A.   Mechanic's Lien on Real Property--Aids creditors who furnish labor and materials used in improving real estate. The typical claimant is a contractor. State law determines the procedure for establishing the lien.

    B.   Artisan's Lien on Personal Property--Similar to a mechanic's lien but aids creditors who furnish labor and materials used in improving personal property. An auto mechanic would qualify for the lien. The creditor must also prove that the work was to be performed on a cash basis. The creditor must retain possession of the property unless there is an agreement with the debtor to return the property. In most states, the property can be sold to satisfy the debt.

C.   Innkeeper's Lien on Personal Property--Similar to an artisan's lien. A hotel or motel operator has a lien on the luggage of the guest to pay for room charges. Also a possessory lien.

D.   Writ of Execution--Issued by a court after a creditor has sued the debtor and obtained a judgment against him or her. The writ directs the sheriff to seize property of the debtor and sell it to satisfy the debt. The sale must be public. Certain assets of the debtor are not available to be sold (see Homestead Exemption below). Debtor may redeem (reclaim) the property by paying the judgment before the sale.

E.   Attachment--A pre-judgment remedy designed to keep the debtor from moving property out of reach of the creditor. The creditor must sign a sworn statement that the debt is owed and must post a bond for the value of the property and any loss to the debtor. The writ directs the sheriff to seize the property and hold it until a judgment is reached. If the creditor prevails, the property may be sold to satisfy the debt.

F.   Garnishment--After judgment for the creditor, the court orders a third party in possession of the debtor's assets to pay the creditor. The third party or garnishee is usually the debtor's employer or his bank. State laws vary but usually there is a limit on the amount of wages that can be garnished.

G.   Composition of Creditors--A kind of informal bankruptcy where the creditors agree to take less money than is owed and the debt is extinguished. Even though the debtor is not providing consideration (see Chapter 10), the agreement is enforceable.

H.   Suretyship and Guaranty--In both situations, a third party agrees to become responsible for another's debt. The contract is between the creditor and the third party.

(1)   Primary v. Secondary Liability--A strict surety is a co-signer and is primarily responsible. The creditor can sue either the debtor or the surety as soon as the debt becomes due. A guarantor is secondarily liable and under the terms of the agreement, the creditor must try to collect the money owed from the debtor before proceeding against the guarantor. The agreement between the guarantor and the creditor must be written unless the guarantor's main purpose in making the agreement was personal gain. Review the discussion in Chapter 11.

(2)   Defenses of the Surety and the Guarantor--The surety or guarantor promises to be responsible for the debtor only on the

conditions outlined in the original agreement. If the creditor and debtor make significant changes in the original contract, the third party is discharged. Almost all defenses that the debtor could use against the creditor are available to the surety or guarantor. "Personal" defenses of the debtor such as incapacity and bankruptcy cannot be claimed by the surety. If the surety has a personal defense, the promise to pay the debt may be canceled.

(3)   Rights of the Surety and Guarantor--These rights come into effect after the surety or guarantor has paid the debtor.

    (a)   Subrogation--When the surety pays the creditor, then the surety steps into the creditor's shoes and can sue the debtor. Any rights in the original contract which were given to the creditor can now be enforced by the surety.

    (b)   Reimbursement--The surety is allowed to proceed against the debtor for any payment of the debt or expenses in connection with the debt.

    (c)   Contribution--Applies only when there is more than one guarantor or surety. If one surety pays more than his or her fair share, suit may be brought against the other sureties or guarantors to recover the amount of excess.

I.   Foreclosure--Applies to creditors who have a mortgage on the debtor's property to guarantee repayment. Once the creditor proves that a judgment is owing, the property can be sold (usually at a public sale) to satisfy the debt. If the proceeds of the sale are insufficient to satisfy the debt, the creditor can bring suit to collect the remaining amount (deficiency judgment). If the proceeds of the sale are more than the amount owed, the excess after deduction for expenses is returned to the debtor.

II.   State Exemption Laws (Homestead Laws)--As mentioned earlier, certain property of the debtor cannot be seized to satisfy debts. The law varies from state to state but the family home, household furniture, clothing, and a car are usually protected from seizure. The law may also cover a limited number of livestock and pets.

III.   Consumer Protection Laws

A.   Consumer Credit Protection Act (CCPA)-A federal law which applies to consumer loans. The CCPA requires that credit terms be fully explained.

B.   Uniform Consumer Credit Code (UCCC)--A uniform law which has been proposed for adoption in every state. Only a few states have adopted it. Attempts to establish maximum interest rates and garnishment amounts. The most widely-accepted provision allows consumers to cancel a contract from a door-to-door salesman within three days of the sale.

C.   FTC Rule--Discussed in Chapter 19, this rule applies to consumer credit contracts. Anyone who buys a consumer credit note is subject to all defenses that the consumer could raise against the original seller. In short, there are no holders in due course of a consumer credit note.

IV.   Bankruptcy - Chapter 7 Liquidations--As stated earlier, bankruptcies fall into two classes: liquidation and reorganization. In a liquidation bankruptcy, the debtor's assets are gathered and distributed to the creditors by a trustee. The bankruptcy case begins with the filing of a petition.

A.   Voluntary Bankruptcy--Petition is filed by the debtor. Must file a list of all creditors, their addresses and amounts owed, a list of property owned by the debtor, including property claimed to be exempt, and a list of current income and expenses.

B.   Involuntary Bankruptcy--Creditors can "force" a debtor into bankruptcy only if the following conditions are met. There are penalties for frivolous filings.

(1)   If the debtor has more than twelve unsecured creditors, three or more unsecured creditors with a combined claim of $5,000 may file. If the debtor has fewer than twelve unsecured creditors, any one creditor who is owed $5,000 may file.

(2)   If the debtor challenges the petition the creditors must also prove that the debtor is insolvent--not paying debts as they become due or that a receiver has taken possession of part of the debtor's property within 120 days of the petition.

C.   Automatic Stay

(1)   Voluntary Bankruptcy--If the petition is proper and the required documents are filed, creditors are stayed (prevented) from taking any action to enforce collection of the debt. This includes filing suit, perfecting most liens, and repossessions. The time begins to run from the filing of the petition, not from time the creditor learns of the bankruptcy.

(2)   Involuntary Bankruptcy--The debtor remains in possession of the property until a hearing is held and it is determined that the filing was proper.

(3)   Relief from the Stay--If a secured creditor can prove that the collateral for his debt is declining in value or that he or she is

otherwise in danger of losing his security for repayment, the court can order relief. This may be in the form of a monthly payment equal in decline to the value of the property, a lien on other property of the debtor, or a guaranty by a solvent third party.

D.   Appointment of Trustee and Creditors' Meeting--Shortly after the stay is granted (ten to thirty days, unless extended), the creditors meet to examine the debtor and to elect a trustee to take charge of the debtor's affairs.

E.   Property of the Estate--All of the assets owned by the debtor at the time the petition is filed are the "property of the estate". The estate also includes income from producing property (e.g. rents). Gifts, inheritances and divorce settlements acquired within 180 days after the petition is filed may also be included. The debtor can them exempt certain property and the rest is disbursed to the creditors.

F.   Exemptions--The debtor may choose the state or federal exemption laws. This property does not become a part of the estate. Note that if the debtor chooses to exempt property with a lien on it, the debtor must pay off the lien. The federal exemptions include most household items up to a limited dollar amount and equity in cars and the family home.

G.   Trustee's Powers--The trustee, whether appointed by the court or elected by the unsecured creditors, has the duty to gather the debtor's assets and to distribute them to the debtors. In order to provide for a fair distribution, the trustee can avoid unfair payments to one creditor.

   (1)   Lien Creditor Status--The trustee is given the rights of a creditor who has obtained a judgment against the debtor. This gives the trustee the power to collect property for the estate which is subject to an unperfected security interest (review Chapter 21). The trustee also has the powers of a purchaser of real estate and may defeat an unperfected security interest in fixtures.

   (2)   Debtor Status--The trustee may also step into the debtor's shoes and rescind any contract made on the basis of duress, fraud, incapacity, or other defense available to the debtor. The property recovered is placed in the estate.

   (3)   Voidable Preferences--Bankruptcy attempts to treat creditors equally and any payment made to one creditor in preference to others may be avoided. However, the following requirements must be met in order to prove an illegal preference.

(a)   Transfer while debtor was insolvent (ninety days before petition, one year to insider).

(b)   To pay an antecedent (pre-existing) debt.

(c)   Creditor must receive more than he or she would have under Chapter 7 liquidation.

Exceptions--Debts in the ordinary course of business (e.g., utility bills) and payments by consumer debtors of less than $600.

(4)   Fraudulent Transfers--Trustee can rescind transfers made within one year of filing if the purpose of the transfer was to injure creditors. Applies even if some money was paid for the property transferred if the consideration was not reasonably equivalent and the transfer left the debtor insolvent.

(5)   Liens--Trustee can avoid some mortgages, mechanic's and landlord's liens. Also any unperfected liens may be avoided and the creditor becomes an unsecured creditor.

H.   Property Distribution--Property is distributed in the order below. Each class must be paid fully before anyone in the next class receives payment. Note the elevated status of a secured creditor.

(1)   Secured Creditor--Within a short time after filing, the debtor must tell the trustee how he or she intends to deal with secured collateral. If the debtor decides to claim the property as exempt, the debtor must pay the value of the collateral to the secured party. If the debtor surrenders the property, the secured party may accept the property in payment of the debt or sell it and keep the proceeds necessary to satisfy the debt and expenses of the sale. If the proceeds are insufficient to pay the debt, the lender becomes an unsecured creditor for the amount remaining. Any excess proceeds are gathered into the estate.

(2)   Expenses--Must be connected with the bankruptcy. Includes court costs, reasonable trustee and attorneys' fees.

(3)   Interim Creditors in Involuntary Case--When creditors file an involuntary bankruptcy, there is a lapse of time between the filing and the stay. Any creditor who provides services or goods to the debtor in this interval is entitled to priority if the debt was incurred in the ordinary course of the debtor's business.

(4)   Employee Claims--Salaries and commissions earned within ninety days of the filing; limited to $2,000 per person. Then contributions to employee benefit plans within 180 days of filing; limited to $2,000 times the number of employees. Excess claims are treated as unsecured debts.

(5)   Agricultural Claims--Farmers and fishermen have claims of $2,000 each against debtors who operate storage or processing facilities.

(6)   Customers of the Debtor--Customers of the debtor who have deposited money with the debtor for the purchase or lease of property or services can claim priority limited to $900; e.g., a customer who has paid for a year of janitorial service and the service declares bankruptcy.

(7)   Taxes and Penalties--Must be owed to the state, local, or federal government. Time limits vary on the type of taxes.

(8)   Unsecured Creditors--Includes all creditors without collateral and any excess amounts from priority claims.

Items 2-7 are designated as priority claims.

I.   Discharge--A discharge is granted when the distribution by the trustee is approved by the court. Most debts are canceled at the time of discharge. Some debts are automatically non-dischargeable; bad faith actions on the part of the debtor may void other discharges and the debtor can agree to repay discharged debts.

(1)   Exceptions to Discharge

(a)   Back taxes for three years prior to filing

(b)   Claims based on false representations of the debtor

(c)   Unscheduled claims (not listed by the debtor)

(d)   Fraud or misuse of funds by debtor in a position of trust (e.g., trustee), theft

(e)   Alimony and child support

(f)   Damages for intentional torts

(g)   Certain student loans unless hardship is proved

(h)   Luxury goods purchased within forty days of filing, more than $500 to a single creditor

(i) Consumer credit advances within twenty days of petition if more than $1,000 under an unlimited line of credit

(j) Judgments or settlements reached in connection with driving while intoxicated suit

(2) Objections to Discharge--Based primarily on bad conduct of the debtor. The debtor can always execute a written waiver. The assets of the estate are distributed but the debtor remains liable for any existing debts.

(a) Concealment/destruction of property with intent to harm creditors

(b) Fraudulent tampering with records, including failure to keep records or explain loss of assets

(c) Refusal to obey an order of the court

(d) Previous discharge in bankruptcy within last six years

(3) Revocation--Bankruptcy courts can revoke discharge if it finds that debtor was dishonest in the bankruptcy proceedings. One year time limit.

(4) Reaffirmation Agreement--A promise by the debtor to pay a debt that would have been discharged (that need not be paid). A debtor may choose to repay a supplier or someone whose help will be needed in the future.

Requirements--Must be signed before discharge. If the debtor has an attorney, the attorney must file an affidavit stating that the consequences of the agreement have been explained, the agreement is voluntary, and no hardship will result. If the debtor has no attorney, the court must find that the agreement is in the debtor's best interest and that no hardship will result. The debtor has a right to rescind before discharge or within sixty days of the agreement; the right to rescission must be stated in the reaffirmation agreement.

V. Reorganizations-Chapter 11--Designed to rehabilitate the debtor's business. Eligibility requirements the same as Chapter 7 except that railroads may also file. Only differences between Chapter 7 and Chapter 11 are noted here. In Chapter 11 type cases, creditors may prefer private negotiations with the debtor. These "workouts" cost less and proceed more quickly than formal bankruptcy.

A.   Trustee--Debtor stays in possession of the estate unless mismanagement is shown.

B.   Plan--Debtor is given the exclusive right for 120 days to file a workable plan of rehabilitation. After 180 days, the creditors may also submit proposed plans. The creditors form committees to represent their interests. Any order of the court must be with their approval or after a hearing.

Requirements--Must be workable or the creditors can convert it to a Chapter 7. The plan must designate classes of creditors and all creditors within a class must be treated equally. It is not necessary that all classes be treated equally as long as the plan is "fair and equitable" and "in the best interest of the creditors".

Acceptance and Confirmation--The creditors are allowed to vote by class on the plan. A class is presumed to accept if the entire debt will be repaid. In other cases, a class accepts the plan if one-half of the number of the creditors, who hold two-thirds of the amount of the claims, approve.

Cram-Down--The court can confirm the plan as long as one class has accepted the plan if the plan is fair and equitable. Fair and equitable means that each class must be treated the same or better than the classes below it. This is sometimes called the "cram-down" provision. The plan is crammed down the throats of the creditors at the bottom of the line if some class above accepts the plan.

VI.   Reorganization-Chapter 13--Also called "Adjustment of Debts for Wage Earners"

A.   Eligibility--Individuals only. Must have a regular income because payment is expected. Salary, commissions, alimony, pensions, and welfare will qualify. Debt ceilings of $350,000 secured debts and $100,000 unsecured debts.

B.   Preliminary Procedures--Voluntary petition only. Automatic stay will not apply to co-debtors if creditor requests lift of stay and debtor does not object.

C.   Plan--The debtor must turn over some earnings to the trustee to provide for payment. Must provide for cash payment of all priority claims, even if on deferred basis. Provide for same treatment of creditors within a plan. Three year limit unless extended by the court to five years.

D.   Confirmation--The creditors do not vote. Different tests for secured and unsecured creditors.

(1)   <u>Secured</u>--Will be confirmed if the secured party accepts or the debtor surrenders the property or if secured party retains lien and will receive payment or property equal to the present value of the collateral.

(2)   <u>Unsecured</u>--Will be confirmed if creditor will receive property equal to the value of the claim <u>or</u> all the debtor's disposable income is turned over to the trustee for a period of three years. The debtor's disposable income is money in excess of reasonable living expenses and business expenses.

E.   <u>Discharge</u>--Not granted until all payments have been made under the plan or a "hardship" is found. In order to qualify for a hardship discharge, the events preventing repayment must be beyond control of the debtor. Only alimony, child support and priority claims remain after discharge.

VII.   <u>Reorganizations-Chapter 12</u>--Designed to rehabilitate farmers whose debts exceeded Chapter 13 limits.

A.   <u>Eligibility</u>--Individual, partnership or closely held corporation if 50 percent of income is made from farming and 80 percent of debts are farm related. Total debt limit $1.5 million.

B.   <u>Plan</u>--Same procedure as Chapter 13. Creditor can ask for lift of automatic stay if debt owed is more than value of the collateral. Debtor can then be ordered to pay reasonable rent to creditor during bankruptcy.

<u>Study Questions</u>

<u>Fill-in-the-Blank Questions</u>

Kleen Products, Inc. is a vacuum cleaner retailer and repair shop. It has been experiencing financial difficulties and is contemplating filing for bankruptcy. Among other debts, Kleen owes $5,000 to Hoover for inventory under a security agreement, back wages for two employees in the amount of $4,500 and $10,000 to numerous unsecured creditors including the local newspaper and an office supply company.

If Kleen wishes to rehabilitate the business, it should file a Chapter _____ bankruptcy. (7/11/13)

If Kleen wishes to liquidate the business, it should file a Chapter _____ bankruptcy. (7/11/13)

The _____ is(are) entitled to a priority
claim.   (newspaper/employees)

In a Chapter 7 proceeding, the office supply company will be paid
_____ Hoover is paid.
      (before/after)

True-False Questions

1.   An innkeeper's lien is a possessory lien. _____

2.   A composition of creditors is created during bankruptcy proceedings.
          _____

3.   The right of one surety to recover against a co-surety is reimbursement.
          _____

4.   The UCCC is a federal law. _____

5.   In a Chapter 13 bankruptcy, creditors can file an involuntary petition against
          a debtor. _____

6.   A trustee in bankruptcy can disaffirm any contract made by the debtor.
          _____

7.   The maximum amount of allowable debt in a Chapter 12 bankruptcy is
          $350,000. _____

8.   The automatic stay does not apply to secured creditors. _____

9.   Attachment is a creditor's right to sell the debtor's property if a legal
          judgment is not satisfied. _____

10.   In a Chapter 13 bankruptcy, a discharge is granted after a plan is confirmed.
          _____

Multiple-Choice Questions

1.   Which of the following is a priority claim in bankruptcy?

          a.   Lien creditor
          b.   Child support
          c.   "Gap" creditor
          d.   Unsecured creditor

2.   Jerry, the carpenter, painted Mr. Jones's house and Mr. Jones now refuses to
          pay. Which of the following remedies should Jerry seek?

        a.   Artisan's lien
        b.   Mechanic's lien
        c.   Priority lien
        d.   Guarantee

3.   Robert, age sixteen, is buying his first car. The bank has agreed to lend the money to Robert only if his brother guarantees the loan. Robert's brother is a(n):

        a.   surety.
        b.   guarantor.
        c.   artisan.
        d.   none of the above.

4.   If Robert does not pay the loan and his brother pays it for him, Robert's brother:

        a.   has a right of subrogation and can sue Robert.
        b.   has a right of subrogation but cannot sue Robert.
        c.   has a right of contribution and can sue Robert.
        d.   has a right of contribution but cannot sue Robert.

5.   Which of the following defenses could be raised successfully by Robert's brother?

        a.   The bank did not sue Robert before asking for payment from Robert's brother.
        b.   Robert is a minor and the contract is voidable.
        c.   Robert's brother has received a discharge in bankruptcy.
        d.   Robert has received a discharge in bankruptcy.

6.   Which of the following debts would be non-dischargeable in a Chapter 7 bankruptcy proceeding?

        a.   Credit card bill from MasterCard
        b.   Telephone bill
        c.   Mink stole charged one month before declaring bankruptcy
        d.   Auto loan where the automobile was declared exempt

7.   Which of the following statements regarding a reaffirmation agreement is false?

        a.   The agreement must be signed before a discharge is granted.
        b.   The agreement must be approved by the court if the debtor has no attorney.
        c.   The agreement can be rescinded by the debtor for up to one year after the discharge.
        d.   The right to rescind must be stated in the agreement.

Questions 8-10 are based on the following facts.

Reader's Mecca, a local bookstore owned by Bill Blake, files for Chapter 11 Bankruptcy on March 1, 1990. On February 14, Bill sold the store's computer to his brother for $200. On February 20, Bill transferred $400 to his magazine supplier in payment for magazines delivered in January. Bill's attorney has proposed the following plan: Bill's unsecured creditors are divided into four classes: (1) inventory creditors with debt greater than $5,000; (2) inventory creditors with debt less than $5,000; (3) equipment creditors; and, (4) all other creditors.

8.   The sale of the computer to Bill's brother is:

      a.   a voidable preference and the trustee can recover the computer.
      b.   a voidable preference but the trustee cannot recover the computer.
      c.   a fraudulent transfer and the trustee can recover the computer.
      d.   a fraudulent transfer and the trustee cannot recover the computer.

9.   If the plan is fair and equitable, the plan will be approved if:

      a.   all the unsecured creditors accept the plan.
      b.   one class of unsecured creditors accepts the plan.
      c.   three classes of unsecured creditors accept the plan.
      d.   the judge approves the plan and no creditors accept the plan.

10.   Assume that all creditors in the magazine supplier's class receive nothing under the plan. The payment of $400 to the magazine supplier is:

      a.   a voidable preference and the trustee can recover the $400.
      b.   a voidable preference but the trustee cannot recover the $400.
      c.   a fraudulent transfer and the trustee can recover the $400.
      d.   legitimate and the trustee cannot recover the $400.

11.   Which of the following would be an acceptable payment under the plan:

      a.   Class 1 receives payment of 40 percent of its debts paid and Class 2, 3, and 4 get nothing.
      b.   Class 1 receives payment of 40 percent of its debts, Class 2 receives 50 percent and Classes 3 and 4 receive nothing.
      c.   Class 1 receives 40 percent payment of its debt, Class 2 receives 30 percent and Classes 3 and 4 receive 30 percent.
      d.   Classes 1, 2, 3, & 4 receive 40 percent payment.

12.   Rob owes Cindy $300. He refuses to pay although he has $4,000 in a savings account. If Cindy wants to satisfy her debt from the money in the account, she should file an action for:

      a.   attachment.
      b.   execution.
      c.   garnishment.

d.   subrogation.

13.   Cindy decides to sue Rob. However, she is worried that Rob may move his assets to another state. She should file an action for:

a.   attachment.
b.   execution.
c.   garnishment.
d.   subrogation.

14.   In a Chapter 13 bankruptcy, the plan filed by the debtor will be accepted if:

a.   the creditors vote to approve the plan.
b.   secured creditors receive payment for all debts and unsecured creditors receive payment from the debtor's disposable income.
c.   secured creditors receive the value of their collateral and unsecured creditors receive payment from the debtor's disposable income.
d.   the secured and the unsecured creditors vote to approve the plan.

15.   Which of the following debtors are eligible for a Chapter 12 bankruptcy?

a.   Debtor is an individual, 50 percent of income is made from farming and 50 percent of debts are farm related
b.   Debtor is a partnership, 50 percent of income is made from farming and 50 percent of debts are farm related
c.   Debtor is a partnership, 50 percent of income is made from farming and 80 percent of the debts are farm related
d.   Debtor is a close corporation and 50 percent of income is made from farming and 80 percent of debts are farm related

16.   The law which protects certain assets from seizure by creditors is:

a.   CCPA.
b.   FTC Rule.
c.   execution.
d.   exemption.

17.   Peter has a $12,000 car loan with First Bank. The bank has a perfected security interest in the car. Peter declares bankruptcy. At the time of the bankruptcy, he owes $8,000 to the bank but the car has a value of $4,500. If the bank sells the car for $4,000:

a.   the debt is extinguished and the bank suffers a loss of $4,000.
b.   the bank remains a secured creditor for $4,000 plus the expenses of the sale.
c.   the bank remains an unsecured creditor for $4,000 plus the expenses of the sale.
d.   the bank remains an unsecured creditor for $500 plus the expenses of the sale.

18.   Which of the following is proper grounds for denying a discharge in a Chapter 7 bankruptcy?

a.   The debtor waived the right to a discharge.
b.   The debtor disobeyed an order of the bankruptcy court.
c.   The debtor failed to explain adequately a loss of $50,000.
d.   All of the above.

19.   Cynthia has two secured creditors (house and car) and 5 unsecured credit cards (charge accounts). Her total debt is $300,000. She owes $8,700 to unsecured creditors, including $5,600 to Mastercard. If Cindy is behind in her payments:

a.   Mastercard can file for an involuntary bankruptcy under Chapter 7.
b.   the bank which has a mortgage on Cindy's house can file for involuntary bankruptcy under Chapter 7.
c.   the bank which has a valid security interest in Cindy's car can file for involuntary bankruptcy under Chapter 7.
d.   All of the above; any of the creditors can file.

20.   Which of the following would be entitled to an artisan's lien?

a.   Stereo repair shop
b.   Mortgage company
c.   Newspaper carrier
d.   Credit card company

21.   The right of a mortgage company to sell a house held as collateral is:

a.   garnishment.
b.   foreclosure.
c.   execution.
d.   attachment.

22.   Which of the following bankruptcy procedures is in correct chronological order:

a.   Petition, automatic stay, discharge, reaffirmation agreement
b.   Petition, discharge, automatic stay, reaffirmation agreement
c.   Petition, reaffirmation agreement, automatic stay, discharge
d.   Petition, automatic stay, reaffirmation agreement, discharge

23.   Which of the following would not be part of a debtor's estate in Chapter 7 bankruptcy?

a.   Paycheck received the day before filing
b.   Paycheck received the day after filing
c.   Inheritance from an aunt who died the day before filing
d.   Income from debtor's rental property received the day after filing

24.   Which of the following laws are designed to help debtors?

    a.   UCCC
    b.   FTC Rule
    c.   Exemption
    d.   All of the above

25.   Which of the following is a voidable preference?

    a.   Cash payment for a new stereo purchased for cash by debtor one month before bankruptcy
    b.   Payment of previous month's electric bill
    c.   Payment of $500 by consumer on MasterCard account one month before bankruptcy
    d.   Payment of $500 account payable by corporation one month before bankruptcy

Answers to Study Questions

Fill-in-the-Blank Questions

If Kleen, Inc. wishes to rehabilitate the business, it should file a Chapter 11 bankruptcy. Chapter 7 is a liquidation bankruptcy. Chapter 13 is a reorganization bankruptcy but it is only available to individuals and Kleen, Inc. does not qualify. The employees are entitled to a priority of $2,000 per employee or $4,000. The newspaper is an unsecured creditor. In a Chapter 7 proceeding, Hoover, a secured creditor, will redeem its collateral before unsecured creditors are paid.

True-False Questions

1.   T.

2.   F.   A composition of creditors is an informal agreement between creditors. A creditors' committee is formed during bankruptcy.

3.   F.   The right of one surety to recover against another surety is contribution. Reimbursement is the surety's right to recover against the debtor.

4.   F.   It is a uniform law which has been adopted in a few states.

5.   F.   Only the debtor can file for Chapter 13 protection.

6.   F.   The trustee can disaffirm any contract which the debtor would have the right to disaffirm, e.g., contract based on fraud or undue influence.

7.   F.   It is $1.5 million.

8.   F.   It applies to all creditors.

9.   F.   Attachment is a pre-judgment remedy.

10.   F.   A discharge is granted after the plan is completed by the debtor.

Multiple-Choice Questions

1.	c		14.	c
2.	b		15.	c
3.	b		16.	d
4.	a		17.	d
5.	c		18.	d
6.	c		19.	a
7.	c		20.	a
8.	c		21.	b
9.	b		22.	d
10.	a		23.	b
11.	a		24.	d
12.	c		25.	d
13.	a			

23

The Entrepreneur's Options

General Principles

An entrepreneur is one who undertakes to start and manage a new business. The business can take many forms. The four basic forms of business listed from simplest to most complex are the sole proprietorship, the general partnership, the limited partnership, and the corporation. As a general rule, the simpler the business, the greater the risk to the participants. As the form of business becomes more complex, operating costs and regulations increase. These costs are offset by a reduced liability if the business fails.

The forms of business listed above are only the starting point. The business can contract with other businesses to operate under a syndicate, business trust, or joint stock company. In these cases, the form of the business and the agreement will determine the rights and responsibilities of the parties.

Chapter Outline

I.   Types of Business Organizations

      A.   Sole Proprietorship--No formal mechanism required to create. Usually small businesses with less than $1 million earnings but they make up two-thirds of American businesses. Owner(s) take all risks but keep all profits. Owner(s) determine management and are personally liable for business debts. Sole proprietorships generally pay less income tax and now can establish retirement plans. Business dissolves if all owners change.

      B.   General Partnership--No formal mechanism required to create but there must be an agreement, express or implied, to carry on business for a profit. Partners share profits, losses and management rights. The personal assets of each partner are liable for partnership debts. Partnership dissolves if a partner changes (death, withdrawal, etc.) If no express agreement, rules of the Uniform Partnership Act (UPA) control operation.

C.   Limited Partnership--Creation according to statute only, usually filing with the secretary of state is required. Must be at least one limited and one general partner. Limited partner has liability only to the extent of his or her investment. State law controls operations. Most states have adopted either Uniform Limited Partnership Act (ULPA) or its revised edition (RULPA).

D.   Corporation--Formal mechanism, usually filing with the secretary of state is required to create. Shareholders (owners) have limited liability. General management is performed by a board of directors; officers perform day-to-day operations. Will not dissolve if shareholders die or change (perpetual existence).

III.   Other Organizational Forms

A.   Joint Venture--Basically a partnership formed for completion of one project. Participants share profits and losses but in contrast to a partnership may not have the power to act for each other.

B.   Syndicate--Similar to a joint venture, in that it is usually formed for the completion of one project. Formal ownership may take any form (corporation, partnership, etc.)

C.   Joint Stock Company--No formal mechanism needed to create. Combination of partnership and corporation. Corporate aspects include directors and officers, shareholder's ability to transfer shares and perpetual existence. Members do not have the power to act for the company or each other. Partnership aspects include personal liability of members and property ownership in member's names.

D.   Business Trust--Formal mechanism in the form of a trust agreement where business assets are held in the name of trustee. The owners are beneficiaries. The trustee, not the beneficiaries, has management powers.

E.   Cooperative--Non-profit association designed to provide or receive a service. Can be incorporated (treated as a non-profit corporation) or unincorporated (treated as a partnership). Used primarily to gain greater purchasing or selling power by pooling resources.

II.   Comparison of Business Organizations

A.   Method of Creation--As noted above, corporations and limited partnerships require formal creation. Sole proprietorships and general partnerships do not.

B. Legal Entity--A corporation is a separate "legal person" and can sue and be sued in its own name. The owners of the sole proprietorship are the business; no separate legal entity. Most states do not recognize a partnership as a separate entity.

C. Liability of Owners--Sole proprietors and general partners are individually liable for business debts. Corporate shareholders and limited partners are liable only for the amount invested.

D. Duration--A partnership and sole proprietorship can be terminated by acts of the members, including death, withdrawal and bankruptcy. A corporation continues in existence regardless of a change in shareholders. In most states, a limited partnership is dissolved only by acts of general partners.

E. Transferability of Ownership--If a sole proprietorship changes hands, the original business ceases to exist. A partner can transfer his or her interest but the assignee does not gain full membership rights. Corporate shareholders can transfer all rights.

F. Management--A sole proprietorship and a general partnership are managed by the owners. A limited partnership is managed by the general partners only. In a corporation, management is separated from ownership. Shareholders (owners) elect directors who provide general management and the directors appoint officers to provide daily administration of the business.

G. Need for Capital--Generally partnerships and corporations are able to raise capital by encouraging investment, but control over the business decreases as the number of owners increases. A sole proprietor retains control but may look only to a lender for funds. A lender may require the shareholders of a small and new corporation to guarantee repayment.

H. Fees and Paperwork--A proprietorship and general partnership pay only fees associated with operation of a business (e.g. license to do business). A general partnership and a corporation pay annual fees and taxes to the state and are required to complete reports.

I. Interstate Business--Because a limited partnership and a corporation are created formally, other states may require a certificate of authority to do business.

J. Taxation--As a general rule, a corporation is a separate legal entity and is treated as such. On the other hand, a partnership or sole proprietorship is a channel to the owners and they are taxed directly.

(1) Corporation--Must file a separate federal income tax return. Corporation is taxed on profits when earned and shareholders

are taxed when dividends are received. State income tax is also levied against a corporation. Gains, losses and accumulation of earnings are not passed on to the shareholders. Exempt interest received by the corporation is taxed to the shareholders if it is distributed.

Can establish an exempt pension trust for employees; payments are deductible by the corporation. Social security tax applies to employees. Death benefits up to $5,000 tax free to beneficiaries of employees and shareholders.

(2)   Partnership--Federal income tax return for information purposes only; the partnership does not pay tax. Partners are taxed on business income even if payment is not distributed. Exempt interest flows directly to partner; his or her share is exempt.

Formal pension trust not allowed; partners can file individual retirement plans. Social security tax only for employees who are not partners; partners pay self-employment tax. No exempt death benefits.

IV.   Private Franchise--Defined by agreement. The participants may take any form of business organization (e.g. corporation, sole proprietorship). Used generally in national or regional retail businesses.

A.   Parties--The franchisor is a "parent" who owns a trademark, patent or copyright. The franchisor gives the franchisee ("child") a license or permission to use these rights. Legally, the franchisor and the franchisee are separate but the franchise contract may bind the two economically.

B.   Types of Franchises

(1)   Distributorship--The franchisor is a manufacturer; the franchisee is a retailer or wholesaler. The franchisor gives a license to sell its products to the franchisee.

(2)   Chain-Styles--In addition to the right to sell the franchisor's product, the franchisee generally must maintain standards of operation acceptable to the franchisor. The franchisee may also be required to buy supplies from the franchisor.

(3)   Manufacturing/Plant Agreement--The right to manufacture and to distribute the product is licensed to the franchisee. The franchisee must conduct both aspects of the operation in accordance with the franchisor's standards.

C.   The Franchise Agreement--The primary benefit for the franchisee is name recognition with the parent and an established clientele. The franchisor must be sure that the franchisee conducts business properly. The most common clauses, listed below, are designed to accomplish that purpose.

(1)   Payment--Franchise usually pays a lump sum for start-up costs and supplies. Franchisee will also purchase replacement supplies from the franchisor and the franchisor receives a percentage of the profits from the franchisee. Some agreements also require a franchisee to contribute to advertising and administrative costs.

(2)   Location and Exclusive Territory--This is determined by the franchisor. The franchisee purchases the right to operate in a particular location; this right may be exclusive or non-exclusive. The franchisor may require the franchisee to purchase or lease a particular location for the business.

(3)   Standards of Operation--Varies with each agreement. The franchisor may wish close supervision of employee training, financial management and quality control. As a part of quality control, the franchisor may require that the franchisee purchase supplies from the parent. Price controls are risky because an agreement to set prices is a violation of the antitrust laws; the franchisor may suggest minimum prices.

(4)   Termination--Most initial agreements are short-term. Contracts are prepared by the franchisor and usually state that the agreement may be canceled for any breach of agreement. Courts try to balance the rights of the parties and may imply a reasonable time before cancellation is allowed.

Study Questions

Fill-in-the-Blank Questions

An agreement between two or more persons to carry on a business for profit is a requirement of a _____.
                          (business trust/partnership)

An incorporated cooperative is treated as a _____.
                                        (partnership/corporation)

In a business trust, the management of the business is conducted by the _____.

        (director/trustee/officer/beneficiary)

The owners of a corporation are the _____.
                            (directors/shareholders)

True-False Questions

1.   A corporation must pay federal income tax. _____

2.   In order to create a joint venture, the owner must file with the secretary of state. _____

3.   A franchisor may establish the prices at which the franchisee sells its products. _____

4.   A limited partner is liable for business debts only up to the amount of his or her investment. _____

5.   A corporation is dissolved or terminated when a shareholder sells stock to an outsider. _____

6.   Unless otherwise specified, partners share equally in the management of the business. _____

7.   A joint stock company is a synonym for a corporation. _____

8.   Burger King is an example of a chain-style franchise. _____

9.   One disadvantage of a sole proprietorship is the inability to raise capital. _____

10.   A limited partnership must have at least one general partner and one limited partner. _____

Multiple-Choice Questions

1.   Which of the following terms of business must be created in accordance with a statute?

    a.   General partnership
    b.   Limited partnership
    c.   Joint Venture
    d.   Sole proprietorship

2.   Which of the following are personally liable for the debts of a business organization?

    a.   General partner
    b.   Limited partner
    c.   Beneficiary
    d.   Shareholder

3.   Which of the following is <u>not</u> associated with a corporation?

   a.   Trustee
   b.   Director
   c.   Shareholder
   d.   Officer

4.   Which of the following forms of a business is used to complete a single transaction?

   a.   Joint venture
   b.   Syndicate
   c.   Both a & b
   d.   Neither a nor b

5.   Which of the following is <u>not</u> a characteristic of a general partnership?

   a.   Creation according to statute
   b.   Equal management rights to all partners
   c.   Personal liability for partnership debts
   d.   Partners pay income tax

6.   Which of the following is an example of a cooperative?

   a.   Businessmen pooling assets to build a shopping center
   b.   Consumers pooling assets to buy food at wholesale prices
   c.   Local outlet of fast-food restaurant
   d.   Local distributor of farm equipment

7.   Which of the following establishes general management procedures for a corporation?

   a.   Beneficiaries
   b.   Officers
   c.   Shareholders
   d.   Directors

8.   Which of the following is(are) common clauses in a franchise agreement?

   a.   Franchisee pays lump-sum for start-up costs
   b.   Quality control established by franchisor
   c.   Supplies purchased from franchisor
   d.   All of the above

9.   Which of the following is <u>not</u> required to form a partnership?

   a.   One or more partners
   b.   Agreement to share profit and losses
   c.   Agreement to carry on a business

d.   Written partnership agreement

10.   Which of the following is <u>not</u> a characteristic of a limited partnership?

a.   At least one limited partner and one general partner
b.   All partners are personally liable for business debts
c.   Formal creation according to statute
d.   Limited partners cannot participate in management

11.   Sam, an entrepreneur, is negotiating a contract with a national cosmetics manufacturer, Beautiful You. According to the agreement, Beautiful You will supply the formula and packaging for different products. Sam will purchase a local manufacturing site and will have the right to distribute the cosmetics in a five-state area. Beautiful You will receive 3% of Sam's profits. The agreement between Sam and Beautiful You is a:

a.   manufacturing franchise.
b.   chain-style franchise.
c.   syndicate.
d.   joint venture.

12.   Beautiful You is a:

a.   director.
b.   franchisee.
c.   franchisor.
d.   beneficiary.

13.   Sam is a:

a.   general partner.
b.   limited partner.
c.   franchisor.
d.   franchisee.

14.   Which of the following is a characteristic of a sole proprietorship?

a.   Personal liability of the owner for business debts
b.   Sole management powers
c.   Both a & b
d.   Neither a nor b

15.   Which of the following is <u>not</u> a tax characteristic of a corporation?

a.   Corporation pays annual income tax
b.   Shareholders pay taxes on capital gains earned by corporation
c.   Shareholders pay tax when dividends are distributed
d.   Tax-free pension fund may be established

16.   Which of the following forms of business organizations is most similar to a joint venture?

       a.   Corporation
       b.   General Partnership
       c.   Cooperative
       d.   Business Trust

17.   Which of the following is a characteristic of a joint stock company?

       a.   Equal management rights by all members
       b.   Automatically dissolved when members change
       c.   Members are personally liable for business debts
       d.   Stock is not transferable

18.   Which of the following is a tax aspect of a partnership?

       a.   Partners pay tax on profits of a business whether distributed or not
       b.   Partnership pays separate income tax
       c.   Tax-free pension fund may be established
       d.   Partners must pay social security tax

19.   Which of the following is a characteristic of a corporation and of a joint stock company?

       a.   Members are personally liable for business debts
       b.   Perpetual existence
       c.   All members have equal management rights
       d.   Shares are not transferable

20.   In a business trust, management is directed by the:

       a.   director.
       b.   beneficiaries.
       c.   officers.
       d.   trustee.

21.   If a general partnership has no formal agreement, which of the following will determine the rights of the partners?

       a.   RULPA
       b.   ULPA
       c.   UPA
       d.   none of the above, there is no partnership because a written agreement is required.

22.   A disadvantage of a sole proprietorship is:

       a.   difficulty in raising capital.

b.   owner determines management.
c.   double taxation.
d.   formal creation by filing required.

23.   Which of the following clauses in a franchise agreement is most likely to be found illegal?

a.   Franchisor requires franchisee to purchase supplies from franchisor
b.   Franchisor requires franchisee to keep minimum capital
c.   Franchisor establishes resale price of products
d.   Franchisee given exclusive distributorship

24.   Which of the following forms of business have perpetual existence?

a.   Sole proprietorship
b.   General partnership
c.   Joint stock company
d.   None of the above

25.   Which of the following is an example of a chain-style franchise agreement?

a.   Automobile dealership
b.   Soft-drink bottling plant
c.   Toy manufacturing plant
d.   Fast-food restaurant

Answers to Study Questions

Fill-in-the-Blank Questions

A partnership is an agreement by two or more persons to carry on a business for a profit. A business trust is a more formal arrangement where a trustee holds title to assets and manages the business; the beneficiaries receive the profits.

An incorporated cooperative is treated as a non-profit corporation. An unincorporated cooperative is treated as a partnership.

In a business trust, management is provided by the trustee. Officers and directors manage a corporation. Beneficiaries receive the profits from a business trust but do not participate in management.

The owners are the shareholders; the directors are the managers.

True-False Questions

1.   T.

2.   F.   Only an implied or express agreement is required.

3.   F.   This would be a violation of the antitrust laws. The franchisor may suggest minimum prices.

4.   T.

5.   F.   The shares usually are freely transferable.

6.   T.

7.   F.   A joint stock company combines elements of a corporation and a partnership.

8.   T.

9.   T.

10.   T.

Multiple-Choice Questions

1.	b	14.	c
2.	a	15.	b
3.	a	16.	b
4.	c	17.	c
5.	a	18.	a
6.	b	19.	b
7.	d	20.	d
8.	d	21.	c
9.	d	22.	a
10.	b	23.	c
11.	a	24.	c
12.	c	25.	d
13.	d		

CHAPTER 24

Agency

General Principles

Agency is an agreement between two parties where one person (the agent) agrees to act <u>on behalf of</u> and <u>instead of</u> another (the principal). The relationship between a shop owner and his sales staff is a typical agency relationship. The staff operates on behalf of the owner because all funds received are submitted to the owner. The staff operates instead of the owner when sales are made (i.e. the owner does not have to make all sales in person).

Because the agent works for the principal, there is a trust or <u>fiduciary</u> relationship between the parties. Because the agent deals with third parties in the place of the principal, the principal is held responsible for approved acts of the agent.

Chapter Summary

I. <u>Types of Agency Relationships</u>--There are three types of agency; the type of agency varies with the amount of control exercised by the principal over the agent. The type of agency may determine the extent of the agent's authority and the principal's responsibility for the agent's acts. It is not the title of the agent that determines his or her status but the nature of the agent's duties. Some acts of an independent contractor may be considered acts of an agent.

A. <u>Principal-Agent</u>--Employer has less control over details and agent acts in the place of the principal. Principal is responsible for authorized acts of the agent. EX: corporation-officer, manager-sales staff.

B. <u>Employer-Employee</u>--Also called master-servant relationship. Employer has control over details of the employee's work and employee has little or no judgment in manner of work. Employer is responsible for any acts of employee while working. Some duties of an employee may involve agency. EX: restaurant-busboy.

C.   Employer/Principal - Independent Contractor--Employer has little or no control over the details of the contractor's work. Employer is not responsible for acts of the independent contractor. Sometimes difficult to distinguish between an employee and independent contractor; courts will look at factors below. EX: client-attorney; homeowner-contractor.

Independent Contractor--A specialist with business apart from client's, uses own tools, paid on a project basis.

Employee--Works only for the employer (second job OK), employer provides work space and tools, paid on a salary or commission basis.

II.   Formation of Agency Relationships--Voluntary arrangement implied or expressed between the parties. Similar to contract rules with the following exceptions: no formality required, no consideration required, only principal needs contractual capacity.

A.   Agency by Agreement--Can be expressed or implied by conduct.

B.   Agency by Ratification--Principal consents after the agent has performed. Can be implied if the principal keeps the benefits of the agent's acts.

C.   Agency by Estoppel--Representation by the principal that would lead a third party to believe that an agency relationship exists. Acts of the agent alone are insufficient. Principal is prevented or estopped from denying the relationship.

D.   Agency by Operation of Law--Exception to the voluntariness standard. The law implies an agency relationship between husband and wife and between partners. Officers are considered agents of a corporation.

III.   Agent's Duties

A.   Performance--Paid agent has the duty to use ordinary skill based on experience and expertise. Failure to do so is grounds for breach of contract. A non-paid (gratuitous) agent cannot be sued in contract but may be responsible for negligence or misrepresentation.

B.   Notification--Because the agent acts in the place of the principal, the agent must notify the principal of agency dealings. A third party may assume that notice to the agent is sufficient to notify the principal.

C.   Loyalty--No self-dealing by agent. Agent cannot represent two principals without the consent of all. Includes confidentiality of agency business.

D.   Obedience--Agent must obey lawful orders of the principal except in emergency situations. Failure to do so is grounds for breach of contract.

E.   Accounting--Duty to explain disbursement and receipt of money. No commingling of personal and agency funds. An accounting is also a legal action brought to force agent to explain his or her records.

IV.   Principal's Duties--Based primarily on contract rules.

A.   Compensation--Unless expressly agreed, the principal has the duty to pay for services rendered by the agent. No duty to gratuitous agent.

B.   Reimbursement and Indemnification--If agent uses personal funds on authorized agency business, the principal must repay (reimburse) the agent. If the agent is sued by a third party or otherwise suffers a loss in the course of the agency, the principal has a duty to stand behind (indemnify) the agent for any loss.

C.   Cooperation--Principal must not interfere with agent's acts if the principal has authorized them. Arises in exclusive dealing arrangements; principal cannot allow competition from other agents in exclusive territory.

D.   Safe Working Conditions--Some required by statute, including worker's compensation (employees only). General duty to provide a safe location and equipment.

V.   Scope of Agent's Authority--A principal may be responsible for an agent's dealings with third parties. This responsibility is dependent on three factors: the scope of the agent's authority, the cause of action (contract or tort), and disclosure of the agency to the third party.

It may be helpful to look at this problem from a third party's point of view. If the third party can show authority in any of the ways listed below, the principal will be responsible for the agent's acts. Note also that if the principal is held responsible, he or she may be able to shift the loss to the agent.

A.   Express Authority--Explicit and stated duties. Can be written or oral. If the agent's duties involve written contracts, then the agent's agreement with the principal must be in writing. This is the equal dignity rule. If the agency agreement is not in writing, the agent has no power to conclude a binding contract for which the law requires a writing. The contract is voidable at the option of the principal. Agent may sue principal for reimbursement.

B.   Implied Authority--Unstated but customary duties of a person in the agent's position. Includes any power necessary to carry out express duties. Test is whether it is reasonable for the agent to believe that he or she has the authority to do the act. Agent may sue principal for reimbursement.

C.   Apparent Authority and Estoppel--Similar to rules for creation of an agency discussed above. Based on acts of the principal which would lead a third party to believe (reasonably) that the agent represented the principal. The acts of the agent do not matter. Usually occurs when the agent has possession of the principal's property. When land is involved, possession alone is not enough, the agent must also have some evidence of ownership such as a deed. Agent may not sue for reimbursement.

D.   Ratification--Occurs after the agent's dealing with a third party (retroactive authority). Although the agent may not have had the express or implied authority to act, the principal accepts the acts of the agent. Third party has the right to withdraw before ratification.

In order for a principal to ratify an act, certain requirements must be met: the principal must know all the facts of the transaction with the third party, the transaction can be ratified completely or not at all (no partial acceptance), principal must have contractual capacity to ratify at the time of the act and at the time of the ratification. In addition, if the equal dignity rule would require a writing, the ratification must be in writing. Agent may sue for reimbursement.

VI.   Liability for Contracts--A principal may be responsible for contracts made by the agent. This liability depends on disclosure of the agency relationship to third parties.

A.   Disclosed Principal--If the agency relationship and the name of the principal are known to the third party, the third party can sue the principal only if the agent's authority is shown. If the third party cannot show that the agent acted with authority, neither the principal nor the agent is responsible.

B.   Partially Disclosed Principal--If the third party has knowledge of the agency relationship but does not know the name of the principal, the same rules apply.

C.   Undisclosed Principal--If neither the agency relationship nor the name of the principal is known to the third party, the agent is personally responsible. The principal will be liable if the agent acted with authority. The principal, even though unknown to the third party, can hold the third party to the contract unless: (1) contract specifically excludes principal, (2) agent signs a negotiable instrument with agent's name only, or (3) agent's duty is personal and cannot be delegated.

VII.   <u>Liability for Agent's Torts</u>--Agent is always responsible for his or her own torts, but it may be more lucrative to sue the principal. If the principal is held responsible, he or she can sue the agent for indemnification.

    A.   <u>General Rule</u>--The rule of respondeat superior holds that the principal is responsible for acts of the agent performed while the agent was working for the principal (within the scope of the agent's employment). Usually a close question of fact but the courts will look at the following factors: whether the agent is on company or personal business, whether the employer had reason to know that the agent would do the act, and whether the act had been done before.

    B.   <u>Misrepresentation</u>--Ask if the agent was authorized to make representations (not necessarily <u>mis</u>representations). Some courts hold the principal liable if the agent was put in a position to make misrepresentations or if the principal failed to supervise the agent.

    C.   <u>Negligence</u>--Use scope of employment test.

    D.   <u>Intentional Torts</u>--Although a principal would never authorize an intentional tort, ask if the act was performed while the agent was within the scope of employment.

VIII.   <u>Liability for Independent Contractor's Acts</u>

    A.   <u>General Rule</u>--A principal is not responsible for the acts of an independent contractor.

    B.   <u>Exception</u>--Hazardous activities. Usually courts or statutes hold employers strictly liable.

IX.   <u>Liability for Agent's Crimes</u>--A principle is not responsible for the criminal acts of an agent.

X.   <u>Termination of the Agency</u>--Distinguish between the power to terminate the agency and the right to do so. Because agency is based on the consent of the parties, either the agent or the principal has the power to terminate at any time. However, if the termination is in breach of the agency agreement, the breaching party has no right to terminate and can be sued for losses sustained by the non-breaching party. The events listed below give a party the <u>right</u> to terminate the agency. Also note the effect of termination on the rights of third parties.

    A.   <u>Methods of Termination</u>

        (1)   <u>General Rule</u>--If the agency is for a specified period of time, it will lapse if not revived by the parties. The same is true if the agency was designed to accomplish a specific purpose. When the purpose is achieved, the agency ends. The agency

agreement can always be rescinded by agreement of the parties.

(2)   Termination by Operation of Law--Similar to rules for terminating any contract. Death, insanity, or bankruptcy will terminate the agency immediately--notice is not required. The agency can also be terminated by impossibility of performance or commercial impracticability (changed circumstances). If the agent's and principal's countries are at war with each other, the agency is terminated.

(3)   Agency Coupled With an Interest (Irrevocable Agency)--An agency created solely for the benefit of the agent normally cannot be revoked if as a part of the agreement, the agent has an interest in the property of the agency. The most common example is agency property used as collateral for a loan or property transferred to an agent for the agent's benefit. Commissions do not suffice; the agent must have some type of ownership interest in the property.

(4)   Third-Party Notice--None required if the agency terminates by operation of law. If terminated by an act of the parties, the principal has the duty to notify third parties that the agency has terminated. Otherwise, the agent's apparent authority can bind the principal even after the agency has been terminated.

Type of Notice--Any notice to agent is sufficient unless the agreement was in writing. If so, must be revoked in writing. Third parties who have dealt with the agent are entitled to actual notice. Other third parties are entitled to "constructive notice", that is, notice which is likely to reach third parties. This is usually accomplished by publication in a newspaper or trade journal.

Study Questions

Fill-in-the-Blank Questions

The Yarn Barn, a needleworks store, is owned by Pearl Cotton. She hires Cathy Crochet to act as assistant manager. Although there is no written employment contract, Pearl tells Cathy that her job is to order inventory, to sell supplies to customers, and to keep financial and inventory records. While Pearl is gone to market, the following events occur. Cathy hires Flossie as a sales clerk. Cathy also orders inventory from Sewing Supplies and refunds money to a disgruntled customer.

Pearl is the _____.
                    (agent/principal)

Cathy has _____ authority to order inventory.
      (express/implied/apparent)

Cathy has _____ authority to refund a customer's money.
      (express/implied/no)

Cathy has _____ authority to hire Flossie.
      (express/no)

True-False Questions

1.   An agent always has the power to terminate an agency. _____

2.   The equal dignity rule states that an agent has the same power to make a contract as the principal does. _____

3.   An agency by estoppel is created by the acts of the agent. _____

4.   If an agent makes a contract on behalf of an undisclosed principal, only the agent is liable for performance. _____

5.   When an agency is terminated, the principal must give actual notice to all parties with whom the agent has dealt. _____

6.   A principal is generally liable for the torts of an independent contractor. _____

7.   A gratuitous agent may not be sued for breach of contract even if he or she fails to perform according to the principal's instructions. _____

8.   In an agency by ratification, a third party has the right to withdraw from any contract made by the agent if withdrawal is made before the principal ratifies the agent's acts. _____

9.   The relationship between a patient and a doctor is one between employer-employee. _____

10.   An agent owes a duty of notification to the principal. _____

Multiple-Choice Questions

1.   The authority of a corporate officer to act on behalf of the corporation is an example of an agency formed by:

      a.   ratification.
      b.   estoppel.
      c.   operation of law.
      d.   implication.

2.   Oliver is hired by Dressman Industries to find and purchase a site for Dressman's new manufacturing plant. Oliver finds a suitable site but purchases it in his brother's name. Oliver has breached:

   a.   the duty of obedience.
   b.   the duty of loyalty.
   c.   the duty of accounting.
   d.   no duty.

3.   Assuming that Oliver buys the land for Dressman and that he has no written agency agreement with Dressman:

   a.   Dressman must honor the contract made by Oliver because Oliver had express authority to make the purchase.
   b.   Dressman must honor the contract made by Oliver because Oliver was acting within the scope of his employment.
   c.   The contract is voidable at Dressman's option because a principal can always choose whether or not to accept an act of an agent.
   d.   The contract is voidable at Dressman's option because of the equal dignity rule.

4.   Bob is a salesman for Microfilm Services, Inc. His territory includes several cities and he drives a company car. Bob is on his way to a customer's office when he causes a car accident with Betty. Betty may sue:

   a.   Bob only.
   b.   Microfilm Services only.
   c.   Bob and Microfilm Services.

5.   Microfilm:

   a.   is responsible for Bob's accident because of the doctrine of respondeat superior.
   b.   is responsible for Bob's accident because of the doctrine of agency by estoppel.
   c.   is not responsible for Bob's accident because of doctrine of respondeat superior.
   d.   is not responsible for Bob's accident because of the doctrine of agency by estoppel.

6.   L. Eagle, an attorney, hires Bonnie as his legal assistant. He tells her that her primary duties are to file documents with the clerk's office, to interview witnesses, and to organize documents. L. Eagle also hires Cindy as an assistant for Bonnie. Cindy's job is to make copies of documents and to file incoming mail. The relationship between Eagle and Cindy is:

   a.   employer-employee.
   b.   principal-agent.
   c.   employer-independent contractor.

    d.   none of the above.

7.   The relationship between Eagle and Bonnie is:

    a.   employer-employee only.
    b.   employer-employee and principal-agent depending on which duty Bonnie is performing.
    c.   employer-independent contractor only.
    d.   principal-agent and employer-independent contractor depending on which duty Bonnie is performing.

8.   Bonnie asks Cindy to deliver documents to a client. Bonnie has _____ authority to ask Cindy to deliver documents.

    a.   express
    b.   implied
    c.   apparent
    d.   no

9.   When Cindy delivers the documents to the client, the client gives Cindy a check made out to Eagle for legal services. Cindy cashes the check and moves to Mexico. When Eagle discovers what has happened, he demands a new check from the client.

    a.   Eagle is within his rights because Cindy had no actual authority to receive the check.
    b.   Eagle is within his rights because Cindy had no apparent authority to receive the check.
    c.   Eagle is not within his rights because Cindy had express authority to receive the check.
    d.   Eagle is not within his rights because Cindy had apparent authority to receive the check.

10.   After working for Eagle for two years, Bonnie takes a new job with Abel Advocate, another attorney. While at a former client's office, Bonnie picks up a check meant for Eagle. Bonnie joins Cindy in Mexico. Eagle again demands that the client write a second check.

    a.   Eagle is within his rights because Bonnie's authority terminated when she went to work for Able.
    b.   Eagle is within his rights because Bonnie should have notified the client that she no longer worked for Eagle.
    c.   Eagle is not within his rights because he should have notified the client that Bonnie no longer worked for him.
    d.   Eagle is not within his rights because Bonnie had implied authority to receive the check, even though she no longer worked for Eagle.

11.   Which of the following is most indicative of an employer-independent contractor relationship?

a.   Employee's work space provided by employer
b.   Details of employee's work are controlled by employer
c.   Employee is paid on a commission basis
d.   Employee is paid on a project basis

12.   Elmer is a delivery person for Gordon's milk. His duties are to deliver milk and to take orders. Hannah tells Elmer that she no longer wishes to receive deliveries from Gordon. Elmer says nothing to Gordon's manager. The next day a new route salesman leaves two quarts of milk at Hannah's door.

a.   Hannah must pay for the milk because the new delivery person had apparent authority to deliver milk to Hannah.
b.   Hannah must pay for the milk because she should have called Gordon's manager.
c.   Hannah need not pay for the milk because Elmer violated his duty of obedience.
d.   Hannah need not pay for the milk because Elmer violated his duty of notification.

13.   Belinda is a buyer for a local boutique. While at market, she uses her credit card to pay for the hotel room and meals. The boutique owner's duty to pay Belinda for the hotel room and the meals is the duty of:

a.   cooperation.
b.   reimbursement.
c.   indemnification.
d.   compensation.

14.   Although Belinda is told that she can purchase only clothes, she orders 25 silver bracelets to sell as accessories. The boutique refuses to honor the contract with the bracelet merchant.

a.   The boutique is within its rights because Belinda has no authority to purchase the bracelets.
b.   The boutique is within its rights because Belinda acted outside the scope of her employment.
c.   The boutique is not within its rights because Belinda had apparent authority to purchase the bracelets.
d.   The boutique is not within its rights because Belinda had implied authority to purchase the bracelets.

15.   If the boutique pays for the bracelets:

a.   it can seek reimbursement from Belinda, because Belinda had no implied authority to order the bracelets.
b.   it can seek reimbursement from Belinda because Belinda had no express authority to order the bracelets.
c.   it cannot seek reimbursement from Belinda because Belinda had express authority to order the bracelets.

d.   it cannot seek reimbursement from Belinda because the boutique ratified the purchase.

16.   Without authority, Belinda also orders some pins in the shape of reindeer, thinking that the boutique can sell them during Christmas. Belinda agrees to purchase the pins on consignment. The contract between Belinda and the pin maker states that after initial sales of twenty pins, any extra unsold pins can be returned. The boutique owner also likes the pins and agrees to honor the contract. However, Belinda neglects to tell her the limits of the consignment.

   a.   The boutique owner is bound to the contract because she ratified it.
   b.   The boutique owner is not bound to the contract because she did not ratify the entire contract.
   c.   The pin maker has no power to withdraw from the agreement because the boutique owner has ratified the contract.
   d.   The pin maker has no power to withdraw from the contract because Belinda had the authority to make the contract.

17.   Ann asks Bob, her neighbor, to mail a letter for her. The letter contains an acceptance of employment with an accounting firm. Bob forgets to mail the letter and Ann loses the job.

   a.   Ann can sue Bob for breach of contract and negligence.
   b.   Ann can sue Bob for breach of contract but not for negligence.
   c.   Ann can sue Bob for negligence but not for breach of contract.
   d.   Ann cannot sue Bob for negligence, nor can she sue him for breach of contract.

18.   Ron is a salesman for Mission Motors. He tells Ralph, a customer, that Mission is looking for a new showroom. Ralph offers to sell Ron some land. Ron agrees and signs the contract in the following manner, "Ron, for Mission Motors." When the owner of Mission Motors learns of the contract, he refuses to honor it.

   a.   Ralph can sue Ron and/or Mission Motors for breach of contract.
   b.   Ralph can sue Ron, but not Missions Motors for breach of contract.
   c.   Ralph can sue Mission Motors, but not Ron for breach of contract.
   d.   Ralph can sue neither Ron nor Mission Motors for breach of contract.

19.   Which of the following is an example of an irrevocable agency?

   a.   Homeowner hires real estate salesman to sell house, contract is for a period of six months, salesman will receive 5 percent commission, homeowner breaches after two months.
   b.   Father authorizes his daughter to sell stock to investors in father's corporation. Father tries to revoke daughter's right to sell.
   c.   Barney borrows money from First Bank and uses his vacation home as collateral. The note states that if Barney cannot repay the loan, the bank has the right to sell the property and keep the proceeds to satisfy

the loan. Barney tries to revoke the bank's power to sell.

d.   Door-to-door salesman is hired to sell greeting cards for $4.00 per box. Salesman is allowed to keep $2.50 per box and remits the rest to his employer. Employer fires salesman without cause.

20.   Ralph is the manager of a fast-food restaurant. He has worked at the restaurant and has dealt directly with Farmer Brown, who supplies milk to the restaurant, Linen Supply, which furnishes napkins and paper towels, and the bank, where Ralph has the authority to sign checks. Which of the following are entitled to actual notice if Ralph is fired?

a.   The bank, Farmer Brown and Linen Supply
b.   Farmer Brown and Linen Supply
c.   The bank only
d.   The bank, Farmer Brown, Linen Supply and customers of the restaurant

21.   The agent's duty to return funds collected on behalf of the principal is the duty of:

a.   reimbursement.
b.   accounting.
c.   obedience.
d.   indemnification.

22.   If an agent concludes a contract on behalf of an undisclosed principal, who is responsible to the third party?

a.   The agent only
b.   The principal only, but only if the agent acts with authority
c.   The principal and the agent, but the principal is liable only if the agent acts with authority
d.   Neither the agent nor the principal

23.   A cashier is trying to collect payment from a store customer. The cashier becomes so exasperated that she grabs the customer by the arm. The customer sues the store for assault.

a.   The customer will prevail if the cashier acted within the scope of her employment.
b.   The customer will prevail because a principal is always liable for the torts of his or her agent.
c.   The customer will not prevail because the principal is never liable for the intentional torts of his or her agent.

24.   Which of the following is not a duty owed by an agent to a principal?

a.   Accounting
b.   Obedience

c.   Cooperation
d.   Loyalty

25.   In which of the following cases, is an agent prevented from suing a principal for reimbursement?

a.   Agent had express authority to do the act in question
b.   Agent had implied authority to do the act in question
c.   Agent had apparent authority to do the act in question
d.   Principal ratified the act in question

Answers to Study Questions

Fill-in-the-Blank Questions

Pearl is the principal; Cathy is the agent. Cathy has express authority to order inventory because Pearl specifically listed it as one of her duties. Cathy has implied authority to refund a customer's money. This authority is necessary to carry out her duties as assistant manager. Cathy has no authority to hire employees. It is arguable that she may have apparent authority, but that is not one of the choices listed.

True-False Questions

1.   T.   He or she may not have the right to terminate.

2.   F.   The equal dignity rule states that in order for an agent to have the authority to make written contracts, the agency agreement must also be in writing.

3.   F.   It can be created only by the acts of the principal.

4.   T.

5.   T.

6.   F.   The principal is liable for the torts of an agent or employee but only if the act was done within the scope of employment.

7.   T.   A gratuitous agent has no contract but he or she may be sued for negligence.

8.   T.

9.   F.   It is an employer-independent contractor relationship.

10.   T.

Multiple-Choice Questions

1.	c
2.	b
3.	d
4.	c
5.	a
6.	a
7.	b
8.	b
9.	d
10.	c
11.	d
12.	d
13.	b

14.	c
15.	d
16.	b
17.	c
18.	d
19.	c
20.	a
21.	b
22.	c
23.	a
24.	c
25.	c

Partnerships

General Principles

A partnership is a voluntary agreement between two or more persons to carry on a continuing business. It can be created informally. It can also be terminated or dissolved easily because the continuation of the business depends on the willingness and financial capability of the partners. A limited partnership is somewhat more formal; it consists of general partners, who operate the business in a manner similar to a partnership, and limited partners, who are treated as investors similar to shareholders of a corporation. A limited partnership must be created according to the rules of a statute. Dissolution is regulated by statute and the limited partnership agreement.

A partnership implies an equal right of management in each partner. This arrangement may be modified somewhat by agreement. General partners are agents of each other and the rules of agency apply. Partners owe a fiduciary duty to each other. The power of partners to deal with third parties is also governed by agency and the rules of express, implied, and apparent authority. The liability of partners depends on whether recovery is based on tort or on contract. In contrast, limited partners are liable only for the amount of their investment unless they take an active role in management.

Chapter Outline

I.   Partnerships

      A.   Definition--"An association of two or more persons to carry on as co-owners a business for profit." Each partner must have some ownership interest but the interests do not have to be equal.

B.   Partnership Characteristics--As a general rule, a partnership is treated as an entity (rather than a collection of individuals) for purposes of lawsuits and property ownership. In contrast, individual partners pay income tax on their individual shares of partnership profits.

C.   Governing Law--Usually governed by the partnership agreement. The Uniform Partnership Act (UPA) is used as a gap-filler.

II.   Partnership Formation

A.   Formalities--Usually created by an agreement called the articles of partnership. Can be created orally or by actions as long as parties agree. A writing is not necessary unless the Statute of Frauds requires one. If the partnership is to continue for more than one year or if the partnership intends to buy and sell land, the agreement must be in writing.

B.   Partnership Duration--Can designate specific time limits (partnership for a term), or, if no period is specified, a partnership at will exists. Although a partner cannot be forced to remain in a partnership against his or her will, a partner who withdraws prior to the end of a stated term can be sued for breach of the partnership agreement.

C.   The Corporation as Partner--The capacity of a corporation to be a partner depends on state corporation law. Most states allow a corporation to become a partner; others require a specific provision in the corporate charter. The UPA permits corporations to be partners.

D.   Indications of Partnership--In a partnership, profits and losses must be shared and each partner has a right to manage the business. A sharing of profits only is not enough if the agreement involves payment of a loan, a landlord-tenant relationship, wages on commission, payment of an annuity, or a sale of the business when the owner retires.

E.   Partnership by Estoppel--May be created if a third person reasonably relies on actions of a partner or non-partner. A non-partner who makes representations will be liable for damages caused by his or her actions. If a non-partner is held out as a partner, the non-partner is treated as an agent of the partnership.

III.   Rights Among Partners

A.   Management of a Partnership--Each partner has equal rights in management regardless of percentage of ownership. In the absence of agreement, majority rules. Each partner has the right to examine partnership books and the books are to be kept at the place of business.

(1)   Delegation of Management--The partners may agree to delegate management to one partner but this will not affect liability to an outsider unless he or she knows of the arrangement.

(2)   Fundamental Changes--Unanimous consent of the partners is required to admit a new partner, to change the essential nature of the business, to assign partnership property for the benefit of creditors, to dispose of the partnership's goodwill, to confess judgment against the partnership, to submit claims to arbitration, or to undertake any act which would cause the business to fail.

B.   Interest in Partnership--Percentage of profits and losses due each partner should be in the partnership agreement. If the agreement does not specify, all partners share equally.

C.   Compensation from Partnership--Because partners are owners of the partnership, no compensation can be paid to a partner who performs service on behalf of the partnership. A partnership agreement can, and frequently does, include a salary for a managing partner.

D.   Accounting--This is a legal procedure to determine the value of each partner's ownership interest. May occur on a regular basis, when one or more partners is suspected of withholding funds, or when the circumstances are "just and reasonable."

E.   Property Rights of a Partner

(1)   Partnership Interest--Right to profits and losses are divided equally unless otherwise stated. Can be assigned to third parties; creditors of individual partners can attach by a charging order.

(2)   Right to Specific Partnership Property--All property owned as a tenancy in partnership unless otherwise agreed. Property remains in the partnership when a partner dies or retires; this right cannot be assigned. The remaining partners must account for the value of a deceased partner's interest in specific property. Creditors of a partner cannot attach partnership property until dissolution. Partnership property is all property brought into the partnership or otherwise acquired. Record ownership does not determine whether property is considered an asset of the partnership.

IV.   Powers and Duties of Partners

A.   Fiduciary Duties--Similar to agency powers. A partner must not compete with partnership business or use partnership funds for private use.

B.   Agency Powers--Each partner is the agent of every other partner. A partner may bind the partnership if his or her act is within the scope of the partnership. The only exceptions are those listed above, which require the consent of all partners. There is no implied right to make charitable contributions from partnership funds because partnerships by definition exist to make a profit.

C.   Liability--Partnership can be sued as an entity if state law allows. Otherwise, must sue partners individually.

(1)   Contract--Joint liability. (In some states, contract liability of partners is joint and several, discussed below.) All partners must be sued in the same suit and a judgment against one is a judgment against all. Responsibility for payment may be placed on one or more partners. Then the partners who have paid more than their share are entitled to reimbursement from the other partners.

(2)   Tort--Joint and several liability. Each partner may be sued individually. If one partner wins, a second partner may be sued and found liable. Only partners who are sued may be liable. "Misbehaving" partner may be sued for indemnification by other partners.

(3)   Changing Partners--An incoming partner is liable only to the extent of his or her contribution with regards to events occurring before he or she became a partner. Similarly, an outgoing partner is responsible for events occurring before his or her withdrawal. Assuming proper notice of withdrawal, an old partner is not liable for new debts.

V.   Termination of a General Partnership--Has two parts: dissolution and winding up.

A.   Dissolution--Can occur by acts of the partners, by operation of law, or by a formal court proceeding.

(1)   Acts of the Partners--Admission of a new partner or withdrawal of a partner. A new partnership may continue. Sale or assignment of partner's interest to creditors does not cause dissolution.

(2)   Operation of Law--Death or bankruptcy of a partner. Any event which makes the continuation of the business illegal.

(3)   Judicial Decree--Must formally petition the court. Can occur due to insanity, incapacity, or impropriety of a partner. May also happen when partners disagree as to operation of the business and business is paralyzed.

B.   Notice--Actual notice to partners and third parties with whom the partnership has dealt. Others are entitled to constructive notice, usually by publication in the newspaper.

C.   Winding Up--Purpose is to pay creditors and to distribute assets; no new business may be conducted. Creditors are paid first. Partnership creditors have first right to partnership property but creditors of individual partners may also sue. After creditors are paid, partners receive assets in the following order: repayment of loans made by partners, return of capital contribution, distribution of profits.

VI.   Limited Partnerships

A.   Definition--Must consist of at least one general partner and one limited partner. The general partner is responsible for management of the business; the limited partner cannot manage the business. A general partner's liability for partnership debts is nearly unlimited. A limited partner's liability is limited to the capital he or she contributes to the partnership.

B.   Formation--Must be created in accordance with statute; a certificate of limited partnership which contains the names of the parties and their rights must be filed with a state official.

VII.   Rights and Duties of Limited Partners

A.   Property Rights--Same right to profits and losses as general partners. Interest can be assigned, ownership of partnership property cannot.

B.   Management Rights--Right to accounting of business and to inspect partnership books. No right to management or limited liability will be canceled. Under ULPA only, a limited partner's capital contribution cannot be in the form of services as a manager; a limited partner may be an employee. Limited partner's name cannot appear in the firm name unless that name is also the name of a general partner. Under RULPA, a limited partner who participates in management loses limited liability only if a third party actually knows of the limited partner's management.

C.   Liability for Defective Formation--A limited partnership does not exist technically until a proper certificate of partnership is recorded in a public office. A limited partner is liable for defective filing if he or she knows of the defect and does not withdraw or correct the mistake. If a false statement is knowingly made, a limited partner is liable as a general partner to a third party who relied on the false statement. Good faith compliance will protect the limited partner and will not affect his or her liability.

VIII.   Dissolution of a Limited Partnership

   A.   Dissolution--The death, withdrawal, or insanity of a general partner can cause dissolution but the certificate may provide otherwise. Death, bankruptcy, or sale of the interest of a limited partner does not cause dissolution but illegality and bankruptcy of a general partner automatically causes dissolution. Can also be dissolved by judicial decree as a general partnership can.

   B.   Winding Up--Order of payment depends on statute.

      (1)   ULPA--Outside creditors and creditors of limited partners. Limited partners' profits and capital contributions. Creditors of general partners, profits and capital contribution of general partners.

      (2)   RULPA--Creditors of the partnership and creditors of the partners. Repayment of loans. Capital contributions and profits; limited partners always precede general partners.

Study Questions

Fill-in-the-Blank Questions

Pam and Pat agree to open a gift store. They agree that profits and losses will be shared equally. Pam and Pat each contribute $5,000 to the business and borrow $5,000 from Pat's uncle. The business is successful but after two years, Pat decides that she wants to go to law school and she retires from the business.

Pam and Pat have formed a partnership _____.
                                         (at will/for a term)

The agreement between Pat and Pam _____ be in writing.
                                       (must/need not)

Pat has the _____ to retire.
              (power but no right/power and the right)

When the partnership is dissolved _____ will receive $5,000 before the others.   (Pat/Pam/Pat's uncle)

Sam, Sid, and Rod form a partnership for the purpose of operating an appliance store. The agreement says nothing about division of profits and losses. Sam and Sid work as salesmen; Rod keeps the books and provides the land for location of the store. Betty purchases a steam iron from the store. Sam tells her that the iron is guaranteed for four years and the store will replace any defective iron during that time. Rod is in some financial difficulty and he uses his partnership interest and the entire inventory of the business as collateral for a loan with First Bank.

Sam and Sid are _____ to a salary from the
business.   (entitled/not entitled)

Sam's promise to Betty _____ bind the partnership.
                        (did/did not)

Sid and Rod are _____ liable to Betty.
                 (jointly/not)

Rod _____ assign his partnership interest to the bank.
        (can/cannot)

Rod _____ assign the store's inventory to the bank.
        (can/cannot)

True-False Questions

1.   A limited partnership must consist of at least one general partner and one
      limited partner. _____

2.   The articles of partnership of a general partnership must be filed with the
      appropriate state official._____

3.   When a partnership is dissolved, each partner is entitled to actual notice of
      the dissolution. _____

4.   The bankruptcy of a limited partner will cause dissolution automatically.
      _____

5.   When a partnership is dissolved, loans made by partners are paid before the
      partners' capital contributions are returned. _____

6.   A partnership can be created only if each partner has an ownership interest
      in the business. _____

7.   Death of a general partner automatically causes dissolution of a limited
      partnership. _____

8.   In all states, a corporation can be a partner. _____

9.   Under ULPA, a limited partner may not participate in the management of the
      business. _____

10.   A partnership at will may be terminated at any time by any partner.
      _____

11.   Under both ULPA and RULPA a limited partner may contribute personal or
      real property as part of his or her initial capital contribution _____

12.   If a limited partnership inadvertently submits a certificate of partnership containing a false statement, all limited partners are liable as general partners. _____

13.   Unless otherwise stated, management decisions of the partnership are determined by majority vote. _____

14.   A limited partner is treated as an investor and has limited rights to inspect partnership books. _____

15.   A limited partner cannot be hired as an employee of the business. _____

16.   A partnership's liability for a contract made by a partner depends on whether the contract was made within the scope of the partnership. _____

17.   An outgoing partner is not liable for any lawsuit commenced after he or she withdraws, regardless of when the right to sue arose. _____

18.   For purposes of determining powers to bind the partnership, partners are treated as mutual agents. _____

19.   Under RULPA, a limited partner who participates in management is not liable to third parties unless the outsider had actual knowledge of the limited partner's participation in management. _____

20.   If one partner agrees to submit a partnership claim to arbitration, this decision is binding on the partnership. _____

Multiple-Choice Questions

1.   Which of the following is grounds for dissolution of a partnership by judicial decree?

        a.   Death of a partner
        b.   Bankruptcy of a partner
        c.   Incapacity of a partner
        d.   Illegality of partnership business

2.   A general partnership agreement is also known as:

        a.   the articles of partnership.
        b.   the certificates of partnership.
        c.   the estoppel of partnership.
        d.   the decree of partnership.

3.   Tom and Susan agree to form a partnership for five years for the purpose of manufacturing and marketing false teeth. Tom and Susan have a:

        a.   partnership at will and their agreement need not be in writing.

    b.   partnership for a term and their agreement need not be in writing.

    c.   partnership at will and their agreement must be in writing.

    d.   partnership for a term and their agreement must be in writing.

4.   Which of the following would require a written partnership agreement?

    a.   Partnership to sell real estate for a term of nine months
    b.   Partnership to sell ball point pens for a term of nine months
    c.   Partnership to operate a law practice
    d.   All partnership agreements must be in writing

5.   Betty and Sam orally agree to form a partnership to operate a dry cleaning business. Each contributes $20,000 to start the business. The profits and losses are to be shared equally. Betty is an active partner; she works in the shop and keeps the books. Sam provided financial backing and handles advertising.

    a.   Betty is a general partner; Sam is a limited partner.
    b.   Betty and Sam are general partners.
    c.   Betty and Sam are not partners; Sam is the owner and Betty is an agent.
    d.   Betty and Sam are not partners; they are co-owners of the business.

6.   Sam decides to quit the business and move to Hawaii. He tells no one of his decision. Which of the following are entitled to actual notice of the dissolution of the partnership?

    a.   Betty only
    b.   Betty and anyone with whom Betty and Sam have done business
    c.   Betty and the partnership's creditors only
    d.   No one; constructive notice is always sufficient

7.   Which of the following are stages of termination of a partnership in correct order of their occurrence?

    a.   Dissolution and winding up
    b.   Winding up and dissolution
    c.   Dissolution and distribution
    d.   Winding up and dissolution

8.   Which of the following is <u>not</u> a part of winding up of partnership business?

    a.   Articles of dissolution
    b.   Payment of creditors
    c.   Return of capital contribution
    d.   Payment of profits to partners

9.   Pages, a bookstore operated as a partnership by Bill Blake and Gordy Byron, is dissolving. The partnership has substantial assets including $20,000 cash

and $100,000 in inventory. The partnership owes $1,000 to its supplier. Gordy owes $3,000 to his dentist. Which of the following correctly lists the order of payment upon dissolution?

a. Supplier, Gordy's dentist, Bill and Gordy's profits
b. Gordy's dentist, Bill and Gordy's profits, supplier
c. Supplier, Bill and Gordy's profits, Gordy's dentist
d. Supplier, Bill and Gordy's profits; Gordy's dentist is not entitled to partnership assets

10. Which of the following is not a required element of a partnership?

a. Agreement
b. Co-ownership by partners
c. Management rights of partners
d. Equal distribution of profits and losses

11. Which of the following statements about a limited partnership is false?

a. It must consist of at least one general and one limited partner.
b. All partners, limited and general, have equal management rights.
c. Illegality of the business will cause dissolution automatically.
d. It must be created according to statute.

12. Which of the following is used as a gap-filler when a general partnership agreement is incomplete?

a. UPA
b. ULPA
c. RULPA

13. John and Jerry form a partnership for the purpose of remodeling homes. Jerry's brother Perry tells his bank and several friends that he is a member of the partnership when, in fact, he is not.

a. A partnership by estoppel has been created and Perry is a partner.
b. A partnership by estoppel has not been created and Perry is liable for any damages caused as a result of his representation.
c. A partnership by estoppel has been created; the partnership is liable for any damages caused as a result of Perry's representation.
d. A partnership by estoppel has not been created unless John and Jerry agree to the estoppel.

14. Rudy, Sandy, and Anne have been partners for several years. Anne dies, but Rudy and Sandy agree to continue the business.

a. Anne's death dissolved the partnership by operation of law.
b. Anne's death dissolved the partnership unless the partnership agreement provided for continuation of the business after the death

of a partner

   c.   The partnership may be dissolved if a petition is filed with a court.

   d.   Death of a general partner will not dissolve the partnership.

15.   Assume that Rudy, Sandy, and Anne had formed a limited partnership. Rudy is the limited partner; Sandy and Anne are general partners. Anne dies.

   a.   Anne's death dissolved the partnership by operation of law.

   b.   Anne's death dissolved the partnership unless the partnership agreement provided for continuation of the business after the death of a partner.

   c.   The partnership may be dissolved if a petition is filed with a court.

   d.   Death of a general partner will not dissolve the partnership.

16.   Paul, Peter, and Pinky are partners in an automobile dealership. When the business started, Paul and Peter contributed $10,000 each; Pinky contributed $5,000. However, they agree to split the profits equally. When the partnership needed money, Paul made a loan to the business of $20,000. The partnership has assets of $105,000. When the partnership is dissolved, which of the following is the correct distribution of assets?

   a.   Paul, $50,000; Peter and Pinky $27,000 each

   b.   Paul, Pinky and Peter, $35,000 each

   c.   Paul, $55,000; Peter, $35,000; Pinky $15,000

   d.   Paul, $50,000; Peter, $30,000; Pinky, $25,000

17.   Which of the following is not required for formation of a limited partnership?

   a.   Agreement of the parties

   b.   Filing of certificate of limited partnership

   c.   Registration with RULPA

   d.   Designation of limited and general partners

18.   Which of the following will never cause dissolution of a limited partnership?

   a.   Bankruptcy of a general partner

   b.   Bankruptcy of limited partner

   c.   Illegality of partnership business

   d.   Death of a general partner

19.   A limited partner:

   a.   is not an owner of the limited partnership.

   b.   is allowed to manage the limited partnership.

   c.   is liable only to the amount of his or her contribution of the business.

   d.   is entitled to fewer profits than general partners.

20.   Which of the following may be grounds for dissolution of a partnership by judicial decree?

a.   Death of a partner
b.   Bankruptcy of a partner
c.   Impropriety of a partner
d.   Illegality of partnership business

21.   In a partnership for a term:

a.   each partner has the right and power to withdraw at any time.
b.   there is no right or power to withdraw until the term of the partnership has expired.
c.   there is a power to withdraw at any time but the right to withdraw does not exist until the term of the partnership has expired.
d.   only general partners have the right to withdraw at any time; limited partners have the right to withdraw only after the term of the partnership has expired.

22.   Which of the following correctly described the distribution of assets under RULPA?

a.   Outside creditors of the partnership, limited partners' capital contribution, limited partners' profits, creditors of all partners
b.   Outside creditors of the partnership, creditors of partners, capital contribution of limited and general partners, profits of limited and general partners
c.   Outside creditors of the partnership, creditors of limited partners, limited partners' capital contribution and profits, creditors of general partners
d.   Outside creditors of limited and general partners, outside creditors of the partnership, capital contribution and profits of limited partners, capital contributions and profits of general partners

23.   Which of the following correctly describes the distribution of assets under ULPA?

a.   Outside creditors of the partnership, limited partners' capital contribution, limited partners' profits, creditors of all partners
b.   Outside creditors of the partnership, creditors of partners, capital contribution of limited and general partners, profits of limited and general partners
c.   Outside creditors of the partnership, creditors of limited partners, limited partners' capital contribution and profits, creditors of general partners, general partners' capital contribution and profits
d.   Outside creditors of limited and general partners, outside creditors of the partnership, capital contribution and profits of limited partners, capital contributions and profits of general partners

24.   Sarah, Sally, and Beth form a partnership for the purpose of making and selling novelty sweatshirts. They agree that Sarah will receive 60 percent of the profits, because she will perform most of the work. Sally and Beth are to receive 20 percent each. No provision is made for sharing of losses. Sarah is also given the exclusive power to make all contracts for the partnership if the amount involved is less than $1,000. Because the agreement did not specify the manner in which losses were to be shared:

    a.   Sarah, Sally, and Beth are each liable for one-third of the losses.

    b.   Sarah is responsible for 60 percent of the losses and Beth and Sally are responsible for 20 percent each.

    c.   the agreement is illegal because losses must be apportioned.

    d.   no partnership has been formed because losses must be apportioned.

25.   The partnership of Sarah, Beth, and Sally is sued for breach of contract when one of the sweatshirts is founds to be defective. The partnership is sued for $55, the cost of the sweatshirt.

    a.   Sarah, as the managing partner, has a right to settle the suit because the amount in dispute is less than $1,000.

    b.   All partners must agree to settle the suit, regardless of the amount.

    c.   The liability of the partners for damages is joint and several.

    d.   The plaintiff can sue Sarah or Beth or Sally and recover the full amount.

26.   Which of the following does not require the unanimous consent of the partners?

    a.   Payment of a debt resulting from the action of one partner

    b.   Submission of a claim to arbitration

    c.   Sale of the goodwill of the business

    d.   Admission of a new partner

27.   Which of the following is not a right of a limited partner?

    a.   Inspection of partnership books

    b.   Filing a legal action to account for partnership funds

    c.   Working for the partnership as an employee

    d.   Inclusion of his or her name in the name of the business

28.   Bud, Sam, and John form a limited partnership. Bud is the limited partner; Sam and John are general partners. The partnership is sued when Sam, while conducting partnership business, causes an automobile accident.

    a.   Bud, Sam, and John are jointly liable to the victim of the car accident.

    b.   Sam and John are jointly liable to the victim of the car accident; Bud is not liable.

    c.   Bud, Sam, and John are jointly and severally liable to the victim of the car accident.

    d.   Sam and John are jointly and severally liable to the victim of the car accident; Bud is not liable.

29.   If a judgment is rendered against the partnership:

    a.   Bud will be liable to the extent of his contribution; Sam and John will be personally liable.
    b.   All partners will be personally liable without limit.
    c.   Bud will not be liable but Sam and John will be personally liable without limit.
    d.   All partners will be liable to the amount of money each has contributed to the partnership.

30.   A limited partner who discovers a false statement in the certificate of limited liability:

    a.   will be treated as a general partner.
    b.   will always retain limited partner status if the false statement was not made intentionally.
    c.   will retain limited partner status even if the false statement was made intentionally.
    d.   will be protected from liability if he or she withdraws from the partnership.

31.   A creditor of a partner can attach which of the following to satisfy the debt?

    a.   Partner's interest only
    b.   Partnership property only
    c.   Partner's interest and partnership property
    d.   Only personal assets may be attached to satisfy the debt.

32.   A suit against a partner's interest is a(n)

    a.   order of partnership.
    b.   charging order.
    c.   secured transaction.
    d.   several charge.

33.   A partner's rights include all of the following except:

    a.   interest in profits and losses.
    b.   rights in specific partnership property.
    c.   right of management.

34.   Tom and Lily form a partnership. Lily agrees to transfer some land to the partnership in exchange for her interest. The partnership business uses the land but the land is held in Lily's name.

    a.   The land is probably partnership property.

b.   The land is Lily's property because she holds title.

c.   The land is owned by Tom and Lily as tenants in common.

d.   The land is owned by Tom and Lily as joint tenants.

35.   Rudy, Jacob, and Jill form a partnership which lasts for ten years until Rudy's death. The partnership owns several pieces of land, office equipment, and machinery. Rudy's heirs are entitled to:

a.   Rudy's partnership interest and Rudy's rights in partnership property.

b.   Rudy's partnership interest and the monetary value of Rudy's rights in partnership property.

c.   all of Rudy's rights in the partnership, including management.

d.   nothing; Rudy's partnership interest and his interest in partnership property pass to the remaining partners.

36.   Sid Salt, Bill Pepper, and Cathy Cayenne form a limited partnership. Sid is the limited partner. All of the following would be proper names for the partnership except:

a.   Salt & Pepper.

b.   Pepper Manufacturing.

c.   Pepper & Cayenne.

d.   Spice, etc.

37.   Cathy agrees to purchase $5,000 of advertising from Good Cooks magazine. The partnership is:

a.   bound by Cathy's decision because she is an agent of Salt and Pepper and the contract was within the scope of the partnership business.

b.   bound by Cathy's decision only if she is the managing partner.

c.   not bound by Cathy's decision because contracts require the unanimous consent of the partners.

d.   not bound by Cathy's decision because the contract was not within the scope of the partnership business.

38.   Pepper decides to leave the partnership after Cathy's decision regarding the advertising. Cathy and Sid agree to admit a new partner, Sally Saffron. Which of the following correctly describes liability for the advertising contract?

a.   Pepper is personally liable; Sally is not liable.

b.   Pepper and Sally are personally liable.

c.   Sally is personally liable; Pepper is not liable.

d.   Pepper is personally liable; Sally is liable to the extent that she has contributed to the partnership.

39.   Which of the following statements about partners' joint liability is false?

a.   Each partner may be sued individually.

b.   Joint liability applies to suits for breach of contract but not for suits in negligence.

c.   Res judicata will bar more than one suit.

d.   Each partner is only liable for a percentage of the judgment.

40.   Five brothers in the DeMatto family have operated a restaurant as a partnership for several years. No one has been designated as managing partner. One brother proposes to sell half of the partnership land to outsiders and to use the proceeds of the sale to open a drive-in grocery. The decision to sell the land:

a.   can be carried out by one brother regardless of the consent of the others.

b.   requires a majority of the brothers to agree.

c.   requires the consent of all brothers.

d.   will dissolve the partnership.

41.   One of the DeMatto brothers purchases an ice cream parlor across the street from the restaurant. The new store is not in direct competition with the partnership. The purchase of the ice cream parlor:

a.   is in violation of the partnership agreement, because a partner cannot operate another business.

b.   is a breach of fiduciary duty regardless of the lack of competition between the two businesses.

c.   may be a breach of fiduciary duty if the owner of the ice cream parlor neglects partnership responsibilities.

d.   is not in violation of the partnership agreement; a partner has the right to enter into business for himself.

42.   Res judicata refers to:

a.   the right of partners to demand an accounting of partnership funds.

b.   a judgment against one partner which forecloses suits against other partners.

c.   the rights of a partner's heirs to his or her rights in the business.

d.   the right of a creditor to attach a partner's interest.

43.   Which of the following statements regarding partners' rights and duties is false?

a.   All partners are agents of each other.

b.   Partners owe a fiduciary duty to each other.

c.   Admission of a new partner requires unanimous consent of all partners.

d.   An incoming partner is not liable for actions occurring before his or her admission to the partnership.

44. Paul, Peter, and Susan form a limited partnership and operate a clothing tore. Paul is the limited partner; the others are general partners. Paul is also employed as a salesperson. Paul gives a refund to an angry customer as part of his employment.

    a. Paul will be treated as a general partner because a limited partner cannot be an employee of the business.

    b. Paul will be treated as a general partner because his decision to give a refund involved a management decision.

    c. Paul will retain limited partner status only if he ceases working as an employee.

    d. Paul will retain limited partner status because he has not participated in the management of the business.

45. A dispute develops between Peter, Susan, and Paul. Peter and Susan wish to postpone a distribution of profits and remodel the store. Paul disagrees.

    a. The store can be remodeled because the vote for remodeling is two to one.

    b. The store can be remodeled because Paul is not entitled to vote on this issue.

    c. The store cannot be remodeled because this decision requires the unanimous consent of all partners.

    d. The store can be remodeled but Paul will not be liable for any damages as a result of the decision.

46. Paul is dissatisfied with the earnings of the partnership and begins to take an active role in management. The partnership orders $50,000 of clothing from a manufacturer.

    a. Under ULPA, Paul is liable as a general partner.

    b. Under ULPA, Paul is liable as a limited partner.

    c. Under ULPA, Paul is liable only if the clothing manufacturer is aware of his participation in the business.

    d. Under ULPA, the partnership is dissolved because Paul legally cannot manage the business.

47. Same facts as question 46, but RULPA applies.

    a. Under RULPA, Paul is liable as a general partner.

    b. Under RULPA, Paul is liable as a limited partner.

    c. Under RULPA, Paul is liable only if the clothing manufacturer is aware of his participation in the business.

    d. Under RULPA, the partnership is dissolved because Paul legally cannot manage the business.

Answers to Study Questions

Fill-in-the-Blank Questions

Pam and Pat have a partnership at will because the length of the agreement was not specified. The agreement between Pat and Pam need not be in writing because they do not intend to buy real estate and because they did not specify that the agreement was to last for more than one year. Pat has the right and power to leave because it is a partnership at will. Pat's uncle is a creditor and he will receive his money first.

Sam and Sid are not entitled to a salary from the business unless the agreement provides; each partner is expected to donate time to the business. The partnership is bound by Sam's promise to Betty; the promise was made within the scope of partnership business. The partners are jointly liable to Betty because Sam's promise creates potential contract liability. (In some states, they would be jointly and severally liable, but that wasn't a choice.) Rod can assign his partnership interest (his right to profits) to the bank. He cannot assign the entire inventory of the store; this is an assignment for benefit of Rod's creditor. Rod has no right to bind the entire assets of the partnership.

True-False Questions

1.   T.

2.   F.   The certificate of partnership of a <u>limited</u> partnership must be filed.

3.   T.

4.   F.   The bankruptcy of a <u>general</u> partner will cause dissolution.

5.   T.

6.   T.

7.   F.   The agreement may provide that the business is to continue.

8.   F.   Only some states allow corporations to be partners.

9.   T.

10.   T.

11.   T.

12.   F.   A good-faith error will not result in liability.

13.   T.

14.   F.   A limited partner has the same right to inspect books as general

partner does; this right is absolute.

15.   F.   A limited partner can be hired as an employee; he or she cannot be hired as manager of the business.

16.   T.

17.   F.   An outgoing partner is liable for all acts performed while he or she was a partner; the time the suit is filed is irrelevant.

18.   T.

19.   T.

20.   F.   A decision to submit a claim to arbitration requires the consent of all partners.

Multiple-Choice Questions

1.	c	17.	c	33.	b
2.	a	18.	b	34.	a
3.	d	19.	c	35.	b
4.	a	20.	c	36.	a
5.	b	21.	c	37.	a
6.	b	22.	b	38.	d
7.	a	23.	c	39.	a
8.	a	24.	b	40.	c
9.	a	25.	b	41.	c
10.	d	26.	a	42.	b
11.	b	27.	d	43.	d
12.	a	28.	c	44.	d
13.	b	29.	a	45.	b
14.	a	30.	d	46.	a
15.	b	31.	a	47.	c
16.	d	32.	b		

CHAPTER 26

Corporations-- Introduction, Formation, and Management Powers

General Principles

A corporation is an artificial person; it is created only by a statute which allows for formation or incorporation of the business. It possesses some of the same rights as individuals, for example: the right to make contracts, the right to equal protection and due process, and the right to sue. However, some rights are denied to a corporation. Corporations are classified by purpose, by shareholders, and by taxation.

A promoter is the person responsible for forming the corporation. He or she may sell stock in the corporation which is to be formed and can arrange for services and property to be purchased by the corporation. The liability for contracts made by the promoter remains with him or her until the corporation accepts them.

The powers of a corporation are determined by state and federal law, the charter, and the bylaws. A corporation can do no more than is stated in these documents; the bylaws and the charter cannot conflict with each other or with higher laws. Management of a corporation generally rests with the board of directors. They make general decisions and appoint officers to carry out these decisions. Shareholders are the owners of the corporation and have limited management rights. Most of their rights are exercised by electing the board of directors and voting on major changes which will alter the make-up or existence of the corporation.

Chapter Summary

I. Introduction

    A. History--The joint stock company was the predecessor of the corporation. Until the nineteenth century, only cities or influential persons could incorporate and the legislature had to pass a special law for each corporation.

333

B.   Current Law--All states have incorporation statutes. Most follow the Model Business Corporation Act (MBCA) or its revised version (RMBCA), but specific law in each state controls.

II.   Nature of the Corporation--A corporation is usually considered a "person" under the law and has the same rights as individuals.

A.   Rights Retained--A corporation has the right to equal protection and due process. It is protected against unreasonable search and seizure and double jeopardy (being tried twice for the same criminal offense). Recent court cases have affirmed a corporation's right to freedom of speech; a corporation may advertise and may express political views.

B.   Right Denied--However, only employees and officers retain the privilege against self-incrimination. A corporation also does not benefit from the privileges and immunities clause, which requires all states to treat residents of other states equally. A corporation can be required to register if it does business in a second state.

C.   Tort and Criminal Law--Most states agree that a corporation can violate the criminal law and be assessed a fine; it obviously cannot be imprisoned. If an officer or employee of a corporation is responsible for the crime, he or she can be sentenced to prison as an individual. A corporation can only commit torts and crimes through its agents (directors, officers or employees). The corporation may be held liable under agency law, including failure of corporate officers to supervise other employees.

D.   Corporate Organization--Shareholders own the corporation; it is managed by directors and officers. Shareholders generally are not liable for the debts of a corporation. Shareholders can sue the corporation or on its behalf (derivative suit); the corporation can sue the shareholders. A corporation is treated as a separate individual for tax purposes; it pays taxes on earnings. When the corporation pays a dividend, the shareholders are taxed on the money they receive.

III.   Classification of Corporations

A.   Domestic, Foreign and Alien Corporations--A corporation is a resident of the state in which it is incorporated. It is a domestic corporation in that state; it is a foreign corporation in any other state. An alien corporation is one incorporated under the laws of another country. Before a corporation can do business in another state that state may require a certificate of authority. As with other defendants, a corporation cannot be sued in a state unless it does business there or otherwise meets the minimum contacts rule.

B.   Public, Private, and Non-Profit Corporations--A public corporation is usually formed by a government to meet some public purpose. Private corporations are created by private individuals to benefit themselves. A nonprofit or eleemosynary (charitable) corporation is usually a private corporation; no dividends are paid. Examples of nonprofit corporations include hospitals and private schools.

C.   Close Corporations--In a close corporation, there are only a few shareholders. It may also be referred to as a family corporation although the shareholders need not be related. Most states limit the number of shareholders and stock cannot be offered for sale to the general public. Management is less rigid than in a larger corporation; shareholders can sign an agreement relating to management of the corporation. If an agreement is not signed, shareholders may control the corporation by requiring more than a majority of the board of directors' agreement for important decisions. The corporation may also require that a shareholder who wishes to sell his or her shares must first offer them to the corporation or to other shareholders; this type of provision prevents outsiders from taking control of the corporation.

D.   S Corporations--An S corporation (Subchapter S of the Internal Revenue Code) is treated as a partnership for tax purposes; the "S" designation relates only to tax law and does not affect state law and other classifications. In order to qualify, the corporation must be a domestic corporation and cannot be associated with other corporations. Shareholders are limited to thirty-five and they must be individuals, estates or certain types of trusts. It may have only one class of voting stock. "S" corporations are taxed as partnerships; each shareholder accounts for the profits and losses of the business; there is no double taxation. However, it loses some of the benefits of regular or "C" corporations; less money can be sheltered in pension funds.

E.   Professional Corporations--The shareholders are members of the same profession (e.g. law or medicine). These businesses can only be incorporated as professional corporations (previously, they had to exist as partnerships or sole proprietorships). Some states insist that members are personally liable for malpractice and one shareholder may be liable for the malpractice of another. However, this rule does not apply to other torts.

IV.   Formation of Corporations-Promoters' Activities--A promoter organizes the corporation. These activities usually involve the purchase of goods and services prior to incorporation and the selling of stock.

A.   Promoter's Liability--Promoter remains personally liable even though the act is done on behalf of the corporation. This rule does not apply if the other party to the contract agrees to look only to the corporation or a novation between all three parties occurs. Most states hold that adoption of a contract by the corporation is insufficient. In addition, a promoter cannot be an agent of the corporation because the corporation did not exist at the time the contract was made and it cannot be a principal.

B.   Subscribers and Subscriptions--Subscriptions are sold by the promoter to potential shareholders. Some states hold that the buyer (subscriber) becomes a shareholder when the corporation is formed (the corporation or promoter is the offeror; the shareholder is the offeree). Others hold that the subscription agreement is an option contract which the corporation can reject or accept. It may also be treated as an agreement between subscribers. Under the MBCA, the subscription is irrevocable for six months.

V.   Incorporation--In order for a corporation to exist, it must be chartered under state law by submitting documentation to a state official.

A.   Articles of Incorporation--A general document similar to a charter or constitution. It should contain the following information:

(1)   Name--Cannot be too similar to an already existing corporation; name can usually be reserved for a short period of time prior to actual incorporation. The name must include words indicating that it is a corporation--Corp., Inc., or Ltd.

(2)   Purpose--Should set out the general type of business; most now use "any legal purpose." Professional corporations, banks, and insurance companies may be prohibited from using this broad statement of purpose.

(3)   Duration--Must set a specified time or state that its duration is perpetual.

(4)   Capital Structure--A minimum amount of capital (usually $1,000) is required in a few states. Must also set out the different types of stock and their par value, if any, and voting rights of each class of stock.

(5)   Internal Organization--Number of officers and directors. Usually stated generally because the bylaws are more specific as to the rights and duties of shareholders, directors, and officers.

(6)   Registered Office and Agent--Must be included for purpose of service of citation if the corporation is sued. The agent must be a specific person and his or her address must be included.

(7)   Incorporators--Submit the articles of incorporation for approval. Usually are shareholders or promoters, but this is not required. The number of incorporators required by state law varies.

B.   Certificate of Incorporation (Charter)--Document received from a public officer (usually secretary of state) that certifies that the articles of incorporation are correct, the fees have been paid, and the corporation has the right to do business.

C.   First Organizational Meeting--Required by law. Usually consists of routine initial matters such as issuing of stock, electing directors, and passing bylaws.

D.   Corporate Status--Corporate status is important because it gives the corporation the right to sue. Furthermore, if incorporation is not properly done, shareholders may be liable. In order to prevent unfair decisions, the courts recognize three types of "improper" incorporation.

(1)   De Jure Corporation--Substantially complied with all the requirements for incorporation. Usually has received certificate from the state.

(2)   De Facto Corporation--Occurs when there has been some mistake in incorporation or the charter has expired. An incorporation statute must exist which the incorporators have tried to follow in good faith and the business must have done business as a corporation. Only the state can challenge the corporate status; other parties cannot sue the shareholders personally.

(3)   Corporation by Estoppel--Does not actually exist; it occurs when a third party has been led to believe that a corporation exists when it does not.

VI.   Disregarding the Corporate Entity--Also called piercing the corporate veil; allows a person to sue shareholders if the corporation has no money. Normally occurs only when shareholders are hiding behind a corporate shell. In order to prevent this, shareholders should not commingle personal and corporate funds, should follow all requirements for meetings and documentation, and should properly fund the corporation.

VII.   Corporate Powers

A.   Express Powers--Stated in precise terms. In order of priority, they are: U.S. Constitution, state constitutions, state statutes, charter, bylaws, and resolutions of the board of directors. A lower power cannot conflict with a greater one. Note that the last three are primarily determined by private individuals who form and operate a corporation.

B.   Implied Powers--Includes powers necessary to carry out express powers and purposes. Usually includes the power to lend and borrow money and to make charitable contributions. Officers have implied power to conduct daily business but not more important changes which require the approval of the board of directors and major changes which require the approval of shareholders as well.

C.   Ultra Vires Act--Any act that is not expressed or implied. Most charters contain board purposes and rights to avoid this problem. Most courts allow ultra vires contracts to be voided only if the contract is executory and a shareholder or director objects. If the contract is partially performed, corporation can be released unless the third party would be injured or the corporation would be unjustly enriched. Most courts now hold that any act which benefits the shareholders is not ultra vires.

VIII.   Corporate Management--Shareholders

A.   Powers--Right to vote on merger, dissolution, sale of most of the business assets, and amendment to the articles of incorporation. Power to remove directors for cause by majority vote. Some charters allow for removal at any time if a majority of the shareholders approve. Can sue on behalf of the corporation (derivative suit) if the board of directors is abusing power or fails to correct an ultra vires act.

B.   Relationship Between Shareholders and Corporation --Shareholders are the owners of the corporation and have no specific rights in management. They act by electing the board of directors and voting on fundamental changes. The officers owe no fiduciary duty to the shareholders, but a director may.

C.   Shareholders' Forum (Meeting)--Must be held annually and shareholders receive written notice within a reasonable time. Special meetings may be called on emergency matters and regular notice must state the purpose of the meetings, which is limited to votes on this issue.

D.   Shareholding Voting

(1)   Quorum--In order for a vote to be taken, a certain number of shareholders must be present in person or represented. It is usually more than 50 percent although the articles of incorporation can set a higher number. Shareholders present vote on resolutions; a majority of those present must approve most resolutions but fundamental changes may require a

higher vote.

(2)   <u>Voting Lists</u>--The right to vote is determined by the voting list which states the record (legal) owner and the number of shares.

(3)   <u>Voting Techniques</u>--Number of votes is determined by number of shares held; some shares may be non-voting.

     (a)   <u>Cumulative Voting</u>--Used to help minority shareholders gain a seat on the board of directors. Each shareholder is entitled to vote the number of shares multiplied by the number of directors to be elected. Under the right circumstances, if minority shareholders cast all their votes for one director, majority shareholders must split their votes in order to elect the rest of the board. Therefore, minority can elect at least one director.

     (b)   <u>Shareholder Agreements, Proxies, and Voting Trusts</u>-- All are approved techniques for providing that votes are cast in a certain way. A shareholder agreement obligates shareholders to vote in a particular way. A proxy is a formal written document giving another the right to vote for the shareholder; the holder of the proxy can generally vote as he or she sees fit. Management often solicits proxies. In a voting trust, shareholders transfer legal title to their shares to a trustee, who also holds the stock certificates. The shareholders receive a voting trust certificate. The voting trust is more formal than a proxy.

IX.   <u>Corporate Management--Directors</u>

A.   <u>Election and Term of Office</u>--Initial board is named in the charter or appointed by the incorporators. Shareholders then elect at the annual meeting. The number of directors is set in the charter. Can be elected annually or for longer terms, if the terms are staggered. (E.g. there are nine directors who serve for three years; three directors are elected each year.) Director can be removed for cause as specified in the bylaws or by shareholder vote. Vacancies are filled by the shareholders or current board members, depending on state law and the bylaws.

B.   <u>Directors' Qualifications and Compensation</u>--Most states have no qualification requirements. Compensation, if any, must be stated in the bylaws or charter.

C.   Management Responsibilities--Direct policy of the corporation, including decisions outside the regular course of business. Declare and pay dividends, appoint and remove corporate officers, and issue stocks and bonds. Can delegate some functions to the officers but still have the right and duty to oversee officers. An executive committee may also be appointed.

D.   Board of Directors' Forum--Meeting dates are set in the bylaws, but special meetings can be called. No notice is required for regular meetings and notice can be waived. Voting is proper only in person (no proxies) and each director has only one vote. Quorum is majority or set in the bylaws; voting is done in person; majority vote required for most resolutions.

E.   Delegation of Powers--Board can delegate some functions relating to ordinary, daily affairs to executive committee or officers, but board remains responsible.

Officers serve at the will of the board of directors; can be removed at any time but the corporation may be liable for breach of contract. They are agents of the corporation; directors are not. Qualifications are set by the board. The number and title of officers are set by state law, charter, and bylaws. Usually a person can serve in more than one office.

Study Questions

Fill-in-the-Blank Questions

Paul is helping some friends to form a corporation. He makes a contract with Crook & Law, Attorneys at Law, for their services in drafting the documents necessary to set up the corporation. He also sells thirty shares of stock to his Aunt Millie.

Paul is a(n) _____ .
              (promoter/incorporator)

Before the corporation is formed, _____ is/are responsible for the money
              (Paul/the shareholders)
owed to Crook & Low.

When Aunt Millie agrees to purchase the stock she is a
_____ .
    (shareholder/subscriber)

The document to be drafted by Crook & Low is the_____ .
(articles of incorporation/certificate of incorporation)

Alpha Corporation's bylaws provide for the election of directors in the following manner. There are nine directors; their term of office is three years and three directors are elected every year. Furthermore, each shareholder is entitled to split his or her voting among the directors to be elected. Most of the stock is owned by Beta Corporation, however, Ralph owns fifty shares.

At each annual meeting, Ralph is entitled to cast _____ votes.
(1/50/150/450)

The directors are elected for _____ terms.
(regular/staggered)

Alpha Corporation _____ cumulative voting.
(has/does not have)

Ralph is entitled to vote on _____ .
(policy decisions/fundamental changes/both)

True-False Questions

1.   A de facto corporation is one which has complied with all the requirements for incorporation. _____

2.   A promoter is personally liable for pre-incorporation contracts unless the corporation ratifies the contracts. _____

3.   An eleemosynary corporation is a synonym for a public corporation. _____

4.   An "S" corporation is taxed as a partnership. _____

5.   An alien corporation is one chartered in another country. _____

6.   A corporation cannot be convicted of a criminal offense. _____

7.   The name of the registered agent of a corporation should be stated in the bylaws. _____

8.   The number of shareholders in a close corporation is limited. _____

9.   A court is likely to pierce the corporate veil if the corporation is undercapitalized. _____

10.   A corporation is dissolved or terminated when a shareholder sells stock to an outsider. _____

11.   Corporate directors have a fiduciary duty to the corporation. _____

12.   Directors may vote by proxy. _____

13.   A shareholder vote may remove a director for cause. _____

14.   Most courts would permit an ultra vires act to stand if the act benefits the corporation. _____

15.   A director must be a shareholder of the corporation. _____

16.   A shareholder can bring a derivative suit to enjoin an ultra vires act. _____

17.   Cumulative voting is designed to help management retain control of the corporation. _____

18.   Shareholders can vote to declare dividends. _____

19.   In a voting trust, the trustee holds legal title to the shares of stock. _____

20.   Shareholders are entitled to written notice of special meetings only. _____

Multiple-Choice Questions

1.   The law which contains a codification of corporation law is the:

   a.   Uniform Corporation and Partnership Code.
   b.   Uniform Business Corporation Act.
   c.   Model Business Corporation Act.
   d.   Model Corporation Code.

2.   Which of the following constitutional rights is held by a corporation?

   a.   Privileges and immunities clause
   b.   Right against self-Incrimination
   c.   Freedom of speech
   d.   Right to travel

3.   Which of the following best describes the application of the right of due process to corporations?

   a.   Corporations enjoy the same right as individuals.
   b.   Corporations have limited due process rights.
   c.   Corporations have no due process rights; only employees and officers have a right to due process.
   d.   Corporations have due process rights in some states but not in others.

4.   Which of the following is <u>not</u> a part of the articles of incorporation?

    a.   Registered agent and business address
    b.   Capital structure
    c.   Bylaws
    d.   Names of incorporators

5.   Which of the following documents govern the internal workings of the corporation?

    a.   Articles of incorporation
    b.   Bylaws
    c.   Charter
    d.   Certificate of incorporation

6.   Cathy's Dress Shop is trying to incorporate. Cathy submits the required documents to the proper public officer but neglects to correct a mistake in the address of the registered agent. While waiting to receive authorization from the proper public officer, Cathy does business as a corporation. Cathy's Dress Shop is:

    a.   a de jure corporation.
    b.   a de facto corporation.
    c.   a corporation by estoppel.
    d.   not a corporation.

7.   Which of the following statements about a corporate name is <u>false</u>?

    a.   It must not contain the full name of an individual.
    b.   It must contain the words "company," "corporation," or other words which show that it is a corporation.
    c.   It must not be deceptively similar to the name of another corporation.
    d.   It must be included in the articles of incorporation.

8.   Which of the following correctly describes a foreign corporation?

    a.   A corporation incorporated in Alabama but doing business in Texas
    b.   A corporation incorporated in Alabama and doing business in Alabama
    c.   A corporation incorporated in Mexico and doing business in Alabama

9.   Which of the following statements about a professional corporation is true?

    a.   Its shareholders never have personal liability for torts of other shareholders.
    b.   Its shareholders may be liable for the malpractice of other shareholders, but not for other torts
    c.   Its shareholders may be liable for all torts of other shareholders.

d.   Its shareholders may be liable for all torts and contracts of other shareholders.

10.   Which of the following most likely would be performed by a promoter?

a.   Selling share subscriptions
b.   Purchasing stock in the corporation
c.   Acting as director of the corporation
d.   Submitting the articles of incorporation for approval

11.   In order for a promoter to be released from liability for pre-incorporation contracts, there must be a(n):

a.   novation.
b.   ratification.
c.   adoption.
d.   amendment.

12.   Which of the following is a synonym for a corporate charter?

a.   Articles of incorporation
b.   Bylaws
c.   Certificate of incorporation
d.   Subscription

13.   Which of the following would probably take place at the first organizational meeting of a corporation?

a.   Selection of a registered agent
b.   Selection of a promoter
c.   Selection of the board of directors
d.   Selection of a corporate name

14.   Which of the following is not required for a de facto corporation?

a.   State statute which allows incorporation of the business
b.   Good faith attempt to comply with incorporation statute
c.   Business undertaken in the name of a corporation
d.   Third party deceived as to fact that no corporation exists

15.   Which of the following is an example of an eleemosynary corporation?

a.   Red Cross
b.   Amtrak
c.   Crook & Low, Attorneys at Law
d.   City of Houston, Texas

16.   Which of the following statements regarding an "S" corporation is <u>false</u>?

    a.   The number of shareholders is restricted.
    b.   It enjoys full fringe benefits, including all pension plans.
    c.   It is taxed like a partnership.
    d.   The types of shareholders are limited.

17.   Which of the following terms describe a court's decision to hold a shareholder personally liable for a corporation's debt?

    a.   Novation
    b.   Piercing the corporate veil
    c.   Corporation by estoppel
    d.   Adoption

18.   Which of the following constitutional rights is denied to a corporation?

    a.   Freedom of speech
    b.   Due process
    c.   Privilege against self-incrimination
    d.   Double jeopardy

19.   A corporation which has few stockholders, is governed by shareholder agreements, and restricts sale of stock is a description of a(n):

    a.   "S" corporation.
    b.   close corporation.
    c.   nonprofit corporation.
    d.   eleemosynary corporation.

20.   With regard to subscription agreements, most courts hold that:

    a.   they are prohibited until the corporation is formed.
    b.   they are continuing offers to the corporation.
    c.   they are acceptances of a corporation's offer to sell stock.
    d.   they are invalid.

21.   Under the Model Business Corporation Act:

    a.   share subscriptions are illegal.
    b.   share subscriptions are irrevocable for six months.
    c.   share subscriptions are irrevocable until the corporation is formed.
    d.   a promoter is personally liable for all share subscriptions.

22.   Which of the following is <u>not</u> a synonym for a close corporation?

    a.   "S" corporation
    b.   privately-held corporation

c.   closely-held corporation
d.   closed corporation

23.   Which of the following correctly describes a promoter's liability for pre-incorporation contracts?

a.   The promoter is liable until the corporation ratifies or adopts the contract.
b.   The promoter remains personally liable until the corporation is formed.
c.   The promoter is never personally liable but the incorporators are.
d.   The promoter is personally liable until a novation is concluded.

24.   The duration of most corporations is:

a.   twenty years.
b.   fifty years.
c.   ninety-nine years.
d.   perpetual.

25.   The board of directors can delegate:

a.   all of its power to an executive committee, but it must oversee officers.
b.   all of its power to officers, but it must supervise them.
c.   some of its power to either an executive committee or to officers, but both are limited to ordinary business acts.
d.   some of its power to an executive committee, but it cannot delegate board duties to officers.

26.   Which of the following incorrectly describes the difference between shareholders' and directors' meetings?

a.   Shareholders must receive notice of all meetings; directors need receive notice of only special meetings.
b.   Shareholders may only meet once per year at an annual forum; directors may meet more often for regular and special meetings.
c.   A shareholder's vote is based on the number of shares he or she owns, each director is entitled to only one vote.
d.   Shareholders can vote by proxy; directors cannot.

27.   Which of the following is true?

a.   A corporation has only the powers listed in its articles of incorporation and bylaws; it has no implied powers.
b.   A corporation has express powers which are noted in its articles of incorporation and it has implied powers to carry out express powers.
c.   The express powers of a corporation usually include the right to give

CORPORATIONS--INTRODUCTION, FORMATION, 347
AND MANAGEMENT POWERS

money to charity.

d.   The bylaws of a corporation are superior to its charter.

28.   "Ultra vires" means:

a.   illegal.
b.   unauthorized.
c.   beyond the powers of.
d.   limited.

29.   Audiotronics, Inc. has 100,000 shares which are issued and held by shareholders. In the absence of special bylaws, how many votes are needed to pass a resolution?

a.   25,001
b.   17,001
c.   50,001
d.   75,000

30.   A shareholder gives written consent to another to cast his or her vote at the annual shareholders' meeting. The shareholder retains the stock certificate. This voting technique is a:

a.   shareholder agreement.
b.   voting trust.
c.   shareholder resolution.
d.   proxy.

31.   Which of the following correctly describes the management rights of directors?

a.   They have an absolute right to examine corporate books.
b.   They have an implied right to compensation.
c.   They have the right to vote by proxy.
d.   They have the right to be notified of all meetings.

32.   Which of the following is most likely to result in personal liability of a director?

a.   An expensive mistake of judgment even if fraud is not involved
b.   Failure to attend meetings or supervise employees
c.   Reliance on bad advice of professionals hired by the corporation
d.   Voting for an ultra vires contract which has been executed by both sides

33.   Which of the following correctly lists the order of priority rules governing a corporation?

a.   State statute, state constitution, resolution
b.   State constitution, state statute, charter
c.   State statute, bylaws, charter
d.   State constitution, resolution, bylaws

34.   Which of the following correctly describes the MBCA position on an ultra vires contract of a corporation?

a.   The contract can be voided on principles of agency.
b.   The contract is valid between the parties to the contract.
c.   The contract cannot be voided if unfairness would result.
d.   The corporation can avoid the contract, if it has not yet performed.

35.   Which of the following is not a remedy for correction of an ultra vires act?

a.   Shareholder ratification of the act
b.   Derivative suit brought by the board of directors
c.   Suit against the board of directors
d.   Dissolution by a public official

36.   In the absence of special provision in the bylaws:

a.   shareholders can remove directors for cause by a majority vote at any time.
b.   Shareholders can remove directors at any time for any reason by majority vote.
c.   shareholders can remove directors at any time only if the director has committed a criminal act.
d.   shareholders can remove directors for cause but a two-thirds vote is necessary.

37.   Dumont Corporation has six directors who are elected annually. There are 20,000 outstanding shares of which minority shareholders hold 6,000.

a.   The minority shareholders will be able to elect a director if straight voting is used.
b.   The minority shareholders will be able to elect a director if cumulative voting is used.
c.   The minority shareholders will be able to elect a director regardless of the voting method.
d.   The minority shareholders will not be able to elect a director regardless of the voting method.

38.   Which of the following is true?

a.   Directors may serve for a term of one year and this cannot be altered by corporate bylaws.
b.   Directors may serve for a term of more than one year if state law permits.

c.   Cumulative voting is not allowed in most states.

d.   All directors must be elected at the same time.

39.   Which of the following statements about a voting trust is <u>false</u>?

a.   The shareholder gives his or her right to vote to a trustee, but the shareholder retains the stock certificate.

b.   The shareholder gives his or her right to vote and legal title to the stock to the trustee.

c.   A voting trust is more difficult to revoke than a proxy.

d.   A shareholder retains equitable title to the stock and the right to receive dividends.

40.   Which of the following responsibilities of the board of directors normally requires shareholder approval?

a.   Major policy decisions

b.   Hiring of officers

c.   Declaration of dividends

d.   Amendment of the corporate charter

41.   Ken is president of Mammoth Corporation. He feels that he has been wrongfully dismissed by the board of directors. Which of the following would be a proper remedy for Ken?

a.   Suit against each director personally

b.   Suit against the corporation

c.   Shareholder vote to reinstate Ken

d.   Derivative suit against the board of directors as a whole

42.   Which of the following correctly describes a corporation's liability for wrongful acts of its employees and officers?

a.   The corporation is never liable for their torts; the officers and employees are personally liable.

b.   The corporation is liable for torts committed in the officers' and employees' scope of employment.

c.   The directors may be liable personally if they failed to supervise the employee but the corporation is not liable.

d.   Both the corporation and the directors are protected by the business judgment rule.

43.   Which of the following owe a legally recognized duty to the other?

a.   Officers to shareholders

b.   Officers to corporation

c.   Shareholders to creditors

d.   Shareholders to officers

44.   Which of the following statements regarding shareholders' meetings is correct:

a.   Shareholders are entitled to reasonable notice of annual and special meetings.
b.   The agenda of annual and special meetings must be included in notice to the shareholders.
c.   Special meetings may be called only if two-thirds of the shareholders agree.
d.   A quorum is not required at special meetings.

45.   The number of directors required to take action at a meeting is a:

a.   proxy.
b.   quorum.
c.   quotient.
d.   resolution.

46.   Which of the following correctly describes a proper vote of directors on ordinary business matters?

a.   A majority of the directors must approve the action.
b.   A quorum must be present and all present must approve the action.
c.   A quorum must be present and a majority of those present must approve the action.
d.   A quorum must be present and a majority of the total directors must approve the action.

47.   A voting list:

a.   records the votes of shareholders at annual meetings.
b.   records the votes of directors at annual meetings.
c.   lists the name, address, and number of shares for each shareholder.
d.   lists the directors present at each meeting.

48.   In a voting trust:

a.   the trustee always has discretion to vote as he or she wishes.
b.   the trustee may be told how to vote or have discretion.
c.   the shareholder gives a trust certificate to the trustee.
d.   the shareholder gives a proxy to the trustee.

Answers to Study Questions

Fill-in-the-Blank Questions

Paul is a promoter; an incorporator signs the documents which are submitted to the secretary of state. Paul is personally liable for pre-incorporation contracts unless the corporation, Paul, and the other party sign a novation. Aunt Millie is a subscriber; she does not become a shareholder until the stock is issued. The initial document, which is prepared by the lawyers, is the articles of incorporation; the certificate of incorporation is issued by a public officer.

Ralph is entitled to cast 150 shares (fifty shares X three directors). The directors are elected for staggered terms, three per year. Alpha does use cumulative voting because it allows Ralph to split his shares. Ralph, as a shareholder, is entitled to vote on fundamental changes; directors vote on policy decisions.

True-False Questions

1.   F.   This is the definition of a de jure corporation; a de facto corporation is one which has failed to comply with incorporation requirements.

2.   F.   In most states, ratification is insufficient; a novation is required.

3.   F.   It is a synonym for a charitable or nonprofit corporation.

4.   T.

5.   T.

6.   F.   It can be convicted but punished only by fine.

7.   F.   It should be stated in the articles of incorporation.

8.   T.

9.   T.

10.   F.   It must be dissolved formally. Selling of shares has no effect.

11.   T.

12.   F.   They must vote in person; shareholders may vote by proxy.

13.   T.

14.   T.

15.   F.

16.   T

17.   F.   It is designed to allow minority shareholders to elect a director.

18.   F.   Only the board of directors can declare a dividend.

19.   T.

20.   F.   They are entitled to written notice of all meetings.

Multiple-Choice Questions

1.	c	7.	a
2.	c	8.	a
3.	a	9.	b
4.	c	10.	a
5.	b	11.	a
6.	b	12.	c
13.	c	31.	a
14.	d	32.	b
15.	a	33.	b
16.	b	34.	b
17.	b	35.	b
18.	c	36.	a
19.	b	37.	c
20.	b	38.	b
21.	b	39.	b
22.	a	40.	d
23.	d	41.	b
24.	d	42.	b
25.	c	43.	b
26.	a	44.	a
27.	b	45.	b
28.	c	46.	c
29.	c	47.	c
30.	d	48.	c

27

Corporations--Rights and Duties of Directors, Managers, and Shareholders

General Principles

Directors and officers are fiduciaries of the corporation and they owe a duty to act honestly and with loyalty to the corporation. In some situations, majority shareholders may have a fiduciary duty to minority shareholders.

Directors have the right to participate in management, to inspect corporate books, and to have the corporation stand behind them if they suffer loss because of proper corporate action. In addition to the fiduciary duties outlined above, directors have the duty to attend meetings, to supervise officers, and to act in the best interest of the corporation.

Most shareholders rights are connected with voting but in certain circumstances they have the right to inspect corporate books, to retain relative power within the corporation (pre-emptive rights), and to sue on behalf of the corporation. A shareholder is not liable for the actions of the corporation unless he or she accepts watered stock or abuses the privileges of corporate ownership and a court decides to pierce the corporate veil.

Chapter Summary

I.   Roles of Officers and Directors--Most come from fiduciary duties. A director differs from an agent because he or she can control the corporation-principal; a director differs from a trustee because shareholders do not transfer ownership of the corporation to the directors.

      A.   Duty of Care--Standard is reasonably prudent judgment. Duty to reasonably supervise officers. Permissible to rely reasonably on the opinions of experts. The duty of care also includes the duty to attend meetings and to vote. A director who disagrees or who is absent should record a dissent in order to avoid liability.

B.   Duty of Loyalty--Allegiance to the corporation first. Director must disclose conflicts of interest. Cannot compete with the corporation, steal a corporate opportunity, or use inside information to profit personally. No self-dealing.

C.   Conflict of Interest--Occurs when the corporation and the director personally have competing interests. Disclosure is always required. Contracts between a director and the corporation are allowed if disclosure of self-interest is revealed, the contract is reasonable and, the other directors approve it by a majority. Interlocking directorates (one director sitting on the board of competing corporations) is prohibited by the Clayton Act if either corporation has capital surplus and retained profits of more than $1 million.

II.   Rights of Directors

A.   Participation and Inspection--Includes right to participate in meetings and to vote. Absolute right to corporate books (compare shareholders).

B.   The Business Judgment Rule--Because of fiduciary duty to the corporation, directors can be liable for improper use of corporate funds, lax supervision of officers, and ultra vires acts. Business judgment rules protects honest mistakes; due care and compliance with charter and bylaws is the test.

C.   Indemnification--Most states and the MBCA give a corporation the right to pay directors for cost incurred if a director is sued in connection with his or her appointment with the corporation. This right of indemnification is allowed even if a judgment is made against the corporation as long as the director acted in good faith and the business judgment rule was used. Corporations can purchase insurance specifically tailored for officers and directors.

D.   Compensation--Not granted automatically, although most bylaws provide for it.

III.   Officers' Rights and Duties--Owe a fiduciary duty to the corporation so they may be liable for the same reasons directors may be liable, e.g. conflict of interest, taking a corporate opportunity. In addition, officers must follow properly passed resolutions of the board. An officer's rights are defined in the employment contract with the corporation.

IV.   Rights of Shareholders

A.   Stock Certificates--Right to stock certificate and to vote his or her shares.

B.   Preemptive Rights--The number of shares owned by a stockholder is a measure of his or her voting strength because it is a percentage of the whole. (An owner of ten shares in a corporation with fifty shares owns one-fifth of the corporation.)   Preemptive rights allow a stockholder to purchase stock whenever a new offering is made; this allows the stockholder to keep his or her vote from being diluted. (If the corporation above issues fifty more shares, the stockholder would own ten out of 100 or one-tenth; and that shareholder's strength has been cut in half.) In most states, corporations can deny these rights. In general, the rights apply only when new stock is issued (not authorized).

C.   Stock Warrants--When new stock is issued, a stockholder with preemptive rights receives a stock warrant, which is an option to buy stock for a stated period of time.

D.   Dividends--Board of directors decides when to declare; shareholders cannot challenge unless an abuse of discretion is shown. Responsible for return of dividends which would make the corporation insolvent; dividends paid from illegal funds must be returned only if the shareholders knew the dividend was illegal. However, directors who voted for the decision can be personally liable.

E.   Voting Rights--Some classes of stock, usually preferred, may be denied voting rights.

F.   Inspection Rights--More restricted than those of directors. Has right to minutes of meetings and tax return for proper purpose. MBCA and most states allow the shareholder to inspect books if he or she has been the owner for six months or owns 5 percent of the total shares. Written demand must be made.   There are penalties for denial. Limited because shareholders could use information wrongfully or for harassment. List of shareholders must be kept open for inspection at the annual meeting.

G.   Transfer of Shares--General right to sell because shares are personal property. Most close corporations limit transfer; corporation may have the first right to buy (first refusal). Ownership determined by the corporate records; notification is the duty of the shareholders.

H.   Dissolution--Right to vote on this issue and to receive pro rata share of any remaining assets. Preferred shareholders may be given the right to come first.   Can sue for dissolution on behalf of the corporation if the directors are deadlocked, the shareholders cannot break it, and the corporation is suffering irreparable injury or if a specified time period has passed. Can also sue if the directors are acting illegally, fraudulently, wastefully, or against the interest of minority shareholders.

I.   Derivative Suit--Suit brought by shareholders for the benefit of the corporation. Usually occurs when the directors or officers are allowing the corporation to suffer. Any money recovered goes to the corporation. It is called a derivative suit because the shareholders are allowed to sue because they own the corporation and derive the right to sue from corporation ownership.

V.   Liabilities of Shareholders

    A.   Stock Subscriptions--Contract liability to pay for stock subscriptions or purchase agreement.

    B.   Watered Stock--If a shareholder purchases par value stock for less than par value or if an inflated value is placed on property transferred in exchange for no par value stock, he or she can be held liable for the difference (watered stock).

VI.   Duties of Major Shareholders--Shareholder is usually not liable for corporate actions except when a minority shareholder acts for personal benefit and to the detriment of minority shareholders or creditors.

Study Questions

Fill-in-the-Blank Questions

Bubba owns 20 percent (200 shares) of a corporation which manufactures football equipment. The par value of the shares is $1, for which Bubba paid $100. The corporation decides to issue an additional 1,000 shares. It sends a notice to Bubba telling him that he has the right to buy 200 more shares if he returns the enclosed document.

Bubba _____ the owner of watered stock.
          (is/is not)

Bubba has _____ rights.
              (preferred/preemptive)

Bubba purchased his initial stock two months ago. Under the MBCA, he _____ have the right to look at the corporate books.
      (does/does not)

The document which allows Bubba to purchase more shares is a _____.
      (subscription option/stock warrant)

True-False Questions

1. At common law, shareholders had no right to inspect corporate books. _____

2. A director's right to be reimbursed for losses in connection with corporate business is the right of participation. _____

3. If a director does not attend a meeting, he or she will be presumed to have approved any resolutions passed at the meeting. _____

4. Certain rights of officers are automatic, e.g. the right to hire and fire subordinate employees. _____

5. A contract between a director and a corporation is prohibited unless the other directors unanimously vote to approve the contract. _____

6. Directors owe a fiduciary duty to the corporations; officers do not. _____

7. A shareholder can be held personally liable for the amount of any dividend which causes the corporation to be insolvent. _____

8. Dividends are declared by a majority vote of shareholders at the annual meeting. _____

9. Usurping of a corporation opportunity occurs when a director sits on the board of more than one corporation. _____

10. A director can operate a business which competes with the corporation if the other directors and the stockholders approve. _____

Multiple-Choice Questions

1. The rule against interlocking directorates is found in:

    a. MBCA.
    b. Securities and Exchange Act.
    c. Clayton Act.
    d. court decisions.

2. A contract between a director and a corporation:

    a. is always valid.
    b. is always void.
    c. is always voidable.
    d. is valid, if certain requirements are met.

3.   The power of a corporation to purchase insurance for its directors and officers is:

    a.   proper only if the charter so permits.
    b.   proper only if the bylaws so permit.
    c.   part of a corporation's implied powers.
    d.   improper; directors and officers must purchase their own insurance.

4.   Which of the following correctly describes the right of access to corporate books?

    a.   Directors and shareholders have an absolute right to inspect the books.
    b.   Directors have an absolute right to inspect the books; shareholders have no right to inspect the books.
    c.   Directors have an absolute right to inspect the books; shareholders have limited rights.
    d.   Directors and shareholders have limited rights.

5.   In which of the following situations would indemnification of a corporate director be improper?

    a.   Director is sued as part of a products liability suit against the corporation.
    b.   Director is sued for fraud in a shareholder's derivative suit.
    c.   Director pleads guilty to fraud.
    d.   Director is sued but the case is settled out of court.

6.   Betty, a shareholder of Mega Corporation, loses her stock certificate. Which of the following is correct?

    a.   She cannot vote or receive dividends.
    b.   Betty remains the record owner of the stock, but she cannot vote.
    c.   Betty can vote and receive dividends.
    d.   Betty must present her certificate in order to receive a dividend.

7.   Preemptive rights:

    a.   give the shareholder the right to remove directors without cause.
    b.   give the shareholder the right to transfer his or her stock.
    c.   give the corporation the right of first refusal if a shareholder decides to sell his or her stock.
    d.   give the shareholder the right to purchase more stock when the corporation issues it.

8.   Mary receives a notice that Alpha Corporation has declared a dividend which will be paid in one month. Mary's right to a dividend:

    a.   became final when the board of directors declared the dividend.

b.   becomes final when the dividend is paid.
c.   is not absolute; the board of directors can revoke the declaration.
d.   is absolute; she is entitled to be paid a dividend every year but the board of directors can set the amount.

9.   The authority to preemptive rights is contained in a:

a.   stock dividend.
b.   stock rights.
c.   stock warrant.
d.   dividend right.

10.   The transfer (sale or gift) of stock certificates:

a.   is an absolute right of the shareholder.
b.   may be banned totally in a close corporation.
c.   may be subject to reasonable restrictions.
d.   may not be limited except in a close corporation.

11.   Which of the following statements about watered stock is <u>incorrect</u>?

a.   A shareholder who receives watered stock is liable to the corporation for the difference between the value paid and the true value.
b.   It cannot occur if the stock has no par value.
c.   In some states, a shareholder who receives watered stock may be liable to the creditors of the corporation.
d.   It occurs if stock is issued in exchange for future services to be rendered by the shareholder.

12.   Allan owns 90 percent of the stock in Beta Corporation. He decides to sell his shares to Chris. Allan owes a fiduciary duty to:

a.   Chris only.
b.   the minority shareholders only.
c.   the minority shareholders and the corporation.
d.   no one.

13.   Which of the following correctly describes the relationship of a director to a corporation?

a.   The director is a trustee of the corporation.
b.   The director is an agent of the corporation.
c.   The director is both an agent and trustee of the corporation.
d.   The director is a fiduciary, but is neither a trustee nor an agent.

14.   Bob is a director of Gamma Corporation. While Bob is on vacation, the other directors vote to issue a stock dividend from improper funds. Bob:

a. is personally liable because a majority of the directors approved the dividend.
b. is personally liable unless he recorded his dissent.
c. is not personally liable because he did not attend the meeting.
d. is not personally liable if he did not know that the directors were going to authorize the dividend.

15. Meg is a director of Lambda Corporation, which manufactures household appliances. She hears that Price, an investor, has created a new portable dishwasher. Meg buys the patent rights from Price.

a. Meg has breached her fiduciary duty to Lambda Corp.
b. Meg has not breached her fiduciary duty to Lambda Corp.
c. Meg has breached her fiduciary duty unless she discloses her interest to Lambda Corp.
d. Meg has breached her fiduciary duty unless she receives the consent of the other directors.

16. Sam is a director of two corporations. Mega Corporation manufacturers auto parts; Minor Corporation is a retail clothing store.

a. Sam has violated the duty of loyalty to both corporations.
b. Sam has not violated the duty of loyalty to either corporation.
c. Sam is in violation of the Clayton Act.
d. Sam is in violation of the Clayton Act only if one of the corporations has assets of $1 million and 500,000 shareholders.

17. The right to declare a dividend:

a. belongs to the board of directors and the shareholders cannot force payment.
b. belongs to the board of directors but the shareholders may override its decision by a unanimous vote.
c. belongs to the board of directors but the shareholders may override its decision if a court finds that the board is abusing its discretion.
d. belongs to the shareholders and directors jointly.

18. All states allow dividends to be paid from which of the following fund(s)?

a. Retained earnings only
b. Capital surplus only
c. Retained earnings and capital surplus
d. Retained earnings and net profits

19. Which of the following correctly describes a shareholder's right to inspect corporate books under the MBCA?

a. The shareholder must hold at least 5 percent of the stock, owned the shares for six months, and have a proper purpose.

b. The shareholder must hold at least 5 percent of the stock or owned shares for six months, and purpose is irrelevant.

c. The shareholder must hold at least 5 percent of the stock or owned shares for six months and his or her reason for inspection must be proper.

d. The shareholder must hold at least 5 percent of the stock or owned shares for six months and receive the permission of the board of directors.

20. Which of the following correctly describes the personal liability of shareholders?

a. Watered stock, all illegal dividends, and dividends which make the corporation insolvent

b. Watered stock, stock subscriptions, and dividends which make the corporation insolvent

c. Stock subscriptions, all illegal dividends, and dividends which make the corporation insolvent

d. All illegal dividends and watered stock

21. Alice is a shareholder in Gamma Corporation. She has evidence that the board of directors is wasting corporate assets. Alice:

a. cannot sue the corporation but she can sell her stock.

b. can sue in a derivative suit and force the directors to reimburse the corporation or she can sue to dissolve the corporation.

c. can sue in a derivative suit but cannot sue for dissolution.

d. cannot sue the directors because they are protected by the business judgment rule.

22. Anne is a director of Mina Corporation. She is an attorney and the corporation wants to hire her to amend the articles of incorporation and the bylaws.

a. The contract, if approved by the board, will be void.

b. The contract, if reasonable and if approved by a majority of disinterested directors, will be valid.

c. The contract, if approved by a majority of the shareholders, will be valid.

d. The contract, if reasonable, will be valid.

23. Which of the following correctly describes the voting rights of stockholders?

a. All stockholders have the right to vote.

b. The charter may limit the right to vote to certain classes of stock.

c. Treasury stock is voted by the board of directors.

d. Stockholders with preemptive rights are denied the right to vote.

24.   Which of the following is not an automatic right of a shareholder?

    a.   Right to stock certificate
    b.   Right to sell stock, although may be limited
    c.   Right to receive dividends annually
    d.   Right to attend annual and special meetings

25.   Bill is a director of Beta Corporation. He is wrongfully refused entrance to a director's meeting. Bill has been denied his right of:

    a.   indemnification.
    b.   preemption.
    c.   participation.
    d.   inspection.

Answers to Study Questions

Fill-in-the-Blank Questions

Bubba is the owner of watered stock; the stock is valued at $200 and Bubba paid only $100. Bubba has preemptive rights; preferred rights refer to payment of dividends. He does have the right if he has a proper purpose because he owns more than 5 percent of the stock. The stock warrant gives Bubba the right to purchase more stock; a stock subscription is a shareholder's promise to buy stock.

True-False Questions

1.   F.   They always have had the right if their purpose is proper.

2.   F.   It is the right of indemnification.

3.   T.

4.   F.   Their rights are defined in the employment contract.

5.   F.   A majority vote is needed if the contract is reasonable.

6.   F.   Both owe a fiduciary duty to the corporation.

7.   T.

8.   F.   Dividends are declared by the board of directors.

9.   F.   This is a description of an interlocking directorate; usurping of a corporate opportunity occurs when a director competes with a corporation.

10.   F.   This violates the duty of loyalty.

Multiple-Choice Questions

1.	c		14.	b
2.	d		15.	c
3.	c		16.	b
4.	c		17.	c
5.	c		18.	a
6.	c		19.	c
7.	d		20.	b
8.	a		21.	b
9.	c		22.	b
10.	c		23.	b
11.	b		24.	c
12.	c		25.	c
13.	d			

Corporations--Meger, Consolidation, and Termination

General Principles

This chapter deals with fundamental changes within corporations. These changes include merger, consolidation, sale of assets, and dissolutions. The proper procedure may involve approval by one or two board of directors, passage of resolution by shareholders, and approval of the Department of Justice. Shareholders' rights after the change is completed may include buy-out agreements, stock swaps, or nothing at all.

Chapter Summary

I.   Merger and Consolidation

      A.   Merger--Two corporations combine assets and liabilities and only one corporation remains. Articles of merger are filed with the secretary of state. A short-form merger occurs when one corporation (parent), which holds 90 to 95 percent of another corporation (subsidiary), decides to merge. Procedures are different as noted below.

      B.   Consolidation--Two corporations combine assets and liabilities and a new corporation is formed. Articles of consolidation are filed with the secretary of state and are the articles of incorporation for the new corporation.

      C.   Procedure--Boards of directors of both corporations must approve. Shareholders of both corporations must approve, usually by a two-thirds vote, although may be higher. Articles of merger of consolidation are filed; secretary of state issues a certificate of merger or consolidation.

D.   Short-Form Mergers--Short-form mergers can occur without shareholder approval because it would happen even if a vote were taken.

E.   Appraisal Rights

(1)   Stock--In a merger or consolidation, the shareholders of the old or merged corporation receive shares of the surviving or new corporation. When shareholders sell their stock in a tender offer, they may receive cash or stock in the acquiring corporation.

(2)   Appraisal Rights--Used when the shareholder disagrees with the fundamental change; the dissenting shareholder is paid for his or her shares.

(a)   Persons Entitled--Always permitted in mergers and consolidations. In most states, the purchase of assets is treated as a merger and the shareholders of the selling corporation receive appraisal rights. Some states give these rights when the articles of incorporation are amended and a shareholder suffers from the decision. There are no such rights in a tender offer since each stockholder makes the decision whether or not to sell.

(b)   Procedure--Must be followed strictly. Shareholders must file written notice of intent to dissent and written demand for payment after the change has occurred. Usually cannot back out. Entitled to the fair market value of the stock on the day before the vote was taken. If the value is not readily determined, the parties can agree or the court can decide.

F.   Purchase of Assets--One corporation purchases virtually all the assets of another corporation; the legal status of the corporation is not changed. Liabilities are not transferred. Justice Department regulates because it could be a merger in disguise. Purchasing corporation needs only the vote of the directors. The selling (acquired) corporation requires a shareholder vote.

G.   Purchase of Stock (Takeover Bid)--Purchasing corporation makes the offer directly to the shareholders of the selling or target corporation. No formal approval is required but federal securities law regulates public or tender offers. Resistance to a takeover may take several forms. The target company may make a self-tender where the corporation buys the stock back from shareholders. The target may ask a third party or white knight to enter the bidding. Target corporation may also make itself less attractive by selling off assets, taking out loans or changing by-laws to allow shareholders to cash in stock if a takeover occurs (poison pill).

II.   Termination--Includes dissolution and liquidation or winding up.

      A.   Dissolution

          (1)   Voluntary--The board of directors and the shareholders can vote; a unanimous vote of the shareholders will override the board of directors.

          (2)   Involuntary--Legislature passes law which forces dissolution. Court can order dissolution if the corporation does not comply with state requirements, incorporation occurred due to fraud, the directors abuse the ultra vires doctrine, the corporation never does business or ceases to do so. Remember that shareholders can petition for dissolution if the board of directors is deadlocked and the corporation cannot be saved.

      B.   Liquidation--Sale of assets and payment of liabilities; the remainder, if any, is distributed to the shareholders. Usually carried out by the board of directors (as trustees). The court can appoint a receiver if the directors refuse to liquidate, there is reason to believe that the board would not act properly, or when a court dissolves the corporation due to deadlock or mismanagement.

Study Questions

Fill-in-the-Blank Questions

Ruth is a shareholder in Profitable Corporation. The directors of the corporation have voted to combine with Mediocre Corporation. After the combination, only Profitable Corporation will exist.

This is an example of a _____.
                    (merger/consolidation/purchase of assets)

Ruth _____ entitled to vote on the combination.
         (is/is not)

The shareholders of Mediocre Corporation _____ en-titled to vote.
                           (are/are not)

Ruth _____ entitled to appraisal rights.
         (is/is not)

The shareholders of Mediocre Corporation _____
entitled to appraisal rights.   (are/are not)

True-False Questions

1.   The two parts of termination are dissolution and abandonment. _____

2.   In a purchase of assets, the shareholders of the purchasing corporation are entitled to vote. _____

3.   A tender offer is a synonym for a purchase of assets. _____

4.   In a consolidation, the new corporation must file new articles of corporation. _____

5.   Appraisal rights will be awarded only if a dissenting shareholder gives written notice of dissent before the merger. _____

6.   A corporation cannot be terminated voluntarily without the consent of a majority of the board of directors. _____

7.   The value of stock for appraisal purposes is determined on the day before the vote was taken. _____

8.   If a corporation is dissolved involuntarily, a receiver will be appointed to carry out liquidation. _____

9.   In a merger, the surviving corporation absorbs the assets and losses of the merged corporation. _____

10.   A short-form merger can occur only when a parent and subsidiary merge. _____

Multiple-Choice Questions

1.   "The sale of assets of a business or an individual for cash and the distribution of cash to creditors with the balance going to the owners" is a description of:

      a.   preemptive rights.
      b.   termination
      c.   dissolution.
      d.   liquidation.

2.   The right of a shareholder to force the corporation to buy his or her stock after a merger is:

    a.   appropriation rights.
    b.   appraisal rights.
    c.   preemptive rights.
    d.   preferred rights.

3.   "A right which can be enforced in a court to recover a debt or damages" is a definition of:

    a.   appraisal right.
    b.   preemptive right.
    c.   chose in action.
    d.   equity.

4.   Which of the following would be least likely to receive appraisal rights?

    a.   Shareholders of a surviving corporation after merger
    b.   Shareholders of a corporation which has been consolidated
    c.   Shareholders of a corporation which has sold its assets to another corporation
    d.   Shareholders who are the subject of a tender offer

5.   Which of the following is least likely to require a shareholder vote?

    a.   Merger
    b.   Consolidation
    c.   Amendment to the charter
    d.   Amendment of the bylaws

6.   Gamma Corporation and Beta Corporation are planning to merge. Which of the following parties are entitled to vote on the proposal?

    a.   Directors of both corporations only
    b.   Shareholders of both corporations only
    c.   Directors and shareholders of both corporations
    d.   Directors of the surviving corporation; directors and shareholders of the merged corporation

7.   In order for the merger in Question 6 to occur:

    a.   the merged corporation must dissolve and the surviving corporation must file an amendment to its charter.
    b.   the merged corporation must sell its assets and liabilities to the surviving corporation and the merged corporation must dissolve.
    c.   the surviving corporation must file an amendment to its charter.
    d.   the surviving corporation must file articles of merger.

8.   After the merger in Question 6 occurs, which of the following have appraisal rights?

    a.   The directors and shareholders of the merged corporation
    b.   The directors and shareholders of both corporations
    c.   The shareholders of the merged corporation
    d.   The shareholders of both corporations

9.   In order to enforce appraisal rights:

    a.   notice must be given before and after the vote.
    b.   notice must be given before the vote.
    c.   notice must be given after the vote.
    d.   the parties must agree on the value of the stock.

10.   X Corporation and Y Corporation are consolidating. Paul, a shareholder of X Corporation, wants to enforce his appraisal rights. The board of directors of both corporations vote to approve the merger on March 10. The shareholders of both corporations vote on May 10. The articles of merger are filed on May 15; the certificate of merger is approved on May 30. For purposes of appraisal rights, Paul's shares will be valued on:

    a.   March 10.
    b.   May 9.
    c.   May 10.
    d.   May 30.

11.   The merger officially occurs on:

    a.   March 10.
    b.   May 9.
    c.   May 10.
    d.   May 30.

12.   Mega Corporation is purchasing the assets of Minor Corporation. In most states, which of the following have the right to vote on the purchase?

    a.   Board of directors of both corporations only
    b.   Board of directors of both corporations and the shareholders of Mega Corporation
    c.   Board of directions of both corporations and shareholders of Minor Corporation
    d.   Board of directions and shareholders of both corporations

13.   Which of the following laws restricts the purchase of assets described in Question 12?

    a.   Justice Department only

          b.   Clayton Act and the Justice Department

          c.   Clayton Act

          d.   Robinson-Patman Act

14.   In most states, approval of a merger or consolidation requires the approval of:

          a.   a majority of the shareholders with voting stock.

          b.   two-thirds of the shareholders with voting stock.

          c.   a majority of the directors.

          d.   two-thirds of the directors.

15.   Which of the following will not cause termination of a corporation?

          a.   Unanimous vote of the board of directors

          b.   Unanimous vote of the shareholders

          c.   Two-thirds vote of the board of directors and shareholders

          d.   Expiration of the time provided in the charter

16.   Which of the following cannot bring about the dissolution of a corporation without the approval of another party?

          a.   The legislature

          b.   The shareholders

          c.   A court

          d.   The board of directors

17.   When a corporation terminates voluntarily, which of the following cannot occur?

          a.   A receiver will be appointed if the board refuses to liquidate.

          b.   Shareholders will receive assets remaining after liquidation.

          c.   The trustees will be personally liable for any breach of duty committed during liquidation.

          d.   Shareholders will be personally liable for any fraud committed during liquidation.

18.   Gamma and Rho Corporations are combining their assets and liabilities in order to form Tau Corporation. This is a description of a:

          a.   merger.

          b.   consolidation.

          c.   purchase of stock.

          d.   tender offer.

19.   When the combination is complete, the secretary of state will issue:

          a.   articles of merger

          b.   articles of consolidation,

c.   certificate of consolidation.
d.   certificate of completion.

20.   The stock of Beta Corporation is valued at $10 per share. Alpha Corporation is planning a takeover bid. The takeover bid will involve:

a.   tender offers to the shareholders of Beta Corporation.
b.   tender offers to the shareholders of Alpha Corporation.
c.   purchase of the assets of Beta Corporation.
d.   filing of articles of merger.

21.   Sally is a shareholder in Beta Corporation. Alpha Corporation will most likely:

a.   give Sally appraisal rights of $10 per share.
b.   give Sally appraisal rights of $12 per share.
c.   offer Sally $8 per share for the purchase of her stock.
d.   offer Sally $12 per share for the purchase of her stock.

22.   Gamma, Inc. owns 85 percent of the stock of Lambda, Inc. The merger of Gamma and Lambda will require approval of:

a.   the board of directors of both corporations, but not the approval of the shareholders.
b.   the board of directors and shareholders of both corporations.
c.   the board of directors and shareholders of Gamma Inc., and the board of directors of Lambda, Inc.
d.   the board of directors and shareholders of Lambda, Inc. and the board of directors of Gamma, Inc.

23.   Tender offers are regulated by:

a.   federal law.
b.   the charter of the acquiring corporation.
c.   state law.
d.   the charter of the target corporation.

24.   A target corporation is:

a.   the corporation which ceases to exist after a merger.
b.   the corporation which is created after a consolidation
c.   the corporation which is the subject of a takeover bid.
d.   the corporation which is conducting a takeover bid.

25. Which of the following would not require filing a document with the secretary of state?

a. Regular merger
b. Short-form merger
c. Consolidation
d. Purchase of assets

Answers to Study Questions

Fill-in-the-Blank Questions

This is an example of a merger; a consolidation causes both corporations to dissolve and a purchase of assets has no effect on legal status. Ruth and the shareholders of Mediocre Corporation are entitled to vote and shareholders of both corporations are entitled to appraisal rights.

True-False Questions

1. F. They are dissolution and liquidation.

2. F. Only the shareholders of the selling corporation are entitled to vote.

3. F. It is a synonym for a public offering for purchase of stock.

4. F. The articles of consolidation become the articles of incorporation.

5. T.

6. F. The shareholders can terminate by unanimous vote.

7. T.

8. T.

9. T.

10. T.

Multiple-Choice Questions

1.	d		14.	d
2.	b		15.	a
3.	c		16.	d
4.	d		17.	d
5.	d		18.	b
6.	c		19.	c
7.	d		20.	a
8.	d		21.	d
9.	a		22.	b
10.	b		23.	a
11.	d		24.	c
12.	c		25.	d
13.	b			

Corporations-- Financing, Financial Regulation, and Investor Protection

CHAPTER

General Principles

Corporations are financed by selling stock and by borrowing money. Bonds are a form of borrowing money from investors. Investors are protected from fraud and bad faith by state (blue sky) and federal laws. The federal laws require large public corporations to disclose financial statements and regulate the sale of stock. These laws also prevent fraud on the part of insiders and others in connection with the sale of stock.

Chapter Summary

I. Corporate Financing--Stocks and bonds are collectively referred to as securities. Stocks (equity securities) represent ownership in the corporation and purchasers are shareholders. Bonds (debt securities) are essentially loans made from bondholders to the corporation and usually are for long periods of time. They must be paid by the corporation; a stockholder receives payment only when and if a dividend is declared. Stockholders vote; bondholders do not. Stockholders may receive assets on dissolution; bondholders receive nothing once the bond has been paid.

    A. Bonds

        (1) Bond indenture--The agreement between the bondholders and the corporation. It usually provides that the bond will be paid back at a stated rate of interest and payment dates. Most bonds are paid in installments semiannually based on the rate of interest on $1,000.

(2)   Payment--A bond has a face (issued) value of $1,000. The corporation promises to pay back this amount and a stated rate of interest. When interest rates change, the relative value (but not the face value) can change. If the bonds are sold below the face value (discount), then the buyer will receive more money (yield) when the bond is paid off. If the bonds are sold above face value (premium), the buyer will receive less money when the bond is paid off.

EX: Paul purchases a bond at face value of $1,000. Before the bond is repaid, he sells his remaining rights to Sharon, who pays the equivalent of $998. When the corporation pays Sharon, she will receive the same amount of money (principal and interest) as if she had paid $1,000.

(3)   Classification

(a)   Debentures v. Mortgage--The latter uses the property of the corporation as security for payment; the former does not.

(b)   Convertible v. Non-Convertible--The former can be converted into stock at a stated rate. This option remains with the shareholders who will probably choose to do so if the corporation is doing well.

(c)   Callable v. Non-Callable--The former allows the corporation to pay off the bonds early (call) and under conditions specified in the indenture.

B.   Stocks

(1)   Common Stock--Owners of the corporation with voting rights and the right to receive dividends. Preferred stock usually receives a dividend first.

(2)   Preferred Stock--May or may not be allowed to vote. Usually generates a fixed-amount dividend. This is more secure but may not receive as much if the corporation is doing well and is paying high dividends. Preferred stockholders are paid dividends before common stockholders receive theirs and come before common stockholders upon distribution of assets at dissolution.

Preferred cumulative stock is entitled to the same rights as a preferred stockholder but if the corporation does not pay a dividend as promised, the right to a dividend accumulates and the owner may be paid two dividends before a common stock-holder receives any. Participating preferred stock allows the owner to share in dividends with common stockholders after both classes have been paid one dividend. Preferred convertible stock can be exchanged for common stock; callable preferred stock can be repurchased by the corporation.

(3) Stock "Owned" by the Corporation--The articles of incorporation state the authorized shares or the number of shares that the corporation can sell. Issued shares are those which have been sold. Treasury shares are issued shares which have been repurchased by the corporation. Outstanding shares are those which have been issued and have not been repurchased.

(4) Value of Shares--Par value is the value given to the stock by the corporation. No par value stock is not assigned a value. Watered stock has been purchased for less than its true value.

II. The Securities and Exchange Commission--A federal administrative agency with the responsibility to regulate sales and trades of stock on formal exchanges or in over-the-counter markets. Also regulates mutual funds and persons who work in securities sales and advisement. Recommends sanctions for criminal violations.

III. Securities Act of 1933--A disclosure statute which requires most large, publicly-held corporations to inform prospective buyers about the corporation. Covers any transaction in which a person invests expecting a profit which is derived from the managerial talents of others.

A. Registration Statement--Must be filed with the SEC before any offering using mail or interstate commerce is made. Investors must be given a prospectus or description of the company and the offer. The registration statement must include a financial statement prepared by a CPA, notice of pending lawsuits, a description of management and its holdings or interests in the corporation, a description of properties and business and facts about the sale.

B. Other Requirements--Before the registration statement is filed, the corporation may hire an underwriter who will oversee the distribution. No written advertising until twenty days after the registration statement is filed. An interim prospectus (red-herring) may be distributed. After the waiting period, the securities can be bought and sold but the only written advertising allowed is a tombstone ad which simply tells investors where they can get a copy of the prospectus.

C. Exemptions--Private offerings, offerings to institutions, to small numbers of investors, offerings to the residents of the state in which the corporation is incorporated and doing most of its business, and sales not generally advertised if the investor is sophisticated. In general, offerings under $500,000 made in one year are exempt and offerings of up to $5,000,000 if made to less than thirty-five investors, without general advertising. Stock dividends and stock splits are exempt as are securities of a reorganized or charitable corporation. There are other minor exemptions, most of which occur in industries which are tightly regulated by other laws. Note that the exemptions above are usually relatively small in amount or are made to sophisticated investors.

IV.   Securities Exchange Act of 1934--An anti-fraud statute.

    A.   General Provisions--Applies to all corporations listed on stock exchanges, and any corporation with assets in excess of $5 million and at least 500 shareholders (Section 12 companies). SEC regulates all aspects including proxy solicitation, brokers, dealers, and operations of the stock exchanges.

    B.   Insider Trading--An insider is a person who has knowledge about a corporation that the general public does not have. An insider can make money by buying and selling the stock before the information is released to the general public.

        (1)   Rule 10b-5--Applies when an insider sells or purchases stock and misrepresents or omits to state a material fact to the other party. An insider can be a director, officer, controlling stockholder, or someone who has learned information before it is released to the general public. Intent to deceive is required and there are criminal and civil penalties.

        (2)   Section 16(b)--Applies to sale or purchase made within six months of each other. The profits must be returned to the corporation; intent is irrelevant. Applies to officers, directors, and some major shareholders. There are some exceptions. Only the corporation or a shareholder can bring suit.

        (3)   Proxy Statements--The Securities Exchange Act of 1934 regulates the content of proxy statements issued by management. Remedies include damages and injunction.

V.   Regulation of Investment Companies--Companies which manage portfolios made up of smaller investors must register with the SEC and its activities are regulated.

    Mutual Funds--A type of investment company which offers the public shares of ownership in a portfolio on a continuing basis. Annual reports must be filed with the SEC and either a bank or a member of the securities exchange must hold the securities. Investment activities and payment of dividends are also restricted.

VI.   State Laws (Blue Sky Laws)--Anti-fraud statutes which usually require registration before the stock can be offered for sale. Filed with corporations commissioner. Some states have absolute requirements; others use good faith standard.

Study Questions

Fill-in-the-Blank Questions

Bill and Sally have purchased securities from Mega Corporation. Bill paid $5,000 and every six months he receives a stated payment for twenty years. The money is paid regardless of whether the corporation makes a profit. Sally also paid $5,000. She received the right to elect directors of Mega Corporation and she will receive money only if the corporation makes money. However, the corporation promises her that if for some reason they cannot pay her every year, she will receive a payment for each year, when payments are finally made.

Bill is a _____.
                    (stockholder/bondholder)

Sally is a _____.
                    (stockholder/bondholder)

Sally's rights are _____.
                          (cumulative/convertible)

The agreement between Bill and the corporation is a(n):_____.
                                              (subscription/prospectus/indenture)

Sally owns _____ securities.
                    (equity/debt)

True-False Questions

1.   Rule 10b-5 applies only to corporations who trade stock on a securities exchange. _____

2.   Authorized shares include treasury shares, issued shares, and unissued shares. _____

3.   A debenture is any bond with a value of more than $1,000. _____

4.   State securities laws are called red-herring laws._____

5   Rule 10b-5 applies to short-swing profits only. _____

6.   A mutual fund is a type of investment security. _____

7.   Proxy statements are required in order to prevent nonstockholders from lobbying stockholders. _____

8.   A callable bond may be paid off early by the corporation. _____

9.   The Securities Exchange Act of 1934 regulates the manner in which corporations can offer stock for sale. _____

10.   Majority shareholders are considered insiders. _____

Multiple-Choice Questions

1.   A bond is classified as a:

        a.   short-term equity security.
        b.   long-term equity security.
        c.   short-term debt security.
        d.   long-term debt security.

2.   Which of the following is not required in the registration statement under the Securities Act of 1933?

        a.   Financial statement certified by a CPA
        b.   Red-herring prospectus
        c.   Description of the corporation's management and its fringe benefits
        d.   List of pending lawsuits

3.   The Securities Act of 1933 is a(n):

        a.   disclosure statute.
        b.   anti-fraud statute.
        c.   blue sky law.
        d.   state law.

4.   Which of the following is not allowed while approval of a registration statement is pending?

        a.   Selection of an underwriter
        b.   Sale to certain institutional investors
        c.   Issuance of red-herring prospectus
        d.   Oral offers between the corporation and investors

5.   Which of the following is automatically exempted from the registration requirements of the Securities Act of 1933?

        a.   Stock dividends

b.   Sale of stock in public corporations
c.   Sale of all commercial paper
d.   Sale of unadvertised stock to **any investor**

6.   Rose and Stan own stock in Mina Corporation. Rose receives a dividend of 8% per year if and when a dividend is paid. If a dividend is not paid, Rose receives nothing. Rose does not vote. Stan is also promised an 8% return on investment but he may also share in extra dividends after all stockholders have been paid. Rose owns:

a.   common, non-voting, non-cumulative stock.
b.   common, non-participating stock.
c.   preferred, non-cumulative stock.
d.   preferred, participating stock.

7.   Stan owns:

a.   common, participating stock.
b.   common, cumulative stock.
c.   preferred, participating stock.
d.   preferred, cumulative stock.

8.   Bob purchased ten $1,000 bonds from Tau Corporation, but he paid only $990 per bond. He is promised a return on investment of 12 percent for a period of fifteen years. Bob purchased the stock:

a.   at face value.
b.   at a discount.
c.   at a premium.

9.   Bob will receive:

a. $9,990 at 12 percent interest.
b. $10,000 at 12 percent interest.
c. $10,200 at 12 percent interest.

10.   A bond which is backed by the personal and real property of the corporation is a(n):

a.   indenture.
b.   debenture.
c.   mortgage bond.
d.   preferred bond.

11.   Which of the following federal laws regulates short-swing profits?

a.   Blue sky laws
b.   Securities Act of 1933
c.   Rule 10b-5

d.   Securities Act of 1934

12.   The short-swing profits rule applies to:

a.   directors and officers only.
b.   directors, officers, and majority shareholders.
c.   the general public.
d.   tippees, officers, and directors.

13.   The time limit applicable to short-swing profits is:

a.   one year.
b.   one month.
c.   six months.
d.   sixty days.

14.   A person who is not affiliated with a corporation but who receives nonpublic information and uses the information to make a profit is best described as a(n):

a.   insider.
b.   red herring.
c.   tippee.
d.   underwriter.

15.   The state official with whom a sale of securities must be registered is the:

a.   underwriter.
b.   registrar.
c.   corporations commissioner.
d.   stock commissioner.

16.   Which of the following correctly describes the difference between Rule 10b-5 and Section 16?

a.   The former applies to insiders only; the latter applies to the general public.
b.   The former requires proof of fraud; the latter does not.
c.   The former is part of the Securities Act of 1933; the latter is part of the Securities Act of 1934.
d.   The former contains numerous exceptions; the latter does not.

17.   Under its articles of incorporation Alpha Corporation can issue 100,000 shares of stock. 50,000 shares are currently held by shareholders; 10,000 shares were recently purchased by Alpha from Samuel, a shareholder. The number of authorized shares is:

a.   10,000.
b.   50,000.

c.   90,000.
d.   100,000.

18.   The number of treasury shares is:

a.   10,000.
b.   50,000.
c.   90,000.
d.   100,000.

19.   The number of outstanding shares is:

a.   50,000.
b.   60,000.
c.   90,000.
d.   100,000.

20.   John purchased a bond from Mega Corporation. The bond agreement states that John may trade his bond in for five shares of common stock. The agreement also gives Mega the right to pay the bond earlier than is stated in the agreement. John's bond is:

a.   preferred and convertible.
b.   callable and convertible.
c.   preferred and callable.
d.   cumulative and convertible.

21.   Participating preferred stock gives the shareholder the right to:

a.   trade in the stock for a bond.
b.   stated dividends every year.
c.   stated dividends and the right to surplus dividends after common stockholders have been paid.
d.   receive dividends for every year in which dividends were not paid.

22.   Outstanding shares equal:

a.   authorized shares less treasury shares.
b.   authorized shares less issued shares.
c.   issued shares less treasury shares.
d.   issues shares plus treasury shares.

23.   The purpose of the Securities Act of 1933 is to:

a.   give unsophisticated investors information.
b.   prevent short-swing profits.
c.   prevent watered stock.
d   regulate proxy statements.

24.   "A type of investment company which continually sells and buys to investors of ownership in a portfolio" is a(n):

    a.   underwriting company.
    b.   Section 12 company.
    c.   blue sky fund.
    d.   mutual fund.

25.   The information which can be released before a registration statement is approved includes which of the following?

    a.   Red-herring prospectus only
    b.   Tombstone ad only
    c.   Red-herring prospectus and tombstone ad
    d.   Portfolio

Answers to Study Questions

Fill-in-the-Blank Questions

Bill is a bondholder; Sally is a stockholder. Sally's rights are cumulative. The agreement between Bill and the corporation is an indenture; a prospectus is used in connection with a stock sale; a stock subscription is an agreement to buy stock. Sally owns equity securities; Bill owns debt securities.

True-False Questions

1.   F.

2.   T.

3.   F.   A debenture is an unsecured bond.

4.   F.   They are called blue sky laws.

5.   F.   It applies to any fraudulent statement or omission.

6.   T.

7.   F.   They are designed to regulate management solicitation of shareholder votes.

8.   T.

9.   F.   The Securities Act of 1933 does this.

10.   T.

Multiple-Choice Questions

1.	d	11.	d	21.	c
2.	b	12.	b	22.	c
3.	a	13.	c	23.	a
4.	b	14.	c	24.	d
5.	a	15.	c	25.	a
6.	c	16.	b		
7.	c	17.	d		
8.	b	18.	a		
9.	b	19.	a		
10.	c	20.	b		

CHAPTER
30

Antitrust

General Principles

The purpose of antitrust laws is to protect the consumer against practices by businesses which would monopolize the economy. When a monopoly occurs, a few sellers can set the price of goods, which consumers will be forced to pay. A business may obtain a monopoly through price-fixing agreements, distribution practices, and mergers. In some cases, concentration of manufacturing and distribution may cut costs and only unreasonable market power is prohibited. Some practices have no purpose except to maintain monopoly power and these actions are absolutely prohibited (violations per se). As in the textbook, this chapter will briefly review the antitrust statutes and will focus on behavior that is prohibited.

Chapter Summary

I.   Sherman Act--Section 1 applies to agreements between two or more persons which restrain trade (cartel). Section 2 applies to monopolies, which can be created by one person. Actions must have a significant effect on interstate commerce, but intrastate transactions can be banned if they have a significant impact on interstate commerce.

      A.   Court Responses--At first, the court interpreted the Sherman Act too narrowly and some anticompetitive acts were allowed to continue. Then, it began to outlaw almost all practices. The courts have adopted the two legal tests listed below.

            (1)   Rule of Reason--Only unreasonable restraints on trade are outlawed. Court will look at the purpose of the agreement, power of the parties, and the effect on commerce.

            (2)   Per Se Rule--Automatically presumed to restrain trade and are automatically illegal. Includes price-fixing arrangements,

387

group boycotts, horizontal market divisions, and resale price maintenance.

B.   Enforcement--Justice Department may sue to enforce criminal provisions: fines, dissolution, or divestiture (forcing a company to give up one of its operations). Private persons who have been injured may sue for treble (triple) damages and attorney's fees.

C.   Section 1 Violations--Horizontal (between competitors) and vertical (distribution agreements between different segments of an industry).

(1)   Horizontal

(a)   Group Boycotts (Joint Refusals to Deal)--Two or more sellers agree to refuse to sell to a buyer. Per se violation. Some exceptions if done to express political opposition to a particular company or product.

(b)   Horizontal Market Division (Territorial or Customer Restrictions)--Two or more sellers divide market into exclusive territories or sell only to one type of customer. Per se violation.

(c)   Trade Associations--Trade associations are organizations formed by members in the same industry. They may share advertising expenses, exchange information and hire a lobbyist. The rule of reason applies; courts will analyze the purpose and impact of actions of a trade association.

(d)   Joint Ventures--Antitrust laws apply if competitors enter a joint venture agreement. Rule of reason applies.

(2)   Vertical

(a)   Territorial/Customer Restrictions--Manufacturer gives retailer or wholesaler exclusive territory or customer list. Rule of reason applies; lawful unless there is an unreasonable restriction of trade.

(b)   Resale Price Maintenance--Occurs when the manufacturer forces the retailer to sell at a maximum or minimum price; only suggested prices are allowed. Per se violation.

(c)   Refusals to Deal--Can also occur between manufacturers who refuse to sell to certain dealers. Manufacturers are protected if the dealer excessively cuts prices.

D.   Section 2 Violations--Monopolization--One or more persons hold a monopoly power over a defined market or deliberately and aggressively exclude another from a particular market. Rule of reason applies.

II.   FTC Act--Gives general power to the agency to investigate antitrust violations and to define unfair competition and deceptive business practices. FTC can issue cease-and-desist orders which order business to stop prohibited action. Violators can be fined; no action for treble damages.

III.   Clayton Act--Passed to fill in gaps left by the Sherman Act.

A.   Price Discrimination--Prohibits this practice unless based on economic factors such as transportation and distribution costs. Also prohibits exclusive dealing arrangements, mergers, and directors who sit on the boards of more than one powerful company.

B.   Exclusive Dealing--Seller tries to prevent buyer from carrying products of other sellers. Modified rule of reason applies; outlawed only if competition is substantially restricted.

C.   Tying Arrangements--Occurs when seller ties the sale of two products together. Rule of reason applies and tying will be unlawful only if the seller holds significant market power in markets for both the tying and the tied product or unlawful purpose is discovered.

D.   Mergers--Rule of reason applied under the Clayton Act.

(1)   Horizontal--Competitors on same level of production. Allowed as long as it does not increase the possibility of monopoly or illegal agreements between competitors. Generally allowed if will increase efficiency of operation.

(2)   Vertical--Company at one level of production acquires a company at a different level. If a manufacturer acquires a retailer, a forward integration exists; if a manufacturer acquires a parts supplier, a backward integration exists. Rule of reason applies; outlawed if competition in either market is substantially restricted.

(3)   Conglomerate--Companies making different products merge. Usually occurs when one company wants to diversify or broaden its product line. Rule of reason applies; usually lawful because market structure (percentage of market) will not change.

IV.   Robinson-Patman Act--Outlaws predatory price-cutting and price discrimination unless based on transportation, production, or distribution costs. Has been criticized because small businesses use it against large businesses when the latter can afford to charge less for a product.

V.   Exemptions from Antitrust Laws

A.   Labor Unions--Allows collective bargaining agreements and strikes. Union collaboration on issues other than labor rights may be prohibited. (Clayton Act)

B.   Farming/Fishing Operations--Allows sellers to act as a cooperative in order to reduce costs. Price-setting is allowed as long as it is done for a proper purpose. Cannot be used to exclude competitors. (Clayton Act, Capper-Volstead Act and Fisheries Cooperative Marketing Act)

C.   Insurance--Exempted whenever state law governs operation of these companies. States usually have extensive regulation. Does not apply to boycotts, coercion, and other wrongful practices. (McCarran-Ferguson Act)

D.   Foreign Trade--Allows exporters to form cooperatives to share costs and to compete with foreign sellers. Outlawed if trade within the United States is restricted or other exporters are injured. (Webb-Pomerane Act and Export Trading Company Act)

E.   Baseball--Court decision ruled that baseball is not part of interstate commerce; although theory has changed, sport is still exempt. Other sports are not.

F.   Oil Marketing--Producers can set quotas for oil to be sold in interstate commerce. (Interstate Oil Compact)

Study Questions

Fill-in-the-Blank Questions

Widget Manufacturing and Thingamabob Creations are manufacturers of small tools used by carpenters. Widget and Thingamabob secretly agree not to sell to Henry's Hardware.

The agreement between Widget and Thingamabob is an example of _____.
                    (joint refusal to deal/customer restriction)

Their action is an example of a _____ activity.
                    (horizontal/vertical)

If Henry sues the court will apply _____.
                    (rule of reason/per se rule)

The _____ will apply.
            (Clayton Act/Sherman Act)

True-False Questions

1. The Sherman Act was the first antitrust act to be passed by United States Congress. _____

2. All activities of fishing and agricultural cooperatives are exempt from the antitrust laws. _____

3. A tying agreement is an example of a horizontal activity. _____

4. The Sherman Act contains both criminal and civil penalties. _____

5. In order to find a violation under the Sherman Act, the Justice Department need only find a restriction of trade; the intent of the actor is irrelevant. _____

6. Price discrimination is legal if a difference in prices is caused by distribution or transportation costs._____

7. Section 1 of the Sherman Act deals with monopolies. _____

8. The FTC has the power to issue guidelines for mergers and other possibly restrictive activities. _____

9. If a restaurant chain merges with a meat-packing plant, a conglomerate merger has occurred. _____

10. An agreement between manufacturers to sell only in certain parts of the country is per se illegal. _____

11. Activities of trade associations are regulated under the rule of reason. _____

Multiple-Choice Questions

1. Which of the following is not permitted under the FTC Act?

    a. Divestiture
    b. Dissolution
    c. Cease-and-desist order
    d. Treble damages

2. Which of the following statements about the Sherman Act is false?

a.   It applies only to monopolies.
b.   Private parties may sue for treble damages.
c.   A rule of reason is applied to monopolies.
d.   It was the first antitrust statute.

3.   Cutlery, Inc., a manufacturer of silverware, sells to thousands of retail outlets. Cutlery and its retailers agree that the forty-piece set of silverware will not sell for more than $200. Cutlery may have committed:

a.   a tying agreement.
b.   resale price maintenance.
c.   a horizontal price agreement.
d.   a group boycott.

4.   Which of the following statutes provides an exemption from the antitrust laws to exporters?

a.   Sherman Act
b.   Volstead Act
c.   Webb-Pomerane Act
d.   FTC Act

5.   Which of the following actions by a labor union is _not_ exempt from the antitrust statutes?

a.   Collective bargaining
b.   Agreements covering activities unconnected with labor
c.   Strikes
d.   All union activities are exempt.

6.   Photo, Inc. produces an automatic camera which is in great demand. It requires retailers who sell the camera to sell only Photo, Inc. film with its camera. The agreement between Photo, Inc. and its retailers is:

a.   resale price maintenance.
b.   vertical customer restriction.
c.   horizontal customer restriction.
d.   tying agreement.

7.   The agreement in Question 6 is:

a.   a per se violation of the Sherman Act.
b.   a per se violation of the Robinson-Patman Act.
c.   a possible violation of the Sherman Act (rule of reason).
d.   exempt under the Clayton Act.

8.   Yard Products, a manufacturer of gardening tools and supplies, distributes its products in all fifty states. As an incentive to retailers, Yard Products agrees to license only one authorized distributor within each town. The

promise by Yard Products is:

a. an example of vertical territorial restriction and the rule of reason applies.
b. an example of horizontal territorial restriction and the per se rule applies.
c. an example of vertical territorial restrictions and the per se rule applies.
d. an example of horizontal territorial restriction and the rule of reason applies.

9. Yannon Yogurt, a manufacturer and distributor of yogurt products, acquires Dan's Dairy Farm. This is an example of a:

a. conglomerate merger.
b. horizontal merger.
c. backward vertical merger.
d. forward vertical merger.

10. The Justice Department will outlaw the merger:

a. automatically; this type of merger is always prohibited.
b. if Yannon has a substantial share of the yogurt and milk market.
c. if Yannon has a substantial share of either the yogurt market or the milk market.
d. unless Yannon can prove that the merger will lower prices and benefit the consumer.

11. If the Justice Department determines that the merger is illegal, the most likely remedy will be a(n):

a, dissolution.
b. divestiture.
c. award of treble damages.
d. cease-and-desist order.

12. Which of the following activities is per se illegal?

a. Tying agreement
b. Monopoly
c. Price-fixing agreement
d. Vertical territorial restriction

13. Which of the following activities is subject to the rule of reason?

a. Resale price maintenance
b. Horizontal market division
c. Vertical merger
d. Group boycott

14.   Which of the following is <u>not</u> exempt from the antitrust laws?

    a.   Insurance
    b.   Fisheries
    c.   Oil Marketing
    d.   Trucking

15.   Which of the following is an example of a horizontal merger?

    a.   Bicycle manufacturer acquires retail outlet
    b.   Bicycle manufacturer acquires tire manufacturer
    c.   Tire manufacturer acquires tire manufacturer
    d.   Tire manufacturer acquires chemical company

16.   Discount Pharmacy writes to Medi-All, a drug manufacturer, requesting permission to carry its product line. Medi-All refuses because it thinks that the personnel at Discount Pharmacy are not trained properly.

    a.   Discount Pharmacy can sue Medi-All for violation of the Sherman Act.
    b.   Discount Pharmacy cannot sue, but Medi-All can be fined for a criminal violation of the Sherman Act.
    c.   Medi-All can be sued only if the personnel at Discount Pharmacy are trained properly.
    d.   Medi-All has not violated an antitrust statute; individual refusals to deal are usually upheld.

17.   Excess Corporation manufacturers over 75% of the robots in the country and is charged with a violation of the Sherman Act. Excess will be found not guilty if:

    a.   it has a monopoly but keeps its prices low.
    b.   the monopoly resulted from superior business practices.
    c.   the monopoly resulted from mergers.
    d.   it has less than 90 percent of the robot market.

18.   Mojo, a manufacturer of motorcycles, distributes its products to several hundred retailers. The retailers must agree to not sell competing motorcycles, although several sell cars. This is an example of:

    a.   resale price maintenance.
    b.   exclusive dealing.
    c.   vertical refusal to deal.
    d.   tying agreement.

19.   Mojo's practice is:

    a.   a per se violation of the Sherman Act.
    b.   a per se violation of the Clayton Act.

c.   a per se violation of the Robinson-Patman Act.
d.   not a per se violation; the rule of reason applies.

20.   Video Manufacturing, a manufacturer of televisions and related products agrees to sell 1,000 sets to X-Mart for $100 each. It agrees to sell ten sets to Y-Mart at $110 each. Video Visions:

a.   has committed a per se violation of the Robinson-Patman Act.
b.   has committed a per se violation of the Sherman Act.
c.   probably has not committed a violation of the Robinson-Patman Act because it probably costs less per set to deal with X-Mart.
d.   has not committed a violation of any antitrust act; price discrimination is never forbidden.

21.   Which of the following has been exempted from the antitrust laws by court rulings?

a.   Baseball
b.   Insurance
c.   Oil marketers
d.   Trucking

22.   Which of the following is a horizontal activity?

a.   Joint refusal to deal
b.   Price discrimination
c.   Resale price maintenance
d.   Tying agreement

23.   Which of the following is subject to a <u>modified</u> rule of reason?

a.   Joint refusal to deal
b.   Price discrimination
c.   Resale price maintenance
d.   Tying agreement

24.   Ula's Unmentionables, a manufacturer of lingerie, acquires New West, a jeans manufacturer. This is an example of a:

a.   forward vertical merger.
b.   backward vertical merger.
c.   horizontal merger.
d.   conglomerate merger.

25.   A product-extension merger is a form of a:

a.   forward vertical merger.
b.   backward vertical merger.
c.   horizontal merger.

d.   conglomerate merger.

Answers to Study Questions

Fill-in-the-Blank Questions

The agreement between Widget and Thingamabob is a joint refusal to deal. A customer restriction is a division of customers between two sellers. This is a horizontal activity because Widget and Thingamabob are at the same level of production. This is a per se violation under the Sherman Act.

True-False Questions

1.   T.

2.   F.   Cannot be used to restrict trade unreasonably or to injure competitors.

3.   F.   It is a vertical activity involving a seller and a buyer.

4.   T.

5.   F.   The Justice Department must also prove intent.

6.   T.

7.   T.

8.   T.

9.   F.   This is an example of a backward vertical merger.

10.   T.   It is a horizontal territorial restriction.

11.   T.

Multiple-Choice Questions

1.	d		14.	d
2.	a		15.	c
3.	b		16.	d
4.	c		17.	b
5.	b		18.	b
6.	d		19.	d
7.	c		20.	c
8.	a		21.	a
9.	c		22.	a
10.	c		23.	d
11.	b		24.	d
12.	c		25.	d
13.	c			

CHAPTER

31

Consumer and Enviromental Law

General Principles

Consumer protection laws protect buyers from false advertising, usury, discrimination, and dangerous products. Consumer protection legislation developed in the 1960's; court opinions also created common law remedies. Today many of the consumer protection laws are created by administrative agencies. Environmental law also emerged in the 1960's. Federal statutes and administrative regulations provide protection against pollution and hazardous waste.

Chapter Summary

I.   Sources of Consumer Protection

   A.   Legislation--Uniform Commercial Code, Consumer Credit Protection Act, Magnuson-Moss Warranty Act. Covers advertising, packaging, warranties, product safety, credit. State and federal laws.

   B.   Administrative Law--Enforcement through rulings of the Federal Trade Commission, other federal agencies and state agencies.

   C.   Private Organizations and Consumers--Better Business Bureau, small-claims court, and class-action suits where one suit is brought on behalf of numerous consumers who have been injured by the same product.

II.   Advertising--Common law fraud protects from deceptive advertising but a violation is easier to prove under statutes (state and federal) because intent is not required. These laws are based on the effect the advertisement may have on the consumer.

A.   Deceptive Advertising--FTC defines as an ad which has more than one meaning. Can be caused by claims about quality, effects, price, origin, or availability. Omissions or incomplete statements may also be misleading.

B.   Bait and Switch--Seller advertises low price on one item (bait) which is usually unavailable and salesperson encourages the buyer to purchase another more expensive item (switch). Can occur if seller doesn't have adequate supply, refuses to supply within a reasonable time, or tells salesperson to sell other products.

C.   Labeling and Packaging--Fur, wool, flammable fabrics, food, and drugs are protected under special statutes. The Fair Labeling and Packaging Act requires labels to be accurate. Consumer goods must identify the product and list the manufacturer, the name and address of the packer or distributor, net quantity of contents, and quantity of servings if number of servings is indicated. Enforced by FTC and Department of Health and Human Services.

III.   Sales

A.   Door to Door--FTC regulation gives consumers three days to cancel any sale. Also notification must be given in Spanish if the sale was made in Spanish. State laws may also require "cooling off" or time for the consumer to reconsider.

B.   Mail-Order--Federal mail fraud statutes prohibit false sales. Post office regulations allow consumers to keep unsolicited merchandise and sellers who send it are subject to prosecution (free samples are excepted). States may also regulate.

IV.   Health Protection--Food and Drug Act and Food, Drug and Cosmetic Act provide for product testing, regulate food additives and marketing of drugs, and protect against dangerous food or medicine. Also includes warning against dangers caused by tobacco. Special Act covers smokeless tobacco. Warnings must appear on packages and advertising (except billboards).

V.   Consumer Product Safety Legislation--Acts involving individual products now combined under the Consumer Product Safety Act which created the Consumer Product Safety Commission. The agency develops safety standards, investigates product-related injuries, and publishes findings so that consumers can comparison shop. Can remove dangerous products from the marketplace and ban the sale of dangerous products.

VI.   Credit Protection

A.   Truth in Lending Act (TILA)--Also known as Consumer Credit Protection Act. (Federal)

(1)   Disclosure of all credit terms required by the Board of Governors of the Federal Reserve System. Advertisement of credit terms must include all information. Retail and installment sales, loans for the purchase of personal or small amounts of real estate are covered. Applies to those who lend money as a regular part of business; individuals only, not corporations are protected.

(2)   Prevents discrimination in granting credit if denial is based on race, religion, age, marital status, and type of income. Questionnaires cannot ask.

(3)   Liability for lost credit cards is limited to $50 per card for unauthorized charges made before credit card company is notified. Consumers are given procedure to follow for disputing errors on credit card bill.

B.   Fair Credit Reporting Act--Applies to credit bureaus, collection agencies, and anyone conducting an investigation. Consumer has the right to be notified of an investigation and has access to files. Procedures for correction of erroneous information are provided. (Federal)

C.   Fair Debt Collection Practices Act--Regulates creditor collection of consumer debts. Creditor cannot use harassment or intimidation or call at inappropriate times. Consumer cannot be contacted at work if the employer objects. Creditor cannot tell third parties about the debt unless the third party is a parent, attorney, spouse, or financial advisor of the consumer unless court approval is received. Creditor cannot communicate with consumer except to give notice of action if consumer refuses to pay debt; creditor cannot contact consumer if the latter is represented by an attorney.

D.   Uniform Consumer Credit Code--Comprehensive law including all of the above. Has been passed by only a few states.

VII.   Environmental Law

A.   Common Law--Before passage of legislation, most environmental pollution issues were resolved by nuisance lawsuits. A private nuisance lawsuit could be brought by one individual against another, if the plaintiff could prove specific injury. If multiple parties were affected, the government had to file a public nuisance lawsuit. It was difficult to sue multiple defendants. Some suits are still brought under negligence; the plaintiff must allege and prove that the defendant acted unreasonably in the use of his or her own property.

B.   Local Regulation--Primarily zoning and land use laws. May include noise pollution, outdoor advertising, and waste disposal.

C.   State Regulation--Can include zoning and land use laws. Also covers disposal of wastes, toxic emissions and recycling.

D.   Federal Regulation

(1)   National Environmental Policy Act (NEPA)--Requires federal agencies to prepare an environmental impact statement, which assesses the effect of major federal action on the environment. Statement required if federal agency controls the action and there is a substantial commitment of resources. Failure to require a statement must be supported in a public statement. The statement must detail adverse effects and highlight irreversible ones. The Environmental Protection Agency (EPA) coordinates enforcement and administration of federal pollution laws.

(2)   Air Pollution

(a)   Types--Carbon monoxide, sulfur oxides, nitrogen oxides, hydrocarbons, and particulates.

(b)   Clean Air Act--Passed in 1960s and amended in 1970s. Federal government, through the Environmental Protection Agency, regulates pollution from industrial operations and from automobiles.

(3)   Water Pollution

(a)   Types--Organic wastes, heated water, sediments, nutrients, toxic chemicals and hazardous waste.

(b)   Clean Water Act--1972 amendments emphasize protecting fish and wildlife, swimming waters and discharge of pollutants. The last must be authorized by permit and injunction and monetary sanctions may be imposed against violators. Previous legislation in this area included the River and Harbor Act of 1886 and the Federal Water Pollution Control Act (1948).

(4)   Toxic Chemicals

(a)   Types--Pesticides and herbicides, toxic substances, and hazardous waste.

(b)   Federal Insecticide, Fungicide and Rodenticide Act of 1947--These products must be registered with the federal government and EPA has the power to revoke registration and to inspect manufacturing plants. Products can be used only if approval is received and use is limited in application to food crops.

(c)   Toxic Control Substances Act of 1976--Regulation and investigation of toxic substances. EPA can require businesses to conduct studies before using chemicals.

(d)   Resource Conservation and Recovery Act of 1976-- Deals with hazardous waste. EPA determines which wastes are hazardous, regulates treatment and storage, packaging and labeling. 1980s amendments expanded definition of toxic chemicals and decreased use of land containment for disposal and storage.

(e)   Comprehensive Environmental Response, Compensation and Liability Act of 1980 (Superfund)--Designed to clean up hazardous waste and to collect costs of clean up from the offending parties. Industries are joint and severally liable. Potential defendants include the company that created the waste, the transporter of the waste, the owners of the waste disposal site (current and at the time of the pollution).

Study Questions

Fill-in-the-Blank Questions

Today modern pollution control is governed mainly by _____.
                                                       (common law/administrative law)

Most consumer protection legislation was passed in the _____.
                                                        (1960s/1980s)

Truth in advertising is enforced by the _____.
                                        (FTC/EPA/CPSC)

Testing of new consumer products is regulated by the _____.
                                                      (FTC/EPA/CPSC)

True-False Questions

1.   Before Congress passed legislation, suits against seller for deceptive advertising were brought on the basis of nuisance. _____

2.   Under the Equal Credit Opportunity Act, an applicant for credit cannot be asked to state the amount of alimony received annually. ____

3.   The Truth-in-Lending Act regulates disputes between a credit card issuer and a consumer. _____

4.   Smokeless tobacco ads do not have to include health warnings. _____

5.   Postal regulations prohibit the mailing of unsolicited merchandise. _____

6.   The Consumer Product Safety Commission cannot recall products. _____

7.   The UCCC is a federal law. _____

8.   The Better Business Bureau is an example of a federal agency which deals with consumer protection. _____

9.   The federal government and most states regulate door-to-door sales by allowing the buyer to cancel within a few days of purchase. _____

10.   The Toxic Control Substances Act deals only with waste disposal. _____

11.   Nitrogen oxides are produced when fuel is burned at high temperatures. _____

12.   Discharge of heated water into rivers and streams is regulated by the Clean Water Act. _____

13.   Liability under Superfund violations is joint and several. _____

14.   An environmental impact statement must list irreversible effects of an action. _____

15.   Local ordinances governing pollution usually include zoning and land use restrictions. _____

Multiple-Choice Questions

1.   A postal regulation provides that unrequested merchandise which is sent to a consumer:

    a.   may be kept by the consumer at no charge and the seller may have committed an unfair trade practice.
    b.   may be kept by the consumer if the consumer wishes to pay the cost and the seller may have committed an unfair trade practice.
    c.   may not be kept by the consumer and the seller has not committed an unfair trade practice.
    d.   may not be kept by the consumer even though the seller may have committed an unfair trade practice.

2.   Which of the following statements about door-to-door sales is _false_?

    a.   They are regulated by the federal government.
    b.   They are regulated by state government.
    c.   The sellers must register with the Federal Trade Commission.
    d.   Most laws provide that the buyer can cancel within three days of the sale.

3.   Which of the following type(s) of tobacco need not post a Surgeon General's warning?

    a.   Cigarettes only
    b.   Smokeless tobacco only
    c.   Small cigars and smokeless tobacco
    d.   All of the above must post warnings.

4.   Which of the following is not a duty of the Consumer Product Safety Commission?

    a.   Research product-related injuries and deaths
    b.   Grant approval for sale of new drugs
    c.   Assist consumers in evaluating the safety of products
    d.   Issue recalls of dangerous consumer products

5.   Another name for the TILA (Truth-in-Lending Act) is:

    a.   CCPA.
    b.   UCCC.
    c.   CPSA.
    d.   FCRA.

6.   Which of the following types of discrimination is not prohibited by the Truth-in-Lending Act?

    a.   Race
    b.   Type of Income
    c.   Amount of Income
    d.   Marital Status

7.   Which of the following is not part of the Clean Air Act?

    a.   Ruling to decrease carbon monoxide emitted by cars
    b.   Ruling to eliminate lead from gasoline
    c.   Provide assistance to states in regulating air pollution
    d.   Ruling to decrease the number of cars on national highways

8.   At common law, legal action against factories which polluted the air of an entire town:

    a.   could be brought by private citizens as a public nuisance suit.
    b.   could be brought by private citizens as a private nuisance suit.

c.   could be brought by city government as a private nuisance suit.

d.   could be brought by city government as a public nuisance suit.

9.   Solid or liquid types of air pollution produced by a factory are:

a.   particulates.

b.   sulfur oxides.

c.   nitrogen oxides.

d.   hydrocarbons.

10.   Which of the following was the first federal statute to regulate water pollution?

a.   Water Pollution Control Act

b.   Clean Water Act

c.   River and Harbor Act

d.   Federal Waterway Regulation Act

11.   Which of the following is not concerned with waste disposal?

a.   RCRA

b.   Superfund

c.   EPA

d.   CPSC

12.   Which of the following is the definition of "deceptive advertising" as adopted by the FTC?

a.   Advertising which the seller intends to induce the buyer to purchase the product

b.   Advertising which is capable of more than one meaning

c.   Advertising which contains an opinion about the quality of a product

d.   Advertising which offers low prices on a product which is not available

13.   Which of the following is a definition of "bait and switch"?

a.   Advertising which the seller intends to induce the buyer to purchase the product

b.   Advertising which is capable of more than one meaning

c.   Advertising which contains an opinion about the quality of a product

d.   Advertising which offers low prices on a product which is not available

14.   Which of the following statements about the Federal Trade Commission is false?

a.   Rulings of the FTC cannot be appealed to the courts.

b.   The FTC has the power to define deceptive advertising.

c.   The FTC has the power to issue cease-and-desist orders.
d.   the FTC has the power to issue decisions on antitrust cases.

15.   Which of the following agency(ies) enforce(s) the Fair Packaging and Labeling Act?

a.   FTC only
b.   FTC and CPSC
c.   FTC and Department of Health and Human Services
d.   FTC and EPA

16.   Which of the following is not a part of the Truth-in-Lending Act?

a.   Counter-advertising procedures
b.   Disclosure of interest rates
c.   Outlaws discrimination in granting of credit
d.   Regulates credit bureaus

17.   Which of the following statements about the UCCC is true?

a.   It is a federal law.
b.   It has been adopted by a few states.
c.   It regulates disposal of hazardous waste.
d.   It gives the government the power to issue an environmental impact statement.

18.   The difference between a case for fraud based on advertising and a case based on deceptive advertising is:

a.   Fraud is based on a statute; deceptive advertising is based on a statute and administrative regulations.
b.   Private persons may sue for fraud; only a government agency may sue for deceptive advertising.
c.   Fraud requires proof of the seller's intent; deceptive advertising does not.
d.   Fraud cases are heard in courts; deceptive advertising cases are heard by administrative agencies and are never heard by courts.

19.   Which of the following is not part of "bait and switch" advertising?

a.   Seller advertises one product at a low price.
b.   Salesperson discourages buyer from purchasing advertised item.
c.   Salesperson refuses to negotiate with buyer for purchase of any item.
d.   Seller fails to have sufficient quantities of the advertised item in stock.

20.   An environmental impact statement:

a.   must be issued when a federal project or law will affect the environment.

b.   must be issued by the EPA for any governmental project.

c.   is required by Superfund.

d.   is required only on federal projects involving more than $1 million.

21.   The CPSC:

a.   regulates advertising of consumer products.

b.   regulates safety of consumer products.

c.   regulates pollution of consumer vehicles.

d.   regulates hazardous waste disposal.

22.   Which of the following is not part of the Clean Water Act or Water Pollution Control Act?

a.   Make water safe for swimming

b.   Regulate traffic on navigable rivers

c.   Regulate pollution of public waters

d.   Issue guidelines for protection of fish in public waters

23.   Environmental law is:

a.   any law which protects the consumer from health hazards.

b.   any law which pertains to health and preservation.

c.   any law which pertains to water, air, or land use.

d.   any law which regulates business use of water, air, or land.

24.   Which of the following is a consumer right under the Fair Credit Reporting Act?

a.   Equal opportunity for credit

b.   Right to see credit reports issued by credit bureau

c.   Right to procedure for settling billing disputes

d.   Right to be free from harassment from creditors

25.   Which of the following statements about the Truth-in-Lending Act is false?

a.   It applies to small real estate loans.

b.   It applies to anyone who arranges for credit as part of a business.

c.   It is a disclosure law.

d.   It protects corporations and individual consumers.

Answers to Study Questions

Fill-in-the-Blank Questions

Modern pollution control is governed by administrative law. Most consumer protection law was passed in 1960s. Truth in advertising is enforced by the FTC (Federal Trade Commission). Testing of new consumer products is regulated by the CPSC (Consumer Product Safety Commission). The EPA is concerned with environmental law.

True-False Questions

1.   F.   They were brought on the basis of fraud.

2.   T.

3.   T.

4.   F.

5.   F.   Unless the merchandise is a free sample.

6.   F.   The CPSC has the power to recall dangerous products.

7.   F.   It is a uniform law adopted by a few states.

8.   F.   It is a private organization.

9.   T.

10.   F.   The law may require businesses to conduct studies before using a chemical.

11.   T.

12.   T.

13.   T.

14.   T.

15.   T

Multiple-Choice Questions

1.	a		14.	a
2.	c		15.	c
3.	d		16.	a
4.	b		17.	b
5.	a		18.	c
6.	c		19.	c
7.	d		20.	a
8.	d		21.	b
9.	a		22.	b
10.	c		23.	b
11.	d		24.	b
12.	b		25.	d
13.	d			

CHAPTER
32

Employee and Labor Law

<u>General Principles</u>

At common law, the employer controlled all aspects of employment. Beginning in the 1930's labor unions were given power to strike and to negotiate with management. Almost all aspects of employment are now regulated by the federal government including employment discrimination, job safety, retirement programs, and other protection for workers.

<u>Chapter Summary</u>

I.   <u>Unions and Collective Bargaining</u>--Initially workers had no rights; then legislation was passed which favored the workers. Corrective legislation was then passed.

    A.   <u>Norris-LaGuardia Act (1932)</u>--First statute gave workers the right to peaceful strikes, picketing and boycotts.

    B.   <u>National Labor Relations Act (1935)</u>--Also known as the Wagner Act. Provided for collective bargaining and prevented owners from interfering in labor activities by influencing workers, contributing to union funds, discrimination against union members, and refusal to bargain collectively. National Relations Labor Board was created to investigate violations and issue complaints. Pro-labor.

    C.   <u>Labor-Management Relations Act (1947)</u>--Also known as the Taft-Hartley Act. Swing back to pro-management. Allowed employers to lobby before union election. Prohibited business which hired only union members (closed shop). Union shops, which require workers to join union some time after beginning work, are allowed but states may pass right-to-work laws which outlaw union shops. President can obtain injunction against strikes for eighty days if a national emergency would otherwise exist.

D.   Labor-Management Reporting and Disclosure Act (1959)--Also known as the Landrum-Griffin Act. Regulates internal union procedures; requires regular and open elections at which no communists or convicts can be elected. Officials are responsible for union funds. Also prohibited hot-cargo contracts under which an employer is induced to boycott non-union products of another. This is a secondary boycott. Under the Taft-Hartley Act a union cannot induce employees to engage in secondary boycotts.

II.   Employment Discrimination--The Civil Rights Act of 1964 was a comprehensive anti-discrimination law; Title VII relates to employment.

A.   Employers--Applies to local, state, and federal governments. Also applies to unions with more than fifteen members or which operate a hiring hall which rations jobs. Private employers with more than fifteen employees are also covered.

B.   Protected Workers--No discrimination on account of race, color, or sex unless it is a bona fide requirement of the job. No advertising separated by sex and must use combined seniority list. Now used to enforce rules against sexual harassment.

C.   Discrimination Methods--Affects not only hiring but benefits and promotions. Job testing and minimal education requirements must be related to duties performed. Distinguish between disparate treatment of employees (intentional) and disparate impact (unintentional). Even the latter can be banned if questioned practices are not legitimately tied to the operation of the business.

D.   Affirmative Action--Designed to correct past discrimination. Minorities and women receive preferred treatment. "Reverse Discrimination" results when majority (white male) workers are discriminated against. Policy is under attack and is examined on a case-by-case basis. Employer is required to consider other factors besides race and sex.

III.   Injury, Compensation, and Safety

A.   Worker's Compensation--State law which provides compensation to workers for injuries received on the job. Strict liability standard; accidental injuries and injuries resulting from negligence are covered, but intentional injuries are not. Some states allow recovery for injuries resulting from preexisting medical problems.

B.   Occupational Health and Safety Act (1970)--Federal law designed to regulate working conditions. Covers all employers who have at least one employee.

    (1)   <u>Agencies</u>--Created administrative agency as part of the department of labor (OSHA). Has the power to issue standards, make inspections, and enforce rules by finding or giving cease-and-desist orders to violators. National Institute for Occupational Safety and Health is part of the Department of Health and Human Services and conducts research on health and safety issues. There is a review commission to hear appeals from action by OSHA employers.

    (2)   <u>Reporting Requirements</u>--Employers with more than ten employees must keep records of job-related illnesses and injury and report them to the agency. Deaths and accidents involving more than five employees must be reported within two days and an inspection is required. Under recent court rulings, the agency cannot search an employer's premises without a search warrant.

C.   <u>Retirement and Security Income</u>--Social Security Act of 1935

    (1)   <u>OASDI</u>--Employers and employees contribute to a fund which pays for loss of income after a worker retires.

    (2)   <u>Medicare</u>--Health insurance administered by the Social Security Administration. Applies to people over sixty-five and disabled persons of any age. Covers hospital and outpatient treatment; can buy additional coverage from the government.

    (3)   <u>Unemployment Compensation</u>--Employers submit taxes to state governments which forward them to the federal government. Funds are used to pay qualified individuals who lose their jobs.

    (4)   <u>Private Retirement</u>--Federal legislation governs activity of persons who administer private pension funds under the Employee Retirement Income Security Act (ERISA).

IV.   <u>Fair Labor Standards Act (1938)</u>

A.   <u>Child Labor</u>--Children under sixteen cannot be employed full-time except for some family businesses. Children between sixteen and eighteen cannot be employed in jobs that would be hazardous to health. Some states require work permits of children under sixteen.

B.   <u>Maximum Hours and Minimum Wages</u>--Most employees must be paid at one and one-half times the usual rate for more than forty hours in more than one week. Professional and union members covered by collective bargaining agreements are exempt. Also sets lowest wage which employer can pay to full-time employees.

C.   Government Contracts--Davis-Bacon Act and Walsh-Healy Public Contract Act regulates wages to employers of contractors and subcontractors on federal projects. Also requires overtime and minimum wage to employees of federal suppliers.

Study Questions

Fill-in-the-Blank Questions

The federal agency which regulates employee safety is _____.
                                             (NLRB/OSHA/OASDI)

Most worker's compensation laws are _____ law.
                            (federal/state)

The _____ Act was the first labor law.
            (Taft-Hartley/Norris-LaGuardia)

Private pension funds are regulated by _____.
                              (FUTA/ERISA/OASDI)

True-False Questions

1.   Hot cargo contracts apply to coercion of employees only. _____

2.   Child labor laws prohibit any child under age sixteen from working. _____

3.   Title VII establishes the national minimum wage. _____

4.   The Occupational Health and Safety Act applies only to employers with more than fifteen employees. _____

5.   Governmental agencies are not prohibited from discriminating against employees on the basis of sex. _____

6.   The National Labor Relations Board has the power to investigate charges of unfair labor practices. _____

7.   Union shops are illegal in all states. _____

8.   The right-to-work law was passed by the United States Congress. _____

9.   Worker's compensation covers injuries received on the job regardless of the

negligence of the injured employee. _____

10.   Management is prohibited from lobbying against unions prior to an election. _____

Multiple-Choice Questions

1.   Which of the following facts about a right-to-work law is true?

     a.   It outlaws union shops.
     b.   It is a part of federal labor law.
     c.   It provides disability payment for injured workers.
     d.   It prevents discrimination on the basis of an employee's sex.

2.   Which of the following acts outlawed hot-cargo contracts?

     a.   Taft-Hartley
     b.   Norris-LaGuardia
     c.   Wagner
     d.   Landrum-Griffin

3.   Which of the following is a duty of the National Labor Relations Board?

     a.   Regulate closed shops
     b.   Investigate unfair labor practices
     c.   Provide unemployment insurance for displaced members
     d.   Represent the employer in a worker's compensation suit

4.   A secondary boycott occurs when:

     a.   union members strike against their own company.
     b.   union members induce other workers to strike against their company.
     c.   union members induce their employer to boycott.
     d.   non-union members boycott union products.

5.   Which of the following statements is _false_?

     a.   Collective bargaining is the right to enter into negotiations with management.
     b.   Collective bargaining was the subject of the first labor laws.
     c.   Right-to-work laws are designed to protect union workers.
     d.   Closed shops are illegal in all states.

6.   Which of the following is in correct chronological order?

     a.   Norris-LaGuardia Act, Wagner Act, Taft-Hartley Act, Landrum Griffin Act
     b.   Landrum-Griffin Act, Norris-LaGuardia Act, Wagner Act, Taft-Hartley Act

c.   Taft-Hartley Act, Wagner Act, Norris-LaGuardia Act, Landrum-Griffin Act

d.   Wagner Act, Taft-Hartley Act, Norris-LaGuardia Act, Landrum-Griffin Act

7.   Which of the following is not an unfair labor practice under the National Labor Relations Act?

a.   Refusal to bargain with union representatives
b.   Management's lobbying against a union
c.   Management's contribution to a labor union
d.   Discrimination against whistleblowers

8.   Which of the following is <u>not</u> a provision of the Taft-Hartley Act?

a.   Cooling-off period if ordered by a federal court
b.   Right of president to request an injunction against strikes for eighty days
c.   Closed shops made illegal
d.   Hot-cargo contracts made illegal

9.   Which of the following regulates the administration of private retirement funds?

a.   OASDI
b.   ERISA
c.   Medicare
d.   FICA

10.   The Fair Labor Standards Act:

a.   established a provision for a national minimum wage.
b.   prohibits children under age sixteen from working in government jobs.
c.   outlawed discrimination against women in the workplace.
d.   established a fund for unemployment compensation.

11.   Title VII of the Civil Rights Act:

a.   banned the use of affirmative action.
b.   banned sex discrimination in the workplace unless a bona fide job qualification is shown.
c.   applies to all employers who use an instrumentality of interstate commerce.
d.   does not apply to state, local, and federal governments.

12.   Paul, a restaurant owner, refuses to hire male waiters. Paul's action is an example of:

a.   affirmative action.

b.   disparate impact.
c.   disparate treatment.
d.   an OSHA violation.

13.   Which of the following describes the federal law relating to job testing?

a.   An employer must show a relationship between the test and the job duties.
b.   An employer may require a high school diploma for any job.
c.   Disparate-impact effects of job testing are never illegal.
d.   An employer may never require that an employee speak English.

14.   Which of the following correctly describes an employer's responsibility under worker's compensation laws?

a.   The employer must pay if the injury was caused by an accident regardless of the time or location.
b.   The employer must pay only if the employee was not negligent.
c.   The employer must pay only if the injury did not result from an intentional tort.
d.   The employer must pay regardless of the employee's intent if the accident occurred on the job.

15.   Which of the following regulates worker safety?

a.   NLRB
b.   Right-to-work law
c.   OSHA
d.   OASDI

16.   Which of the following facts about the OSHA is _false_?

a.   It creates three agencies which deal with worker safety.
b.   It gives administrators the right to investigate job-related injuries and deaths.
c.   It allows administrators to inspect a plant without a warrant.
d.   It requires most businesses to keep records of on-the-job injuries.

17.   Warrantless searches by OSHA administrators:

a.   violate the Fair Labor Standards Act.
b.   violate the Fourth Amendment
c.   violate Title VII of the Civil Rights Act.
d.   are legal if locations are not selected at random.

18.   Which of the following facts about FUTA is _false_?

a.   Employers and employees contribute to the fund.
b.   Funds collected by employers are remitted to insurance companies.

c.   It is a federal law.

d.   It provides for a tax to fund unemployment compensation.

19.   Which of the following correctly describes regulation of child labor?

a.   Children under age sixteen cannot work full-time.

b.   Children under age eighteen cannot work in dangerous jobs.

c.   States may require work permits for children.

d.   Children need not be paid for overtime.

20.   The standard overtime wage is:

a.   twice normal wage.

b.   the same as normal wage.

c.   three times normal wage.

d.   required when an employee works more than forty hours per week.

21.   Medicare is administered by:

a.   OASDI.

b.   Social Security Administration.

c.   NLRB.

d.   OSHA.

22.   Which of the following are the subject of state laws?

a.   Right-to-work law

b.   Worker's compensation

c.   Right-to-work law and worker's compensation

d.   Minimum wage and right-to-work law

23.   If a state has adopted a right-to-work law:

a.   closed shops only are illegal.

b.   union shops only are illegal.

c.   closed shops and union shops are illegal.

d.   employers may refuse to hire nonunion employees.

24.   Which of the following statements about affirmative action is false?

a.   Employers may make hiring decisions based solely on the sex or race of the applicant.

b.   It is being challenged by majority workers.

c.   The United States Supreme Court evaluates affirmative action on a case-by-case basis.

d.   It is designed to correct past discriminatory practices.

25.   Which of the following deals with unemployment compensation?

    a.   ERISA
    b.   FICA
    c.   OSHA
    d.   FUTA

Answers to Study Questions

Fill-in-the-Blank Questions

OHSA (Occupational Safety and Health Administration) regulates employee safety. Worker's compensation is state law. The Norris-LaGuardia Act was first. Private pension funds are regulated by ERISA.

True-False Questions

1.   F.   They also apply to employers.

2.   F.   They cannot work full-time except in certain circumstances.

3.   F.   Title VII regulates employment discrimination.

4.   F.   Only one employee is required.

5.   F.

6.   T.

7.   F.   Closed shops are illegal; union shops are illegal in states with right-to-work law.

8.   F.   It is state law.

9.   T.

10.   F.   This is allowed under the Taft-Hartley Act.

Multiple-Choice Questions

1.	a		14.	c
2.	d		15.	c
3.	b		16.	c
4.	c		17.	b
5.	c		18.	b
6.	a		19.	a
7.	b		20.	d
8.	d		21.	b
9.	b		22.	c
10.	a		23.	c
11.	b		24.	a
12.	c		25.	d
13.	a			

Personal Property and Bailments

General Principles

Personal property includes all property except real estate (land) and items permanently attached to the land (fixtures). It includes chattels (tangible items), rights under a contract, and the use of services. Ownership of property includes the right to use the property and the right to transfer it. Transfer may occur by gift, by sale, or the owner may choose to abandon the property.

A bailment is a transfer of possession of property without transfer of ownership (title). Typical bailments include rental or repair contracts. It may help to think of taking a suit to the dry cleaners or renting a car. In most bailments, the owner of the property (bailor) agrees to pay the transferee (bailee) for the bailee's repair or storage charges. The bailee agrees to take care of the property and to return it to the bailor.

Chapter Summary

I. **Nature of Personal Property**--Personal property includes all property except land (realty or real estate) and items permanently attached to the land (fixtures).

    A.   **Tangible**--Anything that can be touched; for example, a car. A chattel is a good or livestock.

    B.   **Intangible**--Anything that cannot be touched; for example, a patent. It includes ownership in a corporation, rights under a contract, or the right to receive services. Although a corporate stock certificate or a contract may be written on paper and "touchable," the documents only represent ownership. A stock certificate shows the right to vote on corporate policy and to receive dividends; a contract shows the right to sue if the other party does not live up to the agreement.

II.   Property Ownership--Property may be owned by more than one person at a time.

A.   Fee Simple--Complete ownership by one or more persons. The owner has the right to use and dispose of the property as he or she wishes.

B.   Tenancy in Common--Ownership by one or more persons. Each person has an undivided interest in the entire property and may only dispose of his or her portion. When a tenant in common dies, his or her share goes to the heirs. The shares do not have to be equal.

C.   Joint Tenancy with Right of Survivorship--Ownership by two or more persons in equal shares. When one joint tenant dies, his or her share is split between the remaining joint tenants. If a joint tenant transfers his or her interest before death, the joint tenancy is destroyed and the new owners become tenants in common.

D.   Ownership by Husband and Wife--A tenancy by the entirety of a joint tenancy between husband and wife. In a few states, husband and wife own community property, which includes only property acquired during the marriage.

III.   Methods of Acquiring Ownership

A.   Sale, Purchase, or Production--A sale or purchase is the transfer of ownership for a price. Production occurs when the property is created by the owner.

B.   Possession--Applies mainly to capture of wild animals. The person who captures the animal retains ownership unless the capture was made by a trespasser on another's land (the landowner also owns the animal) or unless the capture is in violation of law (the state owns the animal).

C.   Accession--Usually occurs when a non-owner makes changes, addition, or improvements to another's property. The original owner will retain the property unless the person making the improvements acted in good faith and the value of the improved item is substantially higher as a result of the improvement.

D.   Confusion--Occurs when the property of several people is mixed and it is impossible to determine who owns what. If the goods are mixed wrongfully and intentionally, the innocent parties receive title to all of the property. Otherwise, the parties own the goods as tenants in common.

E.   Gifts--Voluntary transfer of ownership without consideration. The donor gives the property to the donee. An inter vivos gift is made while the donor is alive; a gift cause mortis or deathbed gift must be made by the donor when the possibility of death is imminent. This gift is valid only if the donor dies. All three requirements listed below must be met in order for a valid gift to occur.

> (1)   Donative Intent--The donor must intend to give, rather than sell, the property to another. A gift usually will be presumed if the donee is a relative or friend of the donor and if the gift is not most of the donor's assets.

> (2)   Delivery--The donor must give control and possession of the property to the donee. The donor may hand the property to the donee (actual delivery) or give the donee access to the property (constructive delivery). For example, a car could be delivered by giving the keys to the donee. If a third party or agent is used, delivery is complete if the property is transferred to the donee's agent. If the agent is more closely associated with the donor, the agent must transfer the property to the donee.

> (3)   Acceptance--The donee must agree to take the property.

IV.   Mislaid, Lost and Abandoned Property--A person who finds property may acquire title to (ownership) it depending on the status of the property and the intent of the original owner.

> A.   Mislaid Property--The owner deliberately leaves the property but forgets where it is. The finder acquires no rights because the owner will come looking for it. The finder is a bailee of the property.

> B.   Lost Property--The owner involuntarily leaves the property. The finder acquires ownership rights which are good against everyone except the true owner. A finder who knows the owner but does not return the property is liable for conversion. Estray statutes give rewards to finders who turn the property into a governmental agency.

> C.   Abandoned Property--The owner deliberately leaves the property with no intention of recovering it. The finder becomes the owner.

V.   Bailments--Transfer of possession of property; title is retained by the owner.

> A.   Elements of a Bailment--The owner is the bailor; the party with possession is the bailee. The bailor must give the bailee exclusive rights to use and possess the property and the bailee must knowingly accept the property. (Hidden property cannot be the subject of a bailment). The agreement between the parties may be express or implied.

> B.   Ordinary Bailments

> > (1)   Types--Most bailments are for the mutual benefit of both

parties; the bailor transfers the property for repair and the bailee receives no compensation. A bailment for the sole benefit of the bailor occurs when the bailee agrees to act without compensation, e.g. storing goods in a friend's garage. A bailment for the sole benefit of the bailee occurs when the bailor lends the property at no charge.

(2) Rights of the Bailee--The bailee has the right to possession of the property for the time of the bailment. The bailee may have the right to make reasonable use of the property and to be compensated for expenses incurred while using the property. Unless otherwise stated, the bailee is entitled to compensation for his or her services. A bailee may normally limit liability if the limitation is known by the bailor. Exculpatory clauses, which try to relieve a bailee of liability for negligence, are usually not valid.

(3) Duties of the Bailee--The bailee has the duty to take care of the property or risks being sued for negligence. The bailee must also return the property at the end of the bailment; if the bailee does not return the property as promised, he or she will be liable for breach of contract or conversion. The bailee is not liable if a third party with better title takes the property or if the bailee uses due care.

(4) Rights of the Bailor--The bailor has the right to the return of the property in the same or better condition than when it was delivered to the bailee.

(5) Duties of the Bailor--The bailor has the duty to compensate the bailee, unless otherwise agreed. The bailor must notify the bailee of any known defects in the property. In a bailment for mutual benefit, the bailor must also inform the bailee of any defects which could be discovered by a reasonable inspection.

(6) Termination--By agreement, completion of the purpose of the bailment, demand by either party, operation of law, or an act by the bailee that is not a part of the bailment agreement.

B.   Special Bailments--Includes bailments by persons who move or store another's property as a part of their business. The standards of liability depend on the type of bailment.

(1) Common Carriers--Anyone who is publicly licensed to transport goods and persons. Includes airlines, train companies, and bus lines. The bailee is strictly liable for the bailed property unless he or she can show that loss or damage occurred due to an act of God, of the shipper-bailor, of a public authority, or of a public enemy. The bailee will not be

strictly liable if the goods are fragile or easily destroyed. Subject to governmental rules, a common carrier can limit liability if the bailor is made aware of the limitation.

(2)   Warehouse Companies--Warehouse companies are regulated by Article 7 of the UCC. A warehouseman-bailee has the power to issue a negotiable or nonnegotiable warehouse receipt. The warehouse receipt is a document of title and can be used to transfer ownership of the property without moving it. A warehouse company can limit liability if the bailor is given the option of paying extra for more coverage.

(3)   Innkeepers--Includes only those who offer lodging to the public. At common law, an innkeeper was strictly liable for the property of guests but in most states they are only liable for negligence if a safe is provided for the guest's valuables.

Study Questions

Fill-in-the-Blank Questions

Uncle Paul decides to give a car to his favorite niece, Stephanie. He gives the keys to the car to Stephanie's husband, Brad, because Stephanie is out of town on business. When Stephanie returns, Brad hands her the keys.

Uncle Paul is the _____.
                        (donor/donee)

Stephanie is the _____.
                        (donor/donee)

Delivery of the car occurs when _____ receives the
                                          (Stephanie/Brad)
_____.
        (car/keys)

Giving the keys to Stephanie is an example of _____ delivery
of the car.   (constructive/actual)

The gift of the car is an example of a(n) _____
gift.   (cause mortis/inter vivos)

True-False Questions

1.   A stock certificate is an example of tangible personal property. _____

2.   Sid writes a play; his ownership of the play is an example of production. _____

3.   A stereo installed in a car is an example of an accession. _____

4.   Estray statutes apply to lost property only. _____

5.   If confusion of goods is caused by the honest mistake of one party, the innocent party will obtain ownership of all the goods. _____

6.   A finder of mislaid property obtains title against everyone except the true owner. _____

7.   In a gratuitous bailment, the bailor has the duty to warn the bailee of all hidden defects including defects which would be found by a reasonable inspection. _____

8.   As a general rule, warehousemen are strictly liable for the loss of bailed property, although some exceptions exist. _____

9.   Valet parking is an example of a lease; it is not a bailment. _____

10.   An innkeeper is an example of a special bailee. _____

Multiple-Choice Questions

1.   Alice, Beth, and Cecil are co-owners of a horse. Alice owns 60 percent. Beth and Cecil own 20 percent each. When one of the owners dies, his or her share is to be divided equally between the remaining owners. This is an example of:

   a.   a tenancy by the entirety.
   b.   community property.
   c.   a tenancy in common.
   d.   a joint tenancy.

2.   Which of the following is not required for a gift?

   a.   Delivery to the donee or the donee's agent
   b.   Acceptance by the donee
   c.   Donative intent by the donor
   d.   Donative intent by the donee

3.   Which of the following statements about a gift causa mortis is false?

   a.   The donor must die in order for the gift to be valid.
   b.   Donative intent is not required.
   c.   The donor must make the gift thinking that he or she is about to die.
   d.   The gift is automatically revoked if the donor lives.

4.   Cynthia delivers her dog to the Cozy Canine Kennels. She pays the kennel $15 for three nights. The dog is wearing an expensive leather collar. When Cynthia returns, she discovers that the collar is missing and that the dog is sick. The agreement between Cynthia and the kennel is an example of a(n):

    a.   involuntary bailment.
    b.   bailment for mutual benefit.
    c.   bailment for sole benefit of the bailor.
    d.   bailment for sole benefit of the bailee.

5.   Cynthia decides to sue the kennel for the vet bills she incurred in curing the dog. If Cynthia can prove that the kennel did not take reasonable care of the dog, she can sue for:

    a.   breach of contract.
    b.   negligence.
    c.   conversion.
    d.   breach of contract and conversion.

6.   The Cozy Canine Kennel is:

    a.   responsible for the loss of the leather collar.
    b.   not responsible for the loss of the collar because the kennel did not knowingly accept possession of the collar.
    c.   not responsible for the loss of the collar because it is an involuntary bailee.
    d.   not responsible for the loss of the collar because it is an involuntary bailor.

7.   Which of the following is true?

    a.   An ordinary bailee may not limit liability; a special bailee can.
    b.   An ordinary bailee is liable only for negligence; a special bailee is strictly liable.
    c.   An ordinary bailment is one for mutual benefit; a special bailment benefits only one party.
    d.   A special bailee is one who stores or transports goods as part of his or her business; an ordinary bailee is not.

8.   A chattel is a synonym for:

    a.   real estate.
    b.   personalty.
    c.   goods.
    d.   intangible property.

9.   Ann and Mike own a car as joint tenants. Ann sells her share of the car to Pat.

a.   Pat and Mike are joint tenants.
b.   Pat and Mike are tenants in common.
c.   Pat does not own a share in the car; Ann cannot transfer her interest.
d.   Mike owns the car in fee simple.

10.   Sam is preparing to undergo open-heart surgery. He tells Paula that she may have his dog if he dies. Sam recovers.

a.   The gift is valid unless Sam tells Paula he wants to keep his dog.
b.   The gift is valid; Sam cannot revoke the gift.
c.   The gift is invalid; Sam recovered.
d.   The gift is invalid; it was not in writing.

11.   Lucy finds a large tree branch on John's land. Lucy varnishes the branch and attaches felt mushrooms and leaves to the log. She sells it to her mother for $200. Lucy:

a.   acquired title to the log, but she must pay John for this value.
b.   acquired title to the log and owes nothing to John.
c.   did not acquire title to the log because she found it on John's land.
d.   did not acquire title to the log because John did not give her permission to use the log.

12.   Lucy's act of taking the log and improving it is an example of:

a.   ownership by protection.
b.   ownership by accession.
c.   ownership by bailment.
d.   ownership by gift.

13.   Paul lends his bicycle to Renee. Paul does not know that the chain is loose. The chain falls off while Renee is riding to the bank and she suffers minor injuries.

a.   Paul is responsible for Renee's injuries because Paul and Renee had a bailment for mutual benefit and Paul was obliged to warn Renee of any discoverable defects.
b.   Paul is responsible for Renee's injuries because Paul and Renee had a bailment for the sole benefit of the bailee and Paul had an obligation to warn Renee of any discoverable defects.
c.   Paul is not responsible for Renee's injuries because Paul and Renee had a bailment for mutual benefit and he had a duty to warn her of obvious defects only.
d.   Paul is not responsible for Renee's injuries because Paul and Renee had a bailment for the sole benefit of the bailee and he had a duty to warn her of known defects only.

14.   Which of the following is not a right of the bailee?

a.   Right to compensation
b.   Right to exclusive possession of the property during the bailment
c.   Right to any use of the property during the bailment
d.   Right to limit liability within reason

15.   Susan is moving from Georgia to Texas. She packs her china in a box with proper padding and marks "fragile" on the outside of the box. She ships the china by bus. When the china arrives, several pieces are broken.

a.   The bus company is responsible for the china on the basis of strict liability.
b.   The bus company will be responsible only if it was negligent in moving the china.
c.   The bus company is not responsible if Susan did not pack the china correctly.
d.   The bus company is not responsible if it offered Susan more protection in exchange for a higher transportation charge.

16.   Mike attends class in the Fine Arts Auditorium. He places his coat on the chair next to him but forgets to pick it up at the end of class. Barney, the janitor, finds the coat. The coat is:

a.   mislaid property.
b.   lost property.
c.   abandoned property.
d.   bailed property.

17.   Barney:

a.   is an involuntary bailee and has no right to the property.
b.   is an involuntary bailee and has a right to the coat that is good against anyone except Mike.
c.   is a finder and has a right to the coat that is good against anyone except Mike.
d.   is a finder and has absolute right to the coat.

18.   An estray statute:

a.   allows common carriers to limit their liability.
b.   allows warehousemen to issue documents of title.
c.   allows finders of lost property to claim a reward.
d.   allows donors to make gifts after death.

19.   Which of the following is an example of a gratuitous bailment for the sole benefit of the bailor?

a.   Lending a car to a friend
b.   Storing a car in a friend's garage
c.   Renting a car from an agency

d.   Parking a car in a parking place at the airport

20.   Which of the following is not a bailment?

a.   Lending a car to a friend
b.   Storing a car in a friend's garage
c.   Renting a car from an agency
d.   Parking a car in a parking place at the airport

21.   Which of the following is not personalty?

a.   Fixture
b.   Chattel
c.   Good
d.   Intangible Copyright

22.   Which of the following is not an element of a bailment?

a.   Transfer of possession
b.   Transfer of title
c.   Bailment agreement
d.   Personal property

23.   Martin operates a car repair shop. Cindy leaves her car with Martin for repairs. Martin uses Cindy's car to pick up a package in a nearby town. The car is repaired and returned to Cindy. Martin:

a.   has breached the bailment agreement and is liable in tort or contract.
b.   has breached the bailment agreement and is liable in contract only.
c.   has not breached the bailment agreement because he has the exclusive right to use the car during the bailment.
d.   has not breached the bailment agreement because the car was not damaged.

24.   Which of the following is false?

a.   At common law, innkeepers were strictly liable for the possessions of their guests.
b.   An innkeeper is an ordinary bailee.
c.   In most states, an innkeeper is liable only for negligence if the guest has an opportunity to store valuables in a safe.
d.   Many statutes have allowed innkeepers to limit liability for items which cannot be stored in a safe.

25.   Which of the following is true?

a.   A warehouseman is a special bailee.
b.   A warehouseman is not allowed to limit liability.
c.   A warehouseman is strictly liable for goods stored.

d.   A warehouse may issue only nonnegotiable documents of title.

Answers to Study Questions

Fill-in-the-Blank Questions

Uncle Paul is the donor; Stephanie is the donee. Delivery of the car occurs when the keys are given to Brad, who is Stephanie's agent. Transfer of the keys is sufficient because it gives Stephanie access to the car. This is an example of constructive delivery. The gift is inter vivos; a gift causa mortis occurs only when the donor dies.

True-False Questions

1.   F.   It is an example of intangible personal property; a stock certificate represents ownership in the corporation.

2.   T.

3.   T.

4.   T.

5.   F.   The innocent party acquires title to the whole only if the goods are wrongfully and intentionally mixed.

6.   F.   A finder of mislaid property acquires no title; he or she is an involuntary bailee.

7.   F.   In a gratuitous bailment, the owner need only warn of known defects.

8.   F.   A warehouseman is liable under a negligence standard; this sentence describes the liability of a common carrier.

9.   F.   The valet keeps the keys, so it is a bailment.

10.   T.

Multiple-Choice Questions

1.	c		14.	c
2.	d		15.	c
3.	b		16.	a
4.	b		17.	a
5.	b		18.	c
6.	a		19.	b
7.	d		20.	d
8.	b		21.	a
9.	b		22.	b
10.	c		23.	b
11.	a		24.	b
12.	b		25.	a
13.	d			

Real Property

General Principles

You have seen that ownership of property includes not only the right to possess the property, but the right to use it or dispose of it. Ownership of real property includes the right to live on the land, the right to use it for production of minerals or crops, and the right to sell it or give it away.

One person can own land in the present and another person can own it in the future. Non-owners, including tenants, neighbors, and the government may also have rights. Rights in land may be transferred by deed or by will. An owner can lose his or her rights if non-owners use the land for a long period of time without the owner's permission.

Chapter Summary

I.   The Nature of Real Property

    A.   Land--Ownership includes rights to surface, the subsurface, items attached to the land, and to a limited extent, space above the land (air rights).

    B.   Air and Subsurface Rights--Air rights are not absolute, but the owner has the right to be free from low flying planes and other uses which destroy the enjoyment of the property. The subsurface includes water, oil, gas, and other minerals. The subsurface and the surface may be owned by different people.

    C.   Crops and Fixtures--As a general rule, the land also includes items attached to the land such as growing crops or fixtures. A fixture is an item of personal property that has been attached to the land more or less permanently; the intent of the owner to treat it as real or personal property is the test. The more firmly attached, the more likely the property is a fixture.

II.   Estates in Land

    A.   Freehold Estates--Ownership of land is called an estate. A freehold estate is one where the person on the land has ownership rights in contrast to a tenant who has the right to use the land but does not own it. Ownership in land may also be divided along a time span; some people may own the land for a limited period of time. Remember that the land always has to belong to someone.

        (1)   Fee Simple Absolute--Owner has all present and future rights, can dispose of the land as he or she wishes.

        (2)   Fee Simple Defeasible--The current owner has the right to the land as long as a specified condition exists. If the condition fails to exist, the property may go back to the original owner or to a third person.

        (3)   Life Estate--Owner has the land only until he or she dies. The rights of a life tenant are restricted because another has a future right to the land. As a general rule, the life tenant can receive income from the land but cannot injure it.

    B.   Nonfreehold Estates (Tenancies)--The possessor of the land (the tenant) and the owner of the land (landlord) are different people. The tenant has a nonfreehold estate because he or she does not own the property.

        (1)   Tenancy for Years--Has a definite termination date; it need not be in multiples of a year. The tenancy survives the death of either party.

        (2)   Periodic Tenancy--Has no definite termination date but the tenant pays rent on a regular basis. Either party must give notice before terminating the lease.

        (3)   Tenancy at Will--Exists when the landlord consents to the tenant's occupancy. If no definite termination date is specified, the lease can be ended without notice. If rent is paid on a regular basis, the tenancy at will may become a periodic tenancy.

        (4)   Tenancy by Sufferance--Exists without permission of the landlord and usually exists when a tenant wrongfully stays after the expiration of a lease.

III.   <u>Relationship of Landlord and Tenant</u>--Each party has corresponding duties.

    A.   <u>Possession</u>--Must promise that the premises have been rented to only one party (covenant of possession) and that a tenant's lawful possession will not be disturbed (covenant of quiet enjoyment). Otherwise, breach of this last clause may result in constructive eviction of the tenant and the tenant may sue.

    B.   <u>Using the Premises</u>--The tenant must take reasonable care of the premises. A landlord is required to keep the structure and all common areas in good repair.

    C.   <u>Maintaining the Premises</u>--The landlord promises that the premises will be livable (warranty of habitability). In addition, most cities have housing codes with which the landlord must comply.

    D.   <u>Rent</u>--The tenant must pay rent as it comes due. If the tenant wrongfully leaves, he or she still owes the rent. At common law, the landlord had no duty to try to find another tenant; statutes in many states have changed this. Also at common law, destruction of the premises had no effect on the tenant's duty to pay rent; this has also been changed by statute.

    E.   <u>Assignment and Subleasing</u>--An assignment is the transfer of <u>all</u> of the tenant's interest to a third party. A subleasing transfers <u>part</u> of the tenant's interest (usually for less time than the entire lease). In either case, the original tenant remains liable for the rent. Under most leases, the tenant cannot transfer possession without the consent of the landlord although the landlord may waive this right if he or she accepts rent from the tenant's assignee.

IV.   <u>Transfer of Ownership</u>

    A.   <u>By Will or Inheritance</u>--Determined by state statute.

    B.   <u>Eminent Domain</u>--The government takes private property for a valid public purpose. The Constitution requires that the owner be paid just compensation which is usually the market value of the land.

    C.   <u>Adverse Possession</u>--A non-owner may obtain title by living on and using the land for a long period of time (usually three to thirty years). If the true owner checks the land with reasonable frequency, the adverse possessor can be evicted. Therefore, an adverse possessor must meet the following four requirements in order to gain ownership of the land.

        (1)   <u>Actual and Exclusive</u>--Must live on the land and prevent others from occupying it.

(2)   <u>Open and Notorious</u>--Cannot hide when the true owner checks the land.

(3)   <u>Continuous and Peaceable</u>--If the owner evicts the adverse possessor, the time required must begin again.

(4)   <u>Hostile and Adverse</u>--Must claim the property as an owner and not as a tenant; must be adverse to the claims of the true owner.

D.   <u>Conveyance by Deed</u>--Most common way of transferring land.

(1)   <u>Requirements</u>--The deed must be in writing, contain the names of the transferor (grantor) and the transferee (grantee), show an intent to transfer the land, contain a description of the land, and be signed by the grantor.

(2)   <u>Types of Deeds</u>--A general warranty deed is most common and contains the most protection for the grantee. A quit-claim deed promises only to transfer the interest of the grantor which may be full rights or no rights at all. In most states, a deed must be recorded in order to prevent an assertion of the right to the land by third parties.

V.   <u>Future Interests</u>--The owner of a future interest owns a possibility of possessing land at some time in the future.

A.   <u>Reversionary Interests</u>--Future interests that return to the original owner.

(1)   <u>Reversion</u>--Owner transfers land for a period of time. <u>No</u> contingencies. Will eventually return to original owner. If Roger sells Bonnie a life estate, Roger's right to the property is a reversion.

(2)   <u>Possibility of Reverter</u>--Owner transfers land conditionally. If the condition ceases to exist, the original owner will reacquire the land.

B.   <u>Remainders and Executory Interests</u>

(1)   <u>Remainder</u>--Similar to a reversion but the land will go to a third party after a period of time; it will not return to the original owner.

(2)   <u>Executory Interest</u>--Similar to a possibility of reverter but future interest belongs to a third party.

VI.   <u>Nonpossessory Interests</u>--Rights to use the land that belong to outsiders (not owners or tenants).

   A.   <u>Easements and Profits</u>--An easement is a right to use the property but not to take anything from it; it is not revocable. A profit is a right to take items from the land such as soil or minerals. It is not revocable.

      (1)   <u>Classification</u>--An easement appurtenant is one which benefits neighboring land; an easement in gross may benefit anyone. The following requirements relate only to easements and profits.

      (2)   <u>Sale of Property with an Easement Appurtenant</u>--If the easement owner sells his or her land, the easement is transferred to the new owner. If the landowner whose property is burdened by the easement sells his or her land, the new owner must recognize the easement if the easement is publicly recorded or if the new owner knows or should have known that the easement exists.

      (3)   <u>Creation</u>--Expressly by deed or by implication. Also may be created by necessity between two adjacent parcels of land (e.g. a landlocked owner has the right to use a road that goes through another's property). Uninterrupted use may create an easement by prescription (similar to adverse possession but the user does not acquire title).

      (4)   <u>Termination</u>--The easement owner may deed the easement back to the landowner; the easement owner abandons use of the easement; or the easement owner buys the property of the landowner and the rights are merged.

   B.   <u>Licenses</u>--A license differs from an easement and a profit because a license can be revoked at any time. The licensee, or person allowed to use the land, gets <u>no</u> interest in the property.

Study Questions

Oscar owns some land in Georgia. He gives the land to his old high school. The deed contains the following language: "Old High School owns the land as long as it is used for educational purposes. If the land ceases to be used for educational purposes, then the land shall pass to my grandchildren."

Old High School has a_____.
            (fee simple/absolute/fee simple defeasible)

Oscar's grandchildren have a(n) _____.
                 (remainder/executory interest)

The deed _____ be recorded in order to transfer the land.
          (must/need not)

Old High School's estate is_____.
                           (freehold/nonfreehold)

Oscar's grandchildren have a _____ interest.
                             (present/future)

True-False Questions

1.   The surface and subsurface of land may be owned by different people.
      _____

2.   An easement appurtenant can exist only on adjoining land. _____

3.   At common law, a tenant was obliged to pay rent even if the leased premises
      had been destroyed. _____

4.   A tenancy at will exists with the consent of the landlord. _____

5.   A tenancy for years has a definite termination date. _____

6.   A tenancy is a freehold estate. _____

7.   An adverse possessor must live openly on the land._____

8.   An easement by prescription is created by deed. _____

9.   A deed requires the signatures of the grantor and the grantee. _____

10.   When land is taken by eminent domain, the Constitution guarantees just
      compensation for the property owner. _____

Multiple-Choice Questions

1.   Susan rents an apartment from Larry Landlord. The lease states only that
      Susan must pay rent on the first day of every month but does not state when
      the lease expires. Susan has a:

      a.   tenancy for years.
      b.   periodic tenancy.
      c.   tenancy at will.
      d.   tenancy at sufferance.

2.   Susan discovers that the heating in the building does not work and that the
      pipes are rusty. Her bathroom floods whenever she uses the sink. Larry

a. has breached the covenant of quiet enjoyment and Susan has been evicted constructively.
b. has breached the warranty of possession and Susan has been evicted constructively.
c. has breached the covenant of quiet enjoyment but there is not constructive eviction.
d. has not breached any warranty or covenant.

3. Which of the following is least likely to be considered a fixture?

a. Kitchen cabinets
b. Drapes
c. Bed
d. Ceiling fan

4. Which of the following is the highest and most complete form of land ownership and includes present and future rights?

a. Fee simple defeasible
b. Possibility reverter
c. Fee simple absolute
d. Executory interest

5. Randy rents a house from Mrs. Jones for a period of two years. At the end of the first year, Randy decides to move and transfers his interest to Cathy. Randy:

a. has assigned his rights but is still liable for the rent.
b. has subleased his rights but is still liable for the rent.
c. has assigned his rights and is not liable for the rent.
d. has subleased his rights and is not liable for the rent.

6. Which of the following is not required for adverse possession?

a. Visible occupancy of the premises
b. Cultivation or building on the land
c. Possession over a required period of time
d. Exclusive possession of the land

7. Which of the following is not required for a deed?

a. Name of the grantee
b. Signature of the grantee
c. Description of the land
d. Words of conveyance

8. John owns a house near the beach. Every weekend for the last ten years, John's neighbors have crossed John's land to get to the beach. John has never given them permission to do so. The neighbors have:

a.   an easement by prescription.
b.   an easement by implication.
c.   a profit by prescription.
d.   a profit by necessity.

9.   If John does not stop the neighbors from crossing his land, the neighbors will acquire:

a.   adverse possession of the walkway to the beach.
b.   an easement of the walkway to the beach.
c.   a license to use the walkway to the beach.
d.   fee simple absolute of the walkway to the beach.

10.   Which of the following occurs when a tenant holds over without permission of the landlord?

a.   Tenancy by the entirety
b.   Periodic tenancy
c.   Tenancy at will
d.   Tenancy by sufferance

11.   Which of the following is revocable by the action of the landowner?

a.   Profit in gross
b.   Easement appurtenant
c.   License
d.   Life estate

12.   Bob owns some land. He deeds it to Mary. The deed contains the following words, "To Mary for life, then to my cousin Cora." Mary has a(n):

a.   life estate.
b.   executory interest.
c.   fee simple defeasible.
d.   possibility of reverter.

13.   Cora has a(n):

a.   executory interest.
b.   fee simple defeasible.
c.   remainder.
d.   possibility of reverter.

14.   If Mary damages the land, Cora may sue Mary for:

a.   breach of covenant of quiet enjoyment.
b.   breach of warranty for habitability.
c.   breach of warranty of possession.
d.   none of the above.

15.   Beth rents an apartment from Cecil. They agree that Beth can stay as long as she likes. Beth pays rent on the fifth of the month for eight months. When the tenancy was created, Beth and Cecil had a:

    a.   tenancy for years.
    b.   periodic tenancy.
    c.   tenancy at will.
    d.   tenancy at sufferance.

16.   Which of the following cannot be terminated without notice by either party?

    a.   Tenancy for years
    b.   Periodic tenancy
    c.   Tenancy at will
    d.   Tenancy at sufferance

17.   Paul deeds Cindy the right to come onto his land and mine for gold. Cindy has a(n):

    a.   easement appurtenant.
    b.   profit in gross.
    c.   license.
    d.   easement in gross.

18.   Which of the following correctly describes the difference between an easement and adverse possession?

    a.   An adverse possessor may obtain title to the land; an easement owner will not.
    b.   An easement owner may obtain title to the land; an adverse possessor will not.
    c.   An easement owner must live next door to the burdened property; an adverse possessor need not.
    d.   An easement owner must use the land; an adverse possessor need not use the land.

19.   Which of the following will not terminate an easement?

    a.   Merger
    b.   Abandonment
    c.   Deed from easement owner to landowner
    d.   Eviction

20.   Which of the following gives the grantee only the rights possessed by the grantor?

    a.   Warranty deed
    b   Covenant of quiet enjoyment
    c.   Quit-claim deed

d.   Deed of possession

21.   Which of the following is a contingent or conditional future interest?

a.   Fee simple absolute
b.   Executory interest
c.   Reversion
d.   Fee simple defeasible

22.   Which of the following is not a future estate?

a.   Possibility of reverter
b.   Reversion
c.   Remainder
d.   Fee simple defeasible

23.   Which of the following describes a future estate held by the original owner of the property?

a.   Remainder
b.   Executory Interest
c.   Possibility of reverter
d.   Fee simple defeasible

24.   Which of the following is not made by a landlord?

a.   Warranty of habitability
b.   Warranty against waste
c.   Covenant of quiet enjoyment
d.   Warranty of possession

25.   The government's right to take private property for public use is called:

a.   adverse possession.
b.   eminent domain.
c.   adverse domain.
d.   constructive eviction.

Answers to Study Questions

Fill-in-the-Blank Questions

Old High School has a fee simple defeasible because it can lose the right to the land if it is not used for educational purposes. A fee simple absolute has no strings attached to ownership. Oscar's grandchildren have an executory interest; a remainder can only follow a life estate. Old High School has a freehold estate; a nonfreehold estate is a tenancy. Oscar's grandchildren have a future interest.

True-False Questions

1.   T.

2..   T.

3.   T.

4.   T.

5.   T.

6.   F.   A tenancy of any kind is a nonfreehold estate.

7.   T.

8.   F.   It is created by use against the wishes of the landowner.

9.   F.   It requires only the signature of the grantor.

10.   T.

Multiple-Choice Questions

No.	Ans		No.	Ans
1.	b		14.	d
2.	a		15.	c
3.	c		16.	b
4.	c		17.	b
5.	a		18.	a
6.	b		19.	d
7.	b		20.	c
8.	a		21.	b
9.	b		22.	d
10.	d		23.	c
11.	c		24.	b
12.	a		25.	b
13.	c			

Insurance, Wills, and Trusts

General Principles

Insurance is a contract in which one party receives protection against risk in exchange for payment of money. The general rules of contract law apply to insurance policies. This chapter focuses on unique provisions of insurance policies.

Wills and trusts involve transfer of property. A will takes effect at death and transfers the deceased's property to persons named as beneficiaries. Certain formalities are required as protection against fraud. A trust also transfers ownership of property and may take effect during the life of the owner or at his or her death. A trust splits ownership; a trustee holds legal title to the property and manages it for the beneficiaries, who hold equitable title and are entitled to income from the trust property.

Chapter Outline

I.   Insurance--A method of providing security against losses. The insurance company will pay the insured person or the beneficiary if a loss should occur. The process of planning for insurance against losses is risk management.

      A.   Risk Pooling--A process of spreading the risk among insured persons. The insured persons pay premiums every year, but the insurance company pays only when the loss occurs. By pooling or grouping persons in large numbers, the premiums paid should pay for any losses that might occur. Insurance is classified by the type of risk involved.

      B.   Terminology

            (1)   Parties--An insurance contract is a policy. The person covered by the contract (the insured) pays money (premium) to the

insurer. The insurance company (insurer or underwriter) promises to pay a beneficiary if certain contingencies occur. An insured may use a broker or agent to complete the contract.

    (2)   <u>Insurable Interest</u>--In order to obtain an insurance policy, the insured must have a monetary interest or relationship to the subject of the policy. The owners and lienholders of property have a property interest at the time the property is destroyed. Life insurance may be purchased by relatives or by co-owners of a business (key-man insurance); the insured's interest must exist at the time the contract is made. The insurable interest differentiates an insurance contract from gambling.

C.   <u>The Contract</u>--Use general contract principles. False statements by insureds give the insurance company a right to rescind or to cancel the contract.

    (1)   <u>Timing</u>--If a broker is used, no contract exists until the insurer accepts the policy. If an agent is used, the insured is covered when the application is made. A binder is written to insure coverage. Some contracts require payment of a premium or a physical examination before coverage takes effect.

    (2)   <u>Provisions and Clauses</u>--Words are given ordinary meaning and because the insurance companies usually have more knowledge than the insured, any unclear provision will be interpreted in favor of the insured and against the insurance company.

        (a)   <u>Incontestability</u>--After a certain time, insurer cannot challenge statements made by the insured in the original application for insurance.

        (b)   <u>Coinsurance</u>--Owner shares in paying for the loss if policy only covers a certain percentage (usually 80%).

        (c)   <u>Appraisal and Arbitration</u>--Both call for settling disputes by independent, therefore unbiased, third parties. An appraisal is an estimate of the amount of loss covered.

        (d)   <u>Antilapse</u>--"Grace period" for late payment of premiums. Usually thirty or thirty-one days.

        (e)   <u>Cancellation</u>--Insurance company has the right to cancel if premiums are not paid or if false statements are made and discovered before a certain period. Also, negligent actions of the insured, which add to the risk, may be grounds for cancellation. No right to cancel based on race or national origin of the insured or if the insured has appeared in court proceeding against the insurer.

II.   Wills

    A.   Terminology--The maker of a will is called a testator (male) or testatrix (female). A probate court distributes the decedent's property according to the terms of the document; an executor(ix) may be named in the will to pay the debts of the estate and to arrange for the transfer of property. A gift of real estate is a devise; its recipient is a devisee. A gift of personal property is a bequest or legacy; its recipient is a legatee. The Uniform Probate Code (UPC) has been adopted in fourteen states.

    B.   Will Provisions

        (1)   General and Specific Bequests--A specific bequest is an identifiable piece of property. A general bequest usually consists of money.

        (2)   Abatement and Lapsed Legacy--If the estate is insufficient to pay all the general bequests, each legatee takes a reduced share through abatement. If a legatee dies before the testator, the legacy may lapse. The property may then pass with the remainder of the estate or may pass to the heirs of the legatee (if the legatee is a family member of the deceased).

        (3)   Residuary Clause--All property of the estate which is not mentioned in the will passes to a residual legatee. This is usually the last clause in a will.

    C.   Requirements of a Valid Will

        (1)   Writing--A formal will must be in writing and signed by the testator. A will can make reference to another written document which will be incorporated into the provisions of the will. A holographic will is written entirely in the testator's handwriting; it is valid in some states. A nuncupative will is an oral will made by the testator in his or her "last illness"; it can dispose of personal property only and is valid only in some states.

        (2)   Witnessing--A formal will must be witnessed. State law varies on the requirements of witnesses. Usually two or three mentally competent witnesses must watch the testator(ix) and they must sign the will in the presence of each other. Some states require that the witnesses be a certain age and/or disinterested (not receiving a benefit from the will). A witness does not have to read the will

(3)   Publication--Some states require the testator tell the witnesses that the document is his or her will.

(4)   Testamentary Capacity--The testator must be of sound mind and of legal age when the will is made.

D.   Revocation of a Will--A will does not take effect until the testator(ix) dies, so it may be revoked.

(1)   Acts of the Testator(ix)--The maker can revoke it by tearing, cutting, or obliterating it. A single provision cannot be crossed out or an additional term added without the formalities stated above.

(2)   Later Instrument--A codicil, or an amendment to the will, can revoke it in whole or in part if it is executed formally. A new will can also revoke a previous will. An intent to revoke previous wills, usually the first item in a will, is necessary or both wills will be read together although the second will controls in the case of conflict.

(3)   Operation of Law--Can occur if the testator(ix) marries or has children after the will is executed. Unless it appears that the new spouse or child was intentionally omitted, they will be entitled to the share of the estate they would have received if the deceased had died without a will.

E.   Will Substitutes and Probate Substitutes--A testator can avoid the expense of probate by giving his or her property away before death or by placing it in a trust or joint tenancy with right of survivorship. When a will is probated, the executor pays the deceased's creditors and distributes the remaining assets. Some states allow family settlement agreements where the legatees and devisees agree to divide the estate after the deceased's creditors have been paid. Other states allow property to be transferred by filling out forms or making a sworn statement (affidavit).

F.   Intestacy

(1)   Procedure--If a person dies without a will, state law governs the distribution of the estate. An administrator(ix) is appointed to pay debts and distribute the property.

(2)   Order of Distribution

(a)   Wife and children (or grandchildren)--Wife receives one-half if there is one child; one third if there is more than one.

      (b)   <u>Wife and no descendants</u>--Wife takes all.

      (c)   <u>Lineal descendants</u>--If no wife or direct descendants, parents and siblings.

      (d)   <u>Collateral heirs</u>--If no lineal descendants, nieces, nephews, aunts, uncles.

      (e)   <u>Next of kin of collateral heirs</u>--Adopted children may take; stepchildren may not.

      (f)   <u>Escheat</u>--If none of the above can be located, the property passes to the state.

  (3)   <u>Method of Distribution</u>--Problems may arise if a testator(ix)'s child dies first and leaves grandchildren. The estate may be distributed per stirpes (along family lines) or per capita (an equal share to each survivor, regardless of family lines).

III.   Trusts

A.   <u>Parties</u>--The owner of the property, who creates the trust, is the settlor. Legal title and management of the property is given to the trustee, who may receive a fee for services rendered. The beneficiaries acquire equitable title to the property and receive income from the property. Eventually the entire title may pass to the beneficiaries.

B.   <u>Types of Trusts</u>

  (1)   <u>Express</u>--Usually set out in writing and intended to take effect by the settlor.

      (a)   <u>Inter vivos</u>--Created during the life of the settlor.

      (b)   <u>Testamentary</u>--Takes effect at the settlor's death.

      (c)   <u>Charitable</u>--Created for the benefit of the public and is made for educational, religious, or charitable purposes.

      (d)   <u>Spendthrift</u>--Created to protect an imprudent person from creditors; a small amount of the property is distributed at a time and creditors cannot attach the trust.

      (e)   <u>Totten</u>--The settlor is the trustee. Revocable until the settlor dies when the entire property passes to the beneficiary.

    (2)   <u>Implied</u>

        (a)   <u>Constructive</u>--Imposed by the court to prevent wrongdoing. A person wrongfully holding funds will be made into a trustee for the benefit of the rightful owner.

        (b)   <u>Resulting</u>--Occurs when one person holds property for another; it must be clear that a gift was not intended.

Study Questions

Fill-in-the-Blank Questions

Randall is the president of a small engineering firm. The other officers of the corporation are worried that the business may fail if anything happens to Randall. They convince him to buy life insurance which will pay the company if Randall dies. Randall submits an application to Bob, a broker, who forwards the application to Corporate Life Insurance.

Randall is the_____.
           (underwriter/insured/beneficiary)

The engineering firm is the_____.
           (underwriter/insured/beneficiary)

The engineering firm _____ have an insurable interest.
        (does/does not)

Bob is an agent of _____.
        (Randall/Corporate Life Insurance)

The memorandum which Bob will write to cover Randall while the contract is being transmitted is a _____.
        (binder/policy)

True-False Questions

1.   The person who creates a trust is the testator. _____

2.   A formal will must be witnessed. _____

3.   A will may be revoked by burning or tearing it. _____

4.   The Uniform Probate Code has been adopted by all fifty states. _____

5.   A totten trust is a form of express trust. _____

6.   A constructive trust must be in writing.

7.   Collateral heirs are brothers and sisters of the deceased. _____

8.   A gift of real property made in a will is a legacy. _____

9.   If a person dies without a will, an executor(ix) will be appointed to administer the estate. _____

10.   An insurance company spreads the risk of loss among many people by using risk pooling. _____

Multiple-Choice Questions

1.   Which of the following is <u>not</u> a party to a trust?

        a.   Beneficiary
        b.   Trustee
        c.   Testator
        d.   Settlor

2.   Mrs. Adams had her lawyer draft a formal will. After she had signed it in the presence of witnesses, she decided to leave her silverware to her cousin rather than to her daughter. She crossed out her daughter's name and substituted that of her cousin. Who will receive the silverware?

        a.   Mrs. Adams' daughter
        b.   Mrs. Adams' cousin
        c.   Mrs. Adams' heirs because the will is invalid
        d.   The state because the will is invalid

3.   An oral will is called a(n) _____ will.

        a.   holographic
        b.   formal
        c.   codicil
        d.   nuncupative

4.   Which of the following requirements of a formal will is not used in most states?

        a.   Writing
        b.   Witnessing
        c.   Publication
        d   Escheat

5.   Which of the following is <u>not</u> a will substitute?

        a.   Inter vivos trust
        b   Joint tenancy with right of survivorship

c.   Totten trust
d.   Constructive trust

6.   Aunt Mary has just died. In her will she left her ranch to her granddaughter Sally, her diamond ring to her sister Helen, $6,000 to the SPCA, and the remainder of her estate to her grandson, Bob. Bob was also named as the person to distribute the estate. Bob is a(n):

a.   executor and a residuary legatee.
b.   administrator and a residuary devisee.
c.   administrator and specific devisee.
d.   executor and specific legatee.

7.   Sally is a(n):

a.   executrix.
b.   legatee.
c.   devisee.
d.   testatrix.

8.   The SPCA will receive a(n):

a.   specific bequest.
b.   specific devise.
c.   general devise.
d.   general bequest.

9.   Helen predeceased Aunt Mary. Helen's gift is an example of a(n):

a.   abatement.
b.   escheat.
c.   lapsed legacy.
d.   intestate gift.

10.   Bob and Bill are partners. Bob suspects that Bill has been hiding business funds and placing them in a separate bank account. Bob should ask the court for a:

a.   constructive trust
b.   resulting trust.
c.   testamentary trust.
d.   spendthrift trust.

11.   Tom creates a trust for his daughter. He is the settlor and the trustee. Tom has created a:

a.   testamentary trust.
b.   totten trust.
c.   resulting trust.

d.   no trust; Tom cannot be the settlor and the trustee.

12.   In the absence of express agreement, an insurance policy which is obtained through an agent of the insurance company, is:

a.   binding when the application is submitted because the agent works for the company.
b.   binding when accepted by the company because the agent is an independent contractor.
c.   binding when accepted by the company because the agent is an underwriter.
d.   binding when returned to the insured.

13.   Which of the following statements regarding a holographic will is _false_?

a.   It is entirely in the handwriting of the testator.
b.   It must be witnessed.
c.   It is valid in only some states.
d.   It may dispose of real and personal property.

14.   Which of the following may cause a revocation of a will by operation of law?

a.   Tearing the well
b.   Executing a codicil
c.   Marriage after the will has been executed
d.   Marking through the will

15.   The duties of an executor include all of the following _except_:

a.   Paying the debts of the estate
b.   Overseeing the distribution of the estate
c.   Submitting the will to probate
d.   Acting as guardian for the testator's children

16.   Which of the following trusts would be used if you asked your roommate to keep your car for you while you went on vacation?

a.   Resulting trust
b.   Constructive trust
c.   Totten trust
d.   Inter vivos trust

17.   Although requirements for witnesses to a will vary, which of the following is not required in most states?

a.   Witnesses must see the testatrix sign the will.
b.   Witnesses must see each other sign the will.
c.   Witnesses must be of sound mind.
d.   Witnesses must read and verify the will.

18.   Martha dies without a will; she is survived by her husband and two small children. In most states, the distribution will be:

    a.   one-third to Martha's husband; one-third to each child.
    b.   one-half to Martha's husband; one-quarter to each child.
    c.   one-half to each child.
    d.   all of Martha's husband.

19.   Which of the following are collateral heirs?

    a.   Spouse
    b.   Uncles and aunts
    c.   Children
    d.   Grandchildren

20.   Sam executes a simple will which states, "All of my property except for the money in my savings account is left to my wife, Bettina. The money in my savings account is to be apportioned to several charitable agencies as set out by a list in the possession of my attorney." The money in the savings account will go to:

    a.   Bettina, because the gift to the charities is a lapsed legacy.
    b.   Bettina, because the gift to the charities is an abatement.
    c.   The charities; this is an example of incorporation by reference.
    d.   The state; this is an example of an escheat.

21.   When an intestate person has no relatives, his or her property passes to the state. This is an example of a(n):

    a.   abatement.
    b.   escheat.
    c.   lapsed legacy.
    d.   devise.

22.   Sarah executes one will in which she leaves her land to Bud and her personal property to Meg. Sarah has second thoughts and executes a new will in which Bud receives the land, but Meg and Adrienne divide the personal property. Sarah's second will has no revocation clause. How will the estate be divided?

    a.   Bud will receive the land; Meg and Adrienne will receive one-half of the personal property each.
    b.   Meg will receive the personal property and Bud will receive the land.
    c.   Sarah's heirs will receive all the property because the will is invalid.
    d.   The state will receive all the property because the will is invalid.

23.   Which of the following documents must be witnessed?

    a.   Holographic will
    b.   Formal will

c.   Inter vivos trust
d.   Charitable trust

24.   Cindy, who has three children, dies intestate. One child, Mike, has died previously. He left two children (Cindy's grandchildren, Jay and Lonnie). Cindy's other children, Bob and Tom, survived her. Which of the following is the correct distribution of the estate if the distribution is to be made per capita?

    a.   Bob, Tom, Jay, and Lonnie will receive one-fourth each.
    b.   Bob and Tom will receive one-half; Jay and Lonnie will receive nothing.
    c.   Bob and Tom will receive one-third each; Jay and Lonnie will split one-third.
    d.   Bob and Tom will split one-third; Jay and Lonnie will receive one-third each.

25.   Which of the following is a synonym for insurer?

    a.   Broker
    b.   Underwriter
    c.   Administrator
    d.   Trustee

26.   Which of the following is not a clause found in an insurance policy?

    a.   Arbitration clause
    b.   Appraisal clause
    c.   Incontestability clause
    d.   Intestacy clause

27.   Which of the following is/are proper grounds for cancellation of an automobile insurance policy?

    a.   Failure to pay premiums
    b.   Suspension of the insured driver's license
    c.   Both of the above
    d.   Neither of the above

28.   The right of an insured to pay a premium a few days after payment is due is a(n):

    a.   incontestability clause.
    b.   grace period.
    c.   right to an appraisal.
    d.   risk pooling.

29.   A moral hazard is most likely to occur when:

    a.   a key person in a company dies.

    b.   a premium is paid after the due date.

    c.   a building owner has insurance against theft and does not activate the building's security system.

    d.   a person dies without a will.

30.   Which of the following statements is <u>false</u>?

    a.   An ambiguous provision in an insurance policy will be interpreted in favor of the insurance company.

    b.   An incontestability clause does not apply if an insured makes false statements on an application for insurance.

    c.   An appraisal clause provides that a third party will estimate the losses sustained by an insured.

    d.   An insurance company cannot cancel, but can refuse to renew, a contract based on the race of the applicant.

Answers to Study Questions

Fill-in-the-Blank Questions

Randall is the insured; the engineering firm is the beneficiary. The engineering firm does have a monetary and insurable interest. This is an example of key-man insurance. Bob is a broker and is Randall's agent. Bob's memorandum is a binder.

True-False Questions

1.   F.   It is the settlor; a testator makes a will.

2.   T.

3.   T.

4.   F.   It has been adopted by fourteen states.

5.   T.

6.   F.   It is implied by the court and is never in writing.

7.   F.   Collateral heirs are aunts and uncles; siblings are lineal descendants.

8.   F.   It is a devise; a legacy is a gift of personal property.

9.   F.   An administrator will be appointed.

10.   T.

Multiple-Choice Questions

1.	c		16.	a
2.	c		17.	d
3.	d		18.	a
4.	c		19.	b
5.	d		20.	c
6.	a		21.	b
7.	c		22.	a
8.	d		23.	b
9.	c		24.	a
10.	a		25.	b
11.	b		26.	d
12.	a		27.	c
13.	b		28.	b
14.	c		29.	c
15.	d		30.	a

International Law in a Global Economy

General Principles

International law is the set of rules followed in business which crosses borders of countries. It is created primarily by treaties, and unlike national law, compliance is completely voluntarily. International law has developed rules to follow when laws of different countries conflict. In general an act of a foreign government undertaken for a legitimate public purpose will not be questioned by courts of other countries. The last part of this chapter focuses on the process of an international sale of goods and the application of American antitrust laws to transnational business.

Chapter Summary

I. Principles and Sources of International Law--A nation can choose whether or not to follow international law; there is no way to force a nation to comply other than the threat of war.

   A. Definitions--National or domestic law is the law of one country. International law is a set of rules (formal or informal) that are followed by different countries and their peoples.

   B. Treaties--Contract agreed between nations. In the United States, the president negotiates the treaty which must be approved by a two-thirds majority of the Senate. Agreements between two countries are bilateral; agreements among more than two countries are multilateral.

   C. International Court of Justice--A branch of the United Nations, which hears cases involving U.N. resolutions. The parties must agree to allow the court to hear the case (voluntary jurisdiction).

   D. International Organizations--The United Nations issues declarations and resolutions agreed on by its members. The United Nations organization that deals with trade law is called UNCITRAL. A treaty governing the sale of goods, which was proposed by UNCITRAL, has been adopted by sixteen countries.

II.   Legal Principles and Doctrines--When the laws of two nations contradict, the following principles are used to settle disputes.

A.   Comity--Applied when the act of state doctrine does not apply, that is when a government's actions have effects beyond its borders (extra-territorial). A United States court will recognize the decision of a foreign court or government only if that decision is consistent with American policy.

B.   Act of State Doctrine--The courts of one country will not interfere with the decision of a foreign government. This principle applies only if the government is formally recognized and if the action complained of occurs within one nation's borders. Used when private industry is taken for governmental use (expropriation). The private party must be compensated. If not, a confiscation occurs.

C.   Sovereign Immunity--Foreign Sovereign Immunities Act (FSIA) prohibits claims against a foreign state or the state's "instrumentality" in U.S. courts. Exceptions: if the foreign state has waived its immunity or it the claim is based on the foreign state's "commercial activity" in the U.S.

III.   Transacting Business Abroad

A.   Letters of Credit--A buyer and seller use a bank(s) as an intermediary in a sales transaction. The buyer (account party) places an order with the seller (beneficiary) and arranges for a loan from the bank (issuer). When the seller ships the goods and shows the bank the bill of lading, the bank pays the buyer. A bank in the seller's country may help speed the transaction (advising bank). The seller must comply with the terms of the letter of credit in order to receive payment; courts are becoming more lenient and now only require substantial compliance. There are three contracts involved:

1)   contract between buyer and seller
2)   contract between buyer and issuer (loan)
3)   contract between seller and issuer

B.   Sales Contracts--In addition to contract terms discussed in other chapters, international contracts should also include the language of the contract, the currency of payment, and which country's law is to be applied (choice-of-law clause). A choice-of-law clause only determines which courts will hear the case or which countries law will apply. Although a plaintiff may win a lawsuit involving an international dispute, it may be difficult or impossible to collect money to satisfy the judgment if the courts of the defendant's country do not agree. Many also contain arbitration clauses. In case of arbitration, the International Chamber of Commerce or other third party may be designated. The United Nations rules on arbitration have been adopted by fifty countries.

C.   <u>Investment Protection</u>--Used as a hedge against expropriation. May be contained in a national law or treaty. Some countries provide insurance for overseas investors. OPIC (Overseas Private Investment Corporation) insures American businesses.

D.   <u>Antitrust Laws</u>--Sherman Act and other antitrust laws apply to international law whenever a per se violation exists or whenever the effect on American commerce is substantial. Plaintiffs and defendants can be Americans or foreign persons.

Study Questions

Fill-in-the-Blank Questions

Arnold Fabrics, an American manufacturer, is importing jute from India. Arnold arranges with First Bank for a loan and payment to Indian Industries, the jute supplier. First Bank agrees to pay Indian Industries when it has proof that the jute has been shipped to the United States.

This three-party transaction involves a_____.
                                         (bill of lading/letter of credit)

Arnold Fabrics is the_____.
                      (issuer/account party/beneficiary)

First Bank is the _____.
                      (issuer/account party/beneficiary)

Indian Industries will receive payment when it presents a bill of lading to _____.
      (Arnold Fabrics/First Bank)

True-False Questions

1.   The International Court of Justice hears cases only if the parties agree to allow the court to hear the case. _____

2.   Foreigners cannot sue as plaintiffs under American antitrust acts. _____

3.   Expropriation occurs when a government takes private property for public use. _____

4.   Comity is applied only when one country's laws are inconsistent with the laws of the United States. _____

5.   OPIC is an international agency which drafts rules for arbitration between countries. _____

6.   Municipal law is a synonym for foreign law. _____

7.   A government's actions which involve commercial activity are protected by the act of state doctrine. _____

8.   Sovereign immunity applies only to individuals. _____

9.   All treaties entered into by the United States must be approved by both houses of Congress. _____

10.   A choice-of-law clause determines where a case involving two countries will be heard if a dispute develops. _____

Multiple-Choice Questions

1.   Which of the following does not apply to the acts of a foreign government which have extraterritorial effects?

        a.   Act of state doctrine
        b.   Sovereign immunity
        c.   Comity
        d.   Antitrust laws

2.   United States antitrust laws will apply to international transactions if:

        a.   the act complained of has an effect on interstate commerce and the defendants are residents of the United States.
        b.   the act complained of has a substantial effect on interstate commerce and the defendants are residents of the United States.
        c.   the act complained of has an effect on foreign commerce.
        d.   the act complained of has a substantial effect on interstate commerce and the defendants may be residents of any country.

3.   The International Court of Justice is a branch of:

        a.   the United Nations.
        b.   the United States Department of Justice.
        c.   the International Chamber of Commerce.
        d.   OPIC.

4.   A treaty is ratified by:

   a.   the president.
   b.   Congress.
   c.   the Senate.
   d.   the House of Representatives.

5.   Municipal law is a synonym for:

   a.   international law.
   b.   national law.
   c.   antitrust law.
   d.   sovereign immunity.

6.   Which of the following is an international commission on trade law?

   a.   U.N. General Assembly
   b.   UNCITRAL
   c.   FSIA
   d.   OPIC

7.   The judicial rule that a court will not review acts of government which take place within its borders is a description of:

   a.   comity.
   b.   act of state doctrine.
   c.   extraterritoriality.
   d.   sovereign immunity.

8.   Sovereign immunity is not a defense if:

   a.   a foreign state conducts a governmental act which affects United States commerce.
   b.   a foreign state takes private property for a proper public purpose.
   c.   a foreign state conducts commercial business in the United States.
   d.   the United States government takes private property for public use.

9.   Comity:

   a.   states that a government cannot be sued for actions taken which have an effect only within its borders.
   b.   allows the courts of one country to recognize the laws of another country.
   c.   states that a government is always immune from suit.
   d.   is a mandatory provision of international law.

10.   Which of the following statements is <u>false</u>?

    a.   A letter of credit usually involves at least three parties.
    b.   A letter of credit is used in sales agreements.
    c.   A letter of credit is issued by a buyer to a seller.
    d.   The beneficiary of a letter of credit is usually a seller of goods.

11.   Which of the following is not a contract under a letter of credit?

    a.   Bank's promise to pay account party
    b.   Bank's promise to pay beneficiary
    c.   Beneficiary's promise to ship goods
    d.   Beneficiary's promise to pay account party

12.   Which of the following would present a bill of lading in order to receive payment under a letter of credit?

    a.   Issuer
    b.   Buyer
    c.   Account Party
    d.   Seller

13.   FSIA is an abbreviation for:

    a.   Foreign Services Immunity Act
    b.   Foreign State and International Arbitration
    c.   Foreign Sovereign Immunity Act
    d.   Foreign State Immunity Act

14.   United States antitrust laws apply only if a court determines that:

    a.   a per se violation has occurred or an act has a substantial effect on United States commerce.
    b.   a per se violation has occurred.
    c.   an act has an extenuating effect on intrastate commerce.
    d.   an act has a substantial effect on international commerce.

15.   Which of the following is most likely to be involved in international arbitration?

    a.   UNCITRAL
    b.   International Chamber of Commerce
    c.   OPIC
    d.   FSIA

16.   A force majeure clause in an international sales contract:

    a.   specifies that enforcement of the contract will be implemented by the International Court of Justice.

b.   designates the currency of payment.
c.   names the beneficiary of a letter of credit.
d.   protects the parties against acts of God or events beyond their control.

17.   The difference between expropriation and confiscation is:

a.   expropriation is committed by a government; confiscation is committed by an individual.
b.   expropriation refers to acts of a government within its borders; confiscation refers to extraterritorial acts.
c.   expropriation is a public taking of private property with compensation; confiscation is a taking without compensation.
d.   expropriation disputes are submitted to arbitration; confiscation disputes are not.

18.   Which of the following correctly describes the jurisdiction of the International Court of Justice?

a.   Jurisdiction is compulsory and the court interprets national laws.
b.   Jurisdiction is compulsory and the court interprets resolutions of the United Nations.
c.   Jurisdiction is voluntary and the court interprets national laws.
d.   Jurisdiction is voluntary and the court interprets resolutions of the United Nations.

19.   Which of the following is a United States agency which provides protection for overseas investors?

a.   FSIA
b.   OPIC
c.   International Chamber of Commerce
d.   United Nations General Assembly

20.   Which of the following statements regarding sovereign immunity is true?

a.   It can be waived if the defendant conducts commercial activity in another country.
b.   It cannot be waived except by treaty.
c.   It applies to individuals and governments.
d.   It applies to extraterritorial acts.

21.   Which of the following statements about comity is false?

a.   It applies only if actions by a foreign government are consistent with United States law.
b.   It applies only if a foreign government's acts have effects beyond its own borders.
c.   It applies only if a court decides to respect the laws of another nation.
d.   It is a synonym for the act of state doctrine.

22.   Which of the following is an example of extraterritoriality?

    a.   Foreign country appropriates the land of an American investor in its country.
    b.   Foreign country sells goods below cost in the United States.
    c.   Foreign government declares martial law.
    d.   Foreign individual sues his or her government.

23.   Under a letter of credit, an advising bank is:

    a.   usually the seller's bank.
    b.   usually the buyer's bank.
    c.   one who issues a bill of lading.
    d.   one who lends money to the account party.

24.   Which of the following is not used in a letter of credit?

    a.   Note (loan)
    b.   Sales contract
    c.   Bill of lading
    d.   Treaty

25.   Which of the following correctly describes the courts' attitudes toward enforcement of a letter of credit?

    a.   All courts demand strict compliance.
    b.   All courts demand reasonable compliance.
    c.   The courts are split, some courts demand strict compliance and others demand reasonable compliance.

Answers to Study Questions

Fill-in-the-Blank Questions

The transaction involves a letter of credit; a bill of lading is a shipping document which is presented by the buyer to the bank. Arnold Fabrics is the buyer and account party. First Bank is the issuer. Indian Industries will present the bill of lading to First Bank.

True-False Questions

1.   T.

2.   F.   Foreign residents and residents of the United States are protected by the act.

3.   T.

4.   F.   It is applied only when the laws of another country are consistent with the laws of the United States.

5.   F.   It is a United States agency which provides insurance for overseas investors.

6.   F.   It is a synonym for national law.

7.   F.   Only governmental functions are protected.

8.   F.   It applies only to countries or a subdivision of a country.

9.   F.   A treaty must be ratified by a two-thirds vote in the Senate.

10.   T.

Multiple-Choice Questions

1.	b	10.	c	18.	d
2.	d	11.	a	19.	b
3.	a	12.	d	20.	a
4.	c	13.	c	21.	d
5.	b	14.	a	22.	b
6.	b	15.	b	23.	a
7.	b	16.	d	24.	d
8.	c	17.	c	25.	c
9.	b				